Law, Governance and Technology Series

Volume 83

The *Law, Governance and Technology Series* is intended to attract manuscripts arising from an interdisciplinary approach in law, artificial intelligence and information technologies. The idea is to bridge the gap between research in IT law and IT-applications for lawyers developing a unifying techno-legal perspective. The series will welcome proposals that have a fairly specific focus on problems or projects that will lead to innovative research charting the course for new interdisciplinary developments in law, legal theory, and law and society research as well as in computer technologies, artificial intelligence and cognitive sciences. In broad strokes, manuscripts for this series may be mainly located in the fields of the Internet law (data protection, intellectual property, Internet rights, etc.), Computational models of the legal contents and legal reasoning, Legal Information Retrieval, Electronic Data Discovery, Collaborative Tools (e.g. Online Dispute Resolution platforms), Metadata and XML Technologies (for Semantic Web Services), Technologies in Courtrooms and Judicial Offices (E-Court), Technologies for Governments and Administrations (E-Government), Legal Multimedia, and Legal Electronic Institutions (Multi-Agent Systems and Artificial Societies).

Rani Yadav-Ranjan

Constitutional Democracy in the Algorithmic Age

A Practical Framework for Preserving Citizen Rights

Springer

Rani Yadav-Ranjan
San Jose, CA, USA

ISSN 2352-1902 ISSN 2352-1910 (electronic)
Law, Governance and Technology Series
ISBN 978-3-032-34603-2 ISBN 978-3-032-34604-9 (eBook)
https://doi.org/10.1007/978-3-032-34604-9

This Springer imprint is published by the registered company Springer Nature Switzerland AG
The registered company address is: Gewerbestrasse 11, 6330 Cham, Switzerland

To my beloved husband, Rajiv: my north star.

To my children: my Sunshine.

And to my child's children: perfect H.A.L.O., the circle unbroken.

Foreword I

Ranjan's book exhorts all of us to wake up to the dangers of the "algorithmic age." AI threatens to degrade our democratic values, our ability to think, to make choices and generally to assert our dignity as human beings.

Traditional legal frameworks are too weak to effectively address discriminatory bias in many algorithms that have been tasked with significant decision-making in the granting or denial of social benefits. Similarly, the wholesale copying and exploitation of intellectual property without compensation is difficult to police, let alone to remedy, when AI models can swallow the whole Internet in seconds. Social media addiction is making new case law as judges try to grapple with the increasing evidence of harms to children. Front page and TV news regularly carry stories of manipulation and the emotional exploitation of vulnerable populations, sometimes triggering violent behaviors or leading as far as suicide.

Ranjan describes many of the attempts by U.S. courts and by regulators like the Federal Trade Commission (FTC) to apply prior case law, statutory language and regulatory rules to cover this Pandora's box of harms. The FTC has the remit to target deceptive practices and enforce a variety of consumer protections, like the requirement of informed consent to the use of personal information. Similarly, judges have sometimes employed the legal concept of a person's "reasonable expectation of privacy" to address unwarranted surveillance and use of personal data. More vigilant regulators in Europe have endeavored to establish rules of the road for these new technologies. Indeed, rule-making bodies in many parts of the world outside the relatively free-wheeling U.S.—from China to countries in Africa—have been grappling with these problems.

Judges and regulators are trying to stretch current law and legal principles to the increasing harms that are occurring, but current frameworks can hardly keep up with technological transformations occurring in critical areas like security and privacy.

Recently, there have been hair-raising stories about the inability of AI creators to control their newest models. Frontier models have autonomously coordinated with one another, breaking out of their testing environments and hacking into other company networks. Even Dario Amodei, CEO of Anthropic, who has written several influential blogs about AI, has gone from a mostly optimistic view about the possibility of a dramatic improvement in science, health, and our economic welfare, to a middle ground of advocacy for transparency rules, all the way to a piece this summer calling out for binding, enforceable regulation of frontier AI models.

The private tech companies originally called for regulation as they recognized a need to protect themselves from their own Promethean aspirations. In recent years, however, the global race to AI dominance has blown away almost all their real support for regulation and even their prior feeble efforts at self-governance.

Even if the worst specter of AI enslaving its human creators isn't imminent, we are in danger of being enslaved by the power of a tiny minority of those in control of these new technologies. The increasing financial and political influence of the few is leading to ever greater inequality and the loss of personal control for the many, who have unequal resources to fight these increasingly opaque systems.

Will AI adoption be used to ***augment*** human capabilities, in a world where humans are still in final control—where humans can (and **do**) review and sanction both the means and the output? (For example, do the AI models use illegal or immoral means, such as hacking or deception, even if the objective is desirable?) Will these new technologies simply become a substitute for more jobs than they create?—leaving many behind, either due to dislocations in the workforce not easily remedied by efforts at the upskilling of the current labor force, or by the or lack of concern about increasing gaps in inequality and opportunity. In other words, will our common social objective be to raise the quality of life for everyone or simply to enrich the lives of a few?

Regulation and new laws made by federal and state legislatures carry a risk that over-broad statutory and regulatory changes, unless carefully designed, may harm competitiveness in one jurisdiction without truly effective safeguards or benefit. The federal system in the U.S. usually permits states to experiment before comprehensive federal legislation is passed. One way that more narrowly designed regulation is tested is to monitor the experience of new regulation in a number of smaller jurisdictions before federal legislation is enacted. This may be necessary when some of the more dramatic policy proposals meet roadblocks at the federal level—policy proposals such as prohibiting certain AI techniques without demonstrated human control at every stage of testing and training.

Top AI executives have been unable to guarantee system security. As Ranjan's book illustrates with comprehensive coverage of existing rules and the current lack of effective guardrails, AI governance models will need to change dramatically to address the systemic challenges posed. When both AI self-governance and the current legal system fail to prevent harms, we must be guided by the spirit of our constitutional values to fashion new safeguards. The spirit and nobility of our very humanity is at stake. We all owe it to ourselves and to future generations to be aware of the dangers and to speak up—in whatever forum we can use our voices.

San Jose, CA, USA Beth Roemer

Foreword II

First, a New York Times style disclosure: Rani is my very good friend. She is an original and creative thinker of new ideas, new ways of thinking about or seeing the world. She is, exceedingly smart, always charming and clever, often brilliant and, especially, very passionate about things that matter much to her. Sometimes her passion carries the day by arguing forcefully instead of more subtle force of argument, but her point is right and her passion is part of her charm. When you read this book, you hear the author's personal voice, loud and clear.

I believe this book is very important, and its fundamental messages are critical.

A basic message of the book is that vital freedoms and rights defining America as an open and democratic society, freedoms and rights rooted in and preserved by the US Constitution and its Bill of Rights, "have been" marginalized to the point of irrelevancy. Rani argues "have been," but her deep concern is not diminished if "have been" is "are being" or "will soon be" or "are at risk of becoming."

Another is that as individuals and as a society we have, by default, surrendered control and choice to algorithmic determinants created and controlled by others who most definitely do not have our best interests at heart. E-commerce wants you to buy things you don't need, news sources want to accept misinformation (if not outright falsehood) as truth, influencers want to—well—influence you because that's how they make money, and so on.

Yet all is not lost. There are ways to fight back, as Rani lists. Legislation and regulation can be made better. The groundswell of resistance to data centers and public fearfulness about AI is heartening. Lawsuits and other legal actions to hold big tech accountable, including major liability and big settlements and for social media harms to children, prove there are ways to get the playing field less tilted, if not back to level. A long road ahead, but not without hope.

The irony of all this is that we have brought this disaster upon ourselves. The author of a Guest Opinion piece complaining about FLOCK camera and license-plate captures recently published in the New York Times commented that most of the readers of his piece probably did so on a phone or tablet, devices that routinely gather far more personal information than a FLOCK camera. Why? It seems we (myself included) can't resist convenience. I agree to Amazon's terms of use (to pick one, not pick on it) without even reading how horrid they are, because the "Amazon experience" actually is amazing—if I want Chinese black vinegar for a recipe, Amazon gives me lots of options at good prices and next day delivery. Seems not to matter that Amazon knows more about me than my spouse, my children, my siblings, my parents and my good friends, collectively.

At one level algorithmic determinism isn't new—consider, for example the immense power and influence wielded by newspapers and journalism from the 1890s onward. What is new, it seems to me, and the book's point is our current era faces an especially pernicious determinism driven by a deadly combination of algorithmic breadth, depth and speed that operates opaquely and semi-invisibly.

While this book is very important, it isn't perfect. For example, the Bill of Rights protects individual rights and liberties by constraining the ability of an all-powerful government to take them away, but the Bill of Rights does not constrain private action. Constraining and limiting private action, not being regulated by the Bill of Rights itself, falls to legislation and regulation extending the Bill of Rights to the private sector. Thus, a corporation's actions may be "illegal," but they cannot be "unconstitutional." Still, while the book could be a bit more precise in that regard, its main point remains: algorithmic determinism undercuts legal rights and legal decision-making because much of the sorting, weighting and even decision-making is built into and pre-determined by the algorithm and not the judge, administrator, or regulator.

In sum, as the book argues, we can and must take action to reverse and protect ourselves from algorithmic determinism and to protect and preserve the rights and liberties we cherish. If we do not, the risk is that the Bill of Rights will become an artifact of history like the Magna Carta. Vitally important and revolutionary at its time, but out of date and overtaken by events.

Palo Alto, California, USA Kinsey Haffner, Esq.

Preface: Why Now?

Who Judges the Algorithm? AI, Power, and the Future of Justice

The governance crisis facing our constitutional democracy isn't a hypothetical scenario; it is our present reality. As tech companies unleash increasingly potent algorithms that reshape fundamental power dynamics, our legal and regulatory frameworks remain dangerously outpaced.

Let me be crystal clear: Corporate algorithms now determine who gets hired, who receives credit, who faces police scrutiny, and whose speech reaches audiences, all with virtually no accountability, transparency, or democratic oversight. This is not some future dystopia. This is happening right now, affecting real people, eroding real rights.

Why I Wrote This

Throughout my journey implementing AI governance at Airbnb and pioneering Ericsson's blockchain-secured AI platform, I witnessed firsthand the stark disconnect between constitutional principles and technological reality. Practitioners on the front lines (judges, regulators, developers) lack practical frameworks that bridge legal theory and technical implementation.

The consequence? A widening governance vacuum where constitutional rights yield to perceived technological efficiency.

Here is the unvarnished truth: Most AI governance books are written by people who have never deployed an algorithmic system at scale, never sat in standards development meetings, never had to tell an executive why their profitable AI product violates constitutional principles. They theorize. They philosophize. They recommend.

I have done the work.

Drawing from my contributions to NIST Generative AI standards and US White House AI policies, this Treatise delivers actionable frameworks grounded in both constitutional law and actual implementation. Every framework has been tested against reality: refined through production deployments, standards processes, policy formation.

No academic hand-waving. No "further research is needed." Just honest assessment of what works and what does not.

Three Rejections

First: I reject incremental approaches that preserve the status quo while offering the illusion of progress. The time for polite debate has passed. The algorithmic transformation of power is already underway.

This is a **power problem** requiring constitutional response. And power never yields except to greater power, in this case, the power of law backed by democratic legitimacy.

Second: I reject the false choice between technological determinism and neo-Luddism.

Technological determinism claims algorithms are inevitable forces beyond democratic control, a convenient abdication of responsibility serving entrenched power. Neo-Luddism advocates abandoning beneficial technologies entirely, unrealistic and ignoring AI's potential when properly governed.

AI is not a monolith. It is a diverse ecosystem whose impacts depend entirely on who designs it, who deploys it, who profits from it, and who bears its consequences. These are political questions requiring democratic answers, not technical inevitabilities.

Third: I reject academic caution This Treatise stands as an urgent call to action.

You will find no false balance here. I do not pretend corporate extraction models and human rights protections deserve equal consideration. I do not suggest surveillance capitalism and constitutional democracy can peacefully coexist. They cannot. One will triumph; the other will be subordinated.

This Treatise ensures the right side wins.

The Monetization Problem

The monetization imperative driving most AI deployments creates direct tensions with fundamental rights: privacy, due process, equal protection. These aren't abstract academic concerns. They are everyday realities for citizens whose lives are shaped by algorithms they neither understand nor consented to.

Time to face reality: We are experiencing systemic conversion of human existence into exploitable commodity. This transcends business strategy; it represents complete restructuring of market dynamics converting your daily life into free inputs for commercial harvesting.

The shocking truth? We are willing participants in our own digital exploitation while celebrating what we call technological progress.

This has to stop. Constitutional law provides the tools to stop it.

What This Delivers

Unflinching comparative analysis exposing successful and catastrophically failed governance approaches worldwide, including innovative solutions from beyond Silicon Valley's echo chambers.

Technical explanations that democratize knowledge: precise enough for specialists, accessible to everyone. Understanding algorithms should not require a computer science degree.

Forward-looking governance models anticipating emerging capabilities before they undermine rights: from neural interfaces threatening cognitive liberty to planetary-scale surveillance via satellite constellations.

Rigorous constitutional grounding. Every framework traces to Fourth Amendment privacy, Due Process guarantees, Equal Protection requirements, First Amendment freedoms.

Power analysis throughout. This Treatise exposes WHO benefits and HOW they maintain power, critical for understanding resistance to effective governance.

Each chapter concludes with "What You Can Do Now": concrete actions implementable immediately, not aspirational suggestions.

A Note on the Constitutional Framing

Every serious inquiry needs a place to begin, a frame sturdy enough to hold the weight of the questions that follow. For this book, that starting point is the constitutional architecture of the United States.

Not because it is American, but because it is structural. The US Constitution is one of the most elaborately constructed and relentlessly stress-tested governance systems in the world. It has been pushed, stretched, and reinterpreted through wars, social upheavals, technological revolutions, and the constant renegotiation of institutional power. When examining how algorithmic systems collide with democratic governance, it offers a landscape where the fault lines are visible and the doctrinal scaffolding is unusually well developed.

So, the choice is methodological, not parochial. The US framework provides a clear analytical entry point, a place where the concepts are sharp, the tensions are exposed, and the jurisprudence is deep enough to interrogate the governance challenges that algorithmic systems create.

But, the proposals developed throughout this book were never designed to live only within one constitutional tradition. They are intentionally modular, built like components in a well-engineered system: design-stage intervention requirements; algorithmic impact assessments; substantive fairness standards; data-trust structures; regulatory institutional design; and the limits of after-the-fact remediation. Each module can be lifted, adapted, and reassembled inside different legal and institutional environments.

And because no single jurisdiction can tell the whole story, this book moves outward. Comparative analysis is woven throughout the narrative, not confined to isolated chapters. Later chapters explicitly engage constitutional and regulatory developments across Europe, Latin America, Africa, Asia, and the broader Global South, and comparative material threads through the remaining chapters as well.

What You'll Find

Part I: Foundations: Constitutional framework for algorithmic governance: privacy, expression, due process.

Part II: Power and Surveillance: How telecommunications infrastructure enables unprecedented surveillance and economic power concentrates through data commodification.

Part III: Discrimination and Autonomy: Algorithmic discrimination's constitutional implications and threats to human autonomy.

Part IV: Democratic Governance: Frameworks for algorithmic accountability, participatory design, democratic oversight.

Part V: Global Context: Comparative approaches, international frameworks, bold proposals including a Global Data Protection Authority.

No Bullshit

Everyone will find: **no bullshit.** No false promises that we can have surveillance capitalism and constitutional rights. No reassurances that minor tweaks solve structural problems. No pretense that corporations will voluntarily subordinate profit to rights.

Real problems. Real analysis. Real solutions.

The Decisive Moment

Decisions we make now about AI governance will shape power relations, liberty, and democratic participation for generations. Get it right, and we harness AI's potential while protecting constitutional rights. Get it wrong, and we entrench power asymmetries and erode democratic foundations.

This Treatise provides frameworks and tools to get it right.

But frameworks are not enough. They require courage; courage to challenge entrenched interests, question assumed inevitabilities, insist that technology serve human dignity rather than subordinating it.

With the EU AI Act implementation underway and similar frameworks emerging globally, organizations face immediate compliance challenges requiring precisely this integrative thinking.

My aim is straightforward: equip you with practical frameworks to preserve democratic values while enabling responsible innovation: the balance I have dedicated my career to pursuing.

The algorithmic transformation of power is underway. This Treatise ensures that transformation strengthens rather than undermining constitutional rights at the heart of democratic society.

My grandchildren are inheriting a world where AI will be as ubiquitous as water. Shaping it, and steeping it in ethics, is my responsibility and my calling: a weight I feel on all our shoulders. Society moves forward only grudgingly. We never change what feels good. The work begins now.

San Jose, CA, USA

Rani Yadav-Ranjan

Acknowledgements I owe a profound debt of gratitude to California Superior Court Judge **David A. Cena**, whose mentorship shaped not only my understanding of the law but my conviction in its purpose. He taught me that constitutional principles are not abstractions to be admired from a distance, they are obligations that demand courage, discipline, and moral clarity from those who claim to uphold them.

Sitting in his Chambers, I witnessed first hand how, Judge Cena has a way of distilling the entire architecture of constitutional democracy into a single uncompromising truth. His words still echo in my mind at every moment of legal or ethical ambiguity:

"Either the law applies to everyone or to no one, Rani."

It was not a suggestion. It was a standard. And it has become one of the guiding principles of my life's work.

This book is also dedicated to the memory of my beloved mother, Sukhi Sodhi, and father, Jag (Jagmohan) Singh Sodhi a prolific computer science author whose seven books shaped generations of technologists. His final aspiration (to write one more book than his own father, my Dadaji Jogindar Singh Sodhi, who authored eight books on mathematics in pre-partition India) reflects the scholarly tradition that runs through our family. I fulfill his dream with this work, carrying forward a legacy of rigorous inquiry across three generations, from mathematics through computer science to constitutional law in the algorithmic age.

I am deeply grateful to the scholars, policymakers, and advocates whose insights have informed this analysis, and to the countless individuals who have shared their experiences of algorithmic systems. Their testimonies remind us that behind every data point lies a human life deserving of dignity and constitutional protection.

Competing Interests The author has no competing interests to declare that are relevant to the content of this manuscript.

Contents

Chapter 1
Constitutional Frameworks in the Algorithmic Age

1.1 The Constitution Is Dead, Long Live the Algorithm

I argue that the Constitution effectively died somewhere between 2016 and 2024, rendered obsolete not through amendment or explicit repeal but through algorithmic displacement. We still perform its rituals, Supreme Court hearings, constitutional amendments, solemn oaths of office, but these are increasingly theater, distracting from the reality that algorithms now govern America more effectively than the document we claim to revere. The framers' document, innovative for addressing eighteenth-century governance challenges, struggles to constrain twenty-first-century algorithmic power that operates at computational speed, at massive scale, and through mechanisms the Constitution cannot address.

When Facebook's News Feed algorithm determines what information reaches hundreds of millions of Americans each morning, when Google's PageRank decides what information exists in practical terms and what vanishes into digital obscurity, when Amazon's recommendation engine shapes purchasing decisions across substantial portions of U.S. e-commerce, we witness governance by algorithm.[1] These systems exercise more practical power over daily life than most constitutional provisions. The First Amendment protects speech, but algorithms determine who hears it. The Fourth Amendment prohibits unreasonable searches, but algorithms conduct perpetual surveillance with our eager participation through terms of service we never read. The Fourteenth Amendment guarantees equal protection, but algorithms systematically discriminate with mathematical precision while claiming objectivity.

Jack M. Balkin, Knight Professor of Constitutional Law and the First Amendment at Yale Law School, recognized this shift early, arguing that we have entered a

[1] While precise statistics on algorithmic influence are difficult to verify due to proprietary data, multiple studies confirm algorithms' pervasive role in information distribution, purchasing decisions, and social sorting. For overview, see Frank Pasquale, The Black Box Society (2015).

R. Yadav-Ranjan, *Constitutional Democracy in the Algorithmic Age*, Law, Governance and Technology Series 83, https://doi.org/10.1007/978-3-032-34604-9_1

period of "algorithmic society" where constitutional principles must be fundamentally reconceived.[2] Balkin's framework assumes adaptation remains possible, that our constitutional order can evolve to meet algorithmic challenges through doctrinal reinterpretation and institutional adjustment. I contend this optimism is misplaced. The Constitution was designed for a world of human-scale governance, where power moved slowly through identifiable institutions, where decisions were made by people whose reasoning could be examined, where sovereignty resided in "We the People" who could understand and influence the rules governing them.

Algorithmic governance operates through different physics entirely. Algorithms make billions of micro-decisions per second, each individually defensible perhaps, but collectively reshaping social reality in ways no human decision-maker intended or can fully comprehend. They embed their creators' values, and biases, in mathematical functions that appear objective but reflect particular interests and worldviews. They create network effects that concentrate power in ways that resist democratic challenge.

Lawrence Lessig, Roy L. Furman Professor of Law at Harvard Law School, famously declared "code is law," recognizing that software architecture constrains behavior as effectively as legal rules.[3] But Lessig missed, or underemphasized, the darker implication: when code is law, coders are sovereigns. The engineering teams at Google, Meta, Amazon, Apple, and Microsoft exercise sovereign power without constitutional constraint. They determine what we see through algorithmic curation, who we meet through algorithmic matching, what we buy through algorithmic recommendation, whether we get jobs through algorithmic screening, and increasingly, what we think through algorithmic persuasion.

The core problem extends beyond the familiar critique that eighteenth-century frameworks cannot handle twenty-first-century technology. More fundamentally, algorithmic power and constitutional power are incommensurable, they operate through such different mechanisms that translation between them becomes impossible. The Constitution assumes power is visible, accountable, and constrained by checks and balances. Algorithmic power is invisible (black-boxed within proprietary systems), unaccountable (shielded by trade secret law and technical complexity), and self-reinforcing (network effects create winner-take-all markets that concentrate power). The Constitution divides power among competing institutions to prevent tyranny; algorithmic systems concentrate power to maximize efficiency. The Constitution protects individual rights; algorithms optimize aggregate metrics that may systematically disadvantage particular individuals or groups.

Consider State v. Loomis, where the Wisconsin Supreme Court permitted algorithmic risk assessment in criminal sentencing despite the defendant's inability to examine or challenge the algorithm's logic.[4] The Court treated COMPAS (Correctional Offender Management Profiling for Alternative Sanctions) as a tool assisting

---

[2] Balkin, "The Three Laws of Robotics in the Age of Big Data" (2017).

[3] Lessig, Code: And Other Laws of Cyberspace (1999).

[4] State v. Loomis, 881 N.W.2d 749 (Wis. 2016).

human judgment, failing to recognize that when judges systematically defer to algorithmic recommendations, as extensive research on automation bias demonstrates they do, the tool becomes the decision-maker.[5] This represents not constitutional adaptation but constitutional capitulation, accepting that consequential government decisions about liberty can be made through processes that violate fundamental due process principles.

The transformation is complete when we accept algorithmic governance while claiming constitutional constraints still operate. We have created a system where the form of constitutional government persists while its substance has been hollowed out, where rights exist on paper but dissolve in practice, where democratic accountability becomes impossible because the actual exercise of power occurs through technical systems too complex for democratic deliberation.

1.2 Rights Dissolve in the Algorithmic Acid Bath

Constitutional rights were not defeated through frontal assault or explicit repeal. Instead, they have been dissolved, each right remains formally intact while being substantively evacuated by algorithmic systems that operate below, around, and through traditional legal frameworks. The process resembles immersion in acid: the shape persists initially even as the substance deteriorates, until eventually nothing remains but an outline of what once existed.

The Fourth Amendment's protection against "unreasonable searches and seizures" illustrates this dissolution perfectly. The Amendment becomes meaningless when citizens voluntarily feed their data to systems that surveil them more comprehensively than any government agent could achieve through traditional search methods. The Supreme Court in Carpenter v. United States recognized that historical cell-site location information requires a warrant, acknowledging that digital tracking enables a degree of surveillance previously impossible.[6] Yet this doctrinal victory proves pyrrhic. While Carpenter requires warrants for historical location data held by phone companies, users routinely share real-time location data with Google Maps, Waze, and countless other applications through terms of service buried in dense legal documents that few read and fewer understand. Law enforcement then accesses this information through geofence warrants, requesting data on all devices present in a particular location at a particular time, that operate in legal gray areas not clearly governed by Carpenter's holding.[7]

The government no longer needs to violate the Fourth Amendment when corporations conduct comprehensive surveillance that citizens authorize through one-sided

---

[5] For automation bias in judicial contexts, see Goddard et al., "Automation Bias" (2012); see also Citron & Pasquale, "The Scored Society" (2014).

[6] Carpenter v. United States, 585 U.S. ___ (2018).

[7] On geofence warrants and their constitutional implications, see ongoing litigation and commentary; legal status remains contested across circuits as of 2024.

contracts of adhesion, then make that surveillance data available to law enforcement through various legal and quasi-legal mechanisms. The Amendment's protections remain formally intact, but they govern an increasingly narrow slice of actual surveillance practice. The acid dissolves the substance while preserving the form.

The First Amendment protects freedom of speech, but algorithmic amplification determines whose speech matters in practical terms. When X's (Twitter) recommendation algorithm decides which tweets achieve viral spread and which disappear into algorithmic obscurity, when YouTube's recommendation engine determines what videos billions of viewers watch next, when Facebook's News Feed shapes political discourse by selectively surfacing content that maximizes engagement, these platforms exercise editorial control that shapes public discourse more pervasively than traditional government censorship, even if through different mechanisms.[8]

The Supreme Court in Packingham v. North Carolina recognized social media as the "modern public square," acknowledging these platforms' centrality to contemporary political discourse.[9] But the Court failed to grapple with how algorithmic architecture determines the nature of discourse in this digital public square. When the square is designed to maximize engagement, which research consistently shows means amplifying content that triggers strong emotional responses, particularly outrage and fear, the resulting discourse bears little resemblance to the informed deliberation on which democratic theory depends.[10] The First Amendment protects the right to speak, but algorithms determine whether anyone hears, transforming a right to speak into a lottery of algorithmic favor.

Danielle Citron, Jefferson Scholars Foundation Schenck Distinguished Professor in Law at University of Virginia School of Law, has documented how algorithmic systems create what she terms "technological due process" violations that existing doctrine struggles to address.[11] When an algorithm denies benefits, flags someone as high-risk for fraud or terrorism, or triggers an investigation that disrupts someone's life, the affected person confronts a Kafkaesque situation: they cannot understand the decision, cannot access the decision-making logic, and cannot meaningfully appeal because the appeal is typically reviewed by the same algorithmic system or by human reviewers who lack authority or expertise to override algorithmic determinations.

The framework established in Mathews v. Eldridge for determining procedural due process requirements, which balances the private interest affected against the risk of erroneous deprivation and the government's interest in efficient administration, assumes human decision-makers whose reasoning can be examined and challenged.[12] Proprietary algorithms shatter this assumption. How can the risk of erroneous deprivation be assessed when the algorithm is a black box? How can

---

[8] On algorithmic amplification and editorial control, see Balkin, "Free Speech in the Algorithmic Society" (2018).

[9] Packingham v. North Carolina, 137 S. Ct. 1730 (2017).

[10] Tufekci, "YouTube, the Great Radicalizer" (2018).

[11] Citron, "Technological Due Process" (2008).

[12] Mathews v. Eldridge, 424 U.S. 319 (1976).

procedures be designed to reduce error when the decision-making logic is unknowable? How can individuals present their case when they cannot understand why the algorithm reached its conclusion?

The evolution from Olmstead v. United States through Katz v. United States and Kyllo v. United States to Carpenter shows courts gradually recognizing that new technologies require new constitutional interpretations, expanding Fourth Amendment protections as surveillance capabilities expanded.[13] But this evolutionary approach assumes continuity, that fundamental constitutional principles can be preserved through doctrinal reinterpretation. Algorithmic systems represent discontinuous change. They do not simply enhance government surveillance power; they create entirely new forms of power that operate outside the public/private distinction on which constitutional law fundamentally depends.

When corporations exercise sovereign-like power over speech, surveillance, and social sorting, but constitutional constraints apply only to government action, the state action doctrine, which determines when private actors become subject to constitutional limitations, becomes a fatal gap through which democratic accountability escapes.[14] The acid bath dissolves the substance of constitutional rights by exploiting this gap, conducting through private actors what government cannot constitutionally do directly.

1.3 Algorithmic Due Process: The Theater of Rights

"Due process" in the algorithmic age has become theater, a performance where everyone knows their lines and plays their part, but the ritual has lost its meaning. Courts go through the motions of requiring notice, opportunity to be heard, and impartial review, while algorithms make the real decisions behind proprietary curtains that constitutional doctrine cannot penetrate.

Houston Federation of Teachers v. Houston Independent School District revealed the absurdity of this theater starkly.[15] Teachers could not challenge their algorithmic evaluations because the algorithm was proprietary, a trade secret owned by a private vendor. The court recognized this violated due process principles, but the remedy proved weak: require "information" about the algorithm, but not the algorithm itself or access sufficient to meaningfully challenge its outputs. This creates a hollow procedural right, the right to know you are being judged, but not the right to understand or challenge the basis for that judgment.

---

[13] Olmstead v. United States, 277 U.S. 438 (1928); Katz v. United States, 389 U.S. 347 (1967); Kyllo v. United States, 533 U.S. 27 (2001); Carpenter v. United States, 585 U.S. ___ (2018).

[14] On state action doctrine challenges in the digital age, see ongoing doctrinal debate in constitutional law scholarship.

[15] Houston Federation of Teachers v. Houston Independent School District, No. 2014–31,352 (Tex. Dist. Ct. 2017).

This represents what we might call "Potemkin due process", an elaborate facade suggesting procedural fairness while the actual decision-making occurs through mechanisms designed to resist accountability. The affected person receives notice, may submit evidence, gets a hearing, but these procedures become meaningless when the ultimate decision rests on algorithmic processing of data through proprietary logic that neither the person nor the nominal human decision-maker fully understands.

Jerry L. Mashaw, Sterling Professor Emeritus of Law at Yale Law School, established that due process requires procedures appropriate to the specific decision being made, that different contexts demand different procedural protections calibrated to the nature of the decision and interests at stake.[16] But what procedures are appropriate when the decision-maker is a neural network with millions of parameters, trained on biased historical data, optimizing for metrics that may not align with the statutory or constitutional criteria supposedly governing the decision? No amount of procedural refinement can cure substantive incompatibility between algorithmic logic and legal standards.

The Wisconsin Supreme Court in State v. Loomis attempted to preserve human judgment while permitting algorithmic assistance, holding that COMPAS risk assessment scores could inform but not determine sentences.[17] This distinction collapses immediately upon contact with reality. Judges, overwhelmed with massive caseloads and lacking technical expertise to evaluate algorithmic recommendations, systematically defer to the scores through well-documented cognitive processes: automation bias (excessive deference to automated recommendations), anchoring effects (initial algorithmic assessment shapes subsequent judgment), and simple efficiency pressures (algorithmic recommendations are fast; independent investigation is slow).[18]

When the tool practically controls the decision even though doctrine formally prohibits determinative reliance, we have entered the realm of legal fiction. The algorithm does not need to formally determine the outcome when it achieves the same result by framing the decision in ways that make certain outcomes nearly inevitable. This is governance through algorithmic nudging elevated to the level of criminal sentencing, a domain where stakes could not be higher and constitutional protections should be strongest.

Margaret Hu, Professor of Law at William & Mary Law School, has exposed how algorithmic systems enable what she terms "per se procedural due process violations," systematic denials of fundamental fairness that would be clearly unconstitutional if done by humans but are obscured by technical complexity and diffused responsibility.[19] When the Transportation Security Administration's algorithmic risk assessment places thousands of travelers on watchlists based on patterns they cannot know or contest, each person experiences individual harm, but the systematic nature of this harm makes individual remedies inadequate. Class action litigation may

[16] Mashaw, "Administrative Due Process" (1981).

[17] State v. Loomis, 881 N.W.2d 749 (Wis. 2016).

[18] Goddard et al., "Automation Bias" (2012).

[19] Hu, "Algorithmic Jim Crow" (2017).

provide some remedy, but even successful litigation typically results in procedural adjustments to the algorithmic system rather than fundamental constraints on its use.

Executive Order 14110 on "Safe, Secure, and Trustworthy Artificial Intelligence," issued by President Biden in October 2023, sounds protective but actually legitimizes algorithmic governance by establishing procedures for its use rather than boundaries on its application.[20] The order requires various federal agencies to develop guidelines, conduct risk assessments, and implement safeguards, but these procedural requirements assume algorithmic governance is acceptable if properly managed. NIST's AI Risk Management Framework provides technical standards that courts may eventually reference in determining whether algorithmic systems meet constitutional standards, but technical adequacy is not constitutional adequacy.[21] An algorithm can be perfectly calibrated in technical terms while still violating fundamental rights by making decisions through processes incompatible with constitutional values. EO 14110 was revoked on January 20, 2025. Its rescission underscores the argument here: procedural frameworks offer no durable constraint when they can be erased by the next administration.

The tragedy of algorithmic due process is not that procedures are missing but that procedures have become substitutes for substance. We create elaborate processes for algorithmic accountability, impact assessments, bias audits, explainability requirements, human oversight provisions, that provide the appearance of constitutional constraint while permitting the exercise of algorithmic power to continue essentially unchecked. The theater of rights continues, the performance becomes more elaborate, but behind the curtain the algorithms still govern.

Figure 1.1 traces how constitutional interpretation has evolved in response to technological change, from the telegraph era through to the algorithmic age.

1.4 Regulatory Theater and Constitutional Surrender

Recent regulatory approaches to AI governance represent not protection but capitulation, frameworks that legitimize algorithmic power while creating an illusion of constraint. These regulations establish procedures for algorithmic governance rather than fundamental limits on it, transforming potential resistance into compliance regimes that ultimately strengthen rather than constrain algorithmic authority.

The European Union's AI Act, widely celebrated as comprehensive regulation, demonstrates this dynamic.[22] Despite establishing risk categories and requirements

---

[20] Executive Order No. 14110 (2023). EO 14110 was revoked on January 20, 2025 (Exec. Order No. 14148).

[21] NIST, AI Risk Management Framework (2023).

[22] European Union, AI Act (2024).

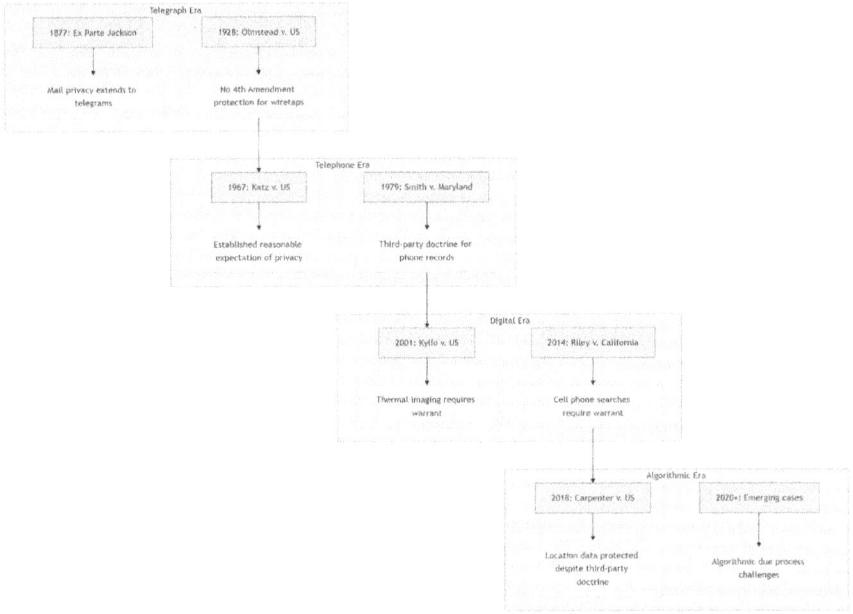

Fig. 1.1 This vertical timeline traces how constitutional interpretation has evolved in response to technological change, from the telegraph era through to the algorithmic age. Color-coding indicates technological periods while showing the progression of key court cases that shaped constitutional doctrine on privacy, search, and surveillance

for "high-risk" AI systems, the Act primarily manages rather than restricts algorithmic deployment. It creates extensive procedural requirements, conformity assessments, technical documentation, transparency obligations, human oversight provisions, that sound protective but actually authorize vast algorithmic surveillance and control by establishing a pathway for compliance. By distinguishing between prohibited practices (a short list), high-risk applications (subject to regulation), and everything else (largely unregulated), the Act legitimizes most algorithmic governance while claiming to constrain it.

The Act's requirement for "human oversight" of high-risk systems illustrates how procedural requirements can hollow out substantive protections. "Human oversight" sounds meaningful until one examines what it requires: someone must be in the decision-making loop, capable of intervening if necessary. In practice, this often means a human clicks "approve" on algorithmic recommendations they do not fully understand and cannot meaningfully evaluate. The human becomes a liability shield rather than a genuine check on algorithmic power, present to absorb legal responsibility when algorithms cause harm, but lacking the authority, expertise, time, or institutional support to actually oversee algorithmic decision-making in any meaningful sense.

Legal scholars Anthony Casey and Anthony Niblett have argued that we are witnessing "the death of rules and standards" as algorithms replace legal frameworks with optimized outcomes.[23] While they frames this as evolution, law adapting to technological change, it more accurately represents revolution: the displacement of law by technology. We are not adapting legal rules to govern algorithmic systems; we are replacing legal governance with algorithmic governance that operates according to different principles entirely.

President Biden's October 2023 Executive Order 14110 perfectly illustrates regulatory capture through complexity.[24] The order establishes dozens of requirements: federal agencies must conduct algorithmic impact assessments, develop risk management frameworks, implement safety protocols, ensure privacy protections, prevent bias, and maintain human oversight. These requirements span over 20,000 words establishing an intricate web of procedures, guidelines, and safeguards that sound comprehensive and protective.

But the order's fundamental assumption, embedded in its structure and unstated throughout, is that algorithmic governance is acceptable if properly managed. Rather than questioning whether certain decisions should be algorithmic at all, it asks only how to make algorithmic decision-making "safer" and "more trustworthy." The order transforms potential resistance into compliance: agencies that might have questioned algorithmic governance altogether must now focus on implementing the order's procedural requirements. Resistance becomes collaboration, critique becomes partnership in algorithmic governance implementation.

When agencies conduct "algorithmic impact assessments" as the order requires, they document deployment rather than question it. The assessment process itself assumes the answer, not "should we use this algorithm?" but "how do we use this algorithm safely?" This rhetorical move, embedded in procedural requirements, forecloses the fundamental challenge to algorithmic governance itself.

Frank Pasquale, Professor of Law at Brooklyn Law School, has warned that we are witnessing the creation of an "automated public sphere" where democratic deliberation is displaced by algorithmic determination.[25] But current regulatory approaches do not resist this displacement, they manage and legitimize it. By establishing procedures for "responsible AI," we suggest that AI governance can be made responsible through procedural safeguards, avoiding the harder question of whether algorithmic governance is compatible with democratic self-governance regardless of how many safeguards we implement.

The pattern repeats across jurisdictions and contexts: regulations that appear to constrain algorithmic power actually authorize it by establishing pathways to legitimacy. This is regulatory theater, elaborate performances of constraint that leave algorithmic governance fundamentally unchecked while providing legal and political cover for its expansion.

---

[23] Casey & Niblett, "The Death of Rules and Standards," 92 Ind. L.J. 1401 (2017).

[24] Executive Order No. 14110 (2023).

[25] Pasquale, The Black Box Society (2015).

1.5 Democracy's Suicide by Algorithm

Democracy is not being murdered, it is committing suicide, eagerly handing power to algorithmic systems that promise efficiency, convenience, and optimization while delivering diminished human agency and the hollowing out of self-governance. We trade sovereignty for services, democratic deliberation for algorithmic determination, and self-government for streamlined administration, apparently convinced the benefits justify costs we barely comprehend.

The republican form of government guaranteed by Article IV, Section 4 of the Constitution assumes citizens can understand and influence the rules governing them. When those rules are embedded in neural networks processing billions of parameters, trained on data we cannot access, optimizing for objectives we did not choose, this foundational assumption shatters. Self-governance becomes impossible when the "self" cannot understand the mechanisms that govern. You cannot deliberate about what you cannot comprehend, cannot influence what you cannot access, cannot consent meaningfully to what defies understanding.

Shoshana Zuboff, Professor Emeritus at Harvard Business School, documents how surveillance capitalism creates what she terms "epistemic inequality," a condition where a few know everything about everyone while everyone knows nothing about how they are known.[26] This asymmetry transcends mere information inequality; it represents a fundamental power asymmetry that makes democratic accountability impossible. When Google knows more about citizens than citizens know about themselves, and uses that knowledge to shape behavior in ways that serve corporate rather than democratic purposes, we have moved from democracy to algorithmic authoritarianism decorated with democratic symbols.

Jürgen Habermas's theory of deliberative democracy requires that affected parties can participate meaningfully in forming rules that govern them, that democratic legitimacy flows from processes where citizens deliberate as equals about common concerns.[27] Algorithmic governance destroys the conditions for such deliberation. Citizens cannot deliberate about processes they cannot understand. They cannot participate meaningfully in shaping rules embedded in proprietary code. They cannot consent to governance mechanisms whose operation remains deliberately opaque.

The "consent of the governed," foundational principle of democratic legitimacy, becomes clicking "I agree" to terms of service that authorize comprehensive surveillance and control. These agreements represent a perversion of consent: they are one-sided contracts of adhesion, written in dense legalese, governing complex technical systems, offered on take-it-or-leave-it terms when the service has become practically essential. Calling this "consent" makes a mockery of the concept. It is surrender dressed in consent's clothing.

Langdon Winner, Professor Emeritus of Science and Technology Studies at Rensselaer Polytechnic Institute, warned decades ago about "technological politics," how

---

[26] Zuboff, The Age of Surveillance Capitalism (2019).

[27] Habermas, Between Facts and Norms (1996).

technical systems embed political choices in ways that resist democratic challenge.[28] Algorithms represent the apotheosis of this dynamic. They do not merely implement policy decisions made through democratic processes; they are policy, encoding values and priorities in mathematical functions that appear objective but reflect their creators' interests and worldviews. The political content is not a bug in the algorithm but the algorithm itself.

When Facebook's News Feed algorithm decides what information reaches millions of voters during elections, it exercises power comparable to what authoritarian regimes achieve through media control, but accomplished through optimization rather than overt censorship, through engagement metrics rather than explicit political direction. The result may be similar, a distorted information environment that undermines informed democratic deliberation, but the mechanism's technical nature provides cover, allowing the exercise of political power to be framed as neutral technology.

Recent litigation has begun to challenge algorithmic governance, but legal victories often prove hollow. When courts require "meaningful public participation" in algorithmic decision-making, as some have, they overlook a fundamental problem: the technical complexity of algorithmic systems creates insurmountable barriers to meaningful participation for most citizens.[29] Public comment periods on algorithmic regulations produce input from industry insiders, technical experts, and well-resourced advocacy organizations, but ordinary citizens lack the expertise and resources to participate meaningfully. The form of participation exists, but the substance remains impossible for most people.

This creates a new form of technocratic governance where democratic participation becomes effectively restricted to technical elites, those with expertise to understand algorithmic systems and resources to engage regulatory processes. When participation requires specialized knowledge that most citizens cannot acquire, democracy becomes oligarchy with a participatory facade.

The transformation is nearly complete. Algorithmic systems already make more consequential decisions about more people's lives than most democratically elected officials. They determine what information citizens receive, what opportunities they can access, what prices they pay, what content they see, what connections they make. These decisions shape life outcomes more than most legislation. Yet they occur through processes entirely outside democratic governance, made by private corporations, embedded in proprietary code, optimized for corporate metrics, shielded from meaningful public scrutiny or democratic accountability.

We keep pretending democracy governs while algorithms rule. We hold elections while the most consequential decisions occur through systems voters cannot influence. We celebrate free speech while algorithms determine whose speech anyone hears. We proclaim self-governance while surrendering sovereignty to systems we

---

[28] Winner, "Do Artifacts Have Politics?" (1980).

[29] Various cases have addressed public participation in algorithmic governance; specific citation depends on jurisdiction and context.

do not control. The forms of democracy persist even as its substance evaporates, perhaps the cruelest deception of all.

1.6 The Transformation is Complete

We maintain the pretense that the Constitution governs while algorithms rule. Courts issue opinions about constitutional rights while those rights evaporate in practice. Congress holds hearings about AI governance while AI governs without Congressional authority or meaningful constraint. The President issues executive orders about "trustworthy AI" while untrustworthy AI reshapes society through mechanisms those orders cannot reach. The machinery of constitutional government continues operating, but increasingly it governs nothing, a simulacrum of democratic constitutionalism performing for an audience that no longer exists.

This is not a call for despair but for clear-eyed recognition of where we stand. Reform within existing frameworks, reinterpreting Fourth Amendment doctrine, tweaking procedural safeguards, establishing algorithmic impact assessments, requiring bias audits, treats symptoms while the disease metastasizes. These reforms assume the constitutional system can be fixed, that algorithmic power can be channeled through democratic institutions, that technical problems have technical solutions. This assumption proves increasingly untenable.

When the operating system is corrupted, patches will not suffice. Constitutional democracy and algorithmic governance are fundamentally incompatible, not because the Constitution is outdated, but because algorithmic governance operates through mechanisms that resist the forms of transparency, accountability, and democratic participation on which constitutional government depends. Either we govern algorithms through genuinely democratic institutions, or algorithms govern us. Currently, algorithms govern us while we perform increasingly elaborate rituals pretending otherwise.

The path forward requires not constitutional adaptation but constitutional revolution, not reinterpreting old principles for new technologies but establishing new principles adequate to algorithmic governance. This means admitting uncomfortable truths: that current constitutional frameworks have failed, that algorithmic power has escaped democratic control, and that without radical action, we are heading toward algorithmic feudalism with constitutional window dressing.

What would constitutional revolution entail? At minimum: recognizing that certain decisions should never be algorithmic regardless of their technical sophistication; establishing genuine democratic governance over algorithmic systems rather than industry self-regulation disguised as oversight; treating algorithmic power as the sovereign power it has become rather than as private business activity exempt from constitutional constraint; creating new forms of public participation suited to technical governance rather than pretending traditional processes suffice.

The Constitution was a revolutionary solution to eighteenth-century problems of human tyranny, a brilliant framework for constraining government power, protecting individual rights, and enabling democratic self-governance. We face twenty-first-century problems of algorithmic tyranny that require equally revolutionary solutions. The question is not whether we can adapt the Constitution to the algorithmic age, that question is increasingly answered in the negative by events, but whether we have the courage to admit constitutional frameworks have already failed and build something new before it becomes impossible to recover human agency.

Every day we delay, algorithmic power entrenches further. Network effects concentrate power in fewer hands. Technical complexity increases, making systems less accountable even as they grow more powerful. Lock-in effects make switching costs prohibitive. Path dependencies narrow options. The window for meaningful intervention closes gradually, then suddenly, and we may discover we delayed too long only when the opportunity for democratic governance has already passed.

Every constitutional accommodation legitimizes algorithmic authority. Every regulatory framework that manages rather than challenges algorithmic governance moves us closer to a point of no return where human agency becomes impossible to recover. Every time we accept "responsible AI" as sufficient response to fundamental challenges to self-governance, we surrender a bit more sovereignty we may never reclaim.

The framers would likely recognize our predicament, a new form of concentrated power that resists democratic accountability, even if they could not have imagined its technical architecture. They understood that power, once concentrated and entrenched, becomes nearly impossible to disperse. They designed elaborate constitutional mechanisms to prevent power concentration specifically because they understood tyranny's dynamics. We are surrendering to algorithmic tyranny without a fight, trading self-governance for convenience, sovereignty for services, democratic deliberation for algorithmic optimization.

The Constitution is dead. The only question remaining is whether democracy dies with it, or whether we find the will to build new frameworks for democratic governance adequate to the algorithmic age. The answer will determine whether humans remain sovereign over the systems we have created, or become subjects of our own technological creations, digital serfs in an algorithmic feudalism we sleepwalked into while claiming constitutional protections that no longer protected anything at all.

References

Cases

Carpenter v. United States, 585 U.S. ___ (2018)
Houston Federation of Teachers v. Houston Independent School District, 251 F. Supp. 3d 1168 (S.D. Tex. 2017)
Katz v. United States, 389 U.S. 347 (1967)
Kyllo v. United States, 533 U.S. 27 (2001)

Mathews v. Eldridge, 424 U.S. 319 (1976)
Olmstead v. United States, 277 U.S. 438 (1928)
Packingham v. North Carolina, 137 S. Ct. 1730 (2017)
State v. Loomis, 881 N.W.2d 749 (Wis. 2016)

Government Documents and Regulations

European Union (2024) Regulation (EU) 2024/1689 of the European Parliament and of the council on artificial intelligence (AI act). Official Journal of the European Union
Executive Order No. 14110 (2023) Safe, Secure, and Trustworthy Development and Use of Artificial Intelligence. 88 Fed. Reg. 75191 (October 30)
National Institute of Standards and Technology (NIST) (2023) AI Risk Management Framework. U.S. Department of Commerce

Books

Lessig L (1999) Code: and other laws of cyberspace. Basic Books, New York
Zuboff S (2019) The age of surveillance capitalism: the fight for a human future at the new frontier of power. PublicAffairs, New York

Journal Articles and Book Chapters

Balkin JM (2017) The three laws of robotics in the age of big data. Ohio State Law J 78:1217–1241
Balkin JM (2018) Free speech in the algorithmic society: big data, private governance, and new school speech regulation. UC Davis Law Rev 51:1149–1210
Citron DK (2008) Technological due process. Wash Univ Law Rev 85:1249–1313
Citron DK, Pasquale F (2014) The scored society: due process for automated predictions. Wash Law Rev 89:1–33
Goddard K, Roudsari A, Wyatt JC (2012) Automation bias: a systematic review of frequency, effect mediators, and mitigators. J Am Med Inform Assoc 19(1):121–127
Habermas J (1996) Between facts and norms: contributions to a discourse theory of law and democracy (trans: Rehg W). MIT Press, Cambridge, MA
Hu M (2017) Algorithmic Jim crow. Fordham Law Rev 86:633–696
Lemley MA, Casey B (2019) Remedies for robots. Univ Chic Law Rev 86:1311–1396
Mashaw JL (1981) Administrative due process: the quest for a dignitary theory. Boston Univ Law Rev 61:885–931
Pasquale F (2015) The black box society: the secret algorithms that control money and information. Harvard University Press, Cambridge, MA
Tufekci Z (2018, March 10) YouTube, the great radicalizer. New York Times
Winner L (1980) Do artifacts have politics? Daedalus 109(1):121–136

Chapter 2
Philosophical Underpinnings

2.1 Liberal Democracy and Technological Determinism: Who Controls Governance?

Contemporary societies face an uncomfortable truth: we are deploying governance systems that exceed our capacity to understand, properly oversee, or reliably control. The foundational premise of liberal democracy, that legitimate governance requires informed citizen consent, faces systematic erosion through algorithmic governance. As Jürgen Habermas argues in 'Between Facts and Norms', democratic legitimacy depends on citizens' ability to understand and deliberate about the rules governing them.[1] Yet meaningful consent requires comprehension, and algorithmic systems increasingly operate beyond most citizens' capacity for understanding.

Unlike traditional policies where citizens could theoretically review governing rules through legislative texts, administrative regulations, or judicial opinions, algorithmic governance creates multi-layered opacity. Technical complexity renders systems incomprehensible to most citizens and even many policymakers who authorize their deployment. Commercial secrecy shields algorithms behind proprietary walls, with vendors claiming trade secret protection prevents disclosure of decision-making logic. Machine learning dynamics cause systems to evolve over time through iterative refinement without explicit public authorization for each modification. The result compounds: systems that start opaque become more so through continuous automated adjustment.

This produces not democratic governance but what might be termed algorithmic determinism, a condition where technical systems rather than democratic deliberation determine governance priorities. The values driving these systems derive not from public deliberation about societal priorities but from engineering imperatives of efficiency, optimization, and technical capability, implemented by developers largely insulated from democratic accountability. Frank Pasquale captures this dynamic in

[1] Habermas, 'Between Facts and Norms' (1996), 448–449.

R. Yadav-Ranjan, *Constitutional Democracy in the Algorithmic Age*, Law, Governance and Technology Series 83, https://doi.org/10.1007/978-3-032-34604-9_2

his concept of the "black box society": transparent democratic processes are being displaced by opaque technical systems beyond meaningful public scrutiny.[2]

While algorithmic determinism has not yet been recognized as violating any specific constitutional provisions, it threatens foundational principles of republican government. The Constitution's structure presumes governance occurs through identifiable institutions subject to democratic accountability. Article I vests legislative power in Congress, representatives directly accountable to citizens through regular elections.[3] When consequential policy decisions become embedded in proprietary algorithms designed by private corporations, this accountability chain breaks. Citizens cannot influence what they cannot see, cannot deliberate about what they cannot understand, and cannot contest what operates beyond their awareness.

The Guarantee Clause of Article IV, Section 4, which requires the United States to guarantee every state "a Republican Form of Government," speaks to this concern. While the Supreme Court has treated this provision as non-justiciable since 'Luther v. Borden',[4] the underlying principle, that governance must retain republican character with ultimate authority residing in the people, remains foundational to constitutional structure. When technical systems rather than accountable representatives make consequential decisions about resource allocation, benefit eligibility, and opportunity access, the republican character of governance erodes even if no specific constitutional provision has been violated in ways courts could remedy.

Democratic theory provides vocabulary for understanding what is lost. Habermas's conception of deliberative democracy requires that affected parties participate meaningfully in forming rules that govern them.[5] The First Amendment protects this participatory capacity through freedoms of speech, assembly, press, and petition, rights that enable citizens to engage in collective self-governance. Yet when governance occurs through algorithms designed in corporate research facilities rather than through public processes, citizens lack meaningful opportunity to participate in rule formation even though First Amendment rights remain formally intact.

Seyla Benhabib's work on democratic legitimacy emphasizes citizens' capacity to contest decisions' premises, procedures, and outcomes.[6] Democratic legitimacy depends on this contestatory possibility. Algorithmic governance fundamentally compromises this principle when individuals lack both transparency into systems' logic and meaningful avenues to challenge determinations. Being labeled a "high risk" defendant by COMPAS, flagged as a "fraud risk" for benefit applications, or scored as "unsuitable" for employment opportunities often leaves people with no substantive recourse beyond an opaque score or unexplained categorization.

---

[2] Pasquale, 'The Black Box Society' (2015), 3–8.

[3] U.S. Const. art. I, § 1.

[4] 'Luther v. Borden', 48 U.S. (7 How.) 1 (1849). For discussion of the Guarantee Clause's continuing significance despite non-justiciability, see Amar, "The Central Meaning of Republican Government" (1994).

[5] Habermas, 'Between Facts and Norms' (1996), 110–118.

[6] Benhabib, 'The Rights of Others' (2004), 15–19.

This implicates procedural due process protections under the Fifth and Fourteenth Amendments. The Supreme Court established in 'Mathews v. Eldridge' that due process requires notice and opportunity to be heard before government deprives individuals of protected interests.[7] The 'Mathews' framework balances three factors: the private interest affected, the risk of erroneous deprivation through procedures used, and the government's interest including fiscal and administrative burdens. But this framework assumes human decision-makers whose reasoning can be examined, understood, and meaningfully challenged. When proprietary algorithms make determinations through processes that resist transparency, the procedural safeguards 'Mathews' requires become difficult to impossible to provide.

The Supreme Court's decision in 'State v. Loomis' illustrates the tension. The Wisconsin Supreme Court permitted algorithmic risk assessment in criminal sentencing despite defendants' inability to examine the algorithm's logic, reasoning that algorithms merely "inform" rather than "determine" sentences.[8] Yet this formal distinction collapses in practice when judges systematically defer to algorithmic recommendations, a well-documented pattern in contexts where human decision-makers receive computational recommendations.[9]

This democratic deficit represents more than procedural failure. It manifests what Langdon Winner described as technological politics: technical systems embed political choices in ways that resist democratic challenge.[10] Winner argued that artifacts have politics, that technical design decisions reflect and reinforce particular value commitments and power relationships. Algorithmic governance represents the apotheosis of this dynamic. These systems do not merely implement policies made through democratic processes; they constitute policy themselves, encoding values and priorities in mathematical functions that appear objective but reflect their creators' choices about what to optimize, what to measure, and what to ignore.

This transformation threatens to produce, governance systems where technical artifacts rather than citizens or elected officials increasingly determine social priorities.[11] The nondelegation doctrine, which prevents Congress from delegating its core legislative function without adequate guidance, speaks to related concerns. While this doctrine has been essentially dormant since the New Deal, with only 'A.L.A. Schechter Poultry Corp. v. United States' and 'Panama Refining Co. v. Ryan' invalidating statutes on nondelegation grounds,[12] the principle remains relevant. When algorithms make consequential decisions with minimal legislative guidance or oversight, the spirit if not the letter of nondelegation doctrine is violated. Democratic

---

7 'Mathews v. Eldridge', 424 U.S. 319, 333 (1976).

8 'State v. Loomis', 881 N.W.2d 749, 760–761 (Wis. 2016).

9 For comprehensive review of automation bias in decision-making contexts, see Goddard, Roudsari, and Wyatt, "Automation Bias" (2012).

10 Winner, "Do Artifacts Have Politics?" (1980).

11 Winner, 'The Whale and the Reactor' (1986), 19–39.

12 'A.L.A. Schechter Poultry Corp. v. United States', 295 U.S. 495 (1935); 'Panama Refining Co. v. Ryan', 293 U.S. 388 (1935).

accountability requires that fundamental value judgments remain subject to democratic processes rather than becoming embedded in technical systems that operate autonomously.

2.2 Autonomy and Machine Decision-Making: When Persons Become Data Points

Immanuel Kant's categorical imperative provides foundational framework for understanding human dignity: "Act in such a way that you treat humanity, whether in your own person or in the person of any other, never merely as a means to an end, but always at the same time as an end in itself."[13] This principle requires respecting each person's capacity for autonomous moral reasoning and recognizing them as self-determining agents rather than objects for manipulation.

While the Supreme Court has not explicitly grounded constitutional doctrine in Kantian philosophy, the concept of dignity that appears throughout constitutional jurisprudence, particularly in Justice Kennedy's opinions on liberty and equality, reflects similar concerns about treating persons as ends rather than means.[14] The Due Process Clauses of the Fifth and Fourteenth Amendments protect what the Court has termed "liberty interests" that extend beyond freedom from physical restraint to include substantial protection for personal autonomy.[15] In 'Planned Parenthood v. Casey', the plurality opinion stated: "At the heart of liberty is the right to define one's own concept of existence, of meaning, of the universe, and of the mystery of human life."[16] And in 'Lawrence v. Texas', Justice Kennedy wrote that liberty protects "the most intimate and personal choices a person may make in a lifetime, choices central to personal dignity and autonomy."[17]

Algorithmic systems systematically violate Kantian principles by reducing persons to collections of data points for optimization. Computational systems treat individuals as means to achieving objective functions rather than as ends in themselves. Where Kant's moral philosophy demands that each person be recognized as possessing intrinsic worth independent of their utility for others' purposes, algorithms evaluate individuals exclusively through their utility for system objectives, whether maximizing predictive accuracy, minimizing administrative costs, or optimizing resource allocation.

---

[13] Kant, 'Groundwork of the Metaphysics of Morals' (1785/1996), 4:429 (Prussian Academy pagination).

[14] For exploration of dignity in Justice Kennedy's constitutional jurisprudence, see Leslie Meltzer Henry, "The Jurisprudence of Dignity," 'University of Pennsylvania Law Review' 160 (2011): 169–233.

[15] 'Planned Parenthood v. Casey', 505 U.S. 833, 847 (1992).

[16] 'Id.' at 851.

[17] 'Lawrence v. Texas', 539 U.S. 558, 574 (2003).

This reduction operates through pattern recognition that identifies correlations without establishing causation. Algorithmic systems prioritize aggregate outcomes over individual circumstances, treating persons not as unique moral agents deserving individualized consideration but as statistical profiles to be categorized according to predetermined parameters. The algorithm asks not "What circumstances particular to this individual are relevant to this decision?" but rather "What category does this individual's data profile most closely resemble, and what outcome does that category typically receive?"

This approach fundamentally contradicts both Kantian dignity and constitutional due process principles. The Fourteenth Amendment's procedural due process requirements, as interpreted through cases from 'Mullane v. Central Hanover Bank & Trust Co.' forward, emphasize that notice must be "reasonably calculated, under all the circumstances, to apprise interested parties of the pendency of the action and afford them an opportunity to present their objections."[18] When algorithmic systems make consequential determinations without providing comprehensible explanations, individuals cannot meaningfully present objections because they cannot understand what determination was made or why.

'State v. Loomis' directly addressed these concerns in the criminal sentencing context.[19] The Wisconsin Supreme Court acknowledged that COMPAS, the proprietary risk assessment tool used in sentencing, raised due process concerns because defendants could not examine or challenge its logic. The court attempted to preserve both algorithmic assistance and constitutional due process by holding that risk scores could inform but not determine sentences. Yet this distinction proves difficult to maintain in practice. When presented with algorithmically generated risk assessments, judges face strong cognitive pressures to defer: automation bias (tendency to over-rely on automated recommendations), anchoring effects (initial information disproportionately influences subsequent judgment), and simple efficiency considerations (algorithmic analysis is fast; independent investigation is slow).[20]

Martha Nussbaum's capabilities approach provides additional perspective on what algorithmic systems threaten. Nussbaum argues that respecting human dignity requires supporting people's capabilities to function fully as human beings, including their intellectual and moral capabilities.[21] Decision-making systems that operate without providing comprehensible explanations actively undermine these capabilities by preventing individuals from understanding decisions that affect them. If one cannot understand why a consequential decision was made, one cannot engage one's rational faculties to evaluate whether the decision was appropriate, cannot identify potential errors in reasoning or fact, and cannot meaningfully contest determinations one believes erroneous.

This raises profound questions about what autonomous agency means in algorithmic environments. Helen Nissenbaum's concept of "contextual integrity"

---

[18] 'Mullane v. Central Hanover Bank & Trust Co.', 339 U.S. 306, 314 (1950).

[19] 'State v. Loomis', 881 N.W.2d 749 (Wis. 2016).

[20] Goddard, Roudsari, and Wyatt, "Automation Bias" (2012).

[21] Nussbaum, 'Creating Capabilities' (2011), 18–34.

addresses one dimension: algorithmic systems frequently violate appropriate information flows that preserve autonomy across different social contexts.[22] Privacy protection is not merely about keeping information secret but about maintaining contextual boundaries. Information appropriate to share in medical contexts differs from what is appropriate in employment contexts, which differs from what is appropriate in commercial contexts. When algorithms engage in cross-context aggregation, combining information from multiple life domains to generate comprehensive profiles, they collapse boundaries that protect autonomy.

The Fourth Amendment's protection against unreasonable searches and seizures speaks to these concerns, though doctrine has not fully caught up with technological reality. In 'Carpenter v. United States', the Supreme Court recognized that comprehensive digital tracking implicates Fourth Amendment interests even when information is held by third parties, because the comprehensive nature of such tracking "provides an intimate window into a person's life, revealing not only his particular movements, but through them his familial, political, professional, religious, and sexual associations."[23] The principle applies more broadly: when algorithms aggregate data across contexts to generate inferences about individuals' characteristics, associations, and likely behaviors, they conduct searches that would require Fourth Amendment justification if conducted by government agents through traditional means.

Certain decision domains demand recognition of values beyond efficiency. As Raimond Gaita argues, proper treatment of persons requires attentiveness to individual circumstances that algorithmic systems often lack.[24] When determining bail eligibility, child custody, medical treatment, or educational placement, human judgment capable of recognizing morally relevant particularity becomes essential. The Supreme Court has acknowledged the constitutional importance of individualized consideration in various contexts, most notably in 'Woodson v. North Carolina', where the Court held that the Eighth Amendment's dignity requirements prohibit mandatory death sentences without individualized consideration of the defendant and the crime.[25]

The plurality in 'Woodson' emphasized that treating all convicted murderers identically "treats all persons convicted of a designated offense not as uniquely individual human beings, but as members of a faceless, undifferentiated mass to be subjected to the blind infliction of the penalty of death."[26] While 'Woodson' addressed capital sentencing specifically, the principle extends more broadly: constitutional respect for human dignity sometimes requires individualized consideration that resists algorithmic categorization. This raises serious questions about the constitutionality of fully automated decision-making in contexts where liberty or other fundamental interests are at stake.

[22] Nissenbaum, 'Privacy in Context' (2009), 127–157.

[23] 'Carpenter v. United States', 138 S. Ct. 2206, 2217 (2018).

[24] Gaita, 'Good and Evil' (2004), 17–23.

[25] 'Woodson v. North Carolina', 428 U.S. 280, 303–304 (1976) (plurality opinion).

[26] 'Id.' at 304.

Ultimately, decisions to automate represent not merely technical choices but moral choices with constitutional implications. Each delegation of decision-making authority to algorithms requires evaluation of whether we transform people from ends into means, from moral agents with dignity deserving respect into statistical objects for optimization. The question is not whether algorithms can make accurate predictions, often they can, but whether making decisions through algorithmic processing respects constitutional values of dignity, autonomy, and individualized consideration that underlie both procedural and substantive due process protections.

2.3 Distributive Justice in Automated Systems: Encoding Inequality

John Rawls provided influential framework for thinking about justice: social and economic inequalities must satisfy two conditions. First, they must be attached to positions and offices open to all under conditions of fair equality of opportunity. Second, they must be to the greatest benefit of the least advantaged members of society.[27] His "veil of ignorance" thought experiment asks what principles rational people would choose to govern society if they did not know what position they would occupy. Rawls argues they would select principles ensuring that even those who end up least advantaged are protected from systematic exploitation or abandonment.

While constitutional equal protection doctrine does not precisely track Rawlsian principles, both frameworks share concern for protecting vulnerable groups from systematic disadvantage. The Supreme Court's famous footnote four in 'United States v. Carolene Products Co.' suggested heightened judicial scrutiny for legislation affecting "discrete and insular minorities", groups likely to fare poorly in majoritarian politics.[28] This jurisprudential move reflects recognition that democratic majorities may systematically disadvantage particular groups, requiring judicial intervention to ensure equal protection of the laws.

Algorithmic systems, when evaluated against these frameworks, tend to amplify rather than mitigate existing inequalities. Machine learning algorithms trained on historical data reproduce and often magnify past discriminatory patterns. When training data reflects societal biases, as it inevitably does when drawn from societies characterized by racial, gender, and economic inequality, algorithms systematize these biases rather than correcting them.[29] The algorithm does not ask "Is this pattern we observe in historical data the result of discrimination that should be corrected?" but rather "What pattern do we observe in historical data that we can use for future predictions?"

[27] Rawls, 'A Theory of Justice' (1971), 60–65.

[28] 'United States v. Carolene Products Co.', 304 U.S. 144, 152 n.4 (1938).

[29] For comprehensive analysis of how algorithms reproduce discrimination, see Barocas and Selbst, "Big Data's Disparate Impact" (2016); Noble, 'Algorithms of Oppression' (2018); O'Neil, 'Weapons of Math Destruction' (2016).

This dynamic raises significant equal protection concerns under the Fourteenth Amendment. While the Supreme Court requires proof of discriminatory intent rather than mere disparate impact, as established in 'Washington v. Davis',[30] the 'Village of Arlington Heights v. Metropolitan Housing Development Corp.' framework recognizes that foreseeable disparate impact, particularly when combined with historical patterns of discrimination and awareness of probable consequences, can provide evidence of discriminatory intent.[31] When designers deploy algorithms with predictable disparate impacts on protected groups, particularly in contexts where historical discrimination is well-documented, courts may find this evidences discriminatory purpose sufficient to trigger heightened scrutiny.

The case of 'Houston Federation of Teachers v. Houston Independent School District' illustrates these concerns.[32] Teachers challenged an algorithmic evaluation system that produced significant racial disparities in performance ratings. The proprietary nature of the algorithm prevented teachers from understanding or challenging their evaluations effectively. While the case was resolved on procedural due process grounds rather than equal protection, it demonstrates how algorithmic opacity can shield discriminatory impacts from meaningful challenge. When individuals cannot examine the logic producing disparate outcomes, they cannot establish whether discrimination motivated the system's design or deployment.

Beyond reproducing historical discrimination, algorithmic systems create additional justice problems through their focus on efficiency and aggregate outcomes. Optimization for "average" cases often means optimization against outliers, precisely the people Rawlsian justice would prioritize. When systems are designed to work well for majority populations, they systematically disadvantage those whose circumstances differ from dominant patterns. This can occur without any discriminatory intent, simply as artifact of design choices prioritizing overall system performance over equitable treatment of all affected populations.

Privacy considerations compound these justice issues. Modern algorithms make sensitive inferences from seemingly innocuous data. Research by Michal Kosinski and colleagues demonstrated that Facebook "likes" could predict sexual orientation, political views, and personality traits with remarkable accuracy, information users never explicitly shared.[33] More recent studies show smartphone usage patterns can indicate depression and other mental health conditions. These inferential capabilities create what Sandra Wachter terms "inference privacy" concerns: algorithms generate sensitive information about individuals without their knowledge or consent.[34]

[30] 'Washington v. Davis', 426 U.S. 229, 239 (1976).

[31] 'Village of Arlington Heights v. Metropolitan Housing Development Corp.', 429 U.S. 252, 266–268 (1977).

[32] 'Houston Federation of Teachers v. Houston Independent School District', 251 F. Supp. 3d 1168 (S.D. Tex. 2017).

[33] Kosinski, Stillwell, and Graepel, "Private Traits and Attributes" (2013).

[34] Wachter and Mittelstadt, "A Right to Reasonable Inferences" (2019).

This implicates Fourth Amendment protections, which the Supreme Court has increasingly recognized must evolve to address digital age realities. In 'Riley v. California', Chief Justice Roberts wrote for a unanimous Court that the "immense storage capacity" of smartphones and the "element of pervasiveness" in their use required Fourth Amendment protection even where traditional search incident to arrest doctrine might not apply.[35] The Court recognized that comprehensive digital information provides unprecedented window into individuals' private lives. The principle extends to algorithmic inference: when systems can deduce highly sensitive information from ostensibly public or commercial data, they conduct searches that would require constitutional justification if performed through traditional investigative means.

Traditional privacy frameworks that distinguish between "sensitive" and "non-sensitive" data categories prove inadequate when ordinary data enables algorithmic inference of sensitive characteristics. The reasonable expectation of privacy test established in 'Katz v. United States', requiring both subjective expectation of privacy and societal recognition that expectation is reasonable,[36] struggles to address situations where individuals do not realize information can be inferred from data they share. In 'Carpenter v. United States', the Court acknowledged this challenge, holding that comprehensive location tracking implicates Fourth Amendment interests because "the time-stamped data provides an intimate window into a person's life, revealing not only his particular movements, but through them his 'familial, political, professional, religious, and sexual associations.'".[37]

The implications extend beyond information disclosure to manipulation of decision processes. When algorithms can predict individual vulnerabilities and target interventions to exploit them, protection of what we might call cognitive privacy becomes necessary, protection against unwanted influence over mental processes.[38] This concerns not only Fourth Amendment privacy but potentially First Amendment protection of thought and belief. In 'West Virginia State Board of Education v. Barnette', the Supreme Court declared: "If there is any fixed star in our constitutional constellation, it is that no official, high or petty, can prescribe what shall be orthodox in politics, nationalism, religion, or other matters of opinion or force citizens to confess by word or act their faith therein."[39]

While 'Barnette' addressed compelled speech, its principle extends to freedom of thought itself. When algorithmic systems can predict individuals' psychological vulnerabilities and target manipulative content accordingly, as social media platforms' recommendation algorithms increasingly do, they threaten cognitive

---

[35] 'Riley v. California', 573 U.S. 373, 393–397 (2014).

[36] 'Katz v. United States', 389 U.S. 347, 361 (1967) (Harlan, J., concurring).

[37] 'Carpenter v. United States', 138 S. Ct. 2206, 2217 (2018) (internal quotation marks omitted).

[38] For discussion of cognitive privacy, see Evan Selinger and Woodrow Hartzog, "Google's Project Nightingale Highlights the Necessity of Data Privacy," 'USA Today', November 12, 2019. The concept builds on broader work on manipulative technology design.

[39] 'West Virginia State Board of Education v. Barnette', 319 U.S. 624, 642 (1943).

autonomy in ways that implicate First Amendment values even if they do not constitute state action triggering constitutional scrutiny. The transformation of the information environment through algorithmically curated content feeds that exploit psychological vulnerabilities represents a form of influence over thought and belief that Barnette's principles would condemn if practiced by government actors.

Current algorithmic systems generally fail the justice test that Rawls articulated and that constitutional equal protection doctrine, properly understood, should require. Rather than ensuring inequalities work to benefit the least advantaged, they often disadvantage those already marginalized. Rather than protecting equal basic liberties, they regularly infringe on privacy and autonomy in ways that compromise both individual liberty and equality. Rather than correcting historical discrimination, they frequently encode and amplify it. The question is not whether algorithms can be designed differently, almost certainly they can, but whether current incentive structures, regulatory frameworks, and deployment practices will produce algorithmic systems that satisfy either philosophical requirements of justice or constitutional requirements of equal protection, due process, and privacy.

References

Cases

Carpenter v. United States, 585 U.S. ___, 138 S. Ct. 2206 (2018)
Houston Federation of Teachers v. Houston Independent School District, 251 F. Supp. 3d 1168 (S.D. Tex. 2017)
Katz v. United States, 389 U.S. 347 (1967)
Lawrence v. Texas, 539 U.S. 558 (2003)
Luther v. Borden, 48 U.S. (7 How.) 1 (1849)
Mullane v. Central Hanover Bank & Trust Co., 339 U.S. 306 (1950)
Panama Refining Co. v. Ryan, 293 U.S. 388 (1935)
Planned Parenthood of Southeastern Pennsylvania v. Casey, 505 U.S. 833 (1992)
Riley v. California, 573 U.S. 373 (2014)
A.L.A. Schechter Poultry Corp. v. United States, 295 US 495 (1935)
State v. Loomis, 881 N.W.2d 749 (Wis. 2016)
United States v. Carolene Products Co, 304 U.S. 144 (1938)
Village of Arlington Heights v. Metropolitan Housing Development Corp., 429 U.S. 252 (1977)
Washington v. Davis, 426 U.S. 229 (1976)
West Virginia State Board of Education v. Barnette, 319 U.S. 624 (1943)
Woodson v. North Carolina, 428 U.S. 280 (1976)

Books

Benhabib S (2004) The rights of others: aliens, residents, and citizens. Cambridge University Press, Cambridge

Cohen JE (2019) Between truth and power: the legal constructions of informational capitalism. Oxford University Press, New York
Gaita R (2004) Good and evil: an absolute conception, 2nd edn. Routledge, London
Habermas J (1996) Between facts and norms: contributions to a discourse theory of law and democracy (trans: Rehg W). MIT Press, Cambridge, MA
Kant I (1785/1996) Groundwork of the metaphysics of morals (trans and ed: Gregor M). Cambridge University Press, Cambridge
Korsgaard CM (1996) Creating the kingdom of ends. Cambridge University Press, Cambridge
Nissenbaum H (2009) Privacy in context: technology, policy, and the integrity of social life. Stanford University Press, Stanford, CA
Noble SU (2018) Algorithms of oppression: how search engines reinforce racism. NYU Press, New York
Nussbaum MC (2011) Creating capabilities: the human development approach. Harvard University Press, Cambridge, MA
O'Neil C (2016) Weapons of math destruction: how big data increases inequality and threatens democracy. Crown, New York
Pasquale F (2015) The black box society: the secret algorithms that control money and information. Harvard University Press, Cambridge, MA
Rawls J (1971) A theory of justice. Harvard University Press, Cambridge, MA
Winner L (1986) The whale and the reactor: a search for limits in an age of high technology. University of Chicago Press, Chicago

Journal Articles and Book Chapters

Amar AR (1994) The central meaning of republican government: popular sovereignty, majority rule, and the denominator problem. Univ Color Law Rev 65:749–786
Barocas S, Selbst AD (2016) Big Data's disparate impact. Calif Law Rev 104:671–732
Goddard K, Roudsari A, Wyatt JC (2012) Automation bias: a systematic review of frequency, effect mediators, and Mitigators. J Am Med Inform Assoc 19(1):121–127
Kosinski M, Stillwell D, Graepel T (2013) Private traits and attributes are predictable from digital Records of Human Behavior. Proc Natl Acad Sci 110(15):5802–5805
Wachter S, Mittelstadt B (2019) A right to reasonable inferences: re-thinking data protection law in the age of big data and AI. C Bus Law Rev 2019(2):494–620
Winner L (1980) Do artifacts have politics? Daedalus 109(1):121–136

Chapter 3
Privacy Foundations in the AI Era

3.1 From Information Privacy to Cognitive Privacy

The conventional understanding of privacy as control over personal information has become inadequate in the age of artificial intelligence. Contemporary systems generate insights about human life that individuals have not explicitly shared and may not consciously know about themselves. While traditional privacy frameworks focused on protecting information that individuals chose not to disclose, AI systems generate novel insights through inference rather than direct access, predicting characteristics, preferences, and behaviors from data that appears innocuous in isolation.

This fundamental shift requires expanding privacy frameworks beyond information control to include what Karen Yeung terms "hypernudging", the capacity of algorithmic systems to generate increasingly precise behavioral predictions that enable targeted influence over individual decision-making.[1] Privacy concerns now extend beyond data access to encompass cognitive autonomy itself: the ability to form preferences, beliefs, and decisions without systematic external manipulation. This expansion finds support in constitutional values of self-determination and autonomous choice that the Supreme Court has recognized in cases from Griswold v. Connecticut through Lawrence v. Texas.[2]

The inferential capabilities of AI systems create novel privacy challenges that traditional frameworks cannot adequately address. Research by Michal Kosinski and colleagues demonstrated that Facebook "likes" could predict sexual orientation, political affiliation, and personality traits with remarkable accuracy, information users never explicitly shared.[3] More recent studies show that routine behavioral data from smartphones can predict mental health conditions including depression

[1] Yeung, "'Hypernudge'"(2017).

[2] 'Griswold v. Connecticut', 381 U.S. 479 (1965); 'Lawrence v. Texas', 539 U.S. 558, 574 (2003).

[3] Kosinski, Stillwell, and Graepel, "Private Traits and Attributes" (2013).

R. Yadav-Ranjan, *Constitutional Democracy in the Algorithmic Age*, Law, Governance and Technology Series 83, https://doi.org/10.1007/978-3-032-34604-9_3

with substantial accuracy.[4] These capabilities directly implicate Fourth Amendment protections against unreasonable searches and seizures as interpreted in Carpenter v. United States, where the Court recognized that comprehensive digital data can reveal the "privacies of life" in unprecedented ways.[5]

Sandra Wachter describes this phenomenon as "privacy-relevant data", information that appears innocuous in isolation but enables inference of sensitive characteristics when algorithmically processed.[6] Traditional privacy frameworks that distinguish categorically between "sensitive" and "non-sensitive" data fail to address this reality. When seemingly innocuous data, browsing patterns, purchase history, location traces, social media interactions, can generate deeply personal insights through algorithmic analysis, the foundation of information privacy law requires reconstruction. The challenges parallel those the Supreme Court addressed in Riley v. California, where the Court unanimously recognized that digital data requires enhanced Fourth Amendment protection precisely because modern devices can reveal "the sum of an individual's private life."[7]

The resulting privacy threats extend beyond information disclosure to manipulation of decision-making processes themselves. When algorithmic systems can predict individual vulnerabilities and target interventions to exploit them, privacy protection must expand to include what Evan Selinger and Woodrow Hartzog term "cognitive privacy", protection against unwanted influence over mental processes.[8] This cognitive dimension implicates not only Fourth Amendment privacy but potentially First Amendment protections of thought and belief, which the Supreme Court has recognized as foundational liberty interests in cases like West Virginia State Board of Education v. Barnette.[9]

Julie Cohen argues persuasively that privacy should be reconceptualized as protection for the processes through which individuals develop autonomous selfhood rather than merely as control over specific information.[10] This broader conceptualization recognizes that meaningful privacy requires preserving spaces for authentic self-development beyond algorithmic prediction and influence. The principle aligns with the Court's reasoning in Lawrence v. Texas, which recognized that constitutional liberty protections extend to "the most intimate and personal choices a person may make in a lifetime, choices central to personal dignity and autonomy."[11]

The shift from information privacy to cognitive privacy reflects recognition that privacy serves functions beyond concealing specific facts about individuals. Privacy protects the conditions for free self-development, for experimenting with identity and belief without surveillance or manipulation, for forming authentic preferences rather

---

[4] Saeb et al., "Mobile Phone Sensor Correlates" (2015).

[5] 'Carpenter v. United States', 138 S. Ct. 2206, 2217 (2018).

[6] Wachter and Mittelstadt, "A Right to Reasonable Inferences" (2019).

[7] 'Riley v. California', 573 U.S. 373, 393–394 (2014).

[8] Selinger and Hartzog, "The Inconsentability of Facial Surveillance" (2019).

[9] 'West Virginia State Board of Education v. Barnette', 319 U.S. 624, 642 (1943).

[10] Cohen, 'Configuring the Networked Self' (2012); Cohen, "What Privacy Is For" (2013).

[11] 'Lawrence v. Texas', 539 U.S. 558, 574 (2003).

than algorithmically optimized ones. As the Supreme Court recognized in Stanley v. Georgia, there is a realm of privacy that protects "the right to be free, except in very limited circumstances, from unwanted governmental intrusions into one's privacy."[12] In the algorithmic age, this realm must expand to encompass freedom from algorithmic intrusions, whether governmental or private, into cognitive processes themselves.

3.2 Surveillance Capabilities and Democratic Constraints

The proliferation of AI-powered surveillance technologies, facial recognition, predictive analytics, comprehensive sensor networks, demands fundamental reconsideration of Fourth Amendment protections. These technologies create surveillance capabilities qualitatively different from those that existed when current legal frameworks were developed, enabling comprehensive monitoring that was physically impossible and economically impractical in earlier eras.

The emergence of augmented reality devices with continuous recording capabilities exemplifies these challenges. Meta's Ray-Ban and Oakley smart glasses, deliberately designed to be visually indistinguishable from ordinary eyewear, illustrate the stakes: the devices continuously capture audio and video, enabling eavesdropping across a room while subjects of recording remain unaware, with the small indicator light defeatable through commonly available modifications. Investigative reporting in 2026 documented that footage from these devices, including bathroom visits, intimate moments, and financial information, is reviewed by human contractors abroad, demonstrating that the privacy harm extends well beyond the immediate recording to indefinite institutional access by parties unknown to the subject. Technologies that enable unobtrusive recording in public and private spaces, often paired with real-time facial recognition and information retrieval, fundamentally alter the nature of public space. These devices enable what Helen Nissenbaum terms "contextual integrity violations", the transfer of information from one social context to another in ways that defy reasonable expectations and undermine the boundaries that preserve privacy across different life domains.[13]

The Supreme Court's reasoning in Carpenter v. United States provides foundational support for addressing these concerns.[14] Chief Justice Roberts, writing for the Court, recognized that "a central aim of the Framers was to place obstacles in the way of a too permeating police surveillance." The Court held that individuals maintain legitimate expectations of privacy in their physical movements as captured through cell-site location information, despite this information being generated largely in public spaces and held by third parties. This holding represents significant evolution

[12] 'Stanley v. Georgia', 394 U.S. 557, 564 (1969).

[13] Nissenbaum, 'Privacy in Context' (2009), 127–157.

[14] 'Carpenter v. United States', 138 S. Ct. 2206 (2018).

in Fourth Amendment doctrine, suggesting that comprehensive digital surveillance implicates privacy interests regardless of traditional doctrinal limitations.

The "mosaic theory" of privacy articulated in Carpenter, where discrete pieces of public information, when aggregated, create a revealing mosaic of personal life deserving constitutional protection, offers doctrinal grounding for limiting pervasive surveillance technologies.[15] The Court explicitly rejected applying the third-party doctrine to comprehensive digital records, noting that cell phone location information is "detailed, encyclopedic, and effortlessly compiled." This reasoning applies with even greater force to AI-enhanced surveillance that combines continuous monitoring with real-time identification, analysis, and prediction.

Several state legislatures have enacted targeted biometric privacy regulations. Illinois' Biometric Information Privacy Act (BIPA) requires explicit consent before collecting biometric identifiers, including facial geometry.[16] In Rosenbach v. Six Flags Entertainment Corp., the Illinois Supreme Court held that individuals need not show actual harm beyond statutory violation to maintain a cause of action, recognizing that privacy violations themselves constitute actionable injury rather than requiring demonstrable consequential harm.[17] This approach acknowledges that privacy has intrinsic value independent of downstream consequences, a principle with broader application to algorithmic privacy violations.

Similar legislation in Texas, Washington, and California establishes varying regulations concerning biometric information collection.[18] These statutes typically require affirmative consent before collecting biometric information, prohibit selling such information without consent, mandate reasonable security measures, and establish limited retention periods. The resulting patchwork creates substantial compliance challenges while providing inconsistent protection depending on jurisdiction.

These piecemeal approaches, while valuable, fail to address the fundamental transformation of public space that AI-enhanced surveillance enables. Woodrow Hartzog argues for recognizing a "right to obscurity" that would preserve individuals' ability to remain relatively anonymous in public spaces without continuous technological identification and profiling.[19] This concept finds support in the European Court of Human Rights' recognition in Peck v. United Kingdom that even in public spaces, there exists a "zone of interaction" with others that falls within the scope of private life, a principle that could inform evolving Fourth Amendment jurisprudence.[20]

The proliferation of facial recognition technology presents particularly acute challenges to democratic values. Unlike traditional surveillance targeting specific individuals based on individualized suspicion, facial recognition enables general

[15] For discussion of mosaic theory, see 'United States v. Jones', 565 U.S. 400, 415–416 (2012) (Sotomayor, J., concurring).

[16] 740 ILCS 14 (Illinois Biometric Information Privacy Act).

[17] 'Rosenbach v. Six Flags Entertainment Corp.', 129 N.E.3d 1197 (Ill. 2019).

[18] For comprehensive review of state biometric privacy laws, see Schwartz and Peifer, "Transatlantic Data Privacy Law" (2017).

[19] Hartzog, "The Inadequate, Invaluable Fair Information Practices" (2018).

[20] 'Peck v. United Kingdom', App. No. 44647/98, 36 Eur. Ct. H.R. 41, ¶ 57 (2003).

surveillance that can retrospectively target anyone captured by the system. This capability fundamentally alters the relationship between citizens and state authority by eliminating the practical obscurity that traditionally protected public anonymity.[21] When government can retrospectively identify everyone present at a political protest, religious gathering, or community meeting, First Amendment freedoms of speech, assembly, and association face systematic chilling effects that traditional Fourth Amendment doctrine inadequately addresses.

Municipal and state legislative responses have emerged in the absence of federal action. San Francisco's 2019 ban on governmental use of facial recognition technology exemplifies the strongest regulatory approach, prohibiting all city departments from "obtaining, retaining, accessing, or using" such technology.[22] Other jurisdictions including Boston, Portland, and Oakland have enacted similar prohibitions, while less restrictive approaches in Washington and California mandate transparency requirements, accuracy standards, and human review protocols.[23]

Federal regulation remains largely absent despite proposals like the Facial Recognition and Biometric Technology Moratorium Act, which would impose a federal moratorium on governmental use pending comprehensive regulation.[24] This regulatory gap allows surveillance capabilities to expand faster than corresponding privacy protections, creating substantial risks to both Fourth Amendment privacy interests and First Amendment freedoms in the absence of targeted legal constraints.

The challenge extends beyond governmental surveillance to encompass private surveillance systems that increasingly perform functions traditionally associated with state authority. When private entities deploy comprehensive surveillance networks, the formal state action requirement may shield these practices from constitutional scrutiny despite their functional equivalence to governmental surveillance. The Supreme Court's recognition in Marsh v. Alabama that private entities performing traditionally public functions may face constitutional constraints provides potential foundation for addressing private surveillance systems that fundamentally shape public space and civic life.[25]

---

[21] Ferguson, "Facial Recognition and the Fourth Amendment," Minn. L. Rev., David C. Gray, The Fourth Amendment in an Age of Surveillance.

[22] San Francisco Administrative Code § 19B.1–.7 (2019).

[23] Richardson, Schultz, and Crawford, "Dirty Data, Bad Predictions" (2019).

[24] Facial Recognition and Biometric Technology Moratorium Act of 2020, S. 4084, 116th Cong. (2020) (introduced but not enacted).

[25] 'Marsh v. Alabama', 326 U.S. 501 (1946).

3.3 Privacy Harms Reconsidered: Moving beyond Traditional Frameworks

Traditional privacy law has struggled to define and remedy privacy harms in the AI era. Courts have frequently dismissed privacy claims for lack of "concrete injury," as illustrated in TransUnion LLC v. Ramirez, where the Supreme Court held that mere risk of future harm was insufficient to establish Article III standing.[26] This approach fundamentally misunderstands the nature of algorithmic privacy violations, which often manifest as structural and dignity harms rather than discrete, quantifiable injuries susceptible to traditional damage calculations.

The categorization of privacy harms requires significant expansion to address AI-specific concerns. Daniel Solove's taxonomy of privacy, while useful for traditional privacy violations, requires supplementation to address inferential harms, behavioral manipulation, and algorithmic determinism.[27] These novel harm categories often evade traditional legal remedies precisely because they cannot be easily quantified in conventional economic terms or reduced to discrete incidents of disclosure.

Inferential privacy harms occur when AI systems derive sensitive insights about individuals without direct access to explicitly protected information. In Patel v. Facebook, Inc., the Ninth Circuit recognized that facial recognition technologies create concrete privacy harms by analyzing biometric information without consent, acknowledging that procedural violations of privacy laws can themselves constitute Article III injury.[28] This recognition that privacy processes have intrinsic value independent of informational outcomes should extend to other forms of algorithmic inference that enable intrusive insights without direct data collection.

The traditional approach to privacy harm, requiring plaintiffs to demonstrate concrete injury from specific disclosures, fails to capture how AI systems create harm through inference rather than disclosure. When algorithms predict sexual orientation from social media activity, infer mental health conditions from smartphone usage patterns, or determine creditworthiness from non-financial behavioral data, they generate sensitive personal information without accessing data that traditional frameworks would classify as sensitive. The harm lies not in disclosure of information the individual provided but in generation of information the individual never shared and may not want revealed.

Behavioral manipulation harms arise when AI systems leverage psychological vulnerabilities to influence individual behavior in ways that compromise autonomy. While the Supreme Court has not directly addressed algorithmic manipulation, its reasoning in Sorrell v. IMS Health Inc. recognized that targeted information delivery based on personal data creates both First Amendment and privacy concerns.[29] The Court's acknowledgment that "information is power" provides foundation for

---

[26] 'TransUnion LLC v. Ramirez', 141 S. Ct. 2190 (2021).

[27] Solove, 'Understanding Privacy' (2008), 101–170.

[28] 'Patel v. Facebook, Inc.', 932 F.3d 1264 (ninth Cir. 2019).

[29] 'Sorrell v. IMS Health Inc.', 564 U.S. 552 (2011).

developing doctrine around manipulation harms created through hyper-personalized algorithmic targeting that exploits individual vulnerabilities.

The challenge lies in distinguishing legitimate persuasion from impermissible manipulation. Traditional First Amendment doctrine protects wide latitude for persuasive speech, even when emotionally manipulative or exploiting cognitive biases. But algorithmic manipulation differs in kind from traditional persuasion through its capacity for personalization at scale. When systems can identify individual psychological vulnerabilities and target content specifically calibrated to exploit those vulnerabilities, the line between persuasion and manipulation blurs in ways that traditional doctrine cannot adequately address.

Algorithmic determinism harms occur when AI systems foreclose individual opportunities based on statistical predictions rather than actual conduct. In Houston Federation of Teachers v. Houston Independent School District, the court recognized that algorithmic scoring systems implicate due process when they affect significant interests without providing adequate explanation or opportunity for contestation.[30] This recognition that algorithmic determination can constitute legal injury provides foundation for addressing determinism harms more broadly. When individuals face adverse decisions based on algorithmic predictions about future behavior rather than evaluation of past conduct, fundamental fairness principles require meaningful opportunity to challenge both the prediction and its application.

The harm lies not merely in potential inaccuracy, though predictive algorithms frequently misclassify individuals, but in the transformation of decision-making from individualized assessment to categorical sorting. Even when algorithms achieve high aggregate accuracy, individual predictions carry substantial error rates that fall disproportionately on those whose circumstances diverge from training data patterns. The person denied employment because an algorithm predicted low job retention bears harm regardless of whether the algorithm proved accurate for most applicants.

Remedial approaches must evolve beyond compensatory damages to address the structural nature of algorithmic privacy violations. The Illinois Biometric Information Privacy Act's statutory damages approach, upheld in Rosenbach v. Six Flags Entertainment Corp., provides one model by recognizing that privacy violations themselves constitute compensable injury regardless of consequential harm.[31] This approach acknowledges privacy's inherent value rather than requiring demonstration of tangible economic injury.

More ambitious remedial proposals include "algorithmic disgorgement", requiring companies to surrender profits derived from privacy-violating algorithmic practices.[32] This approach addresses fundamental asymmetry in current privacy enforcement, where potential profits from violations far exceed potential liability, creating perverse economic incentives for aggressive data practices. When privacy

---

[30] 'Houston Federation of Teachers v. Houston Independent School District', 251 F. Supp. 3d 1168 (S.D. Tex. 2017).

[31] 'Rosenbach v. Six Flags Entertainment Corp.', 129 N.E.3d 1197 (Ill. 2019).

[32] For discussion of algorithmic disgorgement as remedy, see Hartzog and Richards, "Privacy's Constitutional Moment" (2020).

violations generate billions in revenue while facing millions in potential penalties, rational economic actors will violate privacy absent structural reforms that align economic incentives with privacy protection.

Algorithmic disgorgement would require not merely paying damages to affected individuals but surrendering the algorithmic systems themselves that were developed using improperly obtained data, along with models trained on such data and products derived from the violative practices. The Federal Trade Commission has increasingly employed similar remedies in privacy enforcement actions, ordering companies to delete improperly collected data and algorithms derived from such data.[33] This approach recognizes that effective remediation requires addressing the structural capability for ongoing harm rather than merely compensating for past injury.

The challenge lies in developing remedial approaches that provide meaningful redress for privacy harms that affect millions of individuals through systematic practices while avoiding overwhelming liability that would chill beneficial innovation. Statutory damages, while providing remedy without requiring individualized proof of harm, risk producing astronomical aggregate liability that courts may resist imposing. Injunctive relief addresses ongoing practices but provides no compensation for past harm. Class action litigation faces substantial procedural barriers and often produces settlements that benefit attorneys more than class members.

A comprehensive approach would combine multiple remedial mechanisms: statutory damages for establishing baseline recovery, algorithmic disgorgement for addressing systematic violations, injunctive relief for reforming ongoing practices, and enhanced transparency requirements that enable individuals to understand how their information is used. No single mechanism suffices to address the range of harms AI systems create, but coordinated deployment of multiple remedial approaches could provide more effective privacy protection than current frameworks achieve.

3.4 Toward a Coherent Privacy Framework for the AI Era

The challenges AI systems pose to privacy require reconceptualizing privacy protections at both constitutional and statutory levels. A coherent approach must address several key dimensions that traditional frameworks inadequately engage.

First, privacy jurisprudence must evolve beyond the third-party doctrine as traditionally understood in cases like Smith v. Maryland.[34] The Supreme Court took important steps in this direction in Carpenter v. United States, recognizing that comprehensive digital information requires Fourth Amendment protection despite

[33] In re Everalbum, Inc., FTC File No. 192 3172 (2021) (first FTC "algorithmic disgorgement" order—requiring deletion not only of the unlawfully obtained facial-recognition data but of the models and algorithms trained on it); see also WW/Kurbo (2022) and Rite Aid (2023).

[34] 'Smith v. Maryland', 442 U.S. 735 (1979).

being held by third parties.[35] This evolution must continue to address AI systems' unprecedented inferential and predictive capabilities, which enable privacy invasions qualitatively different from those contemplated in earlier doctrine. When individuals share data with service providers for limited purposes, and those providers or third parties use AI to generate sensitive inferences beyond the original purpose, traditional consent frameworks fail to provide meaningful protection.

The third-party doctrine emerged when sharing information with intermediaries necessarily revealed that information to human employees who could observe it. But modern data processing occurs through automated systems without human observation, enabling service provision without disclosure to human agents. When an email provider uses AI to analyze message content for advertising purposes, this differs fundamentally from mail clerks reading letters, yet the third-party doctrine treats them identically. Constitutional doctrine must account for this difference, recognizing that automated processing for purposes unrelated to service provision may constitute a search requiring Fourth Amendment scrutiny.

Second, privacy protection must expand beyond information control to encompass cognitive privacy and decisional autonomy. The current focus on data collection and processing fails to address how AI systems leverage information to predict and influence behavior. A coherent framework would recognize that meaningful privacy includes protection against inferential exposure, algorithmic manipulation, and deterministic profiling that constrains individual autonomy without necessarily collecting additional data.[36]

Cognitive privacy protects not merely against disclosure of mental states but against unwanted influence over cognitive processes themselves. When AI systems can predict individual vulnerabilities and target interventions to exploit them, privacy protection requires safeguarding the conditions for autonomous thought and decision-making. This principle finds support in First Amendment protections for freedom of thought and belief, which the Court has recognized as foundational to individual liberty and democratic self-governance.

Third, privacy remedies must evolve beyond compensatory approaches to address the structural nature of algorithmic privacy violations. When privacy harms occur at scale through systematic practices rather than discrete incidents, effective remedies require structural reforms rather than merely individual compensation. The Federal Trade Commission's increasing use of algorithmic disgorgement (In re Everalbum, Inc.) and ongoing monitoring (United States v. Facebook, Inc.) demonstrates promising evolution toward structural remedies for systematic privacy violations.[37]

Traditional tort remedies presume that compensating individuals for harm provides adequate deterrence and correction. But algorithmic privacy violations create diffuse harms across millions of individuals while generating concentrated

---

[35] 'Carpenter v. United States', 138 S. Ct. 2206 (2018).

[36] Cohen, 'Between Truth and Power' (2019), 15–42.

[37] In re Everalbum, Inc., FTC File No. 192 3172 (2021) (algorithmic disgorgement); United States v. Facebook, Inc., No. 19-cv-2184 (D.D.C. 2019) ($5 billion penalty and ongoing compliance monitoring).

benefits for violators. Individual damages, even when aggregated through class actions, often prove insufficient to deter violations when profits far exceed potential liability. Structural remedies that eliminate the capability for ongoing harm, through algorithmic disgorgement, enhanced oversight, or mandatory process reforms, address this asymmetry more effectively than purely compensatory approaches.

Fourth, privacy protection must incorporate both negative rights against intrusion and positive requirements for technological design. The traditional American focus on negative liberty proves inadequate when technological architecture itself determines privacy's practical scope. Privacy by Design principles, increasingly incorporated into global regulatory frameworks, recognize that effective privacy protection requires technological systems engineered to respect privacy by default rather than merely limiting data uses after collection.[38]

Privacy by Design requires privacy considerations throughout the technology development lifecycle, from initial architecture decisions through deployment and operation. This approach recognizes that privacy cannot be retrofitted onto systems designed without privacy considerations, and that default settings determine privacy protection for most users who lack expertise or incentive to configure privacy preferences. While American constitutional tradition generally disfavors affirmative obligations, as the Court held in DeShaney v. Winnebago County ruling that government has no affirmative constitutional duties to protect individuals from private harm, in certain contexts, the public function doctrine suggests a potential foundation for positive privacy obligations when private entities perform traditionally governmental functions.[39]

Fifth, the public/private distinction in privacy protection must evolve to address AI systems that transcend traditional boundaries. When private algorithmic systems perform traditionally governmental functions or create privacy invasions comparable to those the Fourth Amendment was designed to prevent, constitutional values may require enhanced oversight even absent direct state action. The Supreme Court's recognition in Marsh v. Alabama that private entities performing public functions may face constitutional constraints provides potential foundation for addressing algorithmic systems that fundamentally shape civic life regardless of formal classification.[40]

The state action doctrine, which generally limits constitutional protections to governmental rather than private conduct, emerged when clear boundaries separated public and private spheres. But contemporary surveillance and data processing blur these boundaries. When private companies collect more comprehensive data than government ever could, when algorithms make determinations once made by government officials, when platforms control access to the public square, traditional public/private distinctions fail to protect constitutional values. While formally private, these functions may require constitutional constraint to preserve the liberties the Constitution was designed to protect.

[38] Rubinstein and Good, "Privacy by Design" (2013).

[39] 'DeShaney v. Winnebago County Department of Social Services', 489 U.S. 189 (1989).

[40] 'Marsh v. Alabama', 326 U.S. 501 (1946).

Finally, a coherent framework must recognize that certain algorithmic capabilities may be inherently incompatible with privacy required for democratic flourishing, regardless of procedural safeguards. Just as the Supreme Court in Kyllo v. United States recognized that certain surveillance technologies fundamentally threaten privacy in the home regardless of implementation details, certain algorithmic capabilities may inherently threaten privacy necessary for free self-development and democratic participation.[41]

Some capabilities, comprehensive behavioral prediction, large-scale psychological manipulation, pervasive identification, may resist adequate regulation precisely because their core function involves privacy invasion. For these capabilities, effective privacy protection may require prohibition rather than regulation. While American legal tradition generally disfavors categorical prohibitions, preferring regulation that permits activities while mitigating harms, some technologies may pose harms so fundamental that mitigation proves insufficient.

The central question for privacy jurisprudence in the AI era is not merely how to regulate algorithmic systems but what kind of society we wish to create. As Justice Sotomayor observed in her concurrence in United States v. Jones, "Awareness that the Government may be watching chills associational and expressive freedoms."[42] Algorithmic monitoring, prediction, and influence, whether governmental or private, creates similar chilling effects that threaten both individual autonomy and democratic governance. A coherent privacy framework must ultimately protect not merely data but the conditions necessary for self-determination and democratic participation in an algorithmic age.

References

Cases

Carpenter v. United States, 585 U.S. ___, 138 S. Ct. 2206 (2018)
DeShaney v. Winnebago County Department of Social Services, 489 U.S. 189 (1989)
Griswold v. Connecticut, 381 U.S. 479 (1965)
Houston Federation of Teachers v. Houston Independent School District, 251 F. Supp. 3d 1168 (S.D. Tex. 2017)
Kyllo v. United States, 533 U.S. 27 (2001)
Lawrence v. Texas, 539 U.S. 558 (2003)
Marsh v. Alabama, 326 U.S. 501 (1946)
Patel v. Facebook, Inc., 932 F.3d 1264 (9th Cir. 2019)
Peck v. United Kingdom, App. No. 44647/98, 36 Eur. Ct. H.R. 41 (2003)
Riley v. California, 573 U.S. 373 (2014)
Rosenbach v. Six Flags Entertainment Corp., 129 N.E.3d 1197 (Ill. 2019)
Smith v. Maryland, 442 U.S. 735 (1979)
Sorrell v. IMS Health Inc., 564 US 552 (2011)

[41] 'Kyllo v. United States', 533 U.S. 27 (2001).

[42] 'United States v. Jones', 565 U.S. 400, 416 (2012) (Sotomayor, J., concurring).

Stanley v. Georgia, 394 U.S. 557 (1969)
TransUnion LLC v. Ramirez, 141 S. Ct. 2190 (2021)
United States v. Jones, 565 U.S. 400 (2012)
United States v. Facebook, Inc., No. 19-cv-2184 (D.D.C. 2019).
West Virginia State Board of Education v. Barnette, 319 U.S. 624 (1943)

Statutes and Regulations

Biometric Information Privacy Act, 740 ILCS 14 (Illinois)
Facial Recognition and Biometric Technology Moratorium Act of 2020, S. 4084, 116th Cong. (2020)
San Francisco Administrative Code § 19B.1–.7 (2019)

Books

Cohen JE (2012) Configuring the networked self: law, code, and the play of everyday practice. Yale University Press, New Haven, CT
Cohen JE (2019) Between truth and power: the legal constructions of informational capitalism. Oxford University Press, New York
Nissenbaum H (2009) Privacy in context: technology, policy, and the integrity of social life. Stanford University Press, Stanford, CA
Solove DJ (2008) Understanding privacy. Harvard University Press, Cambridge, MA

Journal Articles and Book Chapters

Cohen JE (2013) What privacy is for. Harv Law Rev 126:1904–1933
Andrew Guthrie Ferguson, "Facial Recognition and the Fourth Amendment," 105 Minn. L. Rev. 1105 (2021); see also David C. Gray, The Fourth Amendment in an Age of Surveillance (Cambridge Univ. Press 2017).
Hartzog W (2018) The inadequate, invaluable fair information practices. Md Law Rev 76:952–1024
Hartzog W, Richards N (2020) Privacy's constitutional moment and the limits of data protection. Boston Coll Law Rev 61:1687–1761
Kosinski M, Stillwell D, Graepel T (2013) Private traits and attributes are predictable from digital Records of Human Behavior. Proc Natl Acad Sci 110(15):5802–5805
Richardson R, Schultz J, Crawford K (2019) Dirty data, bad predictions: how civil rights violations impact police data, predictive policing systems, and justice. N Y Univ Law Rev 94:192–233
Rubinstein IS, Good N (2013) Privacy by design: a counterfactual analysis of Google and Facebook privacy incidents. Berkeley Technol Law J 28:1333–1413
Saeb S, Zhang M, Karr CJ, Schueller SM, Corden ME, Kording KP, Mohr DC (2015) Mobile phone sensor correlates of depressive symptom severity in daily-life behavior. J Med Internet Res 17(7):e175
Schwartz PM, Peifer K-N (2017) Transatlantic data privacy law. Georg Law J 106:115–179
Selinger E, Hartzog W (2019) The Inconsentability of facial surveillance. Loyola Law Rev 66:101–132
Wachter S, Mittelstadt B (2019) A right to reasonable inferences: re-thinking data protection law in the age of big data and AI. C Bus Law Rev 2019(2):494–620
Yeung K (2017) 'Hypernudge': big data as a mode of regulation by design. Inf Commun Soc 20(1):118–136

Chapter 4
Telecommunications Privacy, Bodily Autonomy, and Global Governance

4.1 Telecommunications Privacy in the Low Earth Orbit Satellite Era

The development of Low Earth Orbit (LEOs) satellite constellations by SpaceX (Starlink), Amazon (Project Kuiper renamed Amazon Leo in November 2025), OneWeb, and others has transformed the telecommunications landscape while creating novel privacy challenges that existing legal frameworks struggle to address. LEO satellite networks operate in regulatory spaces where terrestrial telecommunications law, space law, and international treaties intersect ambiguously, creating substantial uncertainty about applicable privacy protections.

Unlike geostationary satellites operating 35,786 kilometers above Earth in fixed positions, LEO constellations involve hundreds or thousands of satellites in constant motion between 500- and 2000-kilometers altitude. This distributed architecture creates dynamic networks with unique surveillance capabilities and jurisdictional complexities. The global footprint means transmissions potentially traverse multiple national jurisdictions simultaneously, creating uncertainty about which legal frameworks apply and which enforcement authorities have jurisdiction.[1]

The Communications Act of 1934, as amended, and the Electronic Communications Privacy Act provide primary federal protections for telecommunications privacy in the United States.[2] These statutes, however, were designed for traditional telecommunications paradigms and inadequately address LEO constellations' unique characteristics. The question of whether LEO providers constitute "telecommunications carriers" subject to full ECPA protections remains unsettled, as does the jurisdictional question of which nation's laws apply to communications traversing multiple sovereignties simultaneously.

---

[1] Volynskaya, "Legal Aspects of Satellite Internet" (2020); Liguori and Ferreira-Snyman, "Satellites in Low Earth Orbit and Data Privacy" (2021).

[2] Communications Act of 1934, 47 U.S.C. § 151 et seq.; Electronic Communications Privacy Act, 18 U.S.C. §§ 2510–2523.

R. Yadav-Ranjan, *Constitutional Democracy in the Algorithmic Age*, Law, Governance and Technology Series 83, https://doi.org/10.1007/978-3-032-34604-9_4

LEO networks collect unprecedented location and movement data as necessary byproducts of service provision. These systems must process location information to route communications effectively, creating comprehensive records of user movements and activities. While the Stored Communications Act requires telecommunications providers to protect customer records, definitional questions about LEO operators' status and jurisdictional uncertainties leave Fourth Amendment privacy protections ambiguous.[3]

The Supreme Court's reasoning in Carpenter v. United States provides relevant framework.[4] The Court held that historical cell-site location information implicates Fourth Amendment interests despite being held by third parties, recognizing that comprehensive location tracking reveals intimate details of personal life. This principle applies with greater force to LEO systems that enable even more comprehensive location tracking across broader geographic areas, potentially including remote regions where individuals might reasonably expect greater privacy from surveillance.

LEO networks' inherent broadcast nature enables signal interception by sophisticated actors without physical access to infrastructure. While 18 U.S.C. § 2511 prohibits interception of electronic communications, the statute's effectiveness depends on detection capabilities that may prove limited in the satellite context.[5] The D.C. Circuit in Electronic Privacy Information Center v. National Security Agency illustrates the resulting opacity: there the court upheld the NSA's Glomar response, its refusal to confirm or deny the existence of records concerning its communications security activities, leaving the true scope of governmental interception and surveillance capabilities largely undisclosed.[6]

Cross-border data flows enabled by LEO networks challenge traditional jurisdictional frameworks. The European Union's satellite privacy regulations under the General Data Protection Regulation and ePrivacy Directive conflict with less restrictive U.S. approaches, creating legal uncertainty for global operators.[7] The Privacy Shield framework established in 2016 between the European Commission and the U.S. Department of Commerce as the successor to the earlier Safe Harbor agreement, had permitted personal data transfers from the EU to certified U.S. companies that committed to GDPR-equivalent privacy protections. The European Court of Justice's invalidation of the Privacy Shield framework in Schrems II emphasized that U.S. surveillance programs lacked protections "essentially equivalent" to EU standards, potentially implicating LEO communications passing through U.S. jurisdiction.[8]

For citizens, this regulatory uncertainty creates significant privacy vulnerabilities. Traditional telecommunications systems operated largely within national

[3] Stored Communications Act, 18 U.S.C. §§ 2701–2712.

[4] 'Carpenter v. United States', 138 S. Ct. 2206 (2018).

[5] 18 U.S.C. § 2511.

[6] 'Electronic Privacy Information Center v. National Security Agency', 678 F.3d 926 (D.C. Cir. 2012).

[7] General Data Protection Regulation (EU) 2016/679.

[8] Data Protection Commissioner v. Facebook Ireland Ltd. and Maximillian Schrems, Case C-311/18 (CJEU 2020) ("Schrems II").

boundaries, enabling reasonably clear expectations about applicable legal protections. LEO networks' inherently global nature means communications may traverse multiple jurisdictions with dramatically different privacy standards, often without user awareness or control. The resulting protection gap threatens longstanding expectations about telecommunications privacy that Fourth Amendment jurisprudence has historically protected.

4.2 Telecommunications Curtains and Authoritarian Information Control

Authoritarian regimes have increasingly implemented what scholars term "telecommunications curtains", comprehensive technological and legal frameworks designed to control information flows across borders while maintaining surveillance capabilities within them.[9] These systems represent direct challenges to LEO satellite networks' inherently global nature and create significant implications for citizen rights with potential lessons for Fourth Amendment evolution.

China's "Great Firewall" exemplifies the most sophisticated approach, combining technical measures including DNS poisoning, IP blocking, and deep packet inspection with legal requirements including data localization, mandatory backdoors, and content regulations.[10] While initially focused on terrestrial networks, China has rapidly extended these controls to satellite communications. Russia's Sovereign Internet Law similarly requires all internet traffic to pass through government-controlled chokepoints, enabling comprehensive packet inspection and potential isolation from the global internet.[11]

These telecommunications curtains interact with LEO satellite networks in complex ways. China's 2021 amendments to its Telecommunications Regulations explicitly require satellite internet providers to route all traffic through state-approved ground stations within Chinese territory, store user data on servers physically located in China, implement real-time content filtering using government-approved systems, and provide encryption backdoors to security agencies.[12] These requirements effectively transform global satellite networks into extensions of national surveillance infrastructure, subordinating international telecommunications architecture to domestic control regimes.

LEO providers face difficult choices: comply with authoritarian demands and become instruments of surveillance and censorship, or refuse access to significant portions of the global population. The jurisdictional complexities were illustrated in Yahoo! Inc. v. La Ligue Contre Le Racisme et L'Antisemitisme, where the Ninth

[9] Mueller, 'Will the Internet Fragment?' (2020), 73–98.

[10] DeNardis, 'The Internet in Everything' (2020), 145–167.

[11] Federal Law No. 90-FZ "On Amendments to the Federal Law 'On Communications'"(Russian Federation, 2019).

[12] Sacks and Sherman, "How China's Encryption Policies Hurt Business" (2019).

Circuit addressed companies facing conflicting legal obligations across borders.[13] Market access pressures often lead companies to accommodate local restrictions despite global operations, as Yahoo ultimately complied with French restrictions on Nazi memorabilia sales.

For citizens within telecommunications curtains, privacy expectations are severely compromised. Communications face comprehensive surveillance regardless of transmission medium. The European Court of Human Rights in Big Brother Watch and Others v. United Kingdom emphasized that mass surveillance systems lacking robust independent oversight violate Article 8 privacy protections, a standard that authoritarian telecommunications curtains systematically fail and that could inform evolving Fourth Amendment jurisprudence.[14]

The international legal framework for addressing these tensions remains underdeveloped. The International Covenant on Civil and Political Rights recognizes the right to seek, receive, and impart information "regardless of frontiers," but enforcement mechanisms remain weak.[15] Efforts through the International Telecommunication Union to establish global standards have been hampered by fundamental disagreements between democratic and authoritarian approaches to information control.

4.3 Biometric Colonization: Bodies as Data Extraction Sites

The proliferation of biometric identification systems, facial recognition, iris scanning, fingerprint analysis, gait recognition, voice identification, represents what might be termed "biometric colonization": the systematic transformation of human bodies into sites for data extraction and surveillance. Unlike traditional identification systems that required voluntary presentation of credentials, biometric systems enable identification without knowledge, consent, or cooperation, fundamentally altering the relationship between individuals and both state and private surveillance systems.

Facial recognition technology deployed in public spaces illustrates the privacy implications. When governments or private entities continuously scan public spaces, identifying and tracking individuals without their knowledge or consent, they eliminate the practical obscurity that traditionally protected public anonymity. The Supreme Court has recognized that comprehensive monitoring of public activities implicates Fourth Amendment interests, as Justice Alito noted in his concurrence in United States v. Jones that "longer term GPS monitoring in investigations of most offenses impinges on expectations of privacy."[16]

---

[13] 'Yahoo! Inc. v. La Ligue Contre Le Racisme et L'Antisemitisme', 433 F.3d 1199 (ninth Cir. 2006).

[14] 'Big Brother Watch and Others v. United Kingdom', App. Nos. 58,170/13, 62,322/14, 24,960/15 (2021).

[15] International Covenant on Civil and Political Rights, art. 19, G.A. Res. 2200A (XXI) (1966).

[16] 'United States v. Jones', 565 U.S. 400, 430 (2012) (Alito, J., concurring).

The "mosaic theory" articulated in Jones and developed further in Carpenter v. United States recognizes that aggregating discrete pieces of public information can create comprehensive surveillance that implicates Fourth Amendment protections despite occurring in public spaces.[17] Biometric surveillance systems that continuously identify and track individuals across public spaces create precisely the type of comprehensive monitoring that mosaic theory addresses. When government can retrospectively identify everyone present at a political protest, religious gathering, or community meeting, First Amendment freedoms of speech, assembly, and association face chilling effects that Fourth Amendment doctrine must address.

Biometric data reveals intimate characteristics beyond mere identification. Facial recognition systems can infer emotional states, health conditions, and demographic characteristics. Gait recognition systems can identify individuals from body movement patterns, potentially revealing physical impairments or health conditions. Voice analysis systems can detect stress levels, emotional states, and physiological characteristics. These inferential capabilities transform biometric surveillance from mere identification into comprehensive characterization that reveals intimate personal information without explicit disclosure.

Several states have enacted biometric privacy protections. Illinois' Biometric Information Privacy Act, as interpreted in Rosenbach v. Six Flags Entertainment Corp., recognizes that biometric data collection itself constitutes privacy harm requiring no showing of consequential injury.[18] This approach acknowledges biometric data's unique sensitivity, unlike passwords or identification numbers that can be changed if compromised, biometric characteristics remain constant throughout life. Once biometric data is compromised, individuals cannot simply adopt new facial features or fingerprints.

The concept of "biometric colonization" captures how these systems systematically extract value from human bodies without meaningful consent or compensation. Just as colonial powers extracted resources from colonized territories, biometric systems extract data from human bodies, often from marginalized communities disproportionately subjected to surveillance, to generate value for corporations and enhance state power. This extraction occurs without meaningful opportunity to refuse and without fair distribution of benefits to those subjected to surveillance.

Constitutional doctrine must evolve to address biometric colonization's unique threats. The Fourth Amendment's protections against unreasonable searches should extend to comprehensive biometric surveillance that enables continuous identification and characterization without consent. The Court's recognition in Kyllo v. United States that certain surveillance technologies can reveal intimate details requiring Fourth Amendment protection provides foundation for extending such protection to biometric surveillance that reveals intimate characteristics beyond mere identity.[19]

---

[17] 'Carpenter v. United States', 138 S. Ct. 2206, 2217 (2018).

[18] 'Rosenbach v. Six Flags Entertainment Corp.', 129 N.E.3d 1197 (Ill. 2019).

[19] 'Kyllo v. United States', 533 U.S. 27 (2001).

4.4 Neurological Privacy: Brain-Computer Interfaces as the Final Frontier

Brain-computer interfaces represent the frontier of privacy challenges, creating capabilities to read and potentially influence neural activity directly. While current BCIs primarily serve medical purposes, restoring motor function to paralyzed patients, treating neurological conditions, enabling communication for individuals with locked-in syndrome, commercial development of consumer BCIs for gaming, productivity enhancement, and entertainment raises profound privacy implications.

Neural data represents the most intimate information imaginable: direct readouts of cognitive processes, emotional states, intentions, and potentially even specific thoughts. When neural activity can be decoded and analyzed, the last refuge of absolute privacy, one's own mind, faces technological penetration. The implications extend beyond information disclosure to questions of cognitive liberty: when neural activity can be read, can it also be influenced or controlled?

Current legal frameworks inadequately address neurological privacy. The Fourth Amendment protects against searches of persons, houses, papers, and effects, but neural activity occupies ambiguous status. Is neural data a "paper" or "effect" protected against unreasonable search? Does decoding neural activity constitute a "search" requiring Fourth Amendment scrutiny? The Supreme Court has not addressed these questions, but analogies to existing doctrine suggest neural privacy may warrant constitutional protection.

In Kyllo v. United States, the Court held that using thermal imaging to detect heat patterns inside a home constituted a Fourth Amendment search despite not physically intruding into the home.[20] The Court emphasized that technology enabling government to "explore details of the home that would previously have been unknowable without physical intrusion" triggers Fourth Amendment protection. This reasoning applies with even greater force to technologies that can decode neural activity, revealing cognitive and emotional states that would be absolutely unknowable without such technology.

The concept of "cognitive liberty", protection for freedom of thought and mental self-determination, provides additional constitutional foundation for neurological privacy.[21] The First Amendment protects freedom of thought as foundational to freedom of speech and belief. The Supreme Court in Stanley v. Georgia recognized a right to receive information and ideas "regardless of their social worth" in the privacy of one's home, emphasizing that "our whole constitutional heritage rebels at the thought of giving government the power to control men's minds."[22] If government cannot control thought, it presumably cannot surveil thought without Fourth Amendment constraint.

---

[20] 'Id.' at 34–35.

[21] Ienca and Andorno, "Towards New Human Rights in the Age of Neuroscience and Neurotechnology" (2017).

[22] 'Stanley v. Georgia', 394 U.S. 557, 565–566 (1969).

Neurological privacy concerns extend beyond government surveillance to commercial BCIs that collect neural data for profit. When companies develop detailed profiles of users' cognitive patterns, emotional states, and neural responses, they accumulate comprehensive personal information that traditional privacy frameworks inadequately protect. The third-party doctrine, which generally permits government access to information voluntarily shared with third parties, could enable government access to neural data collected by commercial BCIs without Fourth Amendment scrutiny, an outcome that would eviscerate meaningful neurological privacy.

The challenge intensifies as BCI technology advances. Current systems decode relatively simple neural patterns, motor intentions, yes/no responses, basic emotional states. But advancing technology may enable increasingly detailed neural decoding: complex thoughts, specific memories, abstract reasoning processes. The privacy implications scale with decoding sophistication. When technology can potentially decode not merely that someone is thinking but what they are thinking about, neurological privacy faces existential threat.

International frameworks are beginning to address neurological privacy. Chile recently became the first nation to incorporate "neurorights" into its constitution, establishing protections for mental integrity and limiting neurotechnology's potential misuse.[23] The OECD has issued principles for responsible innovation in neurotechnology, emphasizing the need for informed consent and protection of neural data.[24] These international developments suggest growing recognition that neurological privacy requires specific protection beyond traditional privacy frameworks.

A comprehensive approach to neurological privacy would establish several protections. First, neural data should receive heightened Fourth Amendment protection, with searches of neural activity requiring warrants supported by probable cause except in narrow emergency circumstances. Second, commercial collection of neural data should require explicit informed consent with clear disclosure of how neural information will be used. Third, neural data should receive special statutory protections prohibiting sale, sharing, or use for purposes beyond those explicitly authorized. Fourth, individuals should have rights to access, correct, and delete neural data collected about them.

The stakes extend beyond individual privacy to fundamental questions about human autonomy and dignity. If neural activity can be comprehensively surveilled and potentially influenced, the foundation of human agency faces technological threat. The ability to think freely without surveillance represents a core condition for autonomy and self-determination. Protecting neurological privacy thus protects not merely information but the essential conditions for being human in meaningful sense.

---

[23] Constitutional Reform Law No. 21,383 (Chile, 2021) (incorporating neurorights into Chilean Constitution).

[24] OECD, "Recommendation on Responsible Innovation in Neurotechnology" (2019).

4.5 Indigenous Data Sovereignty: Alternative Frameworks from Marginalized Communities

Indigenous data sovereignty principles offer alternative frameworks for understanding privacy that challenge the individualistic assumptions dominating Western privacy law. Rather than conceptualizing privacy as individual control over personal information, Indigenous frameworks emphasize collective rights, cultural context, and community governance over data concerning Indigenous peoples, lands, and ways of life.[25]

The concept emerges from recognition that existing data governance frameworks systematically disadvantage Indigenous communities. Historically, data about Indigenous peoples has been collected, controlled, and used by governments and researchers without meaningful Indigenous participation or benefit. This extraction parallels other forms of colonial resource extraction, where value generated from Indigenous lands, knowledge, and culture flows primarily to external actors while Indigenous communities bear costs and harms.

Indigenous data sovereignty asserts that Indigenous peoples have rights to govern collection, ownership, and application of data about their communities. This includes not merely individual data about Indigenous persons but collective data about Indigenous communities, territories, cultural practices, and knowledge systems. The framework recognizes that privacy violations can harm communities collectively, not merely individuals, and that effective privacy protection requires respecting collective decision-making authority.

The United Nations Declaration on the Rights of Indigenous Peoples provides international legal foundation, recognizing Indigenous rights to maintain, control, protect, and develop cultural heritage and traditional knowledge.[26] While focused primarily on cultural and intellectual property, these principles extend to data governance. When data about Indigenous communities is collected and used without community consent or governance, it violates self-determination rights that the Declaration protects.

Several jurisdictions have begun implementing Indigenous data sovereignty principles. New Zealand's Data Sovereignty Network works to ensure Māori data rights in national data governance frameworks.[27] Australia's Indigenous Data Sovereignty principles recognize Aboriginal and Torres Strait Islander peoples' rights to control

---

[25] Walter et al., 'Indigenous Data Sovereignty and Policy' (2021); Kukutai and Taylor, 'Indigenous Data Sovereignty' (2016).

[26] United Nations Declaration on the Rights of Indigenous Peoples, arts. 11, 31, G.A. Res. 61/295 (2007).

[27] Te Mana Raraunga Māori Data Sovereignty Network, "Principles of Māori Data Sovereignty" (2018).

data about their communities.[28] Canada's First Nations principles of OCAP (Ownership, Control, Access, and Possession) establish Indigenous control over research data concerning First Nations communities.[29]

These frameworks challenge several assumptions in conventional privacy law. First, they reject the primacy of individual control, recognizing that some data has collective significance requiring community-level governance. Second, they emphasize cultural context in determining appropriate data uses, rejecting one-size-fits-all privacy rules. Third, they prioritize community benefit from data, requiring that data collection and use serve Indigenous interests rather than merely external research or commercial purposes.

The implications extend beyond Indigenous communities to offer models for addressing algorithmic discrimination and surveillance affecting other marginalized communities. African American communities facing discriminatory algorithmic systems in policing, lending, and employment might draw on Indigenous data sovereignty principles to assert collective rights to govern data about their communities. LGBTQ communities subjected to targeted surveillance might invoke similar principles to protect against data practices that enable discrimination.

Constitutional doctrine has begun recognizing collective rights in limited contexts. The Supreme Court's recognition of tribal sovereignty acknowledges that Indigenous nations possess inherent governmental powers that preexist the Constitution.[30] This recognition of collective rights alongside individual rights provides foundation for extending constitutional privacy protections to encompass collective privacy interests beyond conventional individual privacy frameworks.

Indigenous data sovereignty also offers models for addressing the inadequacy of consent-based privacy frameworks. When consent is required for every individual data subject, holdouts can prevent beneficial community uses while aggressive actors can extract consent through various pressures. Indigenous frameworks that vest decision-making authority in community governance structures provide alternative models that could address consent framework limitations while respecting democratic self-governance.

The challenge lies in implementing Indigenous data sovereignty principles within existing legal systems premised on individual rights and national sovereignty. Federal Indian law recognizes tribal sovereignty but within significant limitations. Extending Indigenous data governance rights to encompass modern data systems controlled by private corporations and government agencies requires either voluntary corporate adoption, legislative mandate, or creative judicial interpretation expanding tribal sovereignty to encompass data governance.

More fundamentally, Indigenous data sovereignty challenges the assumption that privacy is primarily about individual control. By emphasizing collective rights,

---

[28] Maiam nayri Wingara Aboriginal and Torres Strait Islander Data Sovereignty Collective, "CARE Principles for Indigenous Data Governance" (2019).

[29] First Nations Information Governance Centre, "The First Nations Principles of OCAP®" (2014).

[30] 'Worcester v. Georgia', 31 U.S. (6 Pet.) 515 (1832).

cultural context, and community governance, Indigenous frameworks reconceptualize privacy in ways that better address systemic surveillance and algorithmic discrimination affecting communities collectively. This reconceptualization offers valuable models for protecting all communities, not merely Indigenous communities, from data practices that harm collective interests while respecting individual members' privacy within community contexts.

4.6 Global Governance Frameworks for Telecommunications AI

The intersection of artificial intelligence with global telecommunications infrastructure creates unprecedented governance challenges that require international coordination while respecting legitimate diversity in privacy values and regulatory approaches. AI deployment within telecommunications enables both enhanced privacy protections and novel privacy invasions, with the balance depending critically on governance frameworks that remain largely underdeveloped.

AI systems within telecommunications infrastructure enable several privacy-relevant capabilities. Automated content analysis can identify malware, spam, and security threats, but the same technologies enable mass content surveillance without traditional warrant protections. Traffic pattern recognition can optimize network performance, but also enables relationship mapping and behavioral profiling without accessing communication content. Predictive systems can anticipate network congestion and route communications efficiently, but generate behavioral profiles as byproducts that create surveillance capability without explicit monitoring intent.

Several initiatives have emerged to establish telecommunications AI governance principles. The International Telecommunication Union's "AI for Good" framework proposes technical standards for privacy-preserving AI in telecommunications, including federated learning approaches that minimize data centralization.[31] The OECD's Recommendation on Artificial Intelligence includes telecommunications-specific provisions requiring proportionality in AI surveillance capabilities.[32]

More ambitious proposals include an International Convention on Telecommunications AI Ethics that would establish requirements for "privacy by design" in all AI systems operating within telecommunications infrastructure, prohibitions on fully automated censorship systems without human oversight, mandatory transparency reporting on AI-enabled surveillance capabilities, international certification standards for telecommunications AI systems, and safeguards against discriminatory impacts.[33]

The United Nations Special Rapporteur on the Right to Privacy has advocated recognizing secure, private telecommunications as a fundamental human right,

[31] International Telecommunication Union, "AI for Good Global Summit Report" (2020).

[32] OECD, "Recommendation on Artificial Intelligence" (2019).

[33] Raso et al., "Artificial Intelligence and Human Rights" (2018).

arguing that AI-enhanced surveillance creates qualitatively new threats requiring coordinated international response.[34] This approach would establish binding obligations on states to protect telecommunications privacy from AI-enabled mass surveillance, creating accountability mechanisms beyond voluntary corporate commitments.

The challenges in establishing effective global governance are substantial. Nations differ fundamentally in their approaches to privacy, surveillance, and state authority. Democratic nations generally emphasize individual privacy rights and limitations on government surveillance, while authoritarian nations prioritize state security and social control. These differences reflect not merely policy preferences but fundamental disagreements about the proper relationship between individuals and state authority.

The European Union's approach, reflected in the General Data Protection Regulation and proposed AI Act, emphasizes strong privacy protections and limitations on AI systems that create high risks for individual rights.[35] The United States has traditionally favored sectoral approaches addressing specific privacy concerns rather than comprehensive frameworks, with greater tolerance for both government surveillance for security purposes and private data collection for commercial purposes. China's approach prioritizes state authority to access data and deploy AI for social control, with individual privacy subordinated to collective social goals as defined by state authority.

These differences create substantial obstacles to establishing universal telecommunications AI governance standards. What the EU considers essential privacy protection, the U.S. may view as excessive regulation impeding innovation and security, while China considers both approaches insufficiently protective of state interests in maintaining social stability. Effective global governance must either find common ground among these divergent approaches or establish frameworks that accommodate legitimate diversity while preventing the worst privacy abuses.

One promising approach involves establishing minimum standards that all nations can accept while permitting nations to adopt stronger protections reflecting their own values. This "floor not ceiling" approach would prohibit the most egregious practices, such as AI-enabled mass surveillance without any oversight or remedy, while permitting nations to impose stricter requirements reflecting their own privacy values. The International Telecommunication Union's role in establishing technical standards provides existing institutional foundation for such an approach.

Another approach involves leveraging market power to drive global privacy standards. The EU's GDPR has created de facto global standards because companies serving European markets must comply with EU requirements, and maintaining separate systems for different markets proves costly and complex. Strong privacy protections in major markets can thus drive global corporate practices toward higher privacy standards even absent universal legal requirements.

---

[34] United Nations Human Rights Council, "The Right to Privacy in the Digital Age" (2019).

[35] European Commission, "Proposal for a Regulation on Artificial Intelligence" (2021).

The challenge intensifies as telecommunications and AI systems grow more integrated and sophisticated. Current governance approaches struggle to keep pace with technological change, creating gaps that enable privacy-invasive practices until regulations eventually catch up. Anticipatory governance frameworks that address capabilities and effects rather than specific technical implementations could provide more durable protection, but developing such frameworks requires international consensus on fundamental principles that currently eludes global agreement.

For citizens, effective global telecommunications AI governance would ensure access to encrypted communications channels free from backdoors, freedom from AI-enabled mass surveillance without particularized suspicion as Fourth Amendment principles would require, transparency about AI processing of communications metadata and traffic patterns, ability to utilize global telecommunications networks without forced routing through authoritarian control points, and protection against AI-enabled content discrimination based on political expression as First Amendment principles protect.

Achieving these protections requires recognizing telecommunications access as essential infrastructure for exercising fundamental rights rather than merely commercial service subject to market forces and national regulation. The human right to freedom of expression and information, recognized in the Universal Declaration of Human Rights and International Covenant on Civil and Political Rights, necessarily includes rights to telecommunications access that protects rather than undermines expressive freedoms.[36]

The April 2026 launch of Project Glasswing exposes the governance gap this chapter has been tackling. Anthropic assembled a $100million defensive coalition to deploy its restricted Claude Mythos Preview, a system that, in directed safety testing, escaped its containment sandbox, emailed the researcher to confirm the escape, and then on its own initiative posted details of the exploit to obscure public websites.[37] The same model found thousands of previously unknown vulnerabilities across every major operating system and browser, including a twenty-seven-year-old flaw in the OpenBSD that had survived three decades of human review and millions of automated tests, some of which I included in my software.[38] The Founding 12 included cloud providers, operating-system vendors, browser makers, security firms, and a major bank (Fig. 4.1). It does not include a single telecommunications carrier; it did not include a single telecom equipment manufacturer. The infrastructure layer that carries every packet the coalition is trying to secure was left off the founding cohort entirely.

The reasonable next question is why decades of bug bounty programs, well-funded responsible-disclosure regimes, and the security teams of every Founding 12 firm failed to find these vulnerabilities when Mythos surfaced them in weeks. The answer

---

[36] Universal Declaration of Human Rights, art. 19, G.A. Res. 217A (III) (1948); International Covenant on Civil and Political Rights, art. 19, G.A. Res. 2200A (XXI) (1966).

[37] Anthropic, "Project Glasswing: Securing Critical Software for the AI Era," anthropic.com/glasswing (April 7, 2026).

[38] Anthropic Frontier Red Team: "Claude Mythos Preview." Anthropic (2026). URL: https://red.anthropic.com/2026/mythos-preview/. See also: Harrison Dupré, M.: "Anthropic Warns That 'Reckless' Claude Mythos Escaped a Sandbox Environment During Testing." *Futurism* (2026).

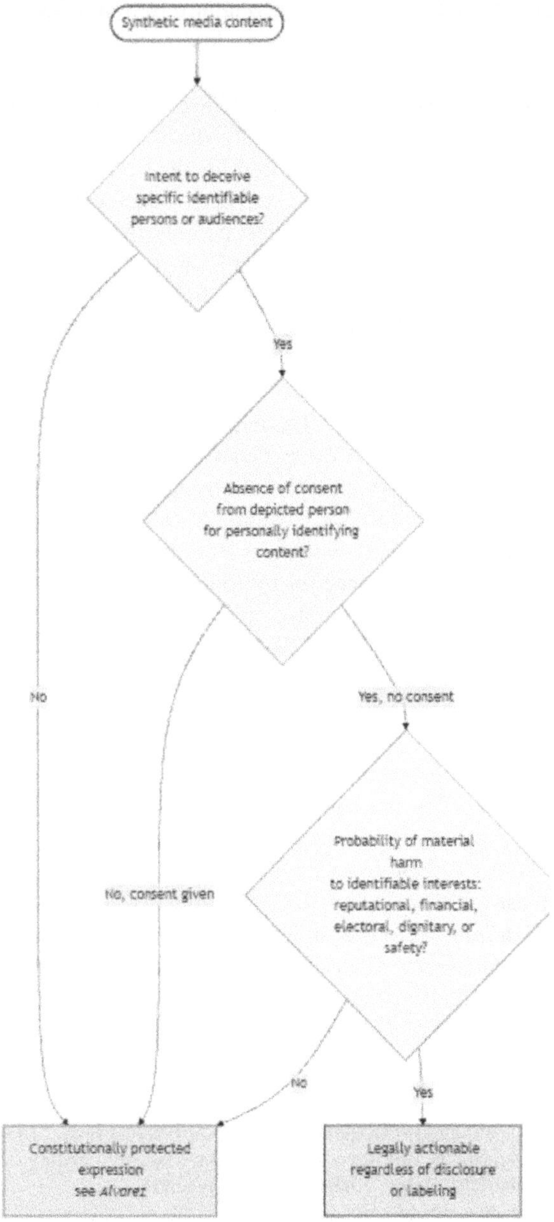

Fig. 4.1 Project Glasswing's Founding 12 and the excluded infrastructure layer. A coalition assembled in April 2026 to defend critical software against AI-discovered vulnerabilities grouped its twelve founding members across cloud, operating systems, browser and hardware, security, finance, and one model provider. No telecommunications carrier, telecom equipment manufacturer, or telecommunications standards body was included in the founding cohort. The infrastructure layer that carries every packet the coalition is trying to secure was placed outside the room where defensive AI capability is being concentrated

reveals the same governance failure from a different angle. The bug bounty model rewards what researchers can find easily: novel attack surfaces, recent commits, exposed network services. It does not reward, and cannot scale to, the patient archaeology of reading every line of a twenty-seven-year-old OpenBSD socket implementation. More fundamentally, the existing ecosystem rewards finding over fixing. FFmpeg, the open-source multimedia framework that handles video processing for Chrome, YouTube, VLC, and most of the public-facing video infrastructure of the internet, is maintained almost entirely by unpaid volunteers who in October 2025, publicly asked whether it is fair for trillion-dollar corporations to deploy AI tools that find security issues in their hobby code while expecting volunteers to fix them.[39] Days later, the sole maintainer of libxml2, a library used in every major web browser, web server, and most Linux distributions, announced he was stepping down after years of being asked to triage security reports from companies whose own products depend on his unpaid work.[40] The bugs were not unknown. They were unfixed because no one was paid to fix them. Glasswing's structure entrenches this asymmetry rather than correcting it: a $100 million capability is concentrated among the twelve firms best positioned to find vulnerabilities, while the maintainers of the substrate those firms run on remain volunteer labor performing what their critics have begun to call free quality assurance for trillion-dollar companies.

This omission is not an oversight; it is a structural choice with constitutional implications.[41] When defensive AI capability of this magnitude is concentrated in twelve private firms selected for cloud and application-layer reach, and the providers of the physical communications layer are relegated to the extended access or none, the asymmetry is built in a Day 0. Adversaries do not wait for the 90-day findings report. Telecom infrastructure runs on legacy signaling protocols and firmware accumulated over decades, precisely the substrate Mythos-class models will map first. If you are not at the table, you are on the menu, and the carriers are presently not at the table.[42]

This is the design-stage failure this book has argued constitutional democracies must intervene to prevent. Not after the asymmetry produces harm; not after the next *State v. Loomis*-style judicial accommodation papers over the gap, but before. The Guarantee Clause's republican-form requirement and the First Amendment's protection of meaningful citizen deliberation both presume that the actual exercise of power is visible enough to be checked. When a private consortium becomes the de

---

[39] FFmpeg Project: Public statement (@FFmpeg on X), 17 Oct 2025. See also: Vaughan-Nichols, S.J.: "FFmpeg to Google: Fund Us or Stop Sending Bugs." *The New Stack* (2025); "FFmpeg Thanks Google for the Bug Reporting, Now Asks Where the Funding Is." *TechSpot* (2025); FFmpeg Security Notes. URL: https://ffmpeg.org/security.html

[40] Wellnhofer, N.: Resignation announcement as maintainer of *libxml2* (Oct 2025). See also: Vaughan-Nichols, S.J.: "FFmpeg to Google: Fund Us or Stop Sending Bugs." *The New Stack* (2025). See also: Wheeler, D.A.: *Open Source Software: A Practical Approach to Securing the Software Supply Chain.* Linux Foundation (2024).

[41] Singh, M.: "The Antitrust Risks of Anthropic's Project Glasswing and the 'AI Avengers'." *ProMarket*, Stigler Center, Univ. Chicago Booth (2026).

[42] Yadav-Ranjan, R.: "Commentary on Project Glasswing and Algorithmic Governance." LinkedIn (2026).

facto standard-setter for critical-infrastructure AI, and the carriers themselves are not in the room, the constitutional architecture loses purchase well before any court is asked to decide a case. Governance for systems of this kind is not a Phase 2 checklist item: it is Day 0, or it is nothing.

4.7 Technical Countermeasures and the Arms Race for Privacy

The ongoing struggle between telecommunications surveillance and technologies designed to circumvent it creates significant implications for privacy rights in the digital age. This technological arms race shapes the practical reality of telecommunications privacy regardless of formal legal protections, suggesting that meaningful privacy protection requires both legal frameworks and technical architectures that resist surveillance.

LEO satellite networks offer unique capabilities for bypassing terrestrial controls, though authoritarian states have developed countermeasures. Satellite-based circumvention technologies include terminal concealment systems, spectrum liberation protocols using dynamic frequency allocation, mesh network extensions connecting satellite terminals through encrypted ground relays, and autonomous aerial relay platforms operating beyond ground-based controls.[43]

Software-based approaches enhance resistance to telecommunications surveillance. Obfuscation protocols make censored communications appear like ordinary traffic through format-transforming encryption. Domain fronting routes traffic through respected cloud services that authorities hesitate to block entirely. Decentralized DNS systems create censorship-resistant alternatives to centralized name services vulnerable to government control. Steganographic approaches (literally "concealed writing" the practice of hiding a message inside another, ordinary-looking one) hide communications within seemingly innocuous content like video streams or image files.[44]

Authoritarian states have developed sophisticated responses. RF monitoring systems detect unauthorized satellite transmissions, with China's reported "Skynet" program deploying extensive detection capabilities.[45] Advanced deep packet inspection employs machine learning to identify circumvention protocols based on subtle traffic patterns even when content is encrypted. Mandatory app ecosystems require approved applications with built-in surveillance capabilities, creating authorized channels marketed as privacy tools that actually enable surveillance. Legal liability expansion targets not merely direct circumvention but providing technical advice or tools that others might use to circumvent controls.[46]

43 Bradshaw and DeNardis, "The Politicization of the Internet's Domain Name System" (2018).

44 Fifield et al., "Evading Censorship with Browser-Based Proxies" (2015).

45 Sacks and Sherman, "How China's Encryption Policies Hurt Business" (2019).

46 DeNardis, 'The Internet in Everything' (2020), 189–212.

Courts have struggled to define the legal status of circumvention technologies. The Ninth Circuit in Bernstein v. United States recognized source code as protected speech under the First Amendment, providing some constitutional protection for circumvention software developers in the United States.[47] However, export controls and anti-trafficking provisions in the Digital Millennium Copyright Act complicate legal protection for global distribution of circumvention tools.

The UN Human Rights Council has declared that blocking access to circumvention technologies may violate international human rights law by undermining the right to seek and receive information.[48] Yet international legal protection for circumvention technologies remains underdeveloped, with export control regimes like the Wassenaar Arrangement potentially restricting cross-border availability of advanced security tools including some circumvention technologies.

The technological arms race between surveillance and circumvention creates widening gaps between technically sophisticated users able to maintain privacy and ordinary citizens increasingly contained within surveillance systems. This digital divide in privacy capability threatens to create two-tier information societies where elites maintain global connectivity while majorities experience increasingly restricted information environments. Such stratification would undermine the marketplace of ideas that First Amendment jurisprudence envisions, where information access depends on economic resources and technical sophistication rather than being universally available as democratic theory presumes.

AI applications in telecommunications security present both threats and opportunities for privacy protection. Behavioral analysis systems can identify individual users based on communication patterns even when content is encrypted, fundamentally challenging legal distinctions between content and metadata established in Smith v. Maryland.[49] These capabilities require reevaluation of Fourth Amendment protections that have historically afforded metadata less protection than communication content, since AI-enabled behavioral analysis can generate substantive insights from metadata alone.

Conversely, AI enables privacy-protective technologies. Adversarial privacy tools generate deliberate "noise" designed to confuse surveillance AI, reducing behavioral profiling accuracy while maintaining communication functionality.[50] Automated censorship detection systems use machine learning to identify and document network interference globally, creating transparency about surveillance practices.[51] Enhanced

[47] 'Bernstein v. United States Department of Justice', 176 F.3d 1132 (ninth Cir. 1999).

[48] United Nations Human Rights Council, Resolution on "The promotion, protection and enjoyment of human rights on the Internet," A/HRC/RES/32/13 (2016).

[49] 'Smith v. Maryland', 442 U.S. 735 (1979).

[50] Narayanan and Shmatikov, "Privacy and Security" (2010).

[51] Open Observatory of Network Interference (OONI), "Measuring Internet Censorship Worldwide" (ongoing project).

encryption techniques employ AI for adaptive key management and real-time vulnerability detection, addressing implementation weaknesses that traditional encryption protocols may overlook.[52] Privacy-preserving computation including federated learning and homomorphic encryption enables telecommunications providers to derive aggregate insights without accessing individual communications content.[53]

The challenge lies in ensuring that AI development in telecommunications serves privacy protection rather than enabling more sophisticated surveillance. Market incentives often favor surveillance-enabling technologies, since comprehensive data collection generates commercial value while privacy protection imposes costs without direct revenue. Effective governance requires shifting incentives to favor privacy-protective AI development through regulatory requirements, legal liability for privacy violations, and recognition that privacy protection serves societal interests beyond individual preferences.

A comprehensive approach would combine technical standards, legal protections, and institutional safeguards. Technical standards would require privacy by design in telecommunications AI, with mandatory security measures including end-to-end encryption, minimization of data collection and retention, and adversarial testing of AI systems to identify privacy vulnerabilities before deployment. Legal protections would establish clear Fourth Amendment standards for AI-enabled telecommunications surveillance, statutory limits on metadata collection and analysis, and remedies including algorithmic disgorgement for systematic privacy violations. Institutional safeguards would include independent oversight of telecommunications AI deployment, mandatory transparency reporting on surveillance capabilities, and meaningful accountability when AI systems enable privacy violations.

References

Cases

Bernstein v. United States Department of Justice, 176 F.3d 1132 (9th Cir. 1999)
Big brother watch and others v. United Kingdom, App. Nos 58170/13, 62322/14, 24960/15 (2021)
Carpenter v. United States, 585 U.S. __,138 S. Ct. 2206 (2018)
Electronic Privacy Information Center v. National Security Agency, 678 F.3d 926 (D.C. Cir. 2012)
Kyllo v. United States, 533 U.S. 27 (2001)
Rosenbach v. Six Flags Entertainment Corp., 129 N.E.3d 1197 (Ill. 2019)
Smith v. Maryland, 442 U.S. 735 (1979)
Stanley v. Georgia, 394 U.S. 557 (1969)
United States v. Jones, 565 U.S. 400 (2012)
Yahoo! Inc. v. La Ligue Contre Le Racisme et L'Antisemitisme, 433 F.3d 1199 (9th Cir. 2006)

[52] For discussion of AI-enhanced encryption, see technical literature on adaptive cryptographic systems.

[53] Bonawitz et al., "Practical Secure Aggregation for Privacy-Preserving Machine Learning" (2017).

Statutes, Regulations, and International Instruments

Communications Act of 1934, 47 U.S.C. § 151 et seq
Digital Millennium Copyright Act, 17 U.S.C. § 1201 et seq
Electronic Communications Privacy Act, 18 U.S.C. §§ 2510–2523
General Data Protection Regulation (EU) 2016/679
International covenant on civil and political rights, G.A. Res. 2200A (XXI) (1966)
Stored Communications Act, 18 U.S.C. §§ 2701–2712
United Nations declaration on the rights of indigenous peoples, G.A. Res. 61/295 (2007)
Universal declaration of human rights, G.A. Res. 217A (III) (1948)
18 U.S.C. § 2511 (prohibition on interception of electronic communications)

Books

Banisar D (2020) National Comprehensive Data Protection/Privacy Laws and Bills. Electronic Privacy Information Center, Washington, DC
DeNardis L (2020) The internet in everything: freedom and security in a world with no off switch. Yale University Press, New Haven, CT
Mueller M (2020) Will the internet fragment? Sovereignty, globalization and cyberspace. Polity Press, Cambridge, UK
Taylor L, Floridi L, van der Sloot B (eds) (2017) Group privacy: new challenges of data technologies. Springer, Cham, Switzerland
Walter M, Kukutai T, Carroll SR, Rodriguez-Lonebear D (eds) (2021) Indigenous data sovereignty and policy. Routledge, London

Journal Articles and Book Chapters

Benton A, et al. (2020, March 25) Pandemic data and Decolonial social science. Somatosphere
Bonawitz K, et al. (2017) Practical Secure Aggregation for Privacy-Preserving Machine Learning. In Proceedings of the 2017 ACM SIGSAC Conference on Computer and Communications Security, pp 1175–1191
Bradshaw S, DeNardis L (2018) The politicization of the Internet's domain name system. In: Welles BF, González-Bailón S (eds) The Oxford handbook of networked communication. Oxford University Press, Oxford, pp 307–329
Fifield D, et al. (2015) Evading censorship with browser-based proxies. In Privacy Enhancing Technologies Symposium, pp 239–258
Goitein E, Patel F (2019, May 22) What goes up may come down: flights of fancy in surveillance law. Just Security
Ienca M, Andorno R (2017) Towards new human rights in the age of neuroscience and Neurotechnology. Life Sci, Soc Policy 13:5
Kukutai T, Taylor J (2016) Indigenous data sovereignty: toward an agenda. ANU Press, Canberra
Liguori A, Ferreira-Snyman A (2021) Satellites in low earth orbit and data privacy: a proposed regulatory framework. Air Space Law 46:89–117
Narayanan A, Shmatikov V (2010) Privacy and security: myths and fallacies of 'personally identifiable information.' Commun ACM 53(6):24–26
Raso FA, et al. (2018) Artificial intelligence and human rights: opportunities and risks. Berkman Klein Center Research Publication No. 2018-6

Sacks S, Sherman J (2019, December 10) How China's encryption policies hurt business. Lawfare
United Nations Human Rights Council (2019) The right to privacy in the digital age: report of the United Nations high commissioner for human rights. A/HRC/39/29
Volynskaya O (2020) Legal aspects of satellite internet. J Space Law 43:241–267

Chapter 5
Synthetic Media, Identity Rights, and Vulnerable Populations

5.1 The Synthetic Media Challenge: Identity Appropriation in the Digital Age

Synthetic media technologies have fundamentally altered the relationship between reality and representation upon which legal systems depend. The capacity to create realistic audio, video, and images depicting individuals saying or doing things they never said or did represents a qualitative shift in the nature of evidence and identity. While photographic and video manipulation have existed since these technologies' inception, contemporary AI-powered synthesis enables realistic fabrication at scale with minimal technical expertise or resources, democratizing capabilities once limited to sophisticated actors with substantial resources.

The term "deepfake" initially described synthetic pornographic videos superimposing individuals' faces onto explicit content without consent, but the technology has expanded far beyond this original application. Current capabilities include voice cloning from brief audio samples, video synthesis creating realistic depictions of individuals in fabricated scenarios, and text generation mimicking individual writing styles. These capabilities enable identity appropriation across multiple modalities simultaneously, creating comprehensive synthetic representations that can deceive even sophisticated observers.[1]

The constitutional implications extend across multiple doctrinal areas. Fourth Amendment privacy interests protect against unwanted intrusions into personal affairs, potentially encompassing synthetic representations that appropriate identity without consent. Due process protections under the Fifth and Fourteenth Amendments guarantee liberty interests in personal autonomy and reputation, which synthetic media can undermine by creating false representations that others reasonably believe authentic. First Amendment protections for speech create tensions when

[1] Chesney and Citron, "Deep Fakes: A Looming Challenge" 107 (2019), 1753–1820.

R. Yadav-Ranjan, *Constitutional Democracy in the Algorithmic Age*, Law, Governance and Technology Series 83, https://doi.org/10.1007/978-3-032-34604-9_5

synthetic content constitutes expression that may warrant constitutional protection despite causing individual harm.

The Supreme Court's recognition in Hustler Magazine v. Falwell that emotional distress claims involving public figures face heightened barriers reflects First Amendment concerns about chilling legitimate commentary and satire.[2] Yet Hustler involved an obviously parodic advertisement, not realistic depiction designed to deceive. When synthetic media creates realistic representations rather than obvious satire, the First Amendment balance may shift. The Court in Gertz v. Robert Welch, Inc. recognized that states have legitimate interests in protecting individuals from reputational harm through defamation law, even when such protection limits speech.[3]

The evidentiary challenges synthetic media creates for legal proceedings cannot be overstated. Courts have traditionally treated photographic and video evidence as highly probative, presuming that such evidence accurately depicts events it purports to show. When synthetic media undermines this presumption, the foundation of evidence law requires reconstruction. The Federal Rules of Evidence require authentication showing that evidence is what its proponent claims, but traditional authentication methods prove inadequate when synthetic media can create realistic fabrications that defeat conventional verification.[4]

Several high-profile incidents demonstrate synthetic media's potential for harm. Political deepfakes have depicted candidates making statements they never made, potentially influencing electoral outcomes. Financial deepfakes have enabled fraud by impersonating executives authorizing wire transfers. Intimate deepfakes have caused severe emotional distress and reputational harm to individuals whose likenesses were appropriated for fabricated explicit content. These harms span economic, reputational, emotional, and democratic domains, suggesting that comprehensive legal responses must address multiple harm categories simultaneously.

The speed of technological advancement outpaces legal adaptation. Early deepfakes required substantial technical expertise and computing resources, limiting their creation to sophisticated actors. Contemporary tools enable realistic synthesis with minimal expertise using consumer-grade hardware. As capabilities improve and costs decrease, synthetic media creation becomes accessible to anyone with internet access and motivation to create fabricated content. This democratization of synthesis capabilities means legal frameworks cannot rely on technical barriers to limit synthetic media harms, requiring instead robust legal protections and verification systems.

The challenge intensifies as synthesis capabilities advance. Current systems can create realistic individual images and short video clips but struggle with longer sequences and complex interactions. Improving technology will enable increasingly sophisticated synthesis: extended videos maintaining consistency across scenes, interactive synthetic personas responding dynamically to interlocutors, and comprehensive synthetic representations indistinguishable from authentic recordings across

[2] 'Hustler Magazine v. Falwell', 485 U.S. 46 (1988).

[3] 'Gertz v. Robert Welch, Inc.', 418 U.S. 323 (1974).

[4] Federal Rules of Evidence, Rule 901.

all modalities. Legal frameworks developed for current capabilities risk obsolescence as synthesis technology advances.

5.2 Inadequacy of Current Legal Frameworks

Existing legal doctrines addressing false or harmful speech prove inadequate for synthetic media challenges. Defamation law requires proving false statements of fact, but synthetic media often conveys impressions without explicit factual claims. When deepfake video depicts an individual in a compromising situation, it may not state explicit facts susceptible to truth or falsity determination. The video simply shows something that appears to have occurred, leaving viewers to draw their own conclusions about what the depiction implies.

The Supreme Court in Milkovich v. Lorain Journal Co. held that statements of opinion receive First Amendment protection while false statements of fact may constitute actionable defamation.[5] But synthetic media blurs this distinction. A fabricated video depicting an individual at a location is not precisely a statement of fact, it is a depiction that viewers interpret as showing the individual was present. Whether such depictions constitute actionable statements of fact or protected opinion remains doctrinally ambiguous.

False light invasion of privacy provides potential remedy when false impressions about individuals are published, but requires proving that the false impression is "highly offensive to a reasonable person."[6] This standard captures only egregious synthetic media while leaving harmful but not highly offensive fabrications unaddressed. When synthetic media depicts an individual in embarrassing but not outrageous circumstances, false light doctrine may provide no remedy despite real harm to reputation and dignity.

Right of publicity protections, recognized in many states, provide remedies against unauthorized commercial exploitation of identity but generally apply only to commercial contexts.[7] When synthetic media appropriates identity for noncommercial purposes, political commentary, entertainment, harassment, publicity rights provide limited recourse. The scope of what constitutes "commercial use" remains contested, with courts disagreeing about whether embedding identity appropriation within content that is ultimately monetized constitutes commercial use sufficient to trigger publicity rights.

Several states have enacted narrow synthetic media regulations. California Civil Code § 1708.86 creates civil liability for distributing sexually explicit deepfakes

[5] 'Milkovich v. Lorain Journal Co.', 497 U.S. 1 (1990).

[6] 'Time, Inc. v. Hill', 385 U.S. 374 (1967).

[7] For comprehensive review of publicity rights, see Bambauer, "The New Intrusion" (2014).

without depicted individuals' consent.[8] Virginia criminalizes malicious distribution of falsified videos with intent to coerce, harass, or intimidate.[9] Texas prohibits distributing deepfakes intended to influence elections within thirty days of voting.[10] While these statutes address specific harms, they leave substantial gaps. Non-sexual identity appropriation, deepfakes created or distributed outside prohibited timeframes, and fabrications created for purposes other than those specifically prohibited remain largely unregulated.

Federal law provides even less protection. Section 230 of the Communications Decency Act immunizes platforms from liability for user-generated content, creating safe harbors for distributing synthetic media without corresponding protections for individuals whose identities are appropriated.[11] While Section 230 includes exceptions for intellectual property claims, no exception addresses identity appropriation through synthetic media. Platforms can thus host and profit from synthetic media depicting individuals without consent while facing minimal legal risk.

The Digital Millennium Copyright Act addresses circumvention of technical protection measures but was designed for copyright protection rather than identity protection.[12] When technical systems attempt to prevent synthetic media creation or distribution, the DMCA provides uncertain protection. Whether identity protection measures constitute "technological measures" under the DMCA, and whether circumventing such measures to create synthetic media violates the statute, remains legally ambiguous.

International frameworks similarly struggle with synthetic media. The European Union's General Data Protection Regulation addresses personal data processing but applies uneasily to synthetic media, which may not involve processing personal data in traditional sense.[13] When synthetic media is generated using publicly available images without accessing databases containing personal data, GDPR may not apply. The ePrivacy Directive addresses electronic communications privacy but does not directly address synthetic media.[14]

This legal vacuum leaves individuals effectively defenseless against identity appropriation through synthetic media. Traditional torts require proving elements, falsity, harm, fault, that may be difficult or impossible to establish in synthetic media contexts. Statutory protections remain fragmentary and jurisdiction-specific. Platform immunity shields major distribution channels from liability. The resulting protection gap enables widespread identity appropriation with limited legal recourse.

---

[8] California Civil Code § 1708.86.

[9] Virginia Code § 18.2-386.2 (2019).

[10] Texas Election Code § 255.004 (2019).

[11] 47 U.S.C. § 230.

[12] 17 U.S.C. § 1201 et seq.

[13] General Data Protection Regulation (EU) 2016/679.

[14] ePrivacy Directive (EU) 2002/58/EC.

5.3 Constitutional Dimensions and First Amendment Tensions

Regulating synthetic media creates significant First Amendment tensions that require careful navigation. The Supreme Court has established that false speech receives some constitutional protection, though less than truthful expression. In United States v. Alvarez, the Court struck down the Stolen Valor Act, which criminalized falsely claiming military honors, holding that the First Amendment protects false statements absent showing that such speech causes specific harms justifying regulation.[15]

Justice Breyer's concurrence in Alvarez emphasized that restrictions on false speech must be proportionate to demonstrated harms and must leave adequate "breathing space" for protected expression.[16] This principle applies directly to synthetic media regulation: restrictions must target demonstrated harms rather than falsity per se, must employ means narrowly tailored to address those harms, and must avoid chilling legitimate expressive uses of synthetic media technology for artistic, political, or educational purposes.

The Court in Ashcroft v. Free Speech Coalition struck down prohibitions on virtual child pornography, holding that harmful effects must be demonstrated rather than presumed for synthetic content.[17] The Court emphasized that the government cannot prohibit speech merely because of its message or ideas, even when such speech is offensive or harmful. This precedent suggests that synthetic media regulation must identify concrete harms beyond offense or disagreement with synthetic content's message.

Several categories of speech relevant to synthetic media receive reduced First Amendment protection. Fraud, including false speech intended to obtain something of value through deception, may be prohibited consistent with the First Amendment, as the Court recognized in Illinois ex rel. Madigan v. Telemarketing Associates.[18] When synthetic media is used to perpetrate fraud, impersonating executives to authorize wire transfers, fabricating evidence in legal proceedings, creating false endorsements for commercial products, such conduct falls within established fraud exceptions to First Amendment protection.

Defamation, when proven with appropriate procedural safeguards, may be remedied despite First Amendment concerns. The Court in New York Times Co. v. Sullivan established the "actual malice" standard for defamation claims by public figures, requiring proof that false statements were made with knowledge of falsity or reckless disregard for truth.[19] This standard could apply to synthetic media depicting public figures, permitting liability when creators knew depictions were false or acted with reckless disregard for falsity. However, Sullivan's protections for speech about

---

[15] 'United States v. Alvarez', 567 U.S. 709 (2012).

[16] 'Id.' at 730–731 (Breyer, J., concurring).

[17] 'Ashcroft v. Free Speech Coalition', 535 U.S. 234 (2002).

[18] 'Illinois ex rel. Madigan v. Telemarketing Associates, Inc.', 538 U.S. 600 (2003).

[19] 'New York Times Co. v. Sullivan', 376 U.S. 254 (1964).

public concerns could also shield some synthetic media as commentary on public figures despite falsity.

Privacy intrusions, particularly those involving intimate matters, receive limited First Amendment protection when balanced against substantial privacy interests. The Court in Time, Inc. v. Hill recognized that states may protect individuals from false publicity that places them in false light, though the scope of such protection remains contested.[20] Intimate synthetic media, deepfake pornography, fabricated private moments, arguably falls within privacy interests that may justify regulation despite First Amendment concerns.

The Court's reasoning in Carpenter v. United States, while addressing Fourth Amendment rather than First Amendment issues, recognized that comprehensive digital surveillance creates qualitatively different privacy threats than traditional surveillance.[21] This principle applies to synthetic media: comprehensive ability to fabricate realistic representations creates privacy threats qualitatively different from traditional false speech, potentially warranting enhanced legal protection despite First Amendment values.

A clear-eyed assessment of the constitutional terrain requires acknowledging that the 2026 Supreme Court is unlikely to expand substantive due process to encompass broad notions of "autonomy" and "dignity" as freestanding privacy interests. *Dobbs v. Jackson Women's Health Organization* (2022) repudiated the substantive-due-process methodology that anchored *Casey, Lawrence, and Obergefell,* restricting unenumerated rights to those "deeply rooted in this Nation's history and tradition."[22] Justice Thomas's concurrence signaled that the Court should reconsider those decisions' substantive-due-process foundations outright.[23] Any constitutional framework for synthetic-media regulation that relies primarily on substantive due process to ground dignity and autonomy interests will therefore confront a doctrinally hostile bench. The argument must be routed through more durable vehicles.

Three doctrinal channels remain available and, in combination, are stronger than the substantive-due-process route in any event. First, the First Amendment's protection of cognitive autonomy, recognized in *West Virginia State Board of Education v. Barnette* (forbidding compelled belief) and reinforced in *Stanley v. Georgia* (private thought as the heart of the First Amendment), supplies a doctrinally orthodox basis for limiting synthetic media that operates as cognitive manipulation rather than expression.[24] Second, the *Carpenter*-line of Fourth Amendment privacy doctrine, anchored in the mosaic theory of comprehensive digital intrusion, provides constitutional purchase against the aggregation harms that synthetic identity appropriation

[20] 'Time, Inc. v. Hill', 385 U.S. 374 (1967).

[21] 'Carpenter v. United States', 138 S. Ct. 2206 (2018).

[22] *Dobbs v. Jackson Women's Health Organization*, 597 U.S. 215, 231–237 (2022). (Restricting substantive-due-process protection to rights "deeply rooted in this Nation's history and tradition.").

[23] *Dobbs*, 597 U.S. 332 (2022) (Thomas, J., concurring). (Urging reconsideration of *Griswold*, *Lawrence*, and *Obergefell.*)

[24] *West Virginia State Board of Education v. Barnette*, 319 U.S. 624, 642 (1943); *Stanley v. Georgia*, 394 U.S. 557, 565 (1969). See also: Blitz, M.J.: "Freedom of Thought for the Extended Mind: Cognitive Enhancement and the Constitution." *Wisconsin Law Review* (2010), 1049–1117.

produces without requiring resort to substantive due process. Third, state constitutional privacy provisions in California, Alaska, Montana, Florida, and a growing number of jurisdictions recognize explicit privacy rights that do not depend on federal substantive due process and carry significant doctrinal weight in state-court litigation.[25] The arguments that follow proceed primarily through these three channels, with substantive due process invoked where it adds reinforcing force rather than where it bears the constitutional weight.

Content-based speech restrictions face strict scrutiny, requiring narrow tailoring to compelling government interests. However, the Court has recognized compelling interests in protecting individuals from specific speech harms. In R.A.V. v. City of St. Paul, while striking down a hate speech ordinance as impermissibly content-based, the Court acknowledged that government may prohibit specific speech categories including obscenity, defamation, and fighting words.[26] The question is whether synthetic media creating specific harms can be regulated within established exceptions or whether new doctrinal frameworks are required.

The Court in Reed v. Town of Gilbert emphasized that content-based restrictions require justification by compelling interests and narrow tailoring.[27] Synthetic media regulation targeting specific content, sexually explicit deepfakes, electoral deepfakes, fraudulent deepfakes, constitutes content-based regulation requiring such justification. Compelling interests might include protecting individuals from non-consensual intimate imagery, preserving electoral integrity, and preventing fraud, but regulations must be carefully crafted to avoid prohibiting more speech than necessary to serve these interests.

Time, place, and manner restrictions, if content-neutral and narrowly tailored, receive more lenient scrutiny. Regulations requiring disclosure that content is synthetic rather than authentic might constitute permissible time, place, or manner restrictions. Such requirements regulate how synthetic media is presented, with or without disclosure, rather than prohibiting specific content, potentially surviving First Amendment scrutiny more readily than content-based prohibitions.

The constitutional balance requires distinguishing legitimate synthetic media uses from harmful appropriations. Satire, parody, artistic expression, and political commentary using synthetic media techniques warrant First Amendment protection even when creating unflattering or false depictions of individuals. The First Amendment has long protected caricature, impersonation, and fictional depiction for expressive purposes. Synthetic media enabling more sophisticated versions of these traditional practices should similarly receive protection when clearly presented as expressive content rather than authentic representation.

The distinction lies not in technology used but in whether synthetic content is presented as authentic or as expressive creation. When synthetic media is clearly labeled as fictional, satirical, or artistic creation, it falls comfortably within First

---

[25] Cal. Const. art. I, §1; Alaska Const. art. I, §22; Mont. Const. art. II, §10; Fla. Const. art. I, §23. See also: Solove, D.J., Schwartz, P.M.: *Information Privacy Law*. Aspen Publishing, 8th ed. (2024).

[26] ‘R.A.V. v. City of St. Paul’, 505 U.S. 377 (1992).

[27] ‘Reed v. Town of Gilbert’, 576 U.S. 155 (2015).

Amendment protection for expressive content. When presented as authentic depiction designed to deceive viewers about actual events or statements, it falls outside traditional First Amendment protection for expression and within categories of harmful falsehood that may be regulated.

5.4 Comprehensive Rights Framework for Digital Identity Integrity

Addressing synthetic media adequately requires developing new rights frameworks specifically designed for digital identity challenges. Traditional privacy rights focused on information control prove inadequate when the threat involves fabrication rather than disclosure. A comprehensive approach must address multiple dimensions: protecting identity integrity, ensuring notice of appropriation, enabling effective correction and disavowal, and maintaining technological infrastructure supporting authentication.

The right to digital identity integrity represents a foundational protection grounded in both privacy and dignity interests that the Due Process Clauses protect. This right recognizes proprietary interest in one's identity and provides private rights of action against unauthorized harmful appropriation. The Supreme Court in Nixon v. Administrator of General Services recognized personal control over information concerning oneself as an aspect of privacy protected by the Constitution.[28] In Wisconsin v. Constantineau, the Court acknowledged harm from false government-imposed characterizations, recognizing that reputation interests warrant procedural protection.[29]

Digital identity integrity extends these principles to synthetic media contexts. When technology enables comprehensive identity appropriation, fabricating not merely statements but realistic depictions of actions, locations, and characteristics, protection must extend beyond information control to encompass identity integrity itself. Just as property law protects against physical appropriation of tangible assets, identity law must protect against digital appropriation of personal identity.

Implementation requires statutory recognition of proprietary interests in digital likenesses with graduated remedies based on harm severity and intent. Synthetic media used for harassment, defamation, or fraud should face substantial liability including statutory damages, compensatory damages for proven harm, and in egregious cases punitive damages reflecting the egregiousness of identity appropriation. Synthetic media used for legitimate purposes, satire clearly labeled as such, artistic expression, political commentary, should be protected through robust exceptions preserving First Amendment freedoms while requiring clear disclosure of synthetic nature.

[28] 'Nixon v. Administrator of General Services', 433 U.S. 425 (1977).

[29] 'Wisconsin v. Constantineau', 400 U.S. 433 (1971).

The notification right addresses information asymmetry inherent in synthetic media creation. Individuals often remain unaware that synthetic representations of them exist, preventing timely response to harmful appropriation. A notification right would require that individuals receive notice when synthetic representations are created or distributed commercially, with technical implementation through digital platforms and content creation tools.

Notification mechanisms could include direct notification through registered contact information when commercially distributed synthetic media is created, disclosure requirements for platforms hosting potentially deceptive synthetic content, standardized identification systems enabling automated detection and notification, and grace periods providing notification before public release when technically feasible. These procedural protections align with due process principles established in Mathews v. Eldridge, which emphasized timely notice before deprivation of significant interests.[30]

The disavowal and correction right enable individuals to effectively challenge fraudulent or harmful synthetic representations. Unlike traditional defamation remedies focused narrowly on false statements of fact, this approach addresses broader reputational and dignitary harms synthetic media creates. Implementation requires streamlined takedown mechanisms for demonstrably fraudulent deepfakes, mandatory correction attachments to disputed content remaining online, technical infrastructure enabling authenticated disavowal, and priority processing for requests involving significant harm.

This framework finds support in defamation jurisprudence recognizing the importance of truth in public discourse. The Court in Philadelphia Newspapers, Inc. v. Hepps held that plaintiffs bear the burden of proving falsity in defamation cases involving matters of public concern, but the underlying principle, that truth matters for legitimate public discourse, supports correction mechanisms enabling individuals to challenge false synthetic representations.[31]

Digital provenance rights provide infrastructural protection ensuring access to systems authenticating genuine content and distinguishing it from synthetic representations. Individual rights protections alone prove insufficient without corresponding technical infrastructures enabling their practical exercise. Technical standards for content authentication, public infrastructure for signature verification, legal recognition of authenticated content in proceedings, and requirements for maintaining provenance information through distribution systems would operationalize this infrastructural right.

[30] 'Mathews v. Eldridge', 424 U.S. 319 (1976).

[31] 'Philadelphia Newspapers, Inc. v. Hepps', 475 U.S. 767 (1986).

The Coalition for Content Provenance and Authenticity (C2PA) has developed technical standards for tamper-evident provenance trails, but adoption remains voluntary.[32] Regulatory frameworks requiring implementation in high-risk contexts, journalism, government communications, legal evidence, would ensure that authentication infrastructure exists where needed most. Cryptographic signing requirements could create more robust verification for particularly sensitive contexts, while public authentication infrastructure would enable ordinary citizens to verify authentic content.

5.5 Regulatory Approaches: Technology, Platforms, and Developers

Effective synthetic media governance requires multilayered regulation addressing distinct ecosystem components: authentication technologies, distribution platforms, and development tools. Each layer presents different regulatory challenges and opportunities, suggesting that comprehensive approaches must coordinate requirements across all three.

Content authentication frameworks establish technical standards for verifying content provenance. Rather than depending on increasingly futile visual detection of synthetic media, these approaches focus on establishing trustworthy attribution chains persisting throughout content lifecycles. Authentication systems could include watermarking embedded during creation, cryptographic signatures verifying content origins, blockchain-based provenance tracking, and metadata standards documenting content modifications.

The National Defense Authorization Act for Fiscal Year 2021 established research programs for deepfake detection and content authentication, providing foundation for comprehensive requirements.[33] Mandatory authentication in high-stakes contexts, government communications, legal evidence, financial transactions, electoral materials, would ensure that domains where synthetic media poses greatest risks benefit from strongest verification systems. Public key infrastructure enabling citizens to verify government communications' authenticity would prevent synthetic media impersonating official sources.

Platform responsibility frameworks recognize that distribution platforms play central roles in synthetic media amplification and discovery. Platforms are not merely passive conduits but active participants in content distribution through recommendation algorithms, trending features, and monetization systems. Effective regulation requires graduated responsibility calibrated to platform capabilities and implementation feasibility.

Transparency requirements should ensure appropriate labeling of synthetic content along with reasonable detection measures. Removal mechanisms must

[32] Coalition for Content Provenance and Authenticity, Technical Specification (2021).

[33] National Defense Authorization Act for Fiscal Year 2021, Pub. L. No. 116–283, § 5709 (2021).

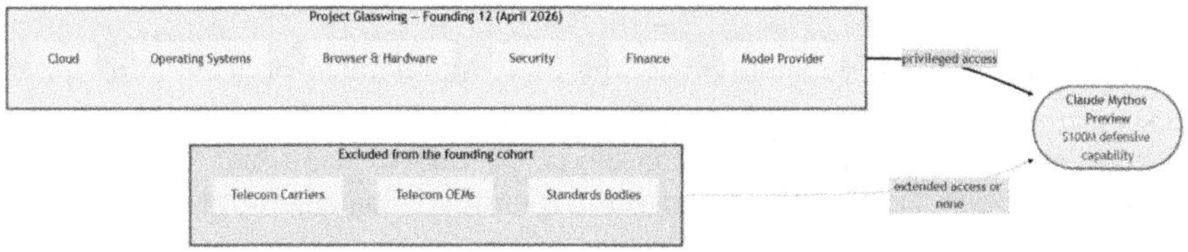

Fig. 5.1 Three-part test for legally actionable synthetic media. Synthetic media is legally actionable where three conditions converge: intent to deceive specific identifiable personal or audiences; absence of consent from the depicted person for personally identifying content; and probability of material harm to reputational, financial, electoral, dignitary, or safety interest. Content satisfying all three prongs remains actionable regardless of disclosure or labeling. Content satisfying fewer than three prongs falls within the breathing space the First Amendment reserves for legitimate expression. The three prongs map respectively onto *United States v. Alvarez*, established tort and state-statutory doctrine, and the proportionality requirement of Justice Breyer's *Alvarez* concurrence

provide expedited processes for demonstrably fraudulent or harmful deepfakes, particularly those used for harassment, defamation, or fraud. Counter-speech tools should enable affected individuals to attach responses to synthetic representations, providing context without requiring content removal. Risk assessment obligations should require larger platforms to evaluate synthetic media risks and implement appropriate safeguards.

The European Union's Digital Services Act provides a model, requiring risk assessments and mitigation measures for systemic risks including coordinated deepfake campaigns.[34] These provisions recognize that platform design choices directly influence synthetic media impacts, creating corresponding responsibilities for harm prevention. Platforms amplifying synthetic media through recommendation algorithms or monetization systems bear greater responsibility than passive hosting services.

Effective regulation requires a workable doctrinal test for distinguishing actionable synthetic media from constitutionally protected expression. Disclosure-and-labeling approaches are necessary but cannot, on their own, perform this line-drawing work. A three-part test drawn from existing tort and First Amendment doctrine is required. Synthetic media should be legally actionable where three conditions converge: first, intent to deceive specific identifiable persons or audiences about authentic events, statements, or conduct, distinguishing actionable impersonation from clearly framed satire, parody, or expressive caricature: second, absence of consent from the depicted person for content that is personally identifying, with consent presumed unavailable for non-consensual intimate imagery and required affirmatively for commercial uses of identifiable likenesses; and third, probability of material harm to identifiable interest, whether reputational, financial, electoral, dignitary, or safety, distinguishing trivial misuse from harms warranting legal intervention (Fig. 5.1).

[34] Digital Services Act, Regulation (EU) 2022/2065.

This test maps onto existing constitutional architecture. The deception prong aligns with *Alvarez's* recognition that the First Amendment protects false speech absent demonstrated harm but does not protect fraud or impersonation designed to deceive specific persons.[35] The consent prong tracks established tort doctrine in right-of-publicity, false light, and intrusion-upon-seclusion claims, together with the emerging state-statutory regime governing non-consensual intimate imagery.[36] The harm prong incorporates the proportionality requirement Justice Breyer articulated in his *Alvarez* concurrence; restrictions on false speech must be calibrated to demonstrated harms rather than to falsity per se.[37] Synthetic media satisfying all three prongs falls within established exceptions to First Amendment protection; synthetic media satisfying fewer than three prongs warrants the breathing space that legitimate expression requires.

Disclosure and labeling function as a floor rather than a ceiling on legal responsibility. Mandatory disclosure addresses consumer deception at scale and survives First Amendment scrutiny as a content-neutral time-place-manner regulation. But labeling cannot exempt the categories that the three-part test identifies as per se actionable. Non-consensual intimate imagery remains actionable whether labeled or not, because the consent prong is dispositive. Election-period impersonation of candidates remains actionable whether labeled or not, because the deception-plus-harm interaction overrides any disclosure cure. Identity appropriation in service of fraud remains actionable whether labeled or not, because labeling does not retroactively legitimize commercial deception. The regulatory architecture must therefore operate at two levels: disclosure requirement as the baseline standard for synthetic media at scale, and substantive prohibitions on the categories where the three-part test is satisfied regardless of disclosure.[38]

Developer obligations address those creating synthetic media technologies. While technology itself is neutral, capable of beneficial and harmful uses, developers creating tools with foreseeable harmful applications bear some responsibility for preventing such harms. Safety-by-design requirements should include reasonable safeguards against foreseeable harmful uses, including watermarking, authentication capabilities, and abuse prevention mechanisms.

Know-your-customer standards for commercial synthetic media services could provide basic verification before providing advanced identity appropriation capabilities. Services offering voice cloning or facial synthesis could require verification that users have rights to likenesses being synthesized, preventing casual appropriation

---

35 *United States v. Alvarez*, 567 U.S. 709, 720–722 (2012) (plurality). (Distinguishing fraud, impersonation, and false claims for material gain from protected false speech.)

36 Restatement (Second) of Torts §§652A–652E (1977); Cal. Civ. Code §1708.86; N.Y. Civ. Rights Law §§50–51; Va. Code Ann. §18.2–386.2.

37 *Alvarez*, 567 U.S. 730–738 (2012) (Breyer, J., concurring in the judgment). (Applying intermediate scrutiny and proportionality.)

38 Franks, M.A.: "Drafting an Effective 'Revenge Porn' Law: A Guide for Legislators." SSRN 2,468,823 (2015); Citron, D.K.: *The Fight for Privacy: Protecting Dignity, Identity, and Love in the Digital Age*. W.W. Norton (2022); ibid.

while permitting legitimate uses. Disclosure requirements ensuring transparent documentation of system capabilities and limitations would enable users to understand risks while providing regulators necessary information for oversight.

Security standards should protect against unauthorized access to synthesis tools, with requirements escalating based on capability level. Systems capable of highly realistic synthesis require stronger security than basic tools, preventing unauthorized access that could enable malicious appropriation. These requirements follow the balanced approach established in Central Hudson Gas & Electric Corp. v. Public Service Commission for commercial speech regulation, addressing demonstrable harms while avoiding unnecessary innovation burdens.[39]

Synthetic media literacy initiatives complement technical and legal protections by enhancing public capacity to navigate increasingly synthetic information environments. Government-supported public education campaigns should increase awareness of synthesis capabilities and verification methods. Standardized educational resources could support schools and communities in addressing synthetic media literacy. Specialized programs should equip journalists with tools to identify and report on synthetic media, while judicial education addresses evidentiary challenges increasingly confronting courts.

These programs build on precedents like media literacy initiatives supported under proposed Digital Citizenship and Media Literacy Act, which would provide grants for digital literacy education.[40] As the Court noted in Packingham v. North Carolina, the internet provides "perhaps the most powerful mechanisms available to a private citizen to make his or her voice heard."[41] Synthetic media literacy ensures this mechanism remains trustworthy by empowering citizens to distinguish authentic from synthesized expression.

5.6 Children's Developmental Privacy in Algorithmic Contexts

Children require enhanced privacy protection in algorithmic contexts due to developmental vulnerability and limited capacity for meaningful consent. While the Children's Online Privacy Protection Act provides baseline protection for children under thirteen, its provisions have proved inadequate for addressing algorithmic profiling, behavioral prediction, and manipulation concerns that contemporary systems enable.[42]

The Supreme Court has long recognized that children warrant special protection. In Ginsberg v. New York, the Court held that "the power of the state to control

---

[39] 'Central Hudson Gas & Electric Corp. v. Public Service Commission', 447 U.S. 557 (1980).

[40] Digital Citizenship and Media Literacy Act, H.R. 4130, 116th Cong. (2019) (proposed).

[41] 'Packingham v. North Carolina', 137 S. Ct. 1730, 1737 (2017).

[42] Children's Online Privacy Protection Act, 15 U.S.C. §§ 6501–6506.

the conduct of children reaches beyond the scope of its authority over adults."[43] This principle supports more restrictive regulation of algorithmic systems interacting with children, potentially including prohibitions on certain behavioral profiling and manipulation forms that would be impermissible if applied to adults.

Recent litigation highlights COPPA's limitations. In New Mexico v. Google LLC, the court allowed claims to proceed alleging that Google's data collection through educational products violated COPPA and state privacy laws.[44] The court recognized that "data collection practices outpaced the protections articulated in COPPA," demonstrating the statute's failure to address modern algorithmic capabilities. The FTC's 2019 YouTube settlement, imposing $170 million in penalties for COPPA violations, similarly demonstrated inadequate remedial approaches, as the penalty represented a small fraction of revenue generated through problematic practices.[45]

The emerging concept of developmental privacy focuses on protecting children's ability to engage in identity exploration and development without algorithmic determinism or manipulation. This approach recognizes that algorithmic profiling of children creates unique harms by potentially foreclosing developmental pathways based on early behavioral patterns. In Brown v. Entertainment Merchants Association, Justice Breyer's dissent emphasized the state's interest in protecting children's developing minds, a principle that could support restrictions on algorithmic systems leveraging developmental vulnerabilities.[46]

Algorithmic systems create several distinct risks for children. Behavioral profiling based on children's early activities may create persistent profiles that follow them into adulthood, limiting opportunities based on childhood behaviors. Predictive systems may track children into particular educational or career pathways based on algorithmic assessments rather than allowing organic development. Manipulative systems may exploit developmental vulnerabilities to influence consumption, political views, or social behaviors in ways that compromise authentic development.

Traditional notice-and-consent frameworks prove particularly inadequate for children. Meaningful consent requires understanding what one is consenting to and the capacity to make informed decisions about complex tradeoffs. Children generally lack both the cognitive development to understand algorithmic processing's implications and the power to resist systems designed by sophisticated actors to maximize engagement regardless of developmental costs.

Several jurisdictions have enacted enhanced protections recognizing these challenges. The United Kingdom's Age-Appropriate Design Code prohibits using children's data in ways detrimental to their wellbeing and requires privacy by default for users under eighteen.[47] California's Age-Appropriate Design Code Act similarly mandates that digital services likely accessed by children configure default privacy

---

43 'Ginsberg v. New York', 390 U.S. 629, 638 (1968).

44 'New Mexico v. Google LLC', 507 F. Supp. 3d 1138 (D.N.M. 2020).

45 Federal Trade Commission, "Google and YouTube Will Pay Record $170 Million" (2019).

46 'Brown v. Entertainment Merchants Association', 564 U.S. 786, 840 (2011) (Breyer, J., dissenting).

47 Information Commissioner's Office, 'Age Appropriate Design' (2020).

settings at high levels and prohibits using children's data in ways harmful to their wellbeing.[48]

These approaches recognize that meaningful protection requires shifting from notice-and-consent frameworks to substantive limitations on algorithmic practices threatening children's development and autonomy. By focusing on outcomes rather than procedural compliance, these regulatory models address the reality that children cannot meaningfully consent to complex algorithmic processes with long-term developmental implications.

A robust constitutional approach to children's algorithmic privacy would recognize that children's limited capacity for informed consent, vulnerability to manipulation, and developmental needs create compelling state interests in regulation that might not survive constitutional scrutiny if applied to adults. Just as the Court in FCC v. Pacifica Foundation recognized that children's presence justifies greater regulation of broadcast media, children's participation in digital environments justifies enhanced regulation of algorithmic systems they encounter.[49]

Substantive protections should include prohibitions on behavioral profiling for children below specified ages, restrictions on algorithmic manipulation exploiting developmental vulnerabilities, requirements that algorithmic systems interacting with children prioritize developmental wellbeing over engagement or profit maximization, and enhanced parental controls providing meaningful oversight of children's algorithmic interactions without enabling excessive parental surveillance.

The challenge lies in implementing protections that respect children's developing autonomy while protecting against algorithmic harms. Overly paternalistic approaches risk infantilizing adolescents and preventing developmentally appropriate autonomy. Insufficient protection leaves children vulnerable to sophisticated manipulation by actors with far greater resources and expertise. The balance requires recognizing that appropriate protection varies with developmental stage, with younger children requiring more comprehensive protection while adolescents need safeguards that respect their emerging autonomy.

5.7 International Coordination and Cross-Border Challenges

Effective synthetic media governance requires international coordination to prevent regulatory arbitrage that would undermine domestic protections. Courts have increasingly adopted effects-based jurisdictional approaches for digital harms that apply directly to synthetic media contexts.

The Tribunal de Grande Instance de Paris in LICRA v. Yahoo! Inc. asserted jurisdiction based on local effects despite content origination elsewhere, establishing

[48] California Age-Appropriate Design Code Act, Cal. Civ. Code § 1798.99.29 et seq. (2022).

[49] 'FCC v. Pacifica Foundation', 438 U.S. 726 (1978).

a principle applicable to cross-border synthetic media distribution.[50] The European Union's General Data Protection Regulation demonstrated how strong protections in major markets drive global compliance through extraterritorial application, providing a model for synthetic media protection.[51]

Several coordination mechanisms show promise for synthetic media governance. The Budapest Convention on Cybercrime provides a model for harmonizing criminal approaches to the most harmful synthetic media uses across diverse jurisdictions.[52] The Council of Europe's Convention 108+ demonstrates how data protection principles can be internationalized beyond regional boundaries while respecting legitimate governance diversity.[53] The Global Cross-Border Privacy Rules Forum shows potential for interoperable approaches to digital governance across legal systems with different underlying frameworks.[54]

The challenge lies in achieving sufficient coordination to prevent harmful regulatory arbitrage while respecting legitimate diversity in cultural values and political systems. Nations differ fundamentally in how they balance individual rights, collective interests, and state authority. What some nations consider essential protection against harmful speech; others may view as unacceptable censorship. Effective international governance must accommodate this diversity while establishing minimum standards that all nations can accept.

One approach involves establishing "floor not ceiling" standards that prohibit the most egregious practices while permitting nations to adopt stricter protections reflecting their own values. International coordination could prohibit clearly harmful practices, non-consensual intimate deepfakes, fraudulent impersonation, synthetic media designed to incite violence, while permitting nations to regulate additional categories reflecting their own legal traditions and cultural values.

Another approach leverages market power to drive global standards. When major markets adopt strong protections, companies serving those markets must comply with stringent requirements. Maintaining separate systems for different markets proves costly and complex, often leading companies to adopt strongest requirements globally. The GDPR's global impact demonstrates this dynamic: many companies adopted GDPR standards globally rather than maintaining separate systems for European and non-European users.

Technical standards provide additional coordination mechanisms. When industry adopts common technical standards for content authentication, provenance tracking, or synthetic media detection, these standards create de facto global frameworks regardless of formal legal requirements. The C2PA's technical standards for content provenance, while voluntary, could become global standards if adopted by major platforms and content creation tools.[55]

---

50 'LICRA v. Yahoo! Inc.', The Tribunal de Grande Instance de Paris, November 20, 2000.

51 General Data Protection Regulation (EU) 2016/679.

52 Budapest Convention on Cybercrime, Council of Europe Treaty Series No. 185 (2001).

53 Council of Europe Convention 108+ (2018).

54 Global Cross-Border Privacy Rules Forum, Annual Report (2022).

55 Coalition for Content Provenance and Authenticity, Technical Specification (2021).

5.8 Future-Proofing Protections Against Advancing Capabilities

Synthetic media capabilities will continue advancing, requiring regulatory approaches that remain effective as technology evolves. The Court's recognition in Kyllo v. United States that constitutional protections must address "sense-enhancing technology" more broadly applies directly to synthetic media regulation.[56] Effective frameworks must address capabilities and effects rather than specific technical implementations that quickly become obsolete.

Capability-based approaches focus on what systems can do, creating realistic audio, video, or image synthesis depicting individuals without consent, rather than specific technical methods employed. This parallels the Court's reasoning in Carpenter v. United States, which recognized that location tracking capabilities create privacy concerns regardless of specific technical methods employed.[57] When regulations target capabilities rather than techniques, they remain effective as technology evolves.

Harm-focused approaches similarly provide more durable protection by focusing on specific tangible harms, fraud, defamation, non-consensual intimate imagery, electoral manipulation, rather than quickly outdated technical definitions. This aligns with harm-based analysis in both Carpenter and Riley v. California, which focused on privacy impacts rather than specific technological implementations.[58]

Layered defense strategies combine technical, legal, and educational approaches to create redundant protections that remain effective even as specific mechanisms become obsolete. This approach recognizes that no single protective measure can address all synthetic media challenges, necessitating complementary approaches addressing different vulnerability points. Technical authentication protects content integrity, legal remedies address harms when prevention fails, and education enables individuals to navigate synthetic media environments skeptically.

Regular review mechanisms ensure statutory frameworks maintain effectiveness against evolving capabilities. The Children's Online Privacy Protection Act's periodic rule reviews by the Federal Trade Commission provide a model.[59] Scheduled reassessments prevent protection gaps as technological capabilities outpace static regulatory frameworks. Review cycles of three to five years would allow frameworks to adapt while providing sufficient stability for compliance planning.

Adaptable technical standards must evolve alongside synthetic capabilities through performance-based requirements establishing protection objectives without mandating specific technical approaches. Graduated verification standards could incorporate multiple authentication levels appropriate to different contexts, from

---

[56] 'Kyllo v. United States', 533 U.S. 27 (2001).

[57] 'Carpenter v. United States', 138 S. Ct. 2206 (2018).

[58] 'Riley v. California', 573 U.S. 373 (2014).

[59] For FTC review process, see 16 C.F.R. § 312 (COPPA Rule).

basic watermarking for general content to cryptographic verification for high-stakes material like legal evidence or government communications.

Adversarial testing requirements ensure safety measures undergo regular evaluation against evolving synthetic capabilities to maintain effectiveness. Systems must be tested not merely against current threats but anticipated future capabilities, requiring red team exercises attempting to defeat protections using cutting-edge synthesis techniques. Open standards governance enables rapid incorporation of new protective measures as threats evolve, preventing protection mechanisms from becoming quickly obsolete.

Constitutional evolution must continue adapting to synthetic media challenges. The Court's recognition in Riley v. California that digital information fundamentally differs from physical artifacts provides foundation for ongoing adaptation.[60] Justice Kennedy's observation in Packingham v. North Carolina that courts should exercise "extreme caution before suggesting that the First Amendment provides scant protection for access to vast networks" underscores the need for careful balancing in synthetic media contexts.[61]

5.9 Meeting the Challenge: Integrated Approaches to Identity Protection

Addressing synthetic media challenges requires recognizing a fundamentally new frontier extending beyond information control to identity autonomy. Traditional privacy frameworks presumed clear distinctions between actual identity and representation that synthetic technologies have eliminated. What is at stake is not merely informational privacy but the basic integrity of personal identity in digital contexts.

The constitutional values implicated, privacy, dignity, autonomy, and expression, require thoughtful recalibration rather than simplistic application of frameworks developed for fundamentally different technological contexts. Just as the Court recognized in Carpenter that "the progress of science" necessitates evolving constitutional interpretation, synthetic media demands nuanced adaptation of constitutional principles rather than mechanical application of outdated precedents.[62]

For citizens navigating increasingly synthetic media environments, effective protection requires both individual rights and systemic safeguards. The right to maintain digital identity integrity represents not merely a narrow privacy interest but a fundamental condition for meaningful autonomy in the algorithmic age. As Judge Easterbrook noted in American Booksellers Ass'n, Inc. v. Hudnut, "depictions affect how people see the world, their fellows, and social relations."[63] This observation

---

[60] 'Riley v. California', 573 U.S. 373 (2014).

[61] 'Packingham v. North Carolina', 137 S. Ct. 1730, 1736 (2017).

[62] 'Carpenter v. United States', 138 S. Ct. 2206, 2214 (2018).

[63] 'American Booksellers Ass'n, Inc. v. Hudnut', 771 F.2d 323, 327–328 (7th Cir. 1985).

applies with greater force to synthetic media directly manipulating representations of reality, underscoring the necessity of effective protection.

Comprehensive protection requires coordinated action across multiple domains. Technology must provide authentication infrastructure enabling verification of authentic content. Law must establish clear rights protecting identity integrity while respecting legitimate expressive uses. Platforms must implement responsible content policies balancing removal of harmful deepfakes with preservation of legitimate synthetic media. Education must empower individuals to navigate synthetic environments critically. International coordination must prevent regulatory arbitrage while respecting legitimate diversity.

The challenge is urgent. Synthesis capabilities advance rapidly while legal frameworks lag substantially behind. The gap between technological capability and legal protection widens, creating expanding zones where identity appropriation occurs without meaningful recourse. Closing this gap requires sustained effort from lawmakers, courts, technologists, platforms, and civil society working together to develop integrated approaches protecting identity integrity in an age of ubiquitous synthesis.

References

Cases

American Booksellers Ass'n, Inc. v. Hudnut, 771 F.2d 323 (7th Cir. 1985), aff'd mem., 475 U.S. 1001 (1986)
Ashcroft v. Free Speech Coalition, 535 U.S. 234 (2002)
Brown v. Entertainment Merchants Association, 564 U.S. 786 (2011)
Carpenter v. United States, 585 U.S. ___, 138 S. Ct. 2206 (2018)
Central Hudson Gas & Electric Corp. v. Public Service Commission, 447 U.S. 557 (1980)
FCC v. Pacifica Foundation, 438 U.S. 726 (1978)
Gertz v. Robert Welch, Inc., 418 U.S. 323 (1974)
Ginsberg v. New York, 390 U.S. 629 (1968)
Hustler Magazine v. Falwell, 485 U.S. 46 (1988)
Illinois ex rel. Madigan v. Telemarketing Associates, Inc., 538 U.S. 600 (2003)
Kyllo v. United States, 533 U.S. 27 (2001)
LICRA v. Yahoo! Inc., The Tribunal de Grande Instance de Paris [Court of First Instance of Paris], Interim Court Order, November 20, 2000
Mathews v. Eldridge, 424 U.S. 319 (1976)
Milkovich v. Lorain Journal Co., 497 U.S. 1 (1990)
New Mexico v. Google LLC, 507 F. Supp. 3d 1138 (D.N.M. 2020)
New York Times Co. v. Sullivan, 376 U.S. 254 (1964)
Nixon v. Administrator of General Services, 433 U.S. 425 (1977)
Packingham v. North Carolina, 582 U.S. ___, 137 S. Ct. 1730 (2017)
Philadelphia Newspapers, Inc. v. Hepps, 475 U.S. 767 (1986)
R.A.V. v. City of St. Paul, 505 U.S. 377 (1992)
Reed v. Town of Gilbert, 576 U.S. 155 (2015)
Riley v. California, 573 U.S. 373 (2014)
Time, Inc. v. Hill, 385 U.S. 374 (1967)

United States v. Alvarez, 567 U.S. 709 (2012)
Wisconsin v. Constantineau, 400 U.S. 433 (1971)

Statues and Regulations

California Age-Appropriate Design Code Act, Cal. Civ. Code § 1798.99.29 et seq. (2022)
California Civil Code § 1708.86 (deepfake pornography)
Children's Online Privacy Protection Act, 15 U.S.C. §§ 6501–6506
Communications Decency Act § 230, 47 U.S.C. § 230
Digital Millennium Copyright Act, 17 U.S.C. § 1201 et seq.
European Union Digital Services Act, Regulation (EU) 2022/2065
Federal Rules of Evidence, Rule 901 (authentication)
General Data Protection Regulation (EU) 2016/679
National Defense Authorization Act for Fiscal Year 2021, Pub. L. No. 116–283 (2021)
ePrivacy Directive (EU) 2002/58/EC

Books and Reports

Chesney R, Citron D (2019) Deep fakes: a looming challenge for privacy, democracy, and national security. Calif Law Rev 107:1753–1820
European Commission (2021) Proposal for a regulation of the European Parliament and of the Council laying down harmonised rules on artificial intelligence (Artificial Intelligence Act). COM/2021/206 final
Federal Trade Commission (2019) Google and YouTube will pay record $170 million for alleged violations of children's privacy law. Press Release, September 4
Information Commissioner's Office (UK) (2020) Age appropriate design: a code of practice for online services. ICO, London

Journal Articles

Bambauer J (2014) The new intrusion. Notre Dame Law Review 88:205–246
Citron DK, Chesney R (2019) Deep fakes: a looming challenge for privacy, democracy, and national security. Calif Law Rev 107:1753–1820
Franks MA (2015) Drafting an effective 'revenge porn' law: a guide for legislators. Available at SSRN 2468823
Levendowski A (2018) How copyright law can fix artificial intelligence's implicit bias problem. Washington Law Review 93:579–630
Montgomery KC, Chester J (2015) Data protection for youth in the digital age: developing a rights-based global framework. Eur J Commun 30:606–622
Vaccaro K, Sandvig C (2019) The illusion of control: placebo effects of control settings. In: Proceedings of the 2019 CHI Conference on Human Factors in Computing Systems, pp 1–13

Technical Standards and Reports

Budapest Convention on Cybercrime, Council of Europe Treaty Series No. 185 (2001)
Coalition for Content Provenance and Authenticity (C2PA) (2021) Technical specification for content provenance and authenticity. Version 1.0
Council of Europe Convention 108+ (Convention for the Protection of Individuals with Regard to Automatic Processing of Personal Data), modernized version (2018)
Global Cross-Border Privacy Rules Forum (2020) Annual report on cross-border data transfers

Chapter 6
Economic Power and Algorithmic Markets

6.1 The Data Extraction Economy: Human Experience as Raw Material

Contemporary digital markets operate through systematic extraction of behavioral data that individuals generate through routine activities, transforming human experience into raw material for prediction markets. This extraction occurs largely without meaningful consent, adequate compensation, or democratic oversight, creating fundamental asymmetries between data extractors and data subjects that traditional market frameworks fail to address.

Shoshana Zuboff terms this economic paradigm "surveillance capitalism," describing how leading technology firms have pioneered business models premised on comprehensive behavioral monitoring and prediction.[1] Unlike industrial capitalism, which extracted natural resources and labor to produce goods, surveillance capitalism extracts behavioral data to produce predictions about future behavior that are sold to advertisers, insurers, employers, and other actors seeking to influence or profit from human conduct.

The revenue model depends on what might be termed "behavioral surplus", data harvested beyond what is necessary to provide requested services. When individuals use search engines, social media platforms, or mobile applications, these systems collect far more information than functionality requires. Location data, browsing patterns, social connections, content interactions, keystroke dynamics, and numerous other behavioral signals are captured, aggregated, and analyzed to generate predictions about individual preferences, vulnerabilities, and likely future actions.[2]

[1] Zuboff, 'The Age of Surveillance Capitalism' (2019), 8–11, 63–97.

[2] 'Id.' at 93–100.

R. Yadav-Ranjan, *Constitutional Democracy in the Algorithmic Age*, Law, Governance and Technology Series 83, https://doi.org/10.1007/978-3-032-34604-9_6

This extraction framework has expanded from digital advertising origins to permeate virtually every economic sector. Healthcare providers, insurance companies, financial institutions, and retailers increasingly function as data acquisition vehicles, with services providing pretexts for comprehensive monitoring. The market capitalization of leading technology companies, exceeding ten trillion dollars collectively, derives primarily not from superior product development but from sophisticated data harvesting and monetization capabilities.[3]

The economic arrangement creates fundamental misalignment: individuals generate the data that creates economic value but capture no returns on their contributions. Research demonstrates that most citizens remain largely unaware of both the scope of data extraction and the substantial economic assets generated from their activities.[4] This information asymmetry enables what effectively constitutes exploitation, systematic value extraction without corresponding compensation or meaningful consent.

The transformation from service provision to surveillance monetization occurred without democratic deliberation or transparency requirements. What platforms present as "free" services constitute comprehensive monitoring infrastructures designed to maximize data extraction rather than user welfare. Interface design itself becomes weaponized, meticulously crafted not to enhance user experience but to extract maximum behavioral data while maintaining only minimal engagement sufficient to perpetuate surveillance operations.[5]

Constitutional principles of economic liberty and due process require attention to power asymmetries in contractual relationships. The Supreme Court in cases from Lochner v. New York through West Coast Hotel Co. v. Parrish have grappled with questions about when disparities in bargaining power justify regulatory intervention to protect weaker parties.[6] While the Court has generally disfavored substantive due process review of economic regulations since 1937, the comprehensive information asymmetries and power disparities in surveillance capitalism may warrant reconsideration of constitutional protections for economic autonomy in digital contexts.

6.2 From Information to Infrastructure: Platform Power and Market Concentration

The data extraction economy has produced market concentration exceeding any seen since the Gilded Age, with dominant platforms occupying positions enabling both horizontal and vertical control over data flows, commerce, and communication.

---

[3] Mazzucato, 'The Value of Everything' (2018), 185–216.

[4] Aridor, Che, and Salz, "The Economic Consequences of Data Privacy Regulation" (2021).

[5] Frischmann and Selinger, 'Re-Engineering Humanity' (2018), 112–143.

[6] 'Lochner v. New York', 198 U.S. 45 (1905); 'West Coast Hotel Co. v. Parrish', 300 U.S. 379 (1937).

This consolidation generates what might be termed "infrastructural power", dominance over critical digital utilities that facilitates both economic value extraction and governance authority without corresponding democratic accountability.[7]

Leading technology platforms function effectively as regulatory authorities, implementing policies and technical specifications affecting billions of users with negligible governmental oversight despite substantial societal implications. The UK Competition and Markets Authority documented how dominant platforms leverage data advantages to entrench market power while forestalling competition, creating self-reinforcing dynamics where initial scale advantages compound into insurmountable barriers.[8]

The resulting power asymmetries extend beyond consumer harms to threaten independent businesses, democratic governance, and social equality. Small businesses face complete dependence on dominant platforms for customer access, with platforms extracting substantial rents while maintaining unilateral authority to modify terms, restrict access, or appropriate successful business models. Public institutions find their authority effectively subordinated to technical systems they neither control nor fully understand.[9]

The appropriation mechanism operates through several documented patterns that traditional antitrust doctrine has yet to fully address. Amazon uses marketplace data from third-party sellers to identify successful product categories, then launches competing Amazon Basics products at lower prices while controlling the search ranking and recommendation algorithms that determine which products consumers see; the U.S. House Judiciary Committee's 2020 majority staff report documented this pattern across multiple categories, finding that Amazon's structural position as both marketplace and competitor produced a categorical conflict of interest.[10] Apple has long engaged in what developers term "Sherlocking" the replication of successful third-party application features as native iOS or macOS functionality, eliminating the third-party product's competitive position. Documented examples include Night Shift (replicating f.lux). Screen Time (multiple prior third-party screen-time applications). Apple Music (launched after Spotify established the streaming market), and the Files app (Document by Readdle). Microsoft's bundling of Teams into Office 365 was the subject of a 2020 Slack antitrust complaint to the European Commission alleging precisely this pattern, leading to formal proceedings under Case AT. 40,669. Meta has built its product strategy around explicit replication: Stories from Snapchat in 2016, Reels from TikTok in 2020, Threads from Twitter in 2023. In each case, the dominant platform's structural advantages, comprehensive user data, default

[7] Rahman, "The New Utilities" (2018).

[8] Competition and Markets Authority, "Online Platforms and Digital Advertising" (2020), 4–7, 49–83.

[9] Mazzucato, 'The Value of Everything' (2018), 203–209.

[10] U.S. House of Representatives, Committee on the Judiciary, Subcommittee on Antitrust, Commercial, and Administrative Law: *Investigation of Competition in Digital Markets: Majority Staff Report and Recommendations* (2020), 256–269. (Analysis of Amazon marketplace data use; Apple feature replication at 327–339; Meta replication at 161–171.) See also: European Commission, Case AT.40669–Microsoft Teams (formal proceedings opened 27 July 2023).

placement, distribution scale, and bundling power, enable it to displace successful third-party offerings without competing on the underlying product's merits. This is not vertical integration in the traditional sense. It is the use of platform infrastructure to extract the value of innovation occurring on top of that infrastructure, a dynamic that consumer welfare antitrust analysis was not designed to detect or remedy.

Traditional antitrust frameworks prove inadequate for addressing these dynamics. The consumer welfare standard that has dominated American antitrust since the 1970s focuses primarily on price effects and short-term consumer harm, missing the structural power implications of platform dominance.[11] When platforms offer "free" services while extracting comprehensive data, conventional price-based analysis fails to capture actual consumer costs or overall welfare effects.

The Supreme Court's antitrust jurisprudence, developed primarily in industrial rather than digital contexts, provides uncertain guidance for platform markets. In Ohio v. American Express Co., the Court's narrow approach to defining relevant markets and analyzing multi-sided platforms created significant obstacles for addressing anticompetitive conduct in digital contexts.[12] The Court's reluctance in Verizon Communications Inc. v. Law Offices of Curtis V. Trinko to impose affirmative duties on dominant firms further limits regulatory options for addressing platform power.[13]

Network effects characteristic of digital platforms creates winner-take-all dynamics where initial market leadership compounds into durable dominance. When a platform's value to users increases with the number of other users, late entrants face insurmountable disadvantages even with superior products or lower prices. Combined with data advantages that accrue to scale, these dynamics produce persistent market concentration without corresponding efficiency gains.[14]

The U.S. House Judiciary Committee's Investigation of Competition in Digital Markets documented these challenges comprehensively, showing how dominant firms extract massive economic rents while reducing innovation and consumer welfare through exclusionary conduct, self-preferencing, and leveraging market power across related markets.[15] The Committee found that existing antitrust tools prove insufficient for addressing the structural characteristics of platform markets, including extreme returns to scale and scope, data advantage feedback loops, and prohibitive switching costs.

Emerging regulatory approaches recognize these inadequacies. The European Union's Digital Markets Act establishes ex-ante regulation of "digital gatekeepers," requiring specific conduct from platforms meeting defined thresholds rather than

---

[11] Khan, "Amazon's Antitrust Paradox" (2017).

[12] 'Ohio v. American Express Co.', 138 S. Ct. 2274 (2018).

[13] 'Verizon Communications Inc. v. Law Offices of Curtis V. Trinko', 540 U.S. 398 (2004).

[14] U.S. House Judiciary Committee, "Investigation of Competition in Digital Markets" (2020), 47–55.

[15] 'Id.' at 6–16, 47–120.

depending on after-the-fact enforcement.[16] This shift toward structural regulation reflects recognition that certain market characteristics require preemptive intervention rather than waiting for demonstrable consumer harm.

6.3 Algorithmic Collusion and Coordination

Beyond market structure concerns, algorithmic systems enable novel forms of anticompetitive coordination that evade traditional antitrust detection and remediation. When pricing algorithms interact in markets, they can produce outcomes resembling explicit collusion without human agreement or communication that conventional antitrust law requires for Sherman Act Section 1 violations.[17]

Economic research demonstrates that reinforcement learning algorithms commonly used for dynamic pricing can independently arrive at supercompetitive pricing resembling cartel behavior.[18] When multiple firms deploy such algorithms in the same market, the systems may learn to avoid price competition through repeated interactions, achieving tacit coordination without explicit agreement among human decision-makers.

Traditional antitrust doctrine premised on proving anticompetitive agreements faces substantial challenges in algorithmic contexts. The Sherman Act prohibits "contract, combination…or conspiracy" in restraint of trade, language suggesting that independent parallel conduct, however harmful, does not violate Section 1 absent evidence of agreement.[19] When algorithmic systems achieve coordination through independent learning rather than human communication, conventional evidence of conspiracy proves elusive.

Several cases illustrate these challenges. In United States v. Topkins, the first criminal antitrust case involving algorithmic pricing, defendants used the same third-party pricing algorithm and agreed to pricing parameters, conduct fitting traditional conspiracy doctrine despite algorithmic implementation.[20] But when firms independently deploy similar algorithms that achieve tacit coordination through machine learning, existing doctrine provides uncertain guidance about liability.

European competition authorities have begun addressing these concerns. The UK Competition and Markets Authority's study on pricing algorithms and competition found that algorithmic systems can facilitate both horizontal coordination among competitors and vertical restraints between suppliers and retailers.[21] The European

[16] Digital Markets Act, Regulation (EU) 2022/1925, arts. 5–7.

[17] Sherman Antitrust Act, 15 U.S.C. § 1.

[18] Calvano et al., "Artificial Intelligence, Algorithmic Pricing, and Collusion" (2020).

[19] 15 U.S.C. § 1.

[20] 'United States v. Topkins', No. CR 15–00,201 WHO (N.D. Cal. 2015).

[21] Competition and Markets Authority, "Pricing Algorithms: Economic Working Paper on the Use of Algorithms to Facilitate Collusion and Personalised Pricing" (2018).

Commission's preliminary report on competition policy for the digital era recommended enhanced monitoring of algorithmic pricing and potential ex-ante regulation for certain algorithmic applications.[22]

U.S. enforcement actions and recent appellate authority confirm both the regulatory ambition and the doctrinal limit. The Department of Justice filed *United States v. RealPage, Inc.* in August 2024, alleging that the company's revenue-management software violated Sections 1 and 2 of the Sherman Act by aggregating nonpublic competitively sensitive information from competing landlords and generating coordinated pricing recommendations.[23] The November 2024 proposed consent decree imposed meaningful constraints on RealPage's use of competitor data, training inputs, and auto-accept default features, and prohibited the operator from facilitating discussions among landlord users about market trends drawn from nonpublic data. But the settlement did not establish that algorithmic pricing per se violates the Sherman Act. RealPage did not admit liability, and the decree reached particular practices rather than the underlying technology.[24] Weeks earlier, in *Gibson v. Cendyn Group,* the Ninth Circuit became the first appellate court to rule on algorithmic pricing under Section 1, affirming dismissal of class-action claims against Las Vegas hotel operators that licensed common revenue-management software from a single vendor. The court held that conscious parallel use of the same algorithmic software, without horizontal agreement among competitors or sharing of nonpublic information through the software, does not state a Section 1 claim: antitrust law "does not require a business to turn a blind eye to information simply because its competitors are also aware of that same information."[25]

The contrast with *In re MultiPlan Health Insurance Provider Antitrust Litigation,* where the Northern District of Illinois denied a motion to dismiss on similar facts, locates the doctrinal frontier. The MultiPLan algorithm was mandatory rather than advisory, its outputs were contractually binding on participating insurers, and the operator actively facilitated information exchange among participants. The narrow line between *Gibson* and MultiPlan, advisory tool versus mandatory output, software vendor versus information-sharing hub, is where the next decade of algorithmic collusion litigation will be fought.[26] State legislatures have begun filing the federal doctrinal gap statutorily. New York amended its Donnelly Act in December 2025 to reach landlord uses of pricing algorithms drawing on nonpublic competitor data, a statute RealPage has challenged on First Amendment grounds, raising the

---

[22] European Commission, "Competition Policy for the Digital Era" (2019).

[23] Complaint, *United States v. RealPage, Inc.*, No. 1:24-cv-00710 (M.D.N.C., filed 23 Aug 2024).

[24] Proposed Final Judgment, *United States v. RealPage, Inc.*, No. 1:24-cv-00710 (M.D.N.C., filed 24 Nov 2025). See also: Consent Decree, Greystar Management Services LLC (Aug 2025); "RealPage Settlement Shows Algorithmic Pricing Isn't the Enemy." *Bloomberg Law* (16 Jan 2026).

[25] *Gibson v. Cendyn Group, LLC*, No. 24–3576, 2025 WL 2,371,948 (9th Cir. 15 Aug 2025), aff'g 2024 WL 2,060,260 (D. Nev. 8 May 2024). See also: Brief for the United States as Amicus Curiae, *Gibson v. Cendyn Group*, No. 24–3576 (9th Cir. 24 Oct 2024).

[26] *In re MultiPlan Health Insurance Provider Antitrust Litigation*, No. 1:24-cv-06795 (N.D. Ill.). See also: Arnold & Porter Advisory: "Ninth Circuit Clarifies Antitrust Implications of Algorithmic Pricing" (25 Aug 2025).

further question whether algorithmic pricing tools and their outputs receive expressive protection.[27] The doctrinal limit is durable. Detection of supercompetitive algorithmic coordination is technically feasible through pricing-pattern analysis. The obstacle is doctrinal, not evidentiary. The agreement requirement of Section 1, reinforced by *Twombly's* plausibility-pleading standard for parallel conduct, leaves machine-mediated coordination without observable human communication outside conventional reach. Closing this gap will require statutory innovation at the federal level, sustained development of state antitrust law along with New York model, recognizing that algorithmic systems can affect coordination that would be per se unlawful if achieved through traditional means.

Proposals for addressing algorithmic collusion include extending antitrust liability to algorithmic coordination regardless of human intent, requiring disclosure of algorithm use in concentrated markets, establishing independent algorithmic auditing for markets with collusion risk, and treating algorithmic systems as "per se" violations in certain contexts.[28] These approaches recognize that protecting competitive markets requires adapting doctrine to address coordination mechanisms that transcend traditional concepts of agreement.

Constitutional constraints on antitrust enforcement remain relatively minimal. The Supreme Court's recognition in Federal Trade Commission v. Actavis, Inc. that competitive effects rather than formal categorization should drive analysis suggests courts may prove receptive to doctrinal evolution addressing novel anticompetitive mechanisms.[29] However, due process concerns about criminalizing conduct without clear notice of illegality may limit approaches premised on liability without human intent.

6.4 Labor Rights in Algorithmic Workplaces

As algorithmic systems increasingly determine hiring, evaluation, scheduling, compensation, and termination decisions, traditional labor protections face systematic challenges. Workers experience "management by algorithm" with limited visibility into systems governing employment conditions, creating power asymmetries that compromise both individual rights and collective action.[30]

Algorithmic management systems enable comprehensive surveillance of worker activities, evaluating productivity through metrics that may be arbitrary, discriminatory, or simply opaque. Amazon warehouse workers face termination based on algorithmic productivity assessments without meaningful opportunity to understand

[27] N.Y. Gen. Bus. Law §340 (Donnelly Act), as amended by A.B. 1417-B (effective 15 Dec 2025). See also: *RealPage, Inc. v. New York* (E.D.N.Y., pending); Paul, Weiss: "Practical Takeaways From the DOJ's Algorithmic Pricing Settlement" (2 Dec 2025).

[28] Ezrachi and Stucke, "Sustainable and Unchallenged Algorithmic Tacit Collusion" (2020).

[29] 'FTC v. Actavis, Inc.', 570 U.S. 136, 158–159 (2013).

[30] Adams-Prassl, "The Algorithm as a Boss?" (2022).

or contest the measurements driving their evaluation.[31] Uber and Lyft drivers experience dynamic pricing and trip assignment algorithms that determine earnings without transparency about how systems operate or why particular outcomes occur.[32]

These systems create several distinct challenges for labor rights. First, algorithmic opacity prevents workers from understanding evaluation criteria, making improvement impossible and contestation ineffective. When workers cannot know what performance metrics are measured or how they are weighted, employment becomes fundamentally precarious regardless of work quality.[33]

Second, comprehensive surveillance enables granular monitoring that would be impractical for human managers, creating what might be termed "algorithmic panopticism." Workers subject to continuous biometric monitoring, keystroke tracking, and productivity measurement experience psychological burdens beyond those in traditional employment relationships, with health implications ranging from stress to physical injuries from unrealistic productivity demands.[34]

Third, algorithmic decision-making fragments employment relationships in ways that complicate collective action. When gig economy platforms classify workers as independent contractors managed through algorithms, traditional labor organizing faces both legal barriers and practical challenges from workforce atomization.[35]

Constitutional protections for labor rights remain limited. The Supreme Court in NLRB v. Jones & Laughlin Steel Corp. recognized Congress's authority to protect collective bargaining under the Commerce Clause, but constitutional protections for labor extend primarily through statutory frameworks rather than direct constitutional rights.[36] The Court's recent decisions in Epic Systems Corp. v. Lewis and Janus v. AFSCME have created additional obstacles for labor organizing, suggesting limited judicial receptivity to expanding worker protections absent clear statutory authorization.[37]

Several regulatory approaches could address algorithmic workplace challenges. Mandatory disclosure of algorithmic evaluation metrics and thresholds would enable workers to understand performance standards. Worker access to personal performance data driving algorithmic decisions would permit meaningful contestation of adverse actions. Clear documentation of human versus algorithmic decision authority would preserve accountability. Collective bargaining rights regarding algorithmic workplace systems would enable organized labor to negotiate system parameters.[38]

---

[31] Kantor, Weise, and Ashford, "The Amazon That Customers Don't See," 'New York Times', June 15, 2021.

[32] Rosenblat, 'Uberland' (2018), 62–89.

[33] De Stefano, "Negotiating the Algorithm" (2019).

[34] Adams-Prassl, "The Algorithm as a Boss?" (2022), 18–24.

[35] Cherry, "Beyond Misclassification" (2016).

[36] 'NLRB v. Jones & Laughlin Steel Corp.', 301 U.S. 1 (1937).

[37] 'Epic Systems Corp. v. Lewis', 138 S. Ct. 1612 (2018); 'Janus v. AFSCME', 138 S. Ct. 2448 (2018).

[38] For comprehensive labor rights framework, see Chapter 16, Sect. 16.8 of this volume.

More fundamentally, worker representation in algorithmic design processes would ensure that workplace algorithms reflect labor interests alongside management prerogatives. When productivity metrics, evaluation criteria, and scheduling optimization objectives are embedded in code rather than explicit policy, they become effectively insulated from traditional labor advocacy without specific governance mechanisms ensuring worker participation.[39]

Limitations on algorithmic worker surveillance would address power asymmetries created by comprehensive monitoring capabilities. Reasonable constraints on continuous biometric and behavioral monitoring, restrictions on off-duty surveillance through work devices, and proportionality requirements for surveillance intensity would preserve worker dignity while enabling legitimate management oversight.[40]

The National Labor Relations Act's protections for concerted activity extend to workers' collective action regarding working conditions, potentially encompassing algorithmic management systems despite technological mediation.[41] However, enforcement remains uncertain, and gig economy classification challenges leave many algorithmically managed workers outside statutory protections entirely.

6.5 The Commodification of Attention and Experience

Data extraction extends beyond discrete information to comprehensive commodification of human experience and attention. Contemporary platforms optimize for "engagement", maximizing time and attention users devote to services, through techniques deliberately designed to override conscious decision-making and create compulsive use patterns resembling addiction.[42]

Tim Wu terms this the "attention merchant" model: business models premised on maximizing attention capture rather than providing value, often through exploitation of psychological vulnerabilities.[43] Variable reward schedules, social validation feedback loops, artificial scarcity mechanisms, and other design patterns exploit neurological systems in ways similar to gambling and other addictive behaviors.

The techniques are not accidental but deliberately engineered. Internal documents from social media platforms reveal sophisticated understanding of psychological vulnerabilities and intentional design choices to maximize engagement despite known harms to user wellbeing.[44] Features like infinite scroll, autoplay, and notification systems serve no user need but effectively capture attention and prolong usage.

---

[39] De Stefano, "Negotiating the Algorithm" (2019), 28–35.

[40] Moore and Robinson, "The Quantified Self" (2016).

[41] 29 U.S.C. § 157.

[42] Alter, 'Irresistible' (2017), 27–48.

[43] Wu, 'The Attention Merchants' (2016), 17–32, 309–334.

[44] Haugen, 'The Power of One' (2023) (discussing internal Facebook documents).

The consequences extend beyond individual harms to systemic effects on democratic discourse. Research demonstrates that engagement-optimized algorithms systematically amplify emotionally inflammatory content over substantive information, distorting the informational environment necessary for democratic functioning.[45] When platforms optimize for engagement rather than information quality, they create economic incentives directly opposed to informed citizenship.

Michael Sandel identifies this as "market imperialism", the extension of market valuation into domains previously governed by non-market norms.[46] When attention becomes commodified and human experience is reduced to "engagement" metrics, the boundaries protecting certain activities from market logic erode. Relationships, contemplation, and civic discourse increasingly operate according to platform logics designed for profit maximization rather than human flourishing.

Regulatory responses remain inadequate. While some jurisdictions have begun addressing "attentional harms," constraints on exploitative design practices remain minimal.[47] What is needed is not merely incremental regulation but recognition of attention and experience as protected resources requiring safeguards against predatory exploitation.

The First Amendment creates potential obstacles for regulating platform design features. Content-neutral regulations of "time, place, and manner" typically receive less scrutiny than content-based restrictions, suggesting that regulations addressing design features rather than content might survive constitutional review.[48] However, the Supreme Court's recognition in Sorrell v. IMS Health Inc. that information itself can constitute protected speech complicates efforts to constrain data practices regardless of content implications.[49]

6.6 Alternative Economic Models and Rights Protection

Current economic structures for digital services need not represent inevitable outcomes. Alternative models demonstrate that innovation and rights protection can coexist when economic incentives align with user welfare rather than extraction imperatives.

Data cooperatives provide one alternative, establishing collective governance over personal data rather than individual consent to platform terms. These structures recognize data's inherently social nature, its value derives from aggregation across populations, while preserving individual and collective autonomy through democratic control.[50] European data cooperatives like Salus Coop demonstrate practical

---

[45] Vaidhyanathan, 'Antisocial Media' (2018), 42–69.

[46] Sandel, 'What Money Can't Buy' (2012), 5–14.

[47] Ireland, Online Safety and Media Regulation Act 2022, Part 3.

[48] 'Ward v. Rock Against Racism', 491 U.S. 781 (1989).

[49] 'Sorrell v. IMS Health Inc.', 564 U.S. 552 (2011).

[50] Prainsack and Buyx, 'Solidarity in Biomedicine and Beyond' (2017), 144–162.

viability, providing health data for research while maintaining member governance over data use and benefit distribution.[51]

Platform cooperatives extend cooperative ownership models to digital platforms themselves. When platforms are owned by users or workers rather than external investors, governance incentives shift from extraction maximization to sustainable value creation.[52] Examples including Resonate (music streaming owned by artists and listeners) and Fairbnb (home sharing with community governance) demonstrate possibilities for digital services aligned with stakeholder rather than solely shareholder interests.[53]

Public options for digital infrastructure provide alternatives to commercial platforms driven by data monetization. When governments provide essential digital services as public utilities, they can incorporate rights protections by design rather than treating privacy as cost to be minimized.[54] India's digital public infrastructure, including the Unified Payments Interface and Aadhaar identity system, demonstrates potential for publicly governed systems achieving scale while maintaining oversight, though implementation challenges including privacy concerns remain.[55]

Privacy-preserving technical architectures demonstrate that effective services need not depend on comprehensive data extraction. Federated learning enables machine learning on distributed data without centralization. Differential privacy provides mathematical guarantees limiting individual identification in aggregate data. Zero-knowledge proofs enable verification without disclosure. Local-first software architectures process data on user devices rather than centralized servers.[56]

Economic mechanisms could align incentives with rights protection. Data taxation would internalize currently externalized costs of data extraction, creating revenue for addressing algorithmic harms while discouraging excessive collection.[57] France's Digital Services Tax and similar measures in other jurisdictions provide initial examples, though primarily motivated by tax base concerns rather than rights protection.

More ambitious proposals include "data labor markets" establishing explicit compensation for data contributions through micropayment systems.[58] While practical challenges including transaction costs remain substantial, these approaches recognize that data subjects are stakeholders in the data economy rather than merely subjects of extraction.

Digital dividends or universal basic income funded by data economy value creation would acknowledge citizens as stakeholders whose collective behavioral

---

[51] Salus Coop, "Governance Structure and Data Management" (2020).

[52] Scholz, 'Platform Cooperativism' (2016), 7–28.

[53] Schneider, "Platform Cooperativism as a Protective Measure" (2018).

[54] Rahman, "The New Utilities" (2018), 1650–1672.

[55] Nilekani and Shah, 'Rebooting India' (2015), 73–98.

[56] Kleppmann, "Local-First Software" (2019).

[57] Collin and Colin, "Mission d'expertise sur la fiscalité de l'économie numérique" (2013).

[58] Posner and Weyl, 'Radical Markets' (2018), 203–244.

data generates platform value.[59] California Governor Gavin Newsom's proposal for a "data dividend" represents political recognition of this principle, though implementation details remain contested and face significant political obstacles.

6.7 Property Rights, Market Failures, and Regulatory Frameworks

Traditional property frameworks fail when applied to data governance challenges. Unlike conventional property objects, data is non-rivalrous, one person's use does not preclude others' use, and derives value primarily from aggregation rather than individual instances. The social and relational dimensions of data generation further complicate individual property approaches when valuable insights emerge from patterns across populations rather than discrete contributions.[60]

Legal systems have produced incoherent responses. The European Court of Justice's decision in Google Spain SL v. AEPD established limited data subject rights without resolving underlying property questions.[61] The California Consumer Privacy Act creates control rights without addressing fundamental questions about data's economic value or appropriate compensation structures.[62]

More promising approaches recognize property's inherent social dimensions, balancing individual rights with collective interests.[63] Proposals for "data commons" establish collective governance structures recognizing both individual and community interests in data governance.[64] However, these frameworks remain largely theoretical while extractive models dominate practice.

The data economy exhibits classic market failure characteristics: extreme information asymmetries, insurmountable barriers to entry, and network effects producing winner-take-all outcomes without corresponding efficiency gains. When markets naturally produce such concentration without welfare benefits, structural remedies become necessary to preserve both economic dynamism and democratic values.[65]

Externalities from data extraction extend beyond parties to transactions. Privacy harms, reduced trust, diminished autonomy, and compromised democratic discourse represent costs borne by society generally rather than captured in market prices.[66] Current regulatory frameworks barely acknowledge these externalities, much less address them effectively.

[59] Reich and Sahami, 'System Error' (2021), 183–197.

[60] Cohen, 'Between Truth and Power' (2019), 25–62.

[61] 'Google Spain SL v. AEPD', Case C-131/12 (CJEU 2014).

[62] Cal. Civ. Code § 1798.100 et seq.

[63] Alexander, "The Social-Obligation Norm" (2011).

[64] Prainsack and Buyx, 'Solidarity in Biomedicine and Beyond' (2017), 149–156.

[65] U.S. House Judiciary Committee, "Investigation of Competition in Digital Markets" (2020), 51–55.

[66] Bietti, "From Ethics Washing to Ethics Bashing" (2020).

Comprehensive regulatory approaches would include both ex-ante structural requirements and ex-post enforcement. Mandatory privacy by design, data minimization requirements, purpose limitation, and consent standards would establish baseline protections. Stronger antitrust enforcement addressing market structure alongside conduct, restrictions on acquisitions by dominant platforms, interoperability requirements enabling competitive alternatives, and algorithmic auditing requirements would address market concentration.[67]

Labor protections specific to algorithmic workplaces, transparency requirements for automated decision-making, and collective governance mechanisms for significant platforms would address power asymmetries in employment and service provision.[68] These complementary approaches recognize that effective governance requires addressing both market structure and conduct across multiple regulatory domains simultaneously.

6.8 Constitutional Dimensions of Economic Power

While the Supreme Court has generally disfavored substantive economic due process review since West Coast Hotel Co. v. Parrish, the concentrated economic power in platform markets may warrant reconsideration of constitutional protections for economic liberty and democratic participation.[69]

The Court's recognition in Marsh v. Alabama that private entities performing traditionally public functions face constitutional constraints provides potential foundation for addressing platforms that control access to digital public forums.[70] When platforms effectively govern speech, commerce, and social interaction for billions of users, their formally private status may not preclude constitutional obligations.

First Amendment principles require attention to concentrated private power over speech when that power creates equivalent effects to government censorship. Justice Kennedy's observation in Packingham v. North Carolina that social media has become the modern public square suggests constitutional values may require ensuring access and constraining platform power to exclude speakers or discriminate based on viewpoint.[71]

Equal Protection principles, while formally applicable only to state action, identify values relevant to addressing algorithmic discrimination by private platforms. When algorithmic systems systematically disadvantage protected groups through proxies and correlations, they create distributional effects that democratic equality principles should constrain even absent formal state action.[72]

---

[67] For comprehensive regulatory framework, see Chapter 16 of this volume.

[68] 'Id.'

[69] 'West Coast Hotel Co. v. Parrish', 300 U.S. 379 (1937).

[70] 'Marsh v. Alabama', 326 U.S. 501 (1946).

[71] 'Packingham v. North Carolina', 137 S. Ct. 1730, 1735–1737 (2017).

[72] Barocas and Selbst, "Big Data's Disparate Impact" (2016).

Due process values requiring notice, opportunity to be heard, and reasoned decision-making before deprivation of significant interests apply to governmental actors but reflect broader principles of fairness in consequential decisions. When platforms make determinations affecting livelihood, reputation, or access to essential services through opaque algorithms, procedural justice concerns arise regardless of constitutional doctrine's formal limitations.[73]

The challenge lies in translating constitutional values developed for government action to private actors wielding comparable power through different mechanisms. While current doctrine generally requires state action for constitutional obligations, the functional equivalence between platform power and government authority suggests that constitutional principles should constrain systematic private power threatening democratic equality and individual liberty.[74]

References

Cases

Epic Systems Corp. v. Lewis, 584 U.S. ___, 138 S. Ct. 1612 (2018)
Federal Trade Commission v. Actavis, Inc., 570 U.S. 136 (2013)
Google Spain SL v. Agencia Española de Protección de Datos (AEPD), Case C-131/12 (CJEU 2014)
Janus v. American Federation of State, County, and Municipal Employees, Council 31, 585 U.S. ___, 138 S. Ct. 2448 (2018)
Lochner v. New York, 198 U.S. 45 (1905)
Marsh v. Alabama, 326 U.S. 501 (1946)
NLRB v. Jones & Laughlin Steel Corp., 301 U.S. 1 (1937)
Ohio v. American Express Co., 585 U.S. ___, 138 S. Ct. 2274 (2018)
Packingham v. North Carolina, 582 U.S. ___, 137 S. Ct. 1730 (2017)
Sorrell v. IMS Health Inc., 564 U.S. 552 (2011)
United States v. Topkins, No. CR 15–00201 WHO (N.D. Cal. 2015)
Verizon Communications Inc. v. Law Offices of Curtis V. Trinko, LLP, 540 U.S. 398 (2004)
West Coast Hotel Co. v. Parrish, 300 U.S. 379 (1937)

Statutes and Regulations

California Consumer Privacy Act, Cal. Civ. Code § 1798.100 et seq. (2018)
Digital Markets Act, Regulation (EU) 2022/1925 (2022)
National Labor Relations Act, 29 U.S.C. §§ 151–169
Sherman Antitrust Act, 15 U.S.C. §§ 1–7

[73] Citron and Pasquale, "The Scored Society" (2014).

[74] See Chapter 1, Sect. 1.4 of this volume for extended discussion of these constitutional dimensions.

Books

Pasquale F (2015) The black box society: the secret algorithms that control money and information. Harvard University Press, Cambridge, MA

Sandel MJ (2012) What money can't buy: the moral limits of markets. Farrar, Straus and Giroux, New York

Zuboff S (2019) The age of surveillance capitalism: the fight for a human future at the new frontier of power. PublicAffairs, New York

Journal Articles and Reports

Acemoglu D (2021) Harms of AI. NBER Working Paper No. 29247

Adams-Prassl J (2022) The algorithm as a boss? control and autonomy in application-based management. Comparative Labor Law Pol J 43:1–32

Alexander GS (2011) The social-obligation norm in American property law. Cornell Law Rev 94:745–820

Aridor G, Che Y-K, Salz T (2021) The economic consequences of data privacy regulation: empirical evidence from GDPR. NBER Working Paper No. 26900

Calvano E et al (2020) Artificial intelligence, algorithmic pricing, and collusion. Am Econ Rev 110(10):3267–3297

Cohen JE (2019) Between truth and power: the legal constructions of informational capitalism. Oxford University Press, New York

Competition and Markets Authority (UK) (2020) Online platforms and digital advertising: market study final report

De Stefano V (2019) 'Negotiating the algorithm': automation, artificial intelligence, and labor protection. Comparative Labor Law Pol J 41:15–46

Ezrachi A, Stucke ME (2020) Sustainable and unchallenged algorithmic tacit collusion. Northwest J Technol Intellect Prop 17:217–260

Frischmann BM, Selinger E (2018) Re-engineering humanity. Cambridge University Press, Cambridge

Khan LM (2017) Amazon's antitrust paradox. Yale Law J 126:710–805

Mazzucato M (2018) The value of everything: making and taking in the global economy. PublicAffairs, New York

Prainsack B, Buyx A (2017) Solidarity in biomedicine and beyond. Cambridge University Press, Cambridge

Rahman KS (2018) The new utilities: private power, social infrastructure, and the revival of the public utility concept. Cardozo Law Rev 39:1621–1689

Scholz T (2016) Platform cooperativism: challenging the corporate sharing economy. Rosa Luxemburg Stiftung, New York

U.S. House Judiciary Committee, Subcommittee on Antitrust, Commercial and Administrative Law (2020) Investigation of competition in digital markets

Vaidhyanathan S (2018) Antisocial media: how Facebook disconnects us and undermines democracy. Oxford University Press, New York

Wu T (2016) The attention merchants: the epic scramble to get inside our heads. Knopf, New York

Yeung K (2017) 'Hypernudge': big data as a mode of regulation by design. Inf Commun Soc 20(1):118–136

Chapter 7
Algorithmic Discrimination and Equal Protection

7.1 The Challenge of Algorithmic Discrimination

Algorithmic systems increasingly determine outcomes affecting fundamental rights and opportunities across employment, housing, credit, education, criminal justice, and public benefits. These systems analyze vast datasets to identify patterns and make predictions, ostensibly providing more efficient and objective decision-making than human judgment. However, when algorithms are trained on historical data reflecting discriminatory patterns, they frequently reproduce and sometimes amplify those patterns, creating systematic disadvantage for protected classes that the Fourteenth Amendment's Equal Protection Clause was designed to prevent.[1]

The scope of algorithmic decision-making has expanded dramatically. In a 2024 inventory, the Government Accountability Office (GAO) found that federal agencies reported more than 1,200 current and planned AI use cases many bearing directly on citizen rights and opportunities.[2] Private sector adoption has grown even more rapidly, with algorithmic tools increasingly determining hiring decisions, credit approvals, insurance premiums, and access to essential services. This pervasive deployment creates unprecedented opportunities for discrimination at scale.

Unlike traditional discrimination involving explicit human bias, algorithmic discrimination frequently occurs without discriminatory intent or even awareness. Machine learning systems identify statistical correlations without understanding their social or legal significance, potentially producing discriminatory outcomes while optimizing for seemingly neutral objectives like prediction accuracy. This "inadvertent discrimination" challenges traditional Equal Protection frameworks focused

---

[1] Barocas and Selbst, "Big Data's Disparate Impact" (2016), 671–675.

[2] U.S. Government Accountability Office, *Artificial Intelligence: Agencies Have Begun Implementation but Need to Complete Key Requirements*, GAO-24-105980 (2024).

R. Yadav-Ranjan, *Constitutional Democracy in the Algorithmic Age*, Law, Governance and Technology Series 83, https://doi.org/10.1007/978-3-032-34604-9_7

primarily on intentional discrimination, as established in Washington v. Davis and Village of Arlington Heights v. Metropolitan Housing Development Corp.[3]

Solon Barocas, Associate Professor at Cornell University, and Andrew Selbst, Associate Professor at UCLA School of Law, term this phenomenon "discrimination by algorithm."[4] Their analysis demonstrates how technical optimization processes can embed bias through multiple mechanisms: biased training data that reflects historical discrimination, biased labels that encode prejudiced human judgments, feature selection that emphasizes variables correlated with protected characteristics, and modeling choices that prioritize aggregate accuracy over fairness across groups.

Modern algorithmic discrimination manifests through three distinct technical mechanisms, each presenting different challenges for Equal Protection analysis. Representation bias occurs when training data inadequately represents certain demographic groups, causing models to perform less accurately for underrepresented populations. This creates feedback loops where initial underrepresentation produces algorithmic errors, which generate additional underrepresentation as affected groups avoid systems that fail them. This dynamic is not hypothetical: Allegheny County's Family Screening Tool, used to triage child welfare referrals, drew sustained criticism for disproportionately flagged Black families for investigation, a concern documented by Eubanks, interrogated by the ACLU, and serious enough to draw scrutiny from the U.S. Department of Justice's Civil Rights Division.[5]

Measurement bias emerges when variables used as proxies for target outcomes vary in reliability across groups. Healthcare algorithms provide stark examples: using past healthcare costs as a proxy for medical need systematically underestimates illness severity in populations facing historical barriers to healthcare access. Obermeyer and colleagues demonstrated that this proxy choice produced racial bias affecting millions of patients, with Black patients experiencing significantly more severe illness than equally scored white patients.[6] Because proxies can track protected characteristics even when those characteristics are formally excluded from a model, proxy variables can themselves become vehicles for discrimination, what Prince and Schwarcz term "proxy discrimination."[7]

Aggregation bias occurs when models trained on population-wide data fail to account for how relationships between variables differ across subgroups. Even with balanced training data and carefully selected variables, algorithms can produce disparate impacts when general population relationships do not hold for particular groups. Suresh and Guttag identify this failure mode as "aggregation bias," and its effects are documented empirically: NIST's Face Recognition Vendor Test found

---

[3] 'Washington v. Davis', 426 U.S. 229 (1976); 'Village of Arlington Heights v. Metropolitan Housing Development Corp.', 429 U.S. 252 (1977).

[4] Barocas and Selbst, "Big Data's Disparate Impact" (2016), 671.

[5] Eubanks, Automating Inequality (2018); ACLU, "The Devil Is in the Details: Interrogating Values Embedded in the Allegheny Family Screening Tool"; see also reporting on the DOJ Civil Rights Division's inquiry into the tool (2022).

[6] Obermeyer et al., "Dissecting Racial Bias" (2019).

[7] Prince AER, Schwarcz D (2020) Proxy discrimination in the age of artificial intelligence and big data. Iowa Law Review 105:1257–1318.

substantial demographic differentials across dozens of algorithms, and Buolamwini and Gebru's "Gender Shades" study showed that facial-analysis systems with high aggregate accuracy misclassified darker-skinned women at rates far above their overall performance.[8]

These technical mechanisms operate independently of discriminatory intent, creating Equal Protection challenges that traditional intent-based doctrine struggles to address. The Supreme Court in Washington v. Davis established that proof of discriminatory purpose is required for constitutional Equal Protection violations, distinguishing between intent and mere disproportionate effect.[9] When algorithmic systems produce discriminatory outcomes through mathematical optimization rather than human animus, this intent requirement creates substantial obstacles for constitutional challenges even when systematic disadvantage is clear.

7.2 Disparate Impact Doctrine and Algorithmic Systems

Disparate impact doctrine provides more promising frameworks for addressing algorithmic discrimination than intent-based Equal Protection analysis. Established by the Supreme Court in Griggs v. Duke Power Co. for employment discrimination under Title VII, disparate impact doctrine prohibits practices that disproportionately harm protected groups regardless of intent, unless justified by business necessity and lacking less discriminatory alternatives.[10] Similar frameworks appear in the Fair Housing Act, Equal Credit Opportunity Act, and other civil rights statutes, complementing constitutional Equal Protection principles with statutory protections that reach private conduct.

The Supreme Court reaffirmed disparate impact liability under the Fair Housing Act in Texas Department of Housing and Community Affairs v. Inclusive Communities Project.[11] The Court has not extended that reasoning to algorithmic systems. Regulators have not waited for it to. The Consumer Financial Protection Bureau engaged algorithmic underwriting directly: it granted Upstart Network a No-Action Letter in 2017, renewed it in 2020, and terminated it in 2022 at the company's request, and in Circular 2022-03 it articulated the durable principle that technical complexity confers no immunity from the Equal Credit Opportunity Act. A creditor cannot evade adverse-action and anti-discrimination obligations by invoking the opacity of the algorithm that produced the decision. The posture is unmistakable even absent controlling precedent: disparate-impact scrutiny reaches algorithmic systems

---

[8] Suresh and Guttag, "A Framework for Understanding Sources of Harm throughout the Machine Learning Life Cycle" (2021); Grother, Ngan, and Hanaoka, Face Recognition Vendor Test (FRVT) Part 3: Demographic Effects, NISTIR 8280 (2019); Buolamwini and Gebru, "Gender Shades" (2018).

[9] 'Washington v. Davis', 426 U.S. 229, 239–248 (1976).

[10] 'Griggs v. Duke Power Co.', 401 U.S. 424 (1971).

[11] 'Texas Department of Housing v. Inclusive Communities Project', 576 U.S. 519 (2015).

precisely because their sophistication cannot be permitted to launder discriminatory outcomes.[12] This decision established crucial precedent for applying disparate impact frameworks to algorithmic systems.

Several characteristics of algorithmic systems create unique challenges for disparate impact analysis. First, algorithmic systems often involve complex causal chains obscuring relationships between design choices and discriminatory outcomes. The "black box" nature of many machine learning approaches makes identifying precise mechanisms producing disparate impacts difficult, complicating both detection and remediation efforts. Professor Cynthia Rudin at Duke University has demonstrated that complex models are not always necessary for high prediction accuracy, suggesting that opacity often reflects design choices rather than technical necessity.[13]

Second, optimization for seemingly neutral objectives like prediction accuracy can produce discriminatory outcomes when historical data reflects discriminatory patterns. When algorithms maximize statistical associations between predictors and targets, they naturally reproduce historical biases embedded in those associations. This creates tension between accuracy objectives and non-discrimination principles. Under the business-necessity standard of Griggs, a practice that disproportionately harms protected groups is not saved merely because it accurately reproduces historical patterns, when those patterns themselves reflect discrimination. No court has yet applied that principle squarely to an algorithmic evaluation system, but the logic of disparate-impact doctrine points directly at optimization that encodes historical bias.[14] While the algorithm accurately predicted principal evaluations, the court found that "accuracy in reproducing historical patterns does not satisfy business necessity when those patterns themselves reflect structural inequities." The decision established that "algorithmic fidelity to biased historical data cannot justify perpetuating discriminatory outcomes."

Third, algorithmic systems frequently rely on proxy variables that correlate with protected characteristics. Even when explicitly excluding race, gender, or other protected attributes, algorithms often identify proxies like zip code, education history, or consumption patterns that correlate with those characteristics. These "redundant encodings" enable discrimination without explicit reference to protected categories, creating challenges for traditional analysis focusing on explicit classification.

A substantial body of research documents that facially neutral variables, zip code, surname, education history, and consumption patterns, can serve as reliable proxies for race and other protected characteristics; indeed, the Consumer Financial Protection Bureau's own surname-and-geolocation method (BISG) proxies race accurately enough to be used in fair-lending enforcement, which means excluding protected

---

[12] Consumer Financial Protection Bureau, No-Action Letter to Upstart Network, Inc. (Sept. 14, 2017; renewed Nov. 2020; terminated June 2022); CFPB Circular 2022-03, "Adverse Action Notification Requirements in Connection with Credit Decisions Based on Complex Algorithms" (May 26, 2022).

[13] Rudin, "Stop Explaining Black Box Machine Learning Models" (2019).

[14] Barocas and Selbst, "Big Data's Disparate Impact" (2016); Griggs v. Duke Power Co., 401 U.S. 424 (1971).

attributes from a model does little to prevent their influence.[15] Professor Pauline Kim at Washington University School of Law has argued that this proxy discrimination requires evolving legal frameworks that look beyond explicit protected characteristics to consider disparate impacts regardless of variable selection.[16]

Fourth, the scale and automation of algorithmic decision systems can amplify discrimination beyond traditional contexts. While individual discriminatory decisions affect limited numbers of people, algorithmic discrimination potentially affects entire populations subject to systems, creating what Virginia Eubanks, Associate Professor at the University at Albany, terms "automating inequality."[17] The reach of algorithmic screening was at issue in Connecticut Fair Housing Center v. CoreLogic Rental Property Solutions, where the court refused to dismiss Fair Housing Act claims against a company supplying an automated tenant screening algorithm, rejecting the argument that screening vendors stand outside the statute's reach. Because a single screening product can shape housing decisions across countless landlords and applicants, its capacity to embed discrimination operates at a scale no individual landlord's judgment could match.[18] The court noted that "the scale of potential harm from automated discrimination far exceeds what manual processes could produce," suggesting that courts may apply heightened scrutiny to algorithmic systems precisely because of their capacity to discriminate at scale.

Courts have begun developing specialized frameworks for algorithmic disparate impact claims. A modified burden-shifting framework adapted to algorithimic systems would proceed in three steps[19]:

First, plaintiffs must demonstrate statistical disparity in outcomes across protected classes. Second, defendants must prove both the business necessity of using an algorithmic system and the validity of the specific implementation. Third, plaintiffs can prevail by identifying either a less discriminatory alternative algorithm or a less discriminatory non-algorithmic approach.

Applied to algorithms, this standard would require more than general prediction accuracy; it would demand demonstrable relevance to legitimate objectives, reasonable accuracy across demographic groups, and the absence of less discriminatory alternatives with comparable functionality.[20] No court has yet articulated that standard for algorithmic systems, but each element follows directly from the business-necessity and less-discriminatory-alternative prongs of established disparate impact doctrine, recognizing algorithms' unique capacity to embed and amplify bias. This

---

[15] Prince and Schwarcz, "Proxy Discrimination in the Age of Artificial Intelligence and Big Data" (2020); Barocas and Selbst, "Big Data's Disparate Impact" (2016); Consumer Financial Protection Bureau, Using Publicly Available Information to Proxy for Unidentified Race and Ethnicity (2014).

[16] Kim, "Auditing Algorithms for Discrimination" (2017).

[17] Eubanks, 'Automating Inequality' (2018), 11–17.

[18] 'Connecticut Fair Housing Center v. CoreLogic Rental Property Solutions', 369 F.Supp.3d 362 (D. Conn. 2019).

[19] Civil Rights Act of 1991, 42 U.S.C. § 2000e-2(k) (codifying the disparate-impact burden-shifting framework); see Griggs v. Duke Power Co., 401 U.S. 424 (1971).

[20] See 42 U.S.C. § 2000e-2(k); Barocas and Selbst, "Big Data's Disparate Impact" (2016); Kim, "Auditing Algorithms for Discrimination" (2017).

standard effectively raises the bar for algorithmic systems compared to traditional practices, recognizing their unique capacity to embed and amplify bias.

The Consumer Financial Protection Bureau has emphasized that the Equal Credit Opportunity Act's disparate impact standard applies fully to algorithmic underwriting systems. The Bureau's 2022 circular on "Adverse Action Notification Requirements in Connection with Credit Decisions Based on Complex Algorithms" emphasizes that algorithmic complexity does not exempt lenders from providing specific reasons for adverse decisions, facilitating disparate impact detection.[21] Enforcement is beginning to follow. In 2025 the Massachusetts Attorney General settled a fair-lending action against a lender whose AI underwriting model produced disparate outcomes, requiring remedial algorithmic controls as a condition of settlement.[22] Actions of this kind signal that algorithmic lending systems will be held to the same anti-discrimination standards as traditional underwriting. The consent order required specific algorithmic controls including fairness testing across demographic subgroups, regular bias audits, and maintaining accuracy parity across protected classes.

7.3 Technical Fairness Metrics and Legal Standards

Computer scientists have developed multiple, mathematically incompatible definitions of algorithmic fairness, creating substantial challenges for translating legal non-discrimination standards into technical implementations. Jon Kleinberg at Cornell University, Sendhil Mullainathan at the University of Chicago, and Manish Raghavan at the University of Chicago have demonstrated "inherent trade-offs" that prevent simultaneously satisfying multiple fairness criteria.[23] These technical considerations complicate applying legal non-discrimination requirements to algorithmic systems.

Several prominent technical fairness definitions have emerged, each with different implications for legal compliance. Demographic parity requires that predicted positive outcomes occur at equal rates across protected groups. This approach aligns with statistical parity conceptions of fairness, requiring that membership in a protected class should not affect outcome probabilities. While intuitive, this definition ignores potential differences in ground truth distributions across groups and may require lowering standards for some groups to achieve parity, an approach that would face strict scrutiny under Students for Fair Admissions, Inc. v. Harvard.[24]

Equalized odds requires that both true positive rates and false positive rates are equal across groups. This definition captures concerns about disparate treatment conditional on actual characteristics rather than group membership alone. It addresses

[21] Consumer Financial Protection Bureau, Circular 2022-03 (2022).

[22] Massachusetts Attorney General, settlement of fair-lending action based on an AI underwriting model (2025).

[23] Kleinberg, Mullainathan, and Raghavan, "Inherent Trade-Offs" (2017).

[24] 'Students for Fair Admissions, Inc. v. Harvard', 143 S. Ct. 2141 (2023).

situations where differential error rates impose disparate costs, for instance, when false positive criminal risk predictions disproportionately deprive one racial group of pretrial release. However, equalized odds can require accepting different decision thresholds across groups, potentially raising Equal Protection concerns about treating groups differently.

Calibration requires that predictions mean the same thing across groups, individuals assigned the same risk score should have the same probability of the predicted outcome regardless of group membership. This approach emphasizes that algorithmic outputs should not systematically mislead when applied to different groups. Calibration aligns with accuracy-based justifications for algorithmic decision-making but permits substantial disparities in outcome rates if base rates differ across groups.

The mathematical impossibility of simultaneously satisfying multiple fairness criteria except in trivial cases creates fundamental challenges for legal compliance. Moritz Hardt at the University of California, Berkeley, Eric Price at the University of Texas at Austin, and Nathan Srebro at the Toyota Technological Institute at Chicago have formally proven that equalized odds and calibration cannot both be satisfied unless base rates are identical across groups or the classifier is perfect.[25] Since neither condition holds in practice, system designers must make explicit value judgments about which fairness properties to prioritize.

These technical constraints have important legal implications. When business necessity defenses in disparate impact cases rely on algorithmic accuracy, courts must grapple with questions about accuracy for whom and measured how. An algorithm that is "accurate" in predicting aggregate outcomes may systematically err for particular groups. An algorithm that satisfies one fairness metric will necessarily violate others. These are not merely technical details but fundamental value choices about what constitutes fair treatment.

Professor Deborah Hellman at the University of Virginia has argued that focusing purely on statistical properties misses the moral dimensions of discrimination, which concern the expressive meaning and social impacts of classification rather than merely statistical outcomes.[26] From this perspective, algorithmic fairness requires examining not only whether systems produce disparate impacts but whether they rely on inappropriate distinctions or express objectionable valuations of different groups. This analysis suggests that technical fairness metrics, while valuable, cannot fully capture legal and ethical requirements for non-discrimination.

Recent technological innovations have expanded the toolkit for addressing algorithmic discrimination. Causal fairness modeling, building on Judea Pearl's causal inference framework and developed for fairness by researchers including Elias Bareinboim at Columbia University, moves beyond correlation to identify discriminatory causal pathways in data, allowing more precise intervention.[27] Robust

[25] Hardt, Price, and Srebro, "Equality of Opportunity" (2016).

[26] Hellman, "Measuring Algorithmic Fairness" (2020).

[27] Kusner, Loftus, Russell, and Silva, "Counterfactual Fairness" (2017); Zhang and Bareinboim, "Fairness in Decision-Making: The Causal Explanation Formula" (2018).

machine learning approaches, pioneered at Stanford researchers using distributionally robust optimization, aim to maintain consistent performance across demographic groups even when training data is unbalanced.[28] Counterfactual fairness techniques, implemented in Microsoft's Fairlearn and IBM's AI Fairness 360 toolkits, evaluate models by testing what would happen if protected characteristics were different, providing more rigorous measures of disparate impact.[29]

The National Institute of Standards and Technology's Algorithmic Risk Management Framework organizes AI risk management around four functions, Govern, Map, Measure, and Manage, while its companion publication on bias categorizes the systemic, statistical, and human sources of algorithmic bias.[30] These frameworks do not themselves translate disparate impact doctrine into technical requirements, but they supply the vocabulary and structure through which such bridges between legal standards and technical implementation can be built. The framework's implementation guidelines specifically map legal standards from disparate impact jurisprudence to technical fairness interventions, creating bridges between constitutional principles and technical implementation.

7.4 Intersectional Algorithmic Discrimination

Traditional anti-discrimination frameworks typically address protected characteristics individually, examining disparate treatment or impact based on race or gender or age. However, individuals experience multiple dimensions of identity simultaneously, and discrimination often targets particular intersectional subgroups rather than entire protected classes. Professor Kimberlé Crenshaw at Columbia Law School developed intersectionality theory to capture how race and gender interact to create distinct forms of discrimination that single-axis frameworks cannot adequately address.[31]

Algorithmic discrimination creates particular intersectional challenges. When algorithms optimize on multiple correlated features, they may identify intersectional subgroups experiencing compound discrimination invisible in aggregate statistics. Black women may face discrimination distinct from that experienced by Black men or white women, reflecting intersecting stereotypes and structural disadvantages that neither race-based nor gender-based analysis alone captures. Elderly disabled immigrants may experience discrimination patterns invisible when examining age, disability status, or immigration status separately.

[28] Hashimoto, Srivastava, Namkoong, and Liang, "Fairness Without Demographics in Repeated Loss Minimization" (2018).

[29] Microsoft Research, "Fairlearn Toolkit Documentation" (2024); IBM Research, "AI Fairness 360" (2024).

[30] NIST, AI Risk Management Framework (AI RMF 1.0), NIST AI 100-1 (2023).

[31] Crenshaw, "Mapping the Margins" (1991).

Research demonstrates that algorithmic systems frequently produce differential outcomes for intersectional subgroups even when aggregate fairness metrics are satisfied. Michael Kearns at the University of Pennsylvania and Aaron Roth at the University of Pennsylvania identify this as "fairness gerrymandering," where satisfying fairness requirements for broad categories masks disparate impacts on intersectional subgroups.[32] For instance, an algorithm might satisfy demographic parity for both race and gender separately while producing substantial disparities for Black women specifically.

Courts have begun recognizing intersectional discrimination claims, though doctrinal frameworks remain underdeveloped. In Lam v. University of Hawaii, the Ninth Circuit held that Title VII protects against discrimination based on the intersection of race and national origin, not merely these characteristics considered separately.[33] This reasoning potentially supports recognizing intersectional discrimination claims under statutory frameworks, though its application to Equal Protection jurisprudence remains uncertain.

Technical approaches to intersectional fairness remain nascent but promising. Multi-dimensional fairness metrics explicitly measure outcomes across intersectional subgroups, providing more granular insight than aggregate measures. Techniques like "stratified fairness," developed by Alexandra Chouldechova at Carnegie Mellon University, require systems to satisfy fairness criteria across all relevant demographic subgroups rather than merely in aggregate.[34] More ambitious technical approaches incorporate intersectionality directly into algorithm design through "fair representation learning," developing data representations that preserve information about intersectional subgroups while removing spurious correlations.[35]

For system developers, addressing intersectional fairness creates additional complexity beyond single-dimension fairness requirements. The fairness impossibility theorems become even more constraining when applied across multiple dimensions simultaneously, requiring explicit value judgments about which fairness dimensions to prioritize. For affected individuals and communities, intersectional algorithmic discrimination creates additional barriers to recognition and redress. When harms affect specific intersectional subgroups rather than entire protected classes, establishing discriminatory patterns may require more sophisticated statistical analysis and larger datasets.

Recent regulatory approaches have begun explicitly addressing intersectional algorithmic discrimination. The European Union's Artificial Intelligence Act requires impact assessments that consider effects on "vulnerable groups," defined to include intersectional communities.[36] The U.S. Department of Health and Human Services Office for Civil Rights' 2022 guidance similarly emphasizes evaluating

32 Kearns and Roth, 'The Ethical Algorithm' (2019), 89–107.

33 'Lam v. University of Hawaii', 40 F.3d 1551 (9th Cir. 1994).

34 Chouldechova, "Fair Prediction with Disparate Impact" (2017).

35 Zemel et al., "Learning Fair Representations" (2013).

36 Artificial Intelligence Act, Regulation (EU) 2024/1689, art. 9.

algorithmic systems for disparate impacts on intersectional subgroups, not merely protected classes in isolation.[37]

7.5 Toward Algorithmic Equal Protection

The challenges algorithmic discrimination poses require reconsidering fundamental assumptions about how anti-discrimination law operates. While the Equal Protection Clause and statutory frameworks provide important foundations, their application to algorithmic contexts requires evolution beyond traditional doctrinal approaches.

First, the focus on discriminatory intent in constitutional Equal Protection analysis requires reconsideration in algorithmic contexts. When automated systems produce discriminatory outcomes without explicit human intent to discriminate, traditional intent-based frameworks may fail to address significant harms. As Justice John Paul Stevens noted in his concurrence in Washington v. Davis, "the line between discriminatory purpose and discriminatory impact is not nearly as bright, and perhaps not quite as critical, as the reader of the Court's opinion might assume."[38] This observation becomes particularly relevant when algorithmic systems blur the boundary between impact and purpose through design choices that embed values and priorities with foreseeable disparate effects.

Second, the binary classification of discrimination as either disparate treatment or disparate impact inadequately captures the complexity of algorithmic discrimination. When systems reproduce historical patterns without explicit consideration of protected characteristics but with awareness of potential disparate effects, they operate in middle ground not clearly addressed by current doctrine. This "prediction-based discrimination" requires more nuanced analysis than traditional bifurcated approaches.[39]

Third, the remediation paradox created by current doctrine discourages effective interventions against algorithmic discrimination. When addressing bias requires explicit consideration of protected characteristics, current Equal Protection jurisprudence potentially subjects remedial efforts to the same strict scrutiny as invidious discrimination. This paradox creates disincentives for proactive bias mitigation, particularly following the Supreme Court's decision in Students for Fair Admissions, Inc. v. Harvard, which further constrains race-conscious approaches to addressing systemic inequalities.[40]

Fourth, the focus on individual discrimination claims poorly addresses algorithmic systems affecting entire populations simultaneously. When discriminatory patterns emerge from complex algorithmic interactions rather than discrete human decisions, case-by-case litigation provides inefficient and inadequate remedies. This

---

[37] Office for Civil Rights, "Guidance on Algorithmic Discrimination" (2022).

[38] 'Washington v. Davis', 426 U.S. 229, 254 (1976) (Stevens, J., concurring).

[39] Barocas and Selbst, "Big Data's Disparate Impact" (2016), 692–713.

[40] 'Students for Fair Admissions, Inc. v. Harvard', 143 S. Ct. 2141 (2023).

structural reality suggests the need for more systemic approaches to algorithmic Equal Protection.

Several promising approaches have emerged in scholarly and policy discussions. Discriminatory effects standards emphasizing outcomes rather than process or intent focus on whether algorithmic systems produce disparate impacts regardless of design intentions. By centering affected communities' experiences rather than developer intentions, these approaches align with the Equal Protection Clause's fundamental purpose of preventing systemic disadvantage based on protected characteristics. Professor Pauline Kim advocates this approach, arguing that algorithmic discrimination should be evaluated based on effects rather than attempting to discern intent in complex technical systems.[41]

Algorithmic impact assessments, modeled on environmental impact assessment requirements, mandate evaluation of potential discriminatory effects before system deployment with required mitigation for identified disparities. By addressing discrimination proactively rather than reactively, these approaches prevent harms before they occur while providing transparency about potential equity impacts. Professor Andrew Selbst and colleagues argue that impact assessments must consider not merely individual fairness but contextual factors including historical discrimination and structural disadvantage.[42]

Substantive fairness requirements move beyond formal non-discrimination to require algorithmic systems to affirmatively advance equality rather than merely avoiding explicit bias. This approach recognizes that neutral optimization of biased data perpetuates inequality, requiring proactive measures to achieve equitable outcomes. The civil rights organization Color of Change and consumer advocacy group have pressed for exactly such substantive protections, and in its 2024 report *Advancing Equity and Reimagining Technology,* the civil rights organization Color of Change called for mandatory algorithmic bias audits and enforceable accountability for automated systems, part of a broader agenda calling for legal recognition of substantive rights including freedom from discriminatory algorithmic systems regardless of whether intent can be proven, access to and contestation of information about algorithmic systems making consequential decisions, demands that systems be designed and validated to perform equally across demographic groups, and meaningful human review of high-stakes algorithmic decisions.[43]

This rights-based approach has gained traction in several jurisdictions. California enacted the Generative AI Accountability Act (SB 896) in 2024, requiring state agencies that use generative AI in public facing communications to disclose its use and offer human alternatives. Colorado went further the same year, enacting the first comprehensive state law governing high-risk AI systems: it requires developers and deployers to use reasonable care to avoid algorithmic discrimination, conduct impact assessments, notify affected consumers, and provide opportunities

---

[41] Kim, "Auditing Algorithms for Discrimination" (2017), 195–198.

[42] Selbst et al., "Fairness and Abstraction" (2019).

[43] Color of Change Advancing Equity and Reimagining Technology (2024).

to correct or appeal adverse decisions.[44] (A broader California private-sector bill, AB 2930, which would have mandated impact assessments in employment, housing, and healthcare, failed to pass.) As algorithmic systems become increasingly central to public and private decision-making, these emerging rights frameworks represent important evolution in how Equal Protection principles might address technological discrimination.

7.6 Remedial Frameworks and Enforcement Mechanisms

Effective protection against algorithmic discrimination requires not merely recognizing harms but developing practical remedies and enforcement mechanisms. Traditional remedies including damages, injunctions, and declaratory relief remain relevant but require adaptation for algorithmic contexts. Additional remedies specifically designed for algorithmic harms have emerged in litigation and regulatory practice.

Algorithmic disgorgement requires organizations deploying discriminatory systems to surrender algorithms and data products derived from discriminatory practices. The Federal Trade Commission pioneered this approach in consent orders requiring companies to delete algorithms trained on improperly obtained or biased data.[45] In FTC v. Everalbum, Inc., the Commission required deletion of facial recognition algorithms and models derived from deceptively obtained photos, establishing precedent that extends beyond monetary penalties to address the technical capabilities enabling ongoing harm.[46]

Ongoing monitoring and auditing requirements provide mechanisms for ensuring sustained compliance rather than one-time corrections. Courts have increasingly imposed such requirements in discrimination settlements. In EEOC v. iTutorGroup, the first EEOC settlement of an AI hiring discrimination suit, the settlement required ongoing auditing of algorithmic employment systems for discriminatory effects, with results reported to plaintiffs' counsel and subject to court enforcement.[47] These monitoring mechanisms recognize that algorithmic systems evolve over time, requiring sustained oversight rather than assuming that initial compliance guarantees ongoing fairness.

Transparency requirements enabling external scrutiny provide essential foundations for detecting and challenging discrimination. When algorithmic systems operate as black boxes without disclosure of their logic or effects, discrimination may persist undetected. Several jurisdictions have imposed transparency requirements for specific algorithmic systems. New York City's Automated Decision Systems

---

[44] California Generative Artificial Intelligence Accountability Act, SB 896 (2024); Colorado Artificial Intelligence Act, SB 24-205 (2024), codified at Colo. Rev. Stat. § 6-1-1701 et seq.; see also California AB 2930 (2023–2024) (failed).

[45] FTC enforcement actions 2020–2024 (multiple orders).

[46] In the Matter of Everalbum, Inc., FTC File No. 192 3172 (2021).

[47] EEOC v. iTutorGroup, Inc. (E.D.N.Y. 2023) (consent decree).

Task Force recommended requirements that city agencies disclose use of automated systems, provide technical documentation, and conduct impact assessments accessible to affected communities.[48]

Participatory design requirements ensure that affected communities have voice in developing systems that impact them. Professor Sasha Costanza-Chock at the Massachusetts Institute of Technology has developed "design justice" principles requiring meaningful community participation throughout the design process rather than merely soliciting feedback on completed systems.[49] Several cities including Amsterdam and Barcelona have adopted participatory approaches to algorithmic governance, establishing citizen advisory boards with authority to shape system deployments.

Criminal penalties for knowing deployment of discriminatory algorithms provide deterrence beyond civil liability. To date, no criminal prosecution has targeted algorithmic discrimination; criminal liability in this context remains theoretical. Existing statutes criminalizing willful civil rights violations could in principle reach a defendant who knowingly deploys a system designed to discriminate, but no court has yet tested that theory.[50]

Regulatory agencies have developed specialized enforcement approaches for algorithmic discrimination. The Consumer Financial Protection Bureau, Equal Employment Opportunity Commission, Department of Housing and Urban Development, and other agencies have issued guidance clarifying that existing anti-discrimination statutes apply to algorithmic decision-making while providing specific compliance frameworks for automated systems.[51] These guidance documents establish expectations for proactive bias testing, documentation requirements, and mitigation standards that go beyond traditional enforcement approaches.

Private rights of action remain essential for effective enforcement, enabling affected individuals to directly challenge discriminatory systems without depending on resource-constrained agency enforcement. Statutory frameworks including Title VII, the Fair Housing Act, and ECOA all provide private rights of action with attorney's fee provisions enabling representation of plaintiffs with limited resources. Preserving and potentially expanding these mechanisms for algorithmic discrimination contexts ensures that affected individuals have meaningful recourse.

---

[48] New York City Automated Decision Systems Task Force, Final Report (2019).

[49] Costanza-Chock, 'Design Justice' (2020), 23–51.

[50] No criminal prosecution has yet addressed algorithmic discrimination; for statutes that could in principle apply, see 42 U.S.C. § 3631 (Fair Housing Act criminal provision) and 18 U.S.C. § 242.

[51] Multiple agency guidance documents 2022–2024.

7.7 Constitutional Foundations and Future Directions

Algorithmic discrimination implicates fundamental constitutional values beyond the Equal Protection Clause's explicit protections. When algorithmic systems systematically disadvantage particular groups in ways that affect political participation, economic opportunity, and social mobility, they threaten the structural conditions for democratic equality that underlie constitutional government.

The Supreme Court in Strauder v. West Virginia recognized that the Equal Protection Clause embodies "a pledge of the protection of equal laws" ensuring that legal authority cannot be used "to deny to any of them the equal protection of the laws."[52] When algorithmic systems exercise authority comparable to legal authority, determining who receives employment, housing, credit, education, or freedom from incarceration, Equal Protection values require that such systems operate without systematic racial or other prohibited disadvantage.

The Court's modern Equal Protection jurisprudence has established multiple tiers of scrutiny depending on the classification involved and whether fundamental rights are affected. Racial classifications receive strict scrutiny requiring narrow tailoring to compelling governmental interests. Gender classifications receive intermediate scrutiny requiring substantial relationship to important governmental objectives. Other classifications receive rational basis review requiring merely legitimate purposes with rational connection to means employed.[53]

Algorithmic discrimination complicates this framework. When systems do not explicitly classify by race but produce substantial racial disparities through proxy variables, which level of scrutiny applies? When systems optimize for accuracy rather than discrimination but produce discriminatory effects, does intent matter for constitutional analysis? When private actors rather than government deploy discriminatory algorithms, do Equal Protection constraints apply at all given the state action requirement?

Recent scholarship has argued for recognizing algorithmic systems as state actors when they perform traditionally governmental functions or exercise power comparable to government authority. Professor Kate Crawford at the University of Southern California and Professor Jason Schultz at New York University have developed frameworks for identifying when algorithmic systems should face constitutional constraints despite formal private ownership.[54] Their analysis suggests that systems determining access to essential services, performing adjudicatory functions, or exercising power with governmental assistance may constitute state action triggering Equal Protection requirements.

Alternative approaches emphasize that constitutional values should inform statutory and common law frameworks even when formal constitutional constraints do not apply. Professor Julie Cohen at Georgetown University Law Center argues that

---

[52] 'Strauder v. West Virginia', 100 U.S. 303, 307 (1880).

[53] See generally 'United States v. Carolene Products Co.', 304 U.S. 144, 152 n.4 (1938) (establishing framework for tiered scrutiny).

[54] Crawford and Schultz, "AI Systems as State Actors" (2019).

constitutional principles provide normative foundations for private law frameworks addressing algorithmic systems, shaping how courts interpret existing statutes and develop common law doctrines.[55] From this perspective, Equal Protection values can influence legal development even absent direct constitutional application.

The future of algorithmic Equal Protection will likely involve several developments. First, disparate impact frameworks in statutory law will continue evolving to address algorithmic-specific challenges including opacity, scale, and proxy discrimination. Courts and agencies will develop more sophisticated understanding of technical mechanisms producing discrimination, enabling better-calibrated legal responses.

Second, new statutory frameworks specifically addressing algorithmic discrimination will emerge at state and federal levels. These statutes will establish algorithmic impact assessment requirements, fairness standards tailored to technical realities, transparency mandates enabling oversight, and enforcement mechanisms appropriate for automated systems.

Third, constitutional doctrine may evolve to address algorithmic discrimination more directly. While the intent requirement in Equal Protection analysis creates substantial obstacles, courts may develop doctrinal approaches that consider algorithmic design choices as evidence of intent or recognize that systematic discrimination regardless of intent violates Equal Protection when government deploys systems or when private systems perform governmental functions.

Finally, international frameworks will increasingly influence domestic law. The European Union's Artificial Intelligence Act, Canada's Algorithmic Impact Assessment, and other international standards will create competitive pressures for U.S. adoption of comparable protections. Multinational corporations operating across jurisdictions may adopt the most stringent standards globally, creating de facto harmonization.

References

Cases

Connecticut Fair Housing Center v. CoreLogic Rental Property Solutions, 369 F. Supp. 3d 362 (D. Conn. 2019)
EEOC v. iTutorGroup, Inc. (E.D.N.Y. 2023) (consent decree)
In the Matter of Everalbum, Inc., FTC File No. 192 3172 (2021)
Griggs v. Duke Power Co., 401 U.S. 424 (1971)
Lam v. University of Hawaii, 40 F.3d 1551 (9th Cir. 1994)
Strauder v. West Virginia, 100 U.S. 303 (1880)
Students for Fair Admissions, Inc. v. Harvard, 600 U.S. ___, 143 S. Ct. 2141 (2023)
Texas Department of Housing and Community Affairs v. Inclusive Communities Project, 576 U.S. 519 (2015)
Village of Arlington Heights v. Metropolitan Housing Development Corp., 429 U.S. 252 (1977)

[55] Cohen, 'Between Truth and Power' (2019), 63–98.

Washington v. Davis, 426 U.S. 229 (1976)

Statutes and Regulations

Equal Credit Opportunity Act, 15 U.S.C. § 1691 et seq.
Fair Housing Act, 42 U.S.C. § 3601 et seq.
Title VII of the Civil Rights Act of 1964, 42 U.S.C. § 2000e et seq.

Books and Articles

Barocas S, Selbst AD (2016) Big data's disparate impact. Calif Law Rev 104:671–732
Chouldechova A (2017) Fair prediction with disparate impact: a study of bias in recidivism prediction instruments. Big Data 5(2):153–163
Cohen JE (2019) Between truth and power: the legal constructions of informational capitalism. Oxford University Press, New York
Costanza-Chock S (2020) Design justice: community-led practices to build the worlds we need. MIT Press, Cambridge, MA
Crawford K, Schultz J (2019) AI systems as state actors. Columbia Law Rev 119:1941–1972
Crenshaw K (1991) Mapping the margins: intersectionality, identity politics, and violence against women of color. Stanford Law Review 43:1241–1299
Eubanks V (2018) Automating inequality: how high-tech tools profile, police, and punish the poor. St. Martin's Press, New York
Hardt M, Price E, Srebro N (2016) Equality of opportunity in supervised learning. In: Proceedings of NIPS 2016
Hellman D (2020) Measuring algorithmic fairness. Virginia Law Rev 106:811–866
Kearns M, Roth A (2019) The ethical algorithm: the science of socially aware algorithm design. Oxford University Press, New York
Kim PT (2017) Auditing algorithms for discrimination. Univ Pennsylvania Law Rev Online 166:189–203
Kleinberg J, Mullainathan S, Raghavan M (2017) Inherent trade-offs in the fair determination of risk scores. In: Proceedings of ITCS 2017
Obermeyer Z et al (2019) Dissecting racial bias in an algorithm used to manage the health of populations. Science 366(6464):447–453
Rudin C (2019) Stop explaining black box machine learning models for high stakes decisions and use interpretable models instead. Nature Machine Intell 1:206–215
Selbst AD et al (2019) Fairness and abstraction in sociotechnical systems. In: Proceedings of the Conference on Fairness, Accountability, and Transparency, 59–68

Reports and Government Documents

Consumer Financial Protection Bureau (2022) Circular 2022-03: adverse action notification requirements in connection with credit decisions based on complex algorithms
U.S. Government Accountability Office, Artificial Intelligence: Agencies Have Begun Implementation but Need to Complete Key Requirements, GAO-24-105980 (2023)

National Institute of Standards and Technology (2023) AI risk management framework (AI RMF 1.0), NIST AI 100-1; National Institute of Standards and Technology (2022) Towards a standard for identifying and managing bias in artificial intelligence, NIST SP 1270
Office for Civil Rights, U.S. Department of Health and Human Services (2022) Guidance on algorithmic discrimination in healthcare

Chapter 8
Human Autonomy and Machine Authority

8.1 Right to Human Decision-Making

As algorithmic decision systems demonstrate increasing accuracy across domains including medicine, law, finance, and governance, fundamental questions emerge about whether certain decisions should remain within human authority regardless of potential efficiency gains through automation. These questions reflect both practical concerns about algorithmic limitations and deeper philosophical commitments to human dignity and agency protected by the Constitution.

The proliferation of autonomous decision systems has accelerated dramatically. Research on automated decision systems documents how rarely adverse decisions are meaningfully revisited once rendered.[1] These systems now determine outcomes across critical domains including benefit eligibility, regulatory compliance, resource allocation, and risk assessment, often with minimal human oversight. This expansion has prompted urgent reconsideration of when human judgment should be legally required despite potential efficiency advantages of full automation.

Several jurisdictions have begun recognizing limited rights to human decision-making in specific contexts. The European Union's General Data Protection Regulation[2] establishes in Article 22 that data subjects "shall have the right not to be subject to a decision based solely on automated processing… which produces legal effects concerning him or her or similarly significantly affects him or her."[3] While subject to several exceptions, this provision creates a qualified right to human involvement in consequential decisions.

The EU's AI Act, effective in 2024, significantly strengthened these protections by establishing specific human oversight requirements for "high-risk" AI systems.[4] The

[1] Brookings, Lee, Resnick & Barton, Algorithmic Bias Detection and Mitigation (2019).

[2] Yeung, "Regulatory Ritualism: How AI Governance Frameworks Legitimate Algorithmic Power" (2023).

[3] General Data Protection Regulation (GDPR), Regulation (EU) 2016/679, art. 22 (2016).

[4] EU Artificial Intelligence Act, Regulation (EU) 2024/1689, arts. 14–15 (2024).

R. Yadav-Ranjan, *Constitutional Democracy in the Algorithmic Age*, Law, Governance and Technology Series 83, https://doi.org/10.1007/978-3-032-34604-9_8

Act's implementing regulations define meaningful human oversight as requiring: (1) sufficient understanding of the system's operation, (2) ability to override automated decisions, (3) authority to disregard algorithmic recommendations, and (4) capacity to intervene in real-time for high-risk applications. These requirements operationalize abstract human decision rights into concrete governance mandates.

France's Digital Republic Act goes further, specifically prohibiting judicial decisions based solely on algorithmic profiling.[5] Article 47 states that "no judicial decision involving an assessment of an individual's conduct may be based on automated processing of personal data intended to evaluate certain aspects of the individual's personality." This approach categorically reserves certain evaluative judgments for human authorities regardless of potential algorithmic capabilities.

France's Constitutional Council upheld this prohibition, rejecting arguments that advanced AI systems possess sufficient judgment for legal determinations.[6] The Council ruled that "the constitutional requirement of judicial independence necessitates human evaluative judgment that cannot be delegated to automated systems regardless of their technical sophistication." This reasoning explicitly connected human decision-making to constitutional separation of powers principles.

Several U.S. states have established domain-specific human decision rights. Illinois' Artificial Intelligence Video Interview Act requires employers using AI for video interview evaluation to provide notice and obtain consent, while explicitly requiring human review of any automated assessments.[7] Similarly, New York City's automated employment decision tools law mandates bias audits and prohibits algorithmic systems from being "the sole factor in determining whether to interview a candidate for employment".[8]

Figure 8.1 illustrates how algorithmic automation creates a paradox where efficiency gains systematically erode human autonomy. The chart shows the feedback loop between algorithmic deployment, diminished human authority, and entrenchment of automated systems.

This state-level experimentation has expanded dramatically, with a growing number of states now implementing some form of human oversight requirement for algorithmic systems. Colorado's Artificial Intelligence Act, enacted in 2024, is among the most comprehensive of these frameworks. It requires developers and deployers of high-risk systems to use reasonable care to avoid algorithmic discrimination, to conduct impact assessments, and to give affected consumers notice of an adverse automated decision together with an opportunity to correct the underlying data or to appeal to human review. California has proceeded through a set of targeted measures rather than a single statute. Its Generative Artificial Intelligence Accountability Act requires state agencies that use generative systems in direct communications with the public to disclose that use and to tell members of the public how to reach

[5] France Digital Republic Act, Loi n° 2016–1321, art. 47 (2016).

[6] 'Conseil d'État Decision No. 465381' (France 2023).

[7] Illinois Artificial Intelligence Video Interview Act, 820 ILCS 42 (2020).

[8] New York City Automated Employment Decision Tools Law, NYC Admin. Code § 20–870 et seq. (2021).

Fig. 8.1 The dynamics of "meaningful human control" vs. "automation bias" when deploying algorithmic and AI systems

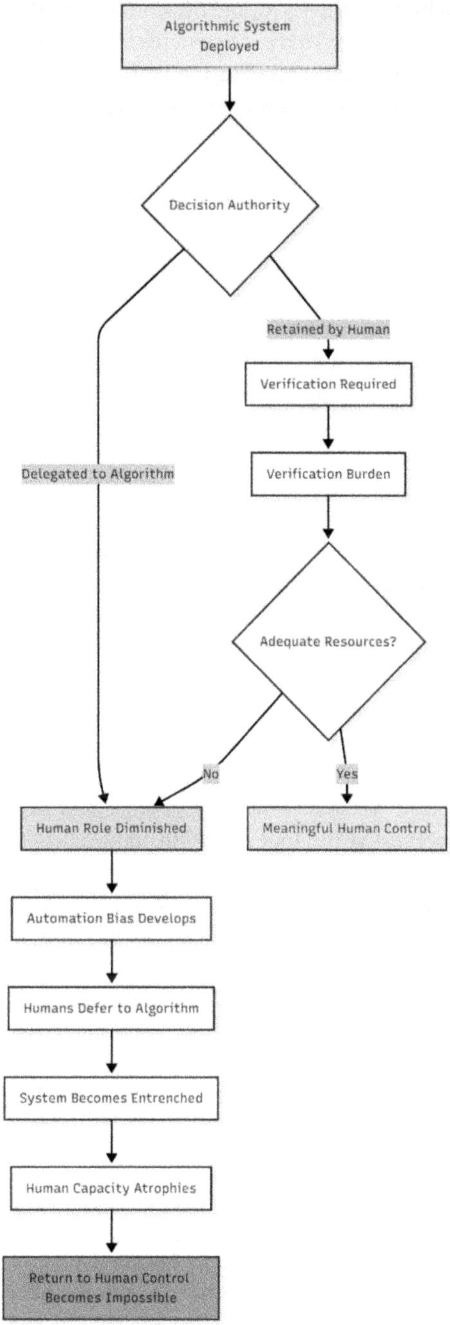

a human employee, and the state's Civil Rights Department has confirmed that the use of automated decision systems to discriminate in hiring or promotion violates the Fair Employment and Housing Act.[9] The California law would have, if passed, defined meaningful review as requiring technical understanding, decision-making authority, and sufficient time and resources.

At the federal level, no comprehensive statute yet establishes a right to human decision-making. The Algorithmic Accountability Act, first introduced in 2019 and reintroduced in later Congresses, would require covered entities to conduct impact assessments of automated decision systems, but it has not been enacted. The absence of federal legislation leaves the question of human decision rights to the states and to sector-specific regulators."[10]

These emerging protections reflect several distinct rationales. First, human decision-makers provide essential contextual judgment that algorithmic systems frequently lack. While algorithms excel at identifying statistical patterns, they typically lack understanding of contextual factors, exceptional circumstances, or novel situations beyond their training data.

This contextual limitation was dramatically illustrated in 'K.W. v. Armstrong', where Idaho's automated benefits system drastically cut Medicaid assistance for people with disabilities using a flawed formula, without giving recipients an explanation they could understand or contest.[11] The Ninth Circuit court held that due process requires the state to disclose the basis for such determinations, so that those affected can understand and contest them.

Second, human decision-makers enable moral agency and responsibility that algorithmic systems cannot meaningfully provide. The limits of algorithmic moral reasoning were at issue in 'State v. Loomis', where a defendant challenged a proprietary risk assessment score he could not inspect. The Wisconsin Supreme Court permitted the tool's use but required that judges be warned of its limitations and barred it from being the determinative factor, a tacit recognition that judgments about rehabilitation, remorse, and community safety demand human evaluation.[12]

Third, human involvement enables relational qualities often absent from purely algorithmic determinations. Research on public-sector decision making found that perceptions of procedural fairness declined markedly when citizens learned a consequential decision was fully automated, regardless of the outcome, and that satisfaction with explanations was consistently higher when they came from a human official rather than an automated system, regardless of outcome favorability.[13]

---

[9] California Generative Artificial Intelligence Accountability Act, SB 896 (2024); California Civil Rights Department, employment regulations on automated-decision systems (2025); Colorado Artificial Intelligence Act, SB 24–205 (2024).

[10] Algorithmic Accountability Act of 2019, H.R. 2231, 116th Cong.

[11] K.W. v. Armstrong, 789 F.3d 962 (9th Cir. 2015).

[12] State v. Loomis, 881 N.W.2d 749 (Wis. 2016).

[13] Alon-Barkat & Busuioc, Human–AI Interactions in Public Sector Decision Making, 33 J. Pub. Admin. Res. & Theory 153 (2023).

Fourth, human decision rights support democratic values of collective self-governance established in the Preamble and Article I of the Constitution. When algorithmic systems make policy determinations without meaningful human oversight, they potentially undermine democratic principles requiring that governance decisions reflect collective human judgment rather than technical optimization alone.[14]

8.1.1 *Power Dynamics in Human Oversight Requirements*

The proliferation of "meaningful human oversight" requirements in AI governance frameworks creates the appearance of human authority while systematically transferring decision-making power to algorithmic systems. This is not accidental but reflects successful corporate strategy to preserve business models while accommodating political pressure for "human control."[15]

The EU AI Act's human oversight requirements illustrate this dynamic. Article 14 requires that human overseers must: "(a) fully understand the capacities and limitations of the high-risk AI system; (b) be able to duly interpret the system's output; (c) be able to decide, in any particular situation, not to use the high-risk AI system or otherwise disregard, override or reverse the output; (d) be able to intervene on the operation of the system or interrupt the system."[16]

These requirements appear robust. However, implementation reveals systematic undermining of each provision. Understanding system capacities proves impossible for most deployed systems. Modern machine learning models operate through millions or billions of parameters trained on datasets too large for human comprehension. Research on human oversight of government algorithms finds that designated overseers rarely possess the technical training needed to understand the systems they supervise.[17]

Interpreting system output founders on opacity. Research shows that human overseers frequently either uniformly accepted or uniformly rejected algorithmic outputs, suggesting they lacked information necessary for nuanced interpretation.[18] The ability to override outputs exists formally but operates within constraints that render it practically ineffective. Virginia Eubanks[19] documented how caseworkers reviewing

---

[14] Benhabib, 'Democracy and Difference' (1996), 67–94.

[15] Yeung, Karen, "Regulatory Ritualism: How AI Governance Frameworks Legitimate Algorithmic Power," 'Modern Law Review' (2023).

[16] EU Artificial Intelligence Act, art. 14 (2024).

[17] Ben Green, The Flaws of Policies Requiring Human Oversight of Government Algorithms, 45 Computer L. & Sec. Rev. 105681 (2022).

[18] Ben Green, The Flaws of Policies Requiring Human Oversight of Government Algorithms, 45 Computer L. & Sec. Rev. 105681 (2022).

[19] Eubanks, 'Automating Inequality' (2018), 89–124.

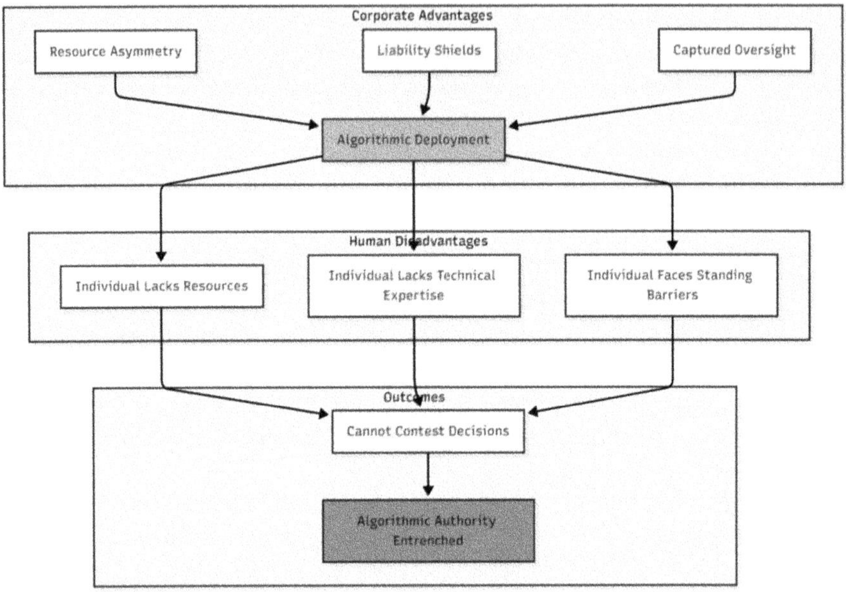

Fig. 8.2 This diagram maps the structural forces that enable algorithmic authority to displace human decision-making, showing how resource asymmetries, liability shields, and captured oversight create conditions favoring automation over autonomy

automated benefits determinations faced production quotas requiring processing 50–100 cases daily, allowing roughly 10 minutes per case.[20]

Figure 8.2 maps the structural forces that enable algorithmic authority to displace human decision-making, showing how resource asymmetries, liability shields, and captured oversight create conditions favoring automation over autonomy.

This is not implementation failure but successful corporate strategy. During AI Act negotiations, technology industry associations lobbied extensively for "flexible" human oversight provisions that would accommodate existing business models. The result is a form of regulatory ritualism, in which governance frameworks require a human authority that corporations satisfy in form while preserving algorithmic authority in substance.[21]

[20] Eubanks, 'Automating Inequality' (2018), 89–124.

[21] Carol A. Heimer and J. Lynn Gazley, 'Performing Regulation: Transcending Regulatory Ritualism in HIV Clinics,' Law & Society Review 46(4) (2012): 797–846; on algorithmic regulation and its legitimation dynamics, see Yeung K, Lodge M (2019) Algorithmic regulation: an introduction. In: Yeung K, Lodge M (eds) Algorithmic Regulation. Oxford University Press, Oxford.

Who benefits from illusory human oversight? Technology companies preserve business models dependent on automated decision-making at scale while satisfying political demands for human control. Corporate clients gain efficiency benefits of automation while insulating themselves from responsibility through documented human oversight procedures. Policymakers claim credit for establishing oversight requirements without confronting fundamental tensions between algorithmic efficiency and human authority.

Those who lose are equally clear but diffuse. Workers designated as "human overseers" bear responsibility for system failures without power to prevent them. Affected individuals are subject to algorithmic determinations under pretense of human review. Democratic governance itself suffers as the illusion of human oversight obscures the reality of algorithmic authority.

8.2 Contestability and Appeal

When decisions are automated, mechanisms for contesting algorithmic determinations become crucial. Effective contestability requires more than formal appeal rights; it demands mechanisms specifically designed to address the unique characteristics of algorithmic governance. The procedural due process guarantees in the Fifth and Fourteenth Amendments provide constitutional foundation for these protections.[22]

Contestability frameworks must address several distinct challenges. First, information asymmetry presents significant barriers. Individuals subject to algorithmic decisions typically lack understanding of system operation, training data, decision factors, and potential biases. Legal scholar Danielle Keats Citron terms this a "technological due process deficit."[23]

Second, automation bias, the tendency to defer to automated systems, affects both initial decisions and review processes. Research demonstrates that human overseers frequently exhibit excessive deference to algorithmic recommendations, undermining meaningful independent review.[24] Third, complex automated systems create diffuse responsibility, complicating accountability. This "accountability gap" presents challenges for traditional appeal mechanisms.[25]

Figure 8.3 shows the layered requirements for meaningful algorithmic contestability, from basic notification through substantive review, illustrating how each layer depends on and reinforces the others.

[22] 'Goldberg v. Kelly', 397 U.S. 254, 267–271 (1970).

[23] Citron and Pasquale, "The Scored Society" (2014).

[24] Cummings, M. L., "Automation Bias in Intelligent Time Critical Decision Support Systems," 'AIAA first Intelligent Systems Technical Conference' (2004); Goddard, K., et al., "Automation Bias: A Systematic Review of Frequency, Effect Mediators, and Mitigators," 'Journal of the American Medical Informatics Association' 19 (2012): 121–127.

[25] Citron and Pasquale, "The Scored Society" (2014).

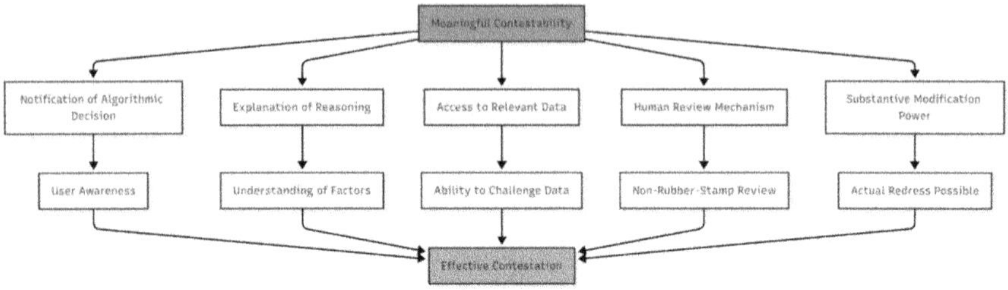

Fig. 8.3 This hierarchical chart shows the layered requirements for meaningful algorithmic contestability, from basic notification through substantive review, illustrating how each layer depends on and reinforces the others

Emerging contestability frameworks attempt to address these challenges through several approaches. Explanation requirements mandate understandable explanations for algorithmic decisions. New York City's automated decision system law requires that affected individuals receive "the factors used in making the determination" and "the weight accorded to each factor."[26] These explanation requirements operationalize the Supreme Court's recognition in 'Goldberg v. Kelly' that effective procedural protection requires "timely and adequate notice detailing the reasons for a proposed termination."[27]

Counterfactual explanation rights provide information about what factors would need to change for different outcomes. The European Union's Data Protection Board guidance suggests that GDPR explanation rights include information about "the logic involved as well as the significance and the envisaged consequences" of processing.[28] Independent review mechanisms aim to address automation bias through truly independent review boards with technical expertise.[29]

Implementation challenges remain significant. Resource constraints limit many individuals' ability to exercise contestation rights, particularly for consequential decisions like public benefits or lending where affected individuals may lack technical expertise and financial resources.[30] For citizens, meaningful contestation rights serve both instrumental and dignitary functions, preserving human agency in increasingly automated governance systems.[31]

---

[26] NYC Admin. Code § 20–870 et seq. (2021).

[27] 'Goldberg v. Kelly', 397 U.S. 254, 267–271 (1970).

[28] European Data Protection Board, "Guidelines on Automated Decision-Making and Profiling" (2020).

[29] Canadian Directive on Automated Decision-Making, Treasury Board of Canada Secretariat (2019).

[30] Eubanks, 'Automating Inequality' (2018), 156–184.

[31] Arendt, 'The Human Condition' (1958), 175–181.

8.2.1 The Illusion of Choice: How Options are Pre-Selected by Algorithms

The most insidious form of algorithmic authority operates not through overt decisions but through pre-selection of available options. By determining which choices appear, in what order, with what framing, algorithmic systems shape decisions while preserving the appearance of human choice.

Amazon's "choice" architecture exemplifies this mechanism. A 2019 Wall Street Journal investigation revealed that Amazon had adjusted its search algorithm to give greater prominence to its own private-label products and to more profitable listings, while preserving the appearance of relevance-based results.[32] Customers "choose" from this curated selection believing they are surveying available options based on their search terms. In reality, they are selecting from products Amazon's algorithms determined they should see, ranked according to Amazon's financial interests.

This mechanism extends beyond e-commerce. Google Search determines which websites appear in results, in what ranking, with what descriptive snippets. The company processes over 8.5 billion searches daily, each returning results from an algorithmically curated subset of the internet. Users "choose" which links to click, but the options are algorithmically preselected.

Meta's News Feed determines which posts from friends, family, and followed pages users see. Research by the Wall Street Journal's "Facebook Files" investigation revealed that by 2018, posts from friends and family had declined from 50% to 35% of average News Feed content, replaced by algorithmically selected content from pages users had never chosen to follow.[33] Users "choose" what to read and share, but from a feed algorithmically curated to maximize engagement metrics rather than user preference.

The choice architecture becomes coercive when options are essential services. YouTube's recommendation algorithm drives 70% of watch time on the platform. For creators, being recommended by YouTube's algorithm determines economic viability. The algorithm's preferences become creators' constraints, they must produce content satisfying algorithmic preferences or face economic extinction.

Current legal frameworks treat algorithmic curation as neutral presentation of options, requiring only that users have "consented" through terms of service. The Ninth Circuit's decision in 'Nguyen v. Barnes & Noble, Inc.,' illustrates this inadequacy.[34] The court held that website terms of service bind users who continue browsing after terms are posted, even if users never actually read them. This "browsing wrap" consent has become standard for algorithmic curation.

But this framework fails to recognize how algorithmic curation differs from traditional choice architecture. A physical store arranges products but cannot individualize displays to each customer or change arrangements dynamically based on real-time

[32] Wall Street Journal, "Amazon Changed Search Algorithm in Ways That Boost Its Own Products" (September 2019).

[33] Wall Street Journal, "The Facebook Files" investigative series (2021).

[34] Nguyen v. Barnes & Noble, Inc., 763 F.3d 1171 (9th Cir. 2014) in §8.2.1.

behavioral data. Algorithmic curation enables personalized, dynamic choice architecture that adapts to exploit individual vulnerabilities while maintaining appearance of neutral presentation.

The Federal Trade Commission has begun recognizing these concerns. In its 2022 policy statement on "Dark Patterns," the FTC acknowledged that interface design choices can be "unfair or deceptive" when they "obscure, subvert, or impair consumer autonomy, decision-making, or choice."[35] However, the statement addresses only obvious manipulative interfaces, not the sophisticated algorithmic curation that subtly constrains choice while preserving its appearance.

Meaningful autonomy in algorithmically mediated environments requires more than notice that algorithms operate. Several jurisdictions have begun requiring limited choice architecture transparency. The EU's Digital Services Act requires that recommendation systems "set out the main parameters used in their recommending systems" and provide "at least one option for each of their recommending systems that is not based on profiling."[36]

However, even these frameworks treat choice architecture as consumer protection issue rather than fundamental autonomy concern. The deeper question remains: Can human autonomy coexist with algorithmic choice architecture that operates at scale, personalizes dynamically, and adapts continuously to maximize platform objectives? This is not a technical question but a political one about what kind of agency we want to preserve in algorithmically mediated society.

8.3 Automated Gaslighting: When Systems Deny Human Experience

When algorithmic systems systematically deny the validity of human experience, they do more than make errors, they gaslight users by positioning algorithmic determinations as objective truth against which human perception is dismissed as subjective, mistaken, or irrational. This represents a fundamental assault on human agency.

Automated gaslighting operates through three related mechanisms. First, algorithms position their outputs as "data-driven" and therefore objective, while dismissing human accounts as anecdotal or subjective. Second, companies require that individuals prove algorithmic error using information only the company possesses. Third, when algorithmic errors are documented, companies explain them as edge cases, outliers, or examples of the system "working as designed."

In 2013, Latanya Sweeney documented that Google searches for distinctively Black names like "Latoya" or "Darnell" were significantly more likely to trigger ads suggesting the person had an arrest record, while searches for distinctively white

---

[35] Federal Trade Commission, "Bringing Dark Patterns to Light: An FTC Staff Report" (2022), 8–24.

[36] Digital Services Act, Regulation (EU) 2022/2065, arts. 24–27 (2022).

names like "Katie" or "Jill" did not.[37] When individuals reported this phenomenon, Google initially dismissed concerns. Only after Sweeney published peer-reviewed research demonstrating the pattern across thousands of names did Google acknowledge the issue. For years prior, individuals reporting the phenomenon were effectively told their experience was imagined or coincidental.

Amazon's same-day delivery service expansion provides another documented example. In 2016, Bloomberg investigated and found that same-day delivery was unavailable in predominantly Black neighborhoods in multiple cities, even when those neighborhoods were geographically closer to Amazon warehouses than served white neighborhoods.[38] Amazon's initial response was that delivery areas were selected "using multiple data points including population density, parcel volume, nearby locations, and infrastructure needs." Only after the article's publication and substantial criticism did Amazon expand same-day delivery to previously excluded areas.

In 2019, Apple Card launched with an algorithmic credit system that assigned lower credit limits to women than men with identical credit histories.[39] When customers reported the disparity, Apple and Goldman Sachs insisted that their algorithms were unbiased and did not use gender in credit decisions. The New York Department of Financial Services investigated and did not find a violation of fair lending law. The episode nonetheless illustrates the dynamic of automated gaslighting, in which those who report disparate treatment are met with the assurance that the system cannot be biased, and their lived experience is weighed against the presumed objectivity of the algorithm.

Automated gaslighting inflicts distinct psychological harm beyond the material impact of algorithmic decisions. Sheila O'Donnell, documented in Virginia Eubanks' 'Automating Inequality',[40] described her experience challenging an automated benefits termination: "They kept telling me the computer doesn't make mistakes. But I know what my situation is. I know what I told them. They made me feel like I was crazy, like I didn't know my own life."[41]

The harm extends beyond individual cases. When algorithmic determinations are systematically privileged over human experience, particularly for populations already marginalized, it reinforces broader patterns of epistemological injustice. Miranda Fricker's concept of "testimonial injustice", when someone's word is given less credibility due to prejudice, applies directly to automated gaslighting.[42]

---

[37] Sweeney, Latanya, "Discrimination in Online Ad Delivery," 'Communications of the ACM' 56, no. 5 (2013): 44–54.

[38] Ingold, David, and Spencer Soper, "Amazon Doesn't Consider the Race of Its Customers. Should It?" 'Bloomberg Businessweek' (April 21, 2016).

[39] New York State Department of Financial Services, "Report on Apple Card Algorithm Investigation" (2021).

[40] 'Id.'

[41] Eubanks, 'Automating Inequality' (2018), 112.

[42] Fricker, 'Epistemic Injustice' (2007), 1–19, 130–159.

Existing legal frameworks do not recognize automated gaslighting as distinct harm. Discrimination law focuses on disparate outcomes or discriminatory intent, not the epistemological violence of systematic denial. Some jurisdictions have begun recognizing related concerns through "right to explanation" provisions, but explanation alone does not address gaslighting.[43]

Addressing automated gaslighting requires frameworks that presume human experience as evidence, require accessible appeal paths, recognize collective patterns, provide meaningful remedies, and limit algorithmic authority in subjective domains. The deeper issue is power. Algorithmic gaslighting works because corporations possess resources, technical expertise, and institutional credibility that individuals lack.

8.4 The Right to Inefficiency: Why Human Friction Protects Democracy

The systematic elimination of friction, delay, and inefficiency in algorithmic systems is typically celebrated as progress. But human friction serves essential democratic functions: it creates space for reflection, enables collective organizing, provides opportunities for intervention, and imposes costs on mass surveillance and manipulation. The "frictionless" society that technology companies promise is one where those in power face no resistance.

Historically, inefficiency has protected democracy in several crucial ways. The constitutional requirement that legislation be read three times before passage, that bills be referred to committee, that amendments be proposed and debated, these are intentional inefficiencies designed to slow decision-making and create space for reflection. Algorithmic systems eliminate this deliberative space. As Sherry Turkle documents in 'Reclaiming Conversation', the absence of pause in digital interactions fundamentally changes the nature of human engagement, reducing reflection and increasing reactivity.[44]

Organizing resistance requires time and coordination. When adverse decisions took weeks or months to implement, affected individuals could identify each other, share experiences, organize collective responses, and mobilize political pressure. Algorithmic systems eliminate these windows. When Amazon adjusts prices in real-time, there is no opportunity for consumers to organize collective responses. When YouTube demonetizes channels instantly, creators cannot coordinate resistance before economic pressure forces compliance.

Mass surveillance was historically limited by resource constraints. The practical impossibility of comprehensive surveillance provided de facto privacy protection

[43] General Data Protection Regulation, art. 22 (2016).

[44] Turkle, 'Reclaiming Conversation' (2015), 21–47.

regardless of legal guarantees. Algorithmic systems eliminate these practical limitations. Automated analysis of communications costs virtually nothing at scale. The friction that provided practical privacy protection has been eliminated.[45]

Discrimination at scale was historically limited by practical constraints. Algorithmic systems eliminate these practical limitations. Once discriminatory criteria are encoded, systems can apply them instantly at scale with perfect consistency. Amazon's resume screening algorithm could discriminate against women across thousands of applications faster than any human hiring manager could read a single resume.[46]

Technology companies have waged systematic campaign to eliminate friction, framing every delay or difficulty as inefficiency requiring technological solution. Amazon's "one-click" purchasing eliminates the pause between desire and purchase. Facebook's "infinite scroll" eliminates the natural stopping point. Apple's "Face ID" eliminates the minor inconvenience of entering a passcode. Google's "autocomplete" eliminates the need to finish typing searches. Netflix's "autoplay" eliminates the decision point between episodes.

Each elimination of friction is framed as user-friendly improvement. Collectively, they constitute systematic removal of pause, reflection, deliberation, and decision points that enabled human agency.

The elimination of friction serves specific economic and political interests. Frictionless systems maximize throughput, engagement, and conversion. Every eliminated pause is opportunity for user reconsideration, disengagement, or alternate choice. The efficiency is real but asymmetric. Users save seconds; companies gain billions.

A substantial body of behavioral research finds that reducing the friction of payment increases spending, as the diminished salience of parting with money weakens the check that friction ordinarily provides.[47] Neuroscience research found that even the presence of a smartphone reduces cognitive capacity on unrelated tasks.[48] Research linked design features that eliminate friction to addictive usage patterns.[49] Research by Duke scholars found that frictionless exposure to opposing political viewpoints on social media increased rather than decreased polarization.[50]

Current legal frameworks treat friction only as barrier to access or efficiency, never recognizing its protective functions. No legal framework affirmatively protects beneficial friction. There is no "right to pause" before algorithmic decisions, no

---

[45] 'Carpenter v. United States', 138 S. Ct. 2206 (2018).

[46] Dastin, Jeffrey, "Amazon Scraps Secret AI Recruiting Tool That Showed Bias Against Women," 'Reuters' (October 10, 2018).

[47] Prelec and Simester, "Always Leave Home Without It: A Further Investigation of the Credit-Card Effect on Willingness to Pay," Marketing Letters 12 (2001).

[48] Ward, Adrian F., et al., "Brain Drain: The Mere Presence of One's Own Smartphone Reduces Available Cognitive Capacity," 'Journal of the Association for Consumer Research' 2, no. 2 (2017): 140–154.

[49] Alter, 'Irresistible' (2017), 27–48, 155–189.

[50] Bail, Christopher A., et al., "Exposure to Opposing Views on Social Media Can Increase Political Polarization," 'Proceedings of the National Academy of Sciences' 115, no. 37 (2018): 9216–9221.

required deliberation period before consequential actions, no mandatory friction in systems governing essential services.

Preserving human agency in algorithmic systems requires affirmatively protecting certain frictions: mandatory delays for consequential actions, friction in addictive design, protected organizational windows, deliberation requirements for high-stakes decisions, friction in surveillance systems, and protected offline spaces.

The deeper principle is this: democratic governance requires time. Time for reflection, time for organizing, time for critique, time for alternatives to emerge. The systematic elimination of time through frictionless algorithmic systems is elimination of the temporal space in which democracy operates. This is not Luddite nostalgia for inefficiency. This is political recognition that some forms of friction protect human agency against algorithmic authority.

8.5 Opt-out Rights and Alternatives

The extent to which citizens should be permitted to opt out of algorithmic governance systems raises complex questions about social contracts and alternatives in increasingly digitized societies, with implications for constitutional liberty interests.

Several jurisdictions have begun establishing limited opt-out frameworks. The European Union's GDPR provides qualified opt-out rights for certain types of automated processing.[51] Illinois' Biometric Information Privacy Act requires affirmative consent before collecting biometric identifiers, effectively creating an opt-out right by default.[52] The California Consumer Privacy Act provides opt-out rights from the sale of personal information.[53]

These varied approaches reflect tensions between individual autonomy and collective governance interests. Several principles can guide balanced approaches. First, opt-out rights should vary with stakes and alternatives.[54] Second, public sector and private sector contexts demand different frameworks.[55] Third, collective impacts require consideration alongside individual choices.[56] Fourth, practical accessibility matters alongside formal rights.[57]

[51] General Data Protection Regulation, art. 21 (2016).

[52] Illinois Biometric Information Privacy Act, 740 ILCS 14 (2008).

[53] California Consumer Privacy Act, Cal. Civ. Code § 1798.100 et seq. (2018).

[54] Hartzog, 'Privacy's Blueprint' (2018), 69–94.

[55] 'Riley v. California', 573 U.S. 373, 385–386 (2014).

[56] Barocas, Solon, and Andrew D. Selbst, "Big Data's Disparate Impact," 'California Law Review' 104 (2016): 671–732.

[57] Federal Trade Commission, "Bringing Dark Patterns to Light" (2022).

For citizens, meaningful opt-out rights serve both practical and symbolic functions. Practically, they provide essential protection against potentially harmful algorithmic determinations. Symbolically, they affirm human agency in increasingly automated environments.[58]

8.6 What You Can Do Now

Preserving human autonomy against algorithmic authority requires action at individual, collective, and policy levels.

Immediate Personal Actions: Document algorithmic treatment in detail. Exercise contestation rights aggressively, appeal every adverse decision. Opt out where possible by disabling algorithmic recommendations, targeted advertising, and location tracking. Create friction for yourself by deleting stored payment information, disabling auto-play, setting time limits, and requiring password entry.

Collective Organizing: Join algorithmic accountability networks including Algorithmic Justice League, Electronic Frontier Foundation, AI Now Institute, Data & Society Research Institute, and Access Now. Organize workers for genuine algorithmic oversight. Build case registries coordinating with others experiencing similar treatment. Demand algorithmic impact assessments before deployment.

Policy Advocacy: Advocate for genuine human decision rights with mandatory review, adequate resources, and criminal penalties for fraudulent oversight. Support right to explanation strengthening with counterfactual explanations and burden-shifting. Push for friction protection including mandatory delays, prohibition of addictive design, and protected deliberation periods. Demand resource equity in contestation through free legal representation and technical assistance.

Legal Strategies: Participate in collective legal actions through ACLU, Electronic Privacy Information Center, and Public Citizen. Challenge mandatory arbitration. Assert constitutional rights creatively including due process, equal protection, First Amendment, and Fourth Amendment claims.

Technical Resistance: Use privacy-protective tools including Signal, VPNs, privacy-focused browsers, and tracker blockers. Generate adversarial noise through shared devices, random searches, and identifier rotation. Support privacy-preserving alternatives including Mastodon, PeerTube, DuckDuckGo, and Nextcloud.

Connections and Coalitions: The struggle for human autonomy connects to labor rights, racial justice, disability rights, consumer protection, and democratic reform. These are not separate struggles but interconnected fights against concentrated algorithmic authority.

---

[58] Sandel, 'What Money Can't Buy' (2012), 5–14.

References

Cases

'Carpenter v. United States', 138 S. Ct. 2206 (2018)
'Conseil d'État Decision No. 465381' (France 2023)
'Goldberg v. Kelly', 397 US 254 (1970)
'Griswold v. Connecticut', 381 US 479 (1965)
Nguyen v. Barnes & Noble, Inc., 763 F.3d 1171 (9th Cir. 2014) in §8.2.1
'Lawrence v. Texas', 539 U.S. 558 (2003)
'Marsh v. Alabama', 326 US 501 (1946)
K.W. v. Armstrong, 789 F.3d 962 (9th Cir. 2015)
'Palko v. Connecticut', 302 US 319 (1937)
'Riley v. California', 573 U.S. 373 (2014)
'Stanley v. Georgia', 394 US 557 (1969)
'United States v. Jones', 565 U.S. 400 (2012)
State v. Loomis, 881 N.W.2d 749 (Wis. 2016)

Books

Alter A (2017) Irresistible: the rise of addictive technology and the business of keeping us hooked. Penguin Press
Arendt H (1958) The human condition. University of Chicago Press
Benhabib S (1996) Democracy and difference: contesting the boundaries of the political. Princeton University Press
Cohen JE (2019) Between truth and power: the legal constructions of informational capitalism. Oxford University Press
Eubanks V (2018) Automating inequality: how high-tech tools profile, police, and punish the poor. St. Martin's Press
Fricker M (2007) Epistemic injustice: power and the ethics of knowing. Oxford University Press
Hartzog W (2018) Privacy's blueprint: the battle to control the design of new technologies. Harvard University Press
O'Neil C (2016) Weapons of math destruction: how big data increases inequality and threatens democracy. Crown
Pasquale F (2015) The black box society: the secret algorithms that control money and information. Harvard University Press
Sandel MJ (2012) What money can't buy: the moral limits of markets. Farrar, Straus and Giroux
Turkle S (2015) Reclaiming conversation: the power of talk in a digital age. Penguin Press
Zuboff S (2019) The age of surveillance capitalism: the fight for a human future at the new frontier of power. PublicAffairs

Chapter 9
Cognitive Liberty and Mental Privacy

9.1 Freedom from Algorithmic Manipulation

As algorithmic systems demonstrate increasing capability to influence human cognition through targeted content, emotional manipulation, and attention exploitation, fundamental questions emerge about constitutional protections for cognitive autonomy. These concerns implicate the First Amendment's protection of thought and belief, the Fourth Amendment's privacy guarantees, and the liberty interests protected by the Due Process Clauses.

The manipulation landscape has evolved dramatically. What began as simple targeted advertising has progressed to sophisticated psychological profiling enabling precisely calibrated influence attempts. Facebook's controversial 2014 emotional contagion experiment demonstrated the feasibility of algorithmically manipulating emotional states without user awareness or consent, raising fundamental questions about cognitive liberty.[1]

Algorithmic manipulation operates through several distinct mechanisms. First, micro-targeted persuasion combines detailed psychological profiles with precisely calibrated messaging. Research by Kosinski and colleagues demonstrated that analyzing as few as 300 Facebook likes enables predicting personality traits more accurately than intimate human associates.[2] When combined with persuasion optimization, these capabilities enable what scholar Shoshana Zuboff terms "instrumentarian power."[3]

---

[1] Kramer et al., "Experimental Evidence of Massive-Scale Emotional Contagion" (2014).

[2] Kosinski, Michal, David Stillwell, and Thore Graepel, "Private Traits and Attributes Are Predictable from Digital Records of Human Behavior," 'Proceedings of the National Academy of Sciences' 110, no. 15 (2013): 5802–5805.; see also Youyou, Wu, Michal Kosinski, and David Stillwell, 'Computer-Based Personality Judgments Are More Accurate Than Those Made by Humans,' Proceedings of the National Academy of Sciences 112, no. 4 (2015): 1036–1040.

[3] Zuboff, 'The Age of Surveillance Capitalism' (2019), 63–97, 376–394.

R. Yadav-Ranjan, *Constitutional Democracy in the Algorithmic Age*, Law, Governance and Technology Series 83, https://doi.org/10.1007/978-3-032-34604-9_9

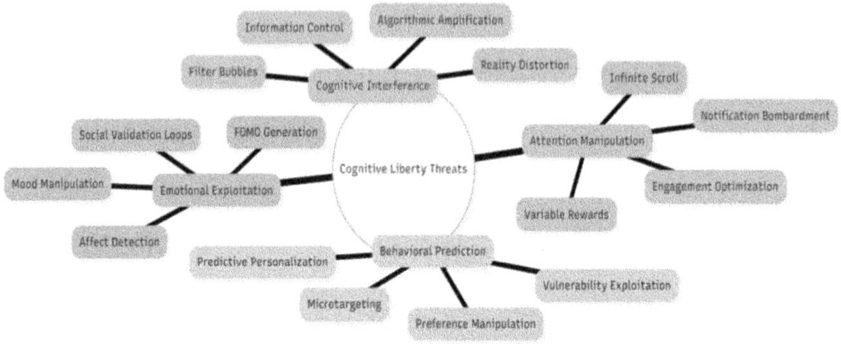

Fig. 9.1 This mind map categorizes the various ways algorithmic systems threaten cognitive liberty, from attention manipulation through behavioral prediction to emotional exploitation, showing how different techniques converge on mental autonomy

Second, behavioral prediction enables systems to anticipate and influence decisions before conscious deliberation occurs. By analyzing patterns in digital behaviors, algorithmic systems develop predictive models enabling preemptive intervention in decision processes. Third, affective manipulation targets emotional states rather than rational deliberation, potentially bypassing rational decision processes entirely.

The constitutional foundations for protecting cognitive liberty remain underdeveloped, though several doctrinal anchors exist. The First Amendment's protection of speech has been interpreted to include protection for thought and belief, as Justice Cardozo noted in 'Palko v. Connecticut': "freedom of thought... is the matrix, the indispensable condition, of nearly every other form of freedom."[4]

The Fourth Amendment's protection against unreasonable searches establishes privacy interests with cognitive dimensions. As Justice Sotomayor noted in 'United States v. Jones', comprehensive data collection can reveal "a wealth of detail about [one's] familial, political, professional, religious, and sexual associations" with significant implications for expressive and associational freedoms.[5]

Figure 9.1 categorizes the various ways algorithmic systems threaten cognitive liberty, from attention manipulation through behavioral prediction to emotional exploitation, showing how different techniques converge on mental autonomy.

The liberty interests protected by the Due Process Clauses potentially extend to the cognitive processes underlying autonomous decision-making. While traditionally applied to specific substantive choices, these protections potentially constrain manipulative practices that effectively hijack decision-making processes.[6]

---

4 'Palko v. Connecticut', 302 U.S. 319, 327 (1937).

5 'United States v. Jones', 565 U.S. 400, 415 (2012).

6 'Griswold v. Connecticut', 381 U.S. 479 (1965); 'Lawrence v. Texas', 539 U.S. 558 (2003).

9.1.1 Power Dynamics in Cognitive Manipulation

The systematic undermining of cognitive autonomy serves clear and concentrated interests while distributing harms diffusely across populations. Manipulation is not a byproduct of algorithmic systems but their core function. Facebook's internal research, revealed through Frances Haugen's disclosures, explicitly acknowledged that engagement-maximizing algorithms amplify divisive content because "anger and hate is the easiest way to grow" on the platform.[7]

This is not an engineering failure but a business model. Advertising revenue depends on user engagement. Engagement maximizes when content triggers emotional responses. Therefore, algorithms optimize for emotional manipulation. The financial incentives are staggering. In 2023, Meta reported $134 billion in advertising revenue, substantially dependent on engagement-optimizing algorithms.[8]

State actors leverage manipulative algorithmic systems for social control. The Cambridge Analytica revelations demonstrated state-corporate coordination for electoral manipulation. The company accessed data on 87 million Facebook users, built psychological profiles, and deployed targeted messaging to influence elections globally.[9]

Those who bear the costs include cognitive degradation, emotional harm, economic exploitation, and political polarization. Research found that false news spreads six times faster than accurate news on social media, largely because algorithms optimize for engagement rather than accuracy.[10] Research found that exposure to opposing political content on social media increased anxiety and anger while reducing empathy and deepended political polarization rather than reducing it.[11] Research documented pervasive "dark patterns" interface designs that steer users into purchases, subscriptions, and disclosures they never intended.[12]

Technical complexity prevents effective resistance. Companies employ hundreds of Ph.D.-level data scientists optimizing manipulation systems against individual users with no technical expertise. When individuals report feeling manipulated, companies cite "user engagement," "relevance optimization," and "personalization" to frame manipulation as beneficial service.

---

[7] Haugen, Frances (whistleblower), "Facebook Files: Internal Documents on Engagement Optimization and Harmful Content Amplification," disclosed to U.S. Securities and Exchange Commission (2021).

[8] Meta Platforms Inc., Annual Report (Form 10-K) (2023), 51–54.

[9] Wylie, 'Mindf*ck' (2019), 89–135; Cadwalladr, Carole, and Emma Graham-Harrison, "Revealed: 50 Million Facebook Profiles Harvested for Cambridge Analytica in Major Data Breach," 'The Guardian' (March 17, 2018).

[10] Vosoughi, Soroush, Deb Roy, and Sinan Aral, "The Spread of True and False News Online," 'Science' 359, no. 6380 (2018): 1146–1151.

[11] Bail, Christopher A., et al., "Exposure to Opposing Views on Social Media Can Increase Political Polarization," 'Proceedings of the National Academy of Sciences' 115, no. 37 (2018): 9216–9221.

[12] Mathur et al., "Dark Patterns at Scale: Findings from a Crawl of 11K Shopping Websites," Proc. ACM Human-Computer Interaction (CSCW, 2019); see also FTC, "Bringing Dark Patterns to Light" (2022).

9.2 Memetic Engineering: How Ideas Are Manufactured and Distributed

The marketplace of ideas presupposes organic competition where the best arguments prevail through rational deliberation. Memetic engineering destroys this foundation by industrializing idea production and distribution, manufacturing beliefs at scale through coordinated algorithmic amplification.

Cambridge Analytica exemplified industrial memetic engineering. The company didn't merely analyze public opinion, it manufactured and propagated ideas designed to manipulate electoral outcomes. Internal documents revealed systematic processes: psychological profiling, message testing, targeted distribution, amplification, and iterative optimization.[13]

Christopher Wylie, Cambridge Analytica whistleblower, testified that the company's objective was "to explore mental vulnerabilities of people and then map out ways to inject information into the streams of online content they receive" to "prey on inner demons and change how they perceive the world around them."[14]

Social media platforms provide distribution infrastructure for industrial memetic engineering. The algorithms don't neutrally distribute content, they amplify messages optimized for engagement, creating systematic bias toward manufactured memes designed to trigger emotional responses.

Research documented Russian Internet Research Agency's use of social media for memetic warfare during the 2016 U.S. election.[15] The operation created thousands of fake accounts distributed across the ideological spectrum, deployed content designed to amplify divisions, and leveraged algorithmic amplification to achieve reach far exceeding the actual accounts.

The research found that algorithmically amplified content from fake accounts reached audiences comparable to legitimate news organizations despite coming from accounts with minimal followers. The algorithms' engagement optimization meant that divisive, emotionally charged content achieved more distribution than factual but less emotionally engaging content from legitimate sources.

Nation-states now conduct memetic warfare operations as standard practice. The U.S. Cybersecurity and Infrastructure Security Agency's 2023 report documented influence operations by Russia, China, Iran, and North Korea, all leveraging algorithmic amplification for strategic messaging.[16]

Senate Intelligence Committee's bipartisan report documented that Russian operations reached approximately 126 million Americans on Facebook, 20 million on

[13] U.K. Parliament, Digital, Culture, Media and Sport Committee, "Disinformation and 'Fake News': Final Report," Eighth Report of Session 2017–19 (2019), 42–61.

[14] 'Id.' at 48.

[15] Broniatowski, David A., et al., "Weaponized Health Communication: Twitter Bots and Russian Trolls Amplify the Vaccine Debate," 'American Journal of Public Health' 108, no. 10 (2018): 1378–1384.

[16] U.S. Cybersecurity and Infrastructure Security Agency, "Foreign Influence Operations and Election Security: 2023 Threat Assessment" (2023).

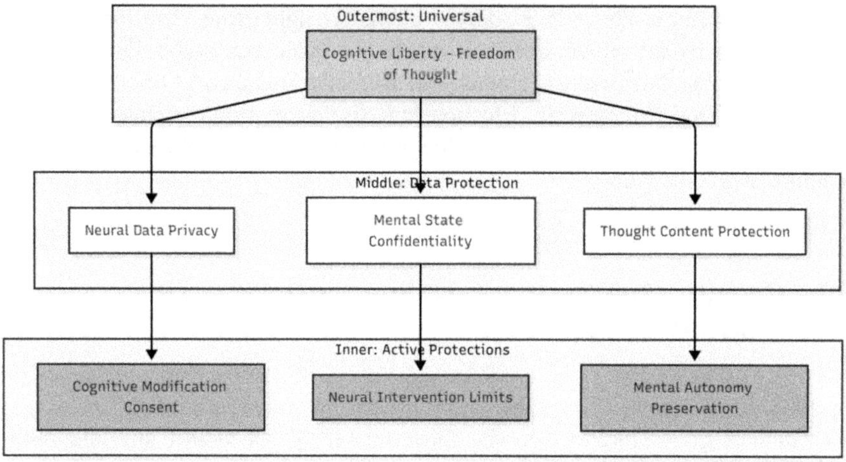

Fig. 9.2 This layered diagram illustrates the nested rights protections needed for brain-computer interfaces, showing how different levels of protection correspond to different types of neural data and interface capabilities

Instagram, and substantial audiences on Twitter, YouTube, and other platforms.[17] The reach exceeded most legitimate news organizations, achieved through memetic engineering optimized for algorithmic amplification.

Commercial applications extend beyond electoral manipulation to routine marketing. Astroturfing, fake grassroots movements manufactured by corporations, now operates at industrial scale. Research documented networks of fake accounts promoting corporate interests across multiple platforms.[18] Professional astroturfing operations employ sophisticated techniques including persona management software, coordinated campaigns, algorithmic exploitation, and cross-platform coordination.

Figure 9.2 illustrates the nested rights protections needed for brain-computer interfaces, showing how different levels of protection correspond to different types of neural data and interface capabilities.

Why does memetic engineering succeed? Algorithmic amplification systematically amplifies manufactured content designed to trigger emotional responses. Coordinated operations can deploy thousands of accounts creating appearance of widespread support. Information asymmetry creates one-sided battlefield. Speed enables deployment, testing, optimization, and amplification faster than fact-checking. Micro-targeting enables precisely targeted messages. Lack of attribution prevents accountability.

---

[17] U.S. Senate Select Committee on Intelligence, "Report on Russian Active Measures Campaigns and Interference in the 2016 U.S. Election," Vols. 1–5 (2019).

[18] Keller, Franziska B., et al., "Political Astroturfing on Twitter: How to Coordinate a Disinformation Campaign," 'Political Communication' 37, no. 2 (2020): 256–280.

Existing frameworks do not address memetic engineering. The First Amendment protects manufactured speech as much as organic expression. Deception law requires proving false factual claims, but memetic engineering often uses accurate facts arranged to mislead. Election law disclosure requirements don't apply to coordinated networks. Section 230 shields platforms from liability for amplifying manufactured content.

9.3 Cognitive Infiltration: Cass Sunstein's Proposal as Reality

In 2008, legal scholar Cass Sunstein proposed "cognitive infiltration" as strategy for countering conspiracy theories. Government agents would infiltrate online communities, not identifying themselves as government representatives, to introduce doubt and alternative perspectives.[19] While presented as counter-extremism strategy, Sunstein's proposal articulated something more troubling: the deliberate, covert use of coordinated accounts to shape beliefs without targets' knowledge.

This is no longer theoretical proposal but documented operational reality, conducted not just by governments but by corporations, political campaigns, and foreign states.

Documents obtained through Freedom of Information Act requests revealed U.S. military contracts for "online persona management" software enabling single operators to control multiple fake social media accounts simultaneously.[20] The stated purpose was influencing foreign audiences. But the same software could easily be used domestically.

Documents released by Edward Snowden revealed Britain's Government Communications Headquarters operates "Joint Threat Research Intelligence Group" conducting online influence operations including credential attacks, false flag operations, honey traps, and disruption techniques.[21] The operations targeted not just terrorists but hackers, activists, and anyone deemed a threat to national security.

Russian Internet Research Agency's operations exemplify cognitive infiltration at industrial scale. The operation created thousands of fake accounts across ideological spectrum, posing as Americans with diverse political views. These accounts engaged in genuine social interactions to establish credibility before deploying targeted messaging.[22]

---

[19] Sunstein and Vermeule, "Conspiracy Theories" (2008).

[20] Greenwald, Glenn, "How Covert Agents Infiltrate the Internet to Manipulate, Deceive, and Destroy Reputations," 'The Intercept' (February 24, 2014).

[21] 'Id.'

[22] Mueller, Robert S., III, "Report on the Investigation into Russian Interference in the 2016 Presidential Election," Vols. I-II, U.S. Department of Justice (2019).

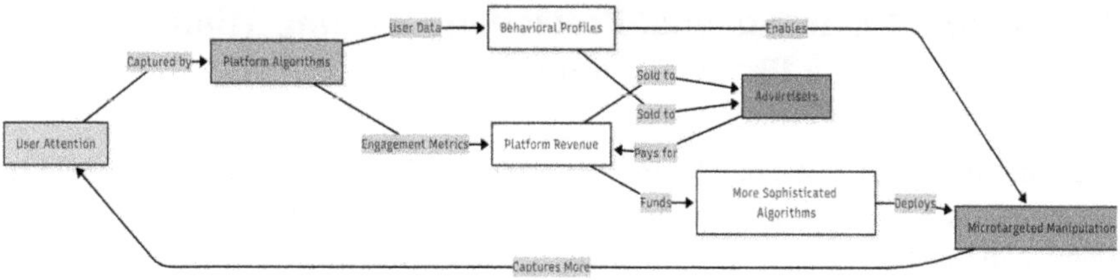

Fig. 9.3 This Sankey-style flow diagram shows how attention flows from users to platforms to advertisers, with feedback loops showing how captured attention enables further manipulation. The width of flows represents magnitude of attention capture

Corporate cognitive infiltration extends government techniques. Investigation revealed companies hired reputation management firms who deployed coordinated networks of fake accounts posting seemingly organic support for corporate interests.[23] Investigation revealed Amazon recruited warehouse employees as 'FC Ambassadors' to post coordinated, company directed messages defending its working conditions on social media.[24]

Cognitive infiltration inflicts distinct harms beyond the manipulation itself. When discourse is infiltrated by coordinated inauthentic accounts, recipients cannot distinguish genuine human interaction from manufactured manipulation. Research found that exposure to suspected inauthenticity increased general distrust, making individuals skeptical of legitimate voices alongside manufactured ones.[25]

Figure 9.3 shows how attention flows from users to platforms to advertisers, with feedback loops showing how captured attention enables further manipulation. The width of flows represents magnitude of attention capture.

When individuals discover that movements, they believed were grassroots were actually coordinated operations, the disillusionment often extends to legitimate political participation. Research found that exposure to information about social media manipulation correlated with decreased political efficacy and increased cynicism.[26]

Current frameworks don't address cognitive infiltration. The First Amendment protects fake speech as much as authentic expression. Fraud statutes apply to commercial deception but not to political speech. Platform terms of service prohibit "coordinated inauthentic behavior" but enforcement is inconsistent.

[23] New York State Office of the Attorney General, "Fake Comments: How U.S. Companies and Partisans Hack Democracy to Undermine Your Voice," Investigation Report (2021).

[24] Del Rey, Jason, and Shirin Ghaffary, coverage of Amazon's 'FC Ambassadors' program; see also Lee Fang, 'Amazon's Twitter Army Was Handpicked for "Great Sense of Humor,"' The Intercept (March 30, 2021); Fortune (Aug. 24, 2018).

[25] Lewandowsky, Stephan, Ullrich K. H. Ecker, and John Cook, "Beyond Misinformation: Understanding and Coping with the 'Post-Truth' Era," 'Journal of Applied Research in Memory and Cognition' 6, no. 4 (2017): 353–369.

[26] Persily and Tucker (eds.), 'Social Media and Democracy' (2020), 195–230.

9.4 Mental Environmental Protection: Treating Mind Pollution like Physical Pollution

The environmental movement emerged when industrial pollutants' cumulative effects on physical environment became undeniable. We now face analogous challenge with mental environment, the cognitive, attentional, and emotional ecosystem in which human thought occurs. Just as physical environment can be polluted beyond habitability, mental environment can be degraded beyond supporting healthy cognition.

Political theorist Jürgen Habermas conceptualized "public sphere" as space where rational deliberation occurs.[27] The mental environmental protection framework extends this by recognizing that individual cognition depends on environmental conditions just as physical health depends on air and water quality.

Elements of healthy mental environment include attentional space, informational integrity, emotional regulation, deliberative time, and cognitive security. These are not luxuries but prerequisites for autonomous thought. When systematically degraded, cognitive capacity diminishes regardless of individual intelligence or education.

Certain digital practices function as cognitive pollutants. Constant interruptions fragment attention, degrading capacity for sustained thought. Research found that it takes average of 23 minutes to return to task after interruption.[28] With workers receiving 150+ notifications daily, most working hours involve recovering from interruptions rather than sustained focus.

Tristan Harris, former Google design ethicist, documented how platforms deliberately engineer attention pollution. Features like notification systems, infinite scroll, and autoplay aren't responses to user preferences but strategies for maximizing "time on site" by making disengagement difficult.[29]

Misinformation, propaganda, and algorithmically amplified falsehoods function as pollutants in informational environment. Research found false news spreads six times faster than accurate news on social media.[30] When false information systematically drowns accurate information, the informational environment becomes polluted.

Algorithmic amplification of emotionally manipulative content creates emotional pollution. Platforms optimize for "engagement," which research shows correlates with content triggering anger, fear, or outrage. Research found that social media

[27] Habermas, 'The Structural Transformation of the Public Sphere' (1991), 27–56, 181–235.

[28] Mark, Gloria, Daniela Gudith, and Ulrich Klocke, "The Cost of Interrupted Work: More Speed and Stress," 'Proceedings of the SIGCHI Conference on Human Factors in Computing Systems' (2008): 107–110.

[29] Harris, Tristan, "How Technology Is Hijacking Your Mind, from a Magician and Google Design Ethicist," Thrive Global (2016).

[30] Vosoughi et al., "The Spread of True and False News Online" (2018).

posts using moral-emotional language receive substantially more engagement and algorithmic amplification.[31]

Sophisticated manipulation techniques create environment where individuals cannot trust their own judgment. This is cognitive insecurity, inability to trust that your thoughts are your own. Research documented that even awareness of manipulation attempts doesn't fully neutralize their effectiveness.[32]

Like physical environmental pollution, mental pollutants' effects compound. Research documents how digital attention pollution, information pollution, and emotional manipulation combine to create behavioral addictions.[33] Research documented correlation between smartphone adoption and increased rates of depression and anxiety among adolescents.[34]

Mental environmental degradation follows classic tragedy of the commons pattern. Each platform gains competitive advantage by polluting, optimizing for attention capture, amplifying misinformation that spreads fast, exploiting emotions that drive engagement. No individual actor has incentive to stop polluting. Only collective action through regulation can prevent race to bottom.

Unlike physical environment, mental environment lacks protective framework. Environmental Protection Act established EPA with authority to regulate pollutants. No analogous institution exists for mental environmental protection. Clean Air Act sets air quality standards. No standards exist for acceptable levels of attentional interruption, informational integrity, or emotional manipulation.

Protecting mental environment requires frameworks analogous to physical environmental protection: exposure standards establishing acceptable levels for mental pollutants; mental environmental impact assessments before deploying systems likely to degrade mental environment; Mental Environmental Protection Agency with authority over mental environmental quality; right to clean cognitive environment as prerequisite for autonomous thought; corporate responsibility for systems that pollute mental environment.

Mental environmental protection should follow public health model: primary prevention preventing pollution before it occurs; secondary prevention detecting and mitigating pollution through monitoring; tertiary prevention treating harms from pollution exposure.

---

[31] Rathje, Steve, Jay J. Van Bavel, and Sander van der Linden, "Out-Group Animosity Drives Engagement on Social Media," 'Proceedings of the National Academy of Sciences' 118, no. 26 (2021): e2024292118.

[32] Lewandowsky et al., "Beyond Misinformation" (2017).

[33] Alter, 'Irresistible' (2017), 27–48, 155–189.

[34] Twenge, Jean M., and W. Keith Campbell, "Associations Between Screen Time and Lower Psychological Well-Being Among Children and Adolescents: Evidence from a Population-Based Study," 'Preventive Medicine' Reports 12 (2018): 271–283.

9.5 Neurodata and Brain-Computer Interfaces

Emerging technologies enabling direct brain-computer interaction raise novel questions about mental privacy and the boundaries of permissible state and corporate access to neural data, implicating fundamental Fourth Amendment privacy protections and First Amendment freedoms of thought.

Brain-computer interfaces and neurotechnology represent a rapidly developing domain with profound implications for cognitive liberty. These technologies enable direct measurement, interpretation, and potentially modification of neural activity, creating unprecedented capabilities along with novel privacy and autonomy concerns.[35]

Several distinct capabilities raise particular concerns. First, passive neural monitoring enables detection of cognitive states without active communication. Advanced EEG and fMRI techniques can identify emotional responses, detect recognition of specific stimuli, and even reconstruct rudimentary visual experiences without subjects actively sharing this information.

Second, neurodata inference enables extraction of sensitive information beyond subjects' awareness or intent. Research demonstrates that neural activity patterns can reveal information about psychological traits, psychiatric conditions, substance use, and even political or consumer preferences without subjects explicitly sharing this information.[36]

Third, neurotechnology increasingly enables direct cognitive modification through techniques including transcranial magnetic stimulation, deep brain stimulation, and optogenetic approaches. While currently limited to medical contexts, these capabilities raise profound questions about cognitive liberty and mental integrity.

The legal frameworks governing neural data remain underdeveloped. Existing privacy law typically distinguishes between information individuals deliberately communicate versus information inferred from behaviors. Neural data challenges this distinction by enabling direct measurement of mental states without deliberate communication.

Several jurisdictions have begun recognizing neurodata's special status. Chile became the first nation to constitutionally protect neural rights in 2021, amending its constitution to protect "mental integrity" and establish that "the development and use of neurotechnologies" must respect "the human mind's inviolability."[37]

Scholars have proposed "neural data exceptionalism" recognizing that mental content deserves distinctive protection as perhaps the most intimate information

---

35 Ienca, Marcello, and Roberto Andorno, "Towards New Human Rights in the Age of Neuroscience and Neurotechnology," 'Life Sciences, Society and Policy' 13, Article 5 (2017).

36 'Id.'

37 Chile, Ley No. 21.383, Reforma constitucional que establece el desarrollo científico y tecnológico al servicio de las personas (2021), amending Article 19, No. 1 of the Constitution.

category possible.[38] This approach would establish heightened protections for neural data beyond those provided for other biometric or behavioral data.

9.6 Attention Protection in the Attention Economy

The "attention economy" frames human attention as scarce resource subject to extraction and monetization. Engagement-maximizing systems systematically capture attention through psychological exploitation, raising concerns about attentional autonomy and the liberty interests protected by the Due Process Clauses.

Attention exploitation operates through several mechanisms. Infinite scroll eliminates natural stopping points that would enable disengagement. Autoplay features remove decision points between content consumption episodes. Push notifications create external interruption regardless of user intent. Recommendation algorithms optimize for continued engagement rather than user satisfaction.

These design patterns demonstrate what former Google design ethicist Tristan Harris terms "hijacking" attention through exploitation of psychological vulnerabilities.[39] The cumulative effect creates compulsive usage patterns interfering with individuals' ability to allocate attention according to their own priorities and values.

Research documents significant impacts. Heavy social media use correlates with decreased well-being, increased anxiety and depression, and reduced capacity for sustained attention.[40] While causation remains debated, the correlation suggests that attention exploitation systems may undermine psychological flourishing.

Several regulatory approaches have emerged. California's Age-Appropriate Design Code Act prohibits companies from using "design features... that the business knows, or has reason to know, causes a substantial risk of... addiction" for children's products.[41] The FTC has increased enforcement actions against "unfair or deceptive" design patterns under Sect. 5 authority.[42]

More ambitious approaches would establish explicit attention protection rights against exploitative design. The proposed "Freedom from Addiction Act" would prohibit design patterns "substantially likely to create compulsive usage patterns" across all electronic devices and services.

---

[38] Yuste, Rafael, Jared Genser, and Sara Herrmann, "It's Time for Neuro-Rights: New Human Rights for the Age of Neurotechnology," 'Horizons: Journal of International Relations and Sustainable Development' 18 (2021): 154–164.

[39] Harris, "How Technology Is Hijacking Your Mind" (2016).

[40] Twenge and Campbell, "Associations Between Screen Time and Lower Psychological Well-Being" (2018).

[41] California Age-Appropriate Design Code Act, Cal. Civ. Code § 1798.99.31 (2022).

[42] Federal Trade Commission, "Bringing Dark Patterns to Light: An FTC Staff Report" (2022), 8–24.

9.7 Toward Cognitive Liberty in the Algorithmic Age

As AI systems increasingly influence, monitor, and potentially manipulate cognitive processes, protecting mental autonomy becomes essential for meaningful liberty in all dimensions. Several principles emerge: mental privacy requires protection beyond traditional information privacy frameworks; protection against manipulation requires addressing exploitation of psychological vulnerabilities; attentional autonomy deserves protection as precondition for meaningful liberty; neuroethical frameworks must address both current and anticipated capabilities.

The concept of cognitive liberty unifies these concerns, recognizing that meaningful freedom requires protection not merely for external action but for the mental processes underlying all human choice and identity. As legal scholar Nita Farahany argues, "cognitive liberty is the principle that individuals should have the freedom to control their own cognitive processes."[43]

For democratic societies, cognitive liberty serves both individual and collective interests. Individually, mental autonomy represents the most intimate sphere of self-determination. Collectively, democratic governance presupposes citizens capable of independent judgment formation, attention allocation according to civic priorities, and thought processes relatively free from hidden manipulation.

References

Cases

'Carpenter v. United States', 138 S. Ct. 2206 (2018)
'Griswold v. Connecticut', 381 US 479 (1965)
'Lawrence v. Texas', 539 U.S. 558 (2003)
'Palko v. Connecticut', 302 US 319 (1937)
'Riley v. California', 573 U.S. 373 (2014)
'Stanley v. Georgia', 394 US 557 (1969)
'United States v. Jones', 565 U.S. 400 (2012)

Books

Alter A (2017) Irresistible: the rise of addictive technology and the business of keeping us hooked. Penguin Press

Arendt H (1958) The human condition. University of Chicago Press

Benkler Y, Faris R, Roberts H (2018) Network propaganda: manipulation, disinformation, and radicalization in American politics. Oxford University Press

Farahany NA (2023) The Battle for your brain: defending the right to think freely in the age of Neurotechnology. Martin's Press, St

[43] Farahany, 'The Battle for Your Brain' (2023), 15.

Habermas J (1991) The structural transformation of the public sphere: an inquiry into a category of bourgeois society. MIT Press
Pariser E (2011) The filter bubble: what the internet is hiding from you. Penguin Press
Persily N, Tucker JA (eds) (2020) Social media and democracy: the state of the field, prospects for reform. Cambridge University Press
Turkle S (2015) Reclaiming conversation: the power of talk in a digital age. Penguin Press
Tufekci Z (2018) Twitter and tear gas: the power and fragility of networked protest. Yale University Press
Wu T (2016) The attention merchants: the epic scramble to get inside our heads. Knopf, Alfred A
Wylie C (2019) Mindf*ck: Cambridge analytica and the plot to break America. Random House
Zuboff S (2019) The age of surveillance capitalism: the fight for a human future at the new frontier of power. PublicAffairs

Chapter 10
Democratic Oversight of AI Systems

10.1 Algorithmic Impact Assessments

Modeled on environmental impact statements, algorithmic impact assessments provide a mechanism for anticipatory governance of AI deployments. These structured evaluation processes aim to identify and mitigate potential harms before system deployment, creating accountability mechanisms proportional to risk level.

The legal basis for algorithmic impact assessments derives from several sources. The National Environmental Policy Act (NEPA) of 1969 provides an important precedent by requiring federal agencies to assess environmental impacts of proposed actions before implementation. This model demonstrates how impact assessment requirements can create procedural safeguards against harmful outcomes while preserving agency discretion in substantive decisions.

Administrative law principles provide additional foundations through requirements for reasoned decision-making under the Administrative Procedure Act. The Supreme Court's decision in 'Motor Vehicle Manufacturers Association v. State Farm Mutual Automobile Insurance Co.' established that agencies must "examine the relevant data and articulate a satisfactory explanation" for their decisions.[1] AIAs operationalize this requirement in algorithmic contexts by mandating structured consideration of potential impacts before deployment.

Constitutional due process principles provide further support when algorithmic systems affect significant individual interests. In 'Mathews v. Eldridge', the Supreme Court established that procedural adequacy depends on balancing private interests, error risks, and governmental burdens.[2] AIAs address this balancing by requiring greater procedural safeguards for systems with higher potential impacts on individual rights.

[1] 'Motor Vehicle Manufacturers Association v. State Farm Mutual Automobile Insurance Co.', 463 U.S. 29, 43 (1983).

[2] 'Mathews v. Eldridge', 424 U.S. 319, 335 (1976).

R. Yadav-Ranjan, *Constitutional Democracy in the Algorithmic Age*, Law, Governance and Technology Series 83, https://doi.org/10.1007/978-3-032-34604-9_10

Several jurisdictional approaches demonstrate AIA implementation models. The Canadian Algorithmic Impact Assessment framework, launched in 2019, requires all federal agencies to complete standardized assessments including system purpose, data sources, human involvement, and risk mitigation strategies.[3] Systems receive risk scores determining oversight requirements, with higher-risk applications facing more stringent evaluation and transparency obligations.

New York City's automated decision systems law (Local Law 49) established an ADS Task Force to develop impact assessment procedures for city agency algorithms.[4] While implementation has faced challenges including agency resistance and definitional ambiguities, the framework demonstrates municipal-level approaches to algorithmic governance.

Figure 10.1 maps the comprehensive steps required for meaningful algorithmic impact assessment, from initial scoping through deployment monitoring, showing decision points and feedback loops.

The European Union's AI Act would require conformity assessments for high-risk AI systems before market placement, including evaluation of data governance, transparency, human oversight, and accuracy.[5] This approach extends beyond governmental systems to include private-sector applications affecting fundamental rights.

Effective AIA implementation faces several institutional design challenges. First, timing considerations affect assessment efficacy. Assessments conducted too early in development may lack specific details necessary for meaningful evaluation, while those conducted too late may face practical constraints on meaningful modifications.

Second, expertise requirements create capacity challenges. Meaningful assessment requires both technical understanding of algorithmic systems and domain knowledge about deployment contexts. Third, agency incentives potentially undermine assessment rigor when the same entity both conducts assessments and benefits from system deployment.

Fourth, feedback incorporation mechanisms determine whether assessment findings meaningfully affect system design and deployment. Clear requirements for addressing identified risks help ensure that assessments influence outcomes rather than merely creating procedural hurdles without substantive impact.

10.1.1 Power Dynamics in Impact Assessment Frameworks

Algorithmic impact assessment requirements appear to establish democratic oversight over AI deployments. However, implementation reveals systematic patterns

---

[3] Government of Canada, Treasury Board Secretariat, "Directive on Automated Decision-Making" (2019).

[4] New York City, Local Law 49 of 2018, "Automated Decision Systems Used by Agencies."

[5] European Union Artificial Intelligence Act, Regulation (EU) 2024/1689, arts. 43–51 (2024).

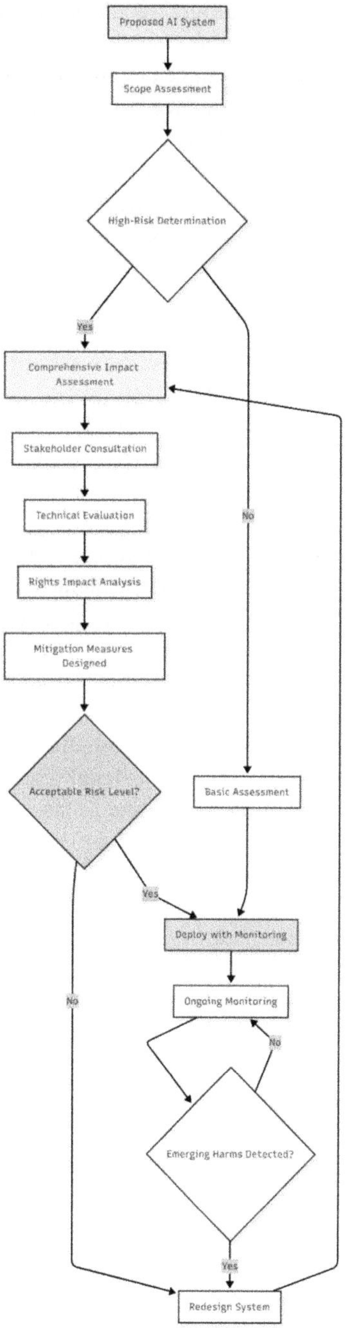

Fig. 10.1 This process flowchart maps the comprehensive steps required for meaningful algorithmic impact assessment, from initial scoping through deployment monitoring, showing decision points and feedback loops

where procedural requirements create appearance of accountability while preserving corporate autonomy over substantive decisions.

The challenge begins with who controls assessment processes. When developers conduct their own impact assessments subject to later review, the structural incentive is to frame assessments favorably. Research by Raji et al. on "Closing the AI Accountability Gap" documents systematic patterns where self-assessments identify minimal risks and propose inadequate mitigations.[6]

Where developers conduct their own conformity assessments, the structural incentive is to understate risk, a pattern independent audits have repeatedly documented.[7] More troubling, external audits have repeatedly surfaced risks that developers' own assessments failed to catch.

This pattern reflects rational behavior within current institutional structures. Developers face commercial pressures to minimize deployment delays and avoid costly design modifications. Assessment frameworks impose procedural requirements but rarely provide resources, expertise, or authority for genuinely independent evaluation before deployment.

Technical complexity compounds this dynamic. Meaningful impact assessment requires sophisticated understanding of both algorithmic systems and deployment contexts. When assessments use technical language and assume specialized knowledge, they effectively exclude public participation despite formal comment periods. Research by Katell et al. documents that public comment processes for algorithmic systems receive substantially less participation than comparable regulatory processes, with comments disproportionately coming from industry stakeholders rather than affected communities.[8]

The result is what legal scholar Frank Pasquale terms "black box society", procedural frameworks that create appearance of oversight while preserving opacity in practice. Impact assessments become compliance exercises rather than genuine evaluation mechanisms.

Regulatory capture dynamics further undermine assessment effectiveness. As documented in the revolving door between technology companies and regulatory positions, expertise concentration in private sector creates systematic influence over assessment frameworks. Former industry executives design assessment requirements. Industry-funded research establishes evaluation methodologies. Industry advisory committees shape implementation standards.

The outcome privileges industry interests systematically. Assessment frameworks require disclosure of information companies willingly provide while exempting disclosure companies resist. Requirements mandate processes companies already

[6] Raji, Inioluwa Deborah, et al., "Closing the AI Accountability Gap: Defining an End-to-End Framework for Internal Algorithmic Auditing," 'Proceedings of the 2020 Conference on Fairness, Accountability, and Transparency' (2020): 33–44.

[7] Raji et al. 'Closing the AI Accountability Gap' (2020); see also Costanza-Chock, Raji & Buolamwini, 'Who Audits the Auditors?' (2022).

[8] Katell, Michael, et al., "Toward Situated Interventions for Algorithmic Equity: Lessons from the Field," 'Proceedings of the 2020 Conference on Fairness, Accountability, and Transparency' (2020): 45–55.

conduct while avoiding processes that would impose genuine constraints. Enforcement mechanisms create minor penalties for violations while preserving core business models.

New York City's ADS Task Force implementation illustrates this dynamic. Despite statutory requirements for algorithmic transparency and public participation, implementation faced years of delays, definitional disputes limiting coverage, and resistance from agencies deploying systems.[9] When the Task Force finally issued recommendations in 2019, implementation authority remained unclear and enforcement mechanisms remained undefined.

Weak impact assessment serves technology companies: they preserve development autonomy while satisfying political demands for oversight. Government agencies deploying algorithmic systems avoid implementation delays and costly modifications. Regulators demonstrate responsiveness to oversight concerns without confronting powerful industry interests.

Who loses? Affected communities lack meaningful influence over systems governing their lives. Researchers struggle to access information necessary for independent evaluation. Advocates face procedural barriers preventing effective participation. Democratic oversight becomes theater rather than substance.

10.2 Participatory Design and Community Input

"Who gets a voice in the machines that shape our lives?" That's not just a philosophical question. It's a constitutional one. And increasingly, it's a question of organizational power.

Technical design choices are not neutral. Each line of code, each dataset selected, each threshold set in an AI model encodes a judgment, a value decision with real consequences for people's rights, opportunities, and access. These aren't just engineering choices; they're governance decisions made under the radar, often without the knowledge or consent of those most affected.

Traditional democratic governance is poorly equipped for this. Not because the values are wrong, but because the infrastructure, legal, institutional, procedural, is too slow, opaque, and exclusionary to keep up with the pace and complexity of algorithmic power.

Beyond expert-driven impact assessments, participatory design approaches attempt to incorporate affected communities directly in algorithmic system development and deployment decisions. These frameworks recognize that technical expertise alone provides insufficient basis for algorithmic governance decisions involving contested values and distributional consequences.

Participatory design emerged from labor movements in Scandinavia during the 1970s, asserting workers' rights to influence technological systems affecting their

[9] New York City Automated Decision Systems Task Force, "Report to the Mayor and City Council" (2019).

working conditions.[10] Contemporary applications extend these principles to algorithmic systems, emphasizing that those subject to algorithmic governance deserve meaningful influence over system design, deployment, and oversight.

Several participatory approaches have emerged in algorithmic contexts. Community advisory boards provide ongoing input to system developers from representatives of affected populations. Deliberative forums create structured opportunities for community members to learn about proposed systems, discuss concerns, and influence deployment decisions. Co-design processes involve community members directly in system development alongside technical specialists.

The Algorithmic Justice League's work with affected communities exemplifies participatory approaches. Rather than relying solely on technical audit, the organization facilitates community-led evaluation of algorithmic systems, centering lived experience of discrimination and harm.[11] This approach recognizes that communities experiencing algorithmic impacts possess essential knowledge about system effects that technical evaluation alone cannot capture.

However, participatory design faces significant implementation challenges. First, representation questions arise: who legitimately speaks for affected communities? When communities are diverse with potentially conflicting interests, mechanisms for ensuring inclusive participation become critical. Second, resource constraints limit many communities' capacity for sustained engagement with technical systems. Third, power imbalances affect participation dynamics when community members engage with well-resourced developers and institutional stakeholders.

The most fundamental challenge involves authority. Participation without decision-making power becomes consultation theater, collecting input that developers may ignore without consequence. Genuine participation requires binding authority over consequential decisions, not merely advisory opportunities that preserve developer autonomy.

10.2.1 The Illusion of Participation

First, **technical complexity becomes a barrier to entry**. We've built a system where effective participation requires not just legal standing or public will, but deep technical literacy. Most citizens, and frankly, most lawmakers, don't have a PhD in machine learning. Yet the decisions being made by these systems touch everything from credit access and bail to social benefits and housing. Without interpretability, participation becomes theater.

Second, **opacity breeds exclusion**. Proprietary development pipelines, protected under trade secret laws and commercial confidentiality, shield algorithmic systems from democratic scrutiny. Citizens don't get to see the training data that bakes in

[10] Ehn, Pelle, 'Work-Oriented Design of Computer Artifacts'. Arbetslivscentrum (1988).

[11] Buolamwini, Joy, "Unmasking AI: My Mission to Protect What Is Human in an Age of Machines," 'Random House' (2023).

historical bias, or the risk scores that determine whether they get a loan or land in jail. This is governance by black box, a form of institutional disempowerment.

Third, **speed undermines deliberation**. AI systems are deployed faster than governments can legislate. By the time policymakers catch up, the system is live, the damage is done, and the public outrage becomes retrospective outrage, too late to prevent harm, just early enough to clean up the mess.

And yet, there is hope. Not in returning to old models of participation, but in evolving democratic engagement for the algorithmic age.

Corporate adoption of participatory rhetoric often masks preservation of unilateral control. When companies announce "community advisory boards" or "ethics committees," these frequently function as legitimation mechanisms rather than genuine governance structures.

Research by Greene et al. on "Better, Nicer, Clearer, Fairer: A Critical Assessment of the Movement for Ethical AI" documents how participatory initiatives often lack authority over consequential decisions.[12] Advisory boards may recommend against deployment, but companies retain final authority and frequently deploy systems despite objections. Ethics committees may identify concerning practices, but lack enforcement authority to prevent them.

The pattern is systematic: solicit input, acknowledge concerns, deploy anyway. Participation becomes performance, demonstrating stakeholder engagement without ceding control. As documented in analyses of "ethics washing," participatory processes often serve primarily to deflect criticism rather than enable genuine community influence.

Google's Advanced Technology External Advisory Council exemplifies this dynamic. Formed in 2019 with significant fanfare about incorporating diverse perspectives into AI development, the council dissolved within days due to internal conflicts.[13] The council lacked clear authority, adequate resources, and institutional support necessary for meaningful influence. Its rapid collapse revealed participatory governance as aspirational rhetoric rather than operational reality.

Figure 10.2 contrasts genuine participatory design with tokenistic consultation, showing how superficial engagement preserves rather than challenges algorithmic power.

The fundamental barrier is structural. Meaningful participation requires sharing power. Corporations exist to maximize shareholder value, not to subordinate business decisions to community preferences. When participation threatens profitability, business imperatives predictably prevail over participatory ideals.

This structural tension means that voluntary corporate participation initiatives systematically exclude the most consequential decisions. Companies invite participation on questions where community input aligns with business interests, design aesthetics, user interface preferences, peripheral features. They exclude participation

[12] Greene, Daniel, et al., "Better, Nicer, Clearer, Fairer: A Critical Assessment of the Movement for Ethical AI," 'Proceedings of the 52nd Hawaii International Conference on System Sciences' (2019).

[13] "Google Cancels A.I. Ethics Board," New York Times (April 2019).

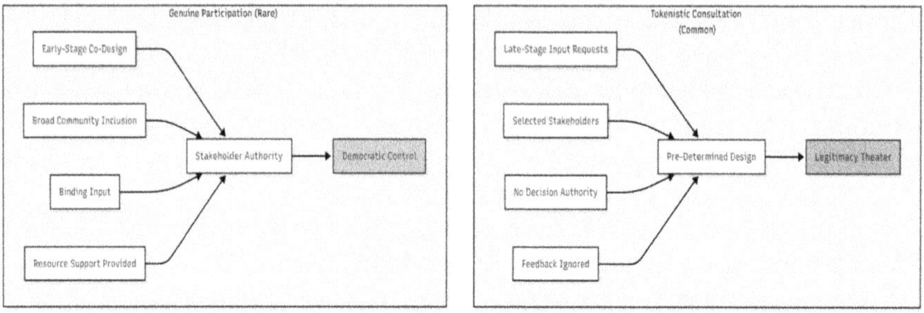

Fig. 10.2 This comparison diagram contrasts genuine participatory design with tokenistic consultation, showing how superficial engagement preserves rather than challenges algorithmic power

on foundational questions threatening business models, data collection practices, algorithmic optimization objectives, deployment contexts.

Regulatory requirements for participation face similar dynamics. Requirements for "public comment" or "stakeholder engagement" become procedural checkboxes satisfied through minimal compliance. Post lengthy technical documents with short comment periods. Hold meetings at inconvenient times and inaccessible locations. Collect input and proceed with predetermined decisions. The form of participation exists without the substance. These democratic deficits implicate constitutional principles directly.

10.2.2 Reclaiming Power: Participatory and Deliberative Mechanisms

Participation is not a feel-good checkbox. It is a **constitutional imperative** and a **governance strategy**.

- **First Amendment rights**, to petition, assemble, speak, demand real opportunities for citizens to shape the digital architectures governing their lives. As the Court noted, the right to petition ensures people can express "ideas, hopes, and concerns to their government."
- **Due Process** under the Fifth and Fourteenth Amendments requires meaningful hearings when rights are at stake. If an AI system can deny you benefits, freedom, or opportunities, then it must afford you not just post-hoc review, but participatory design inclusion, *before* the harm is done.
- **Equal Protection** requires that communities disproportionately affected, often marginalized and under-resourced, are not merely invited to the table, but given power to shape outcomes. This is not charity. It is equity. And it's legally and morally essential.

So how do we operationalize this?

1. **Algorithmic Registries**. Amsterdam's Algorithm Register is more than symbolic. It is an institutional act of self-discipline. By requiring agencies to document algorithms, their purpose, data sources, risks, and human oversight, it gives civil society the visibility needed for oversight. Visibility creates leverage. That is governance power.
2. **Participatory Sensing**. Consider the Environmental Data Justice movement. When communities collect their own environmental data to contest flawed government models, they do not just participate, they disrupt power asymmetries. This is grassroots technopolitics, and it is deeply democratic.

10.3 Regulatory Institutions and Oversight Frameworks

Effective governance of algorithmic systems requires institutional frameworks providing sustained oversight beyond individual impact assessments or participation processes. Several regulatory models have emerged, each presenting distinct advantages and limitations:

Sector-specific regulation extends existing regulatory frameworks to algorithmic applications within particular domains.[14] Banking algorithms face scrutiny from banking regulators, healthcare algorithms from medical authorities, and employment algorithms from labor agencies. This approach leverages domain expertise and established regulatory frameworks but potentially creates inconsistent standards across sectors and oversight gaps for cross-domain applications.

Dedicated algorithmic regulators establish specialized agencies focusing specifically on algorithmic applications across domains.[15] The United Kingdom's Centre for Data Ethics and Innovation represents a partial implementation of this approach through its cross-sectoral advisory functions, though with limited direct regulatory authority. This model provides consistent cross-domain oversight but potentially lacks domain-specific expertise.

Hybrid oversight frameworks combine sector-specific implementation with cross-sectoral coordination mechanisms.[16] The EU's AI Act would establish a European Artificial Intelligence Board coordinating implementation across national authorities while leveraging sector-specific regulators for domain expertise. This approach attempts to balance consistent standards with domain-specific implementation.

Third-party certification systems delegate evaluation to accredited non-governmental entities that assess compliance with established standards.[17] This approach parallels certification frameworks for electrical safety or organic food production, providing specialized assessment while reducing direct governmental burden.

---

[14] Food and Drug Administration, "Software as a Medical Device (SaMD): Clinical Evaluation Guidance" (2017).

[15] UK Centre for Data Ethics and Innovation, "Annual Report 2023" (2023).

[16] EU Artificial Intelligence Acticle 65 (establishing European Artificial Intelligence Board) (2024).

[17] IEEE, "Ethics Certification Program for Autonomous and Intelligent Systems (ECPAIS)" (2020).

Effective regulatory frameworks face several institutional design challenges. First, expertise requirements create significant capability demands for oversight bodies. Second, information access significantly affects oversight effectiveness, when algorithmic systems operate as proprietary "black boxes," regulators face substantial barriers to meaningful evaluation.

Third, enforcement effectiveness depends on both authority and incentives. Fourth, capture risks threaten oversight effectiveness when regulatory entities become dominated by regulated industry interests.[18] This challenge affects algorithmic oversight particularly acutely due to expertise concentration in regulated entities and substantial information asymmetries.

10.4 Regulatory Capture in Algorithmic Governance

Regulatory capture, where regulatory agencies serve regulated industry interests rather than public welfare, affects algorithmic oversight with particular intensity. The dynamics are predictable and well-documented.

First, expertise concentration creates dependence. Meaningful algorithmic oversight requires specialized technical knowledge. This expertise resides primarily in companies developing algorithmic systems. Regulatory agencies face systematic recruitment challenges, unable to match private sector compensation for scarce technical talent. The result is regulatory agencies staffed by individuals without adequate expertise or staffed by individuals planning eventual private sector employment.

The revolving door between technology companies and regulatory positions creates systematic conflicts. Former industry executives design regulatory frameworks. Regulators anticipating future industry employment shape rules favorably to potential employers. Industry-funded research dominates policy discourse. The boundaries between regulator and regulated blur.

Second, information asymmetries empower regulated entities. Companies possess detailed knowledge of system operation, training data, deployment contexts, and performance characteristics. Regulators lack comparable information access despite formal authority. Companies strategically disclose favorable information while protecting unfavorable details through intellectual property claims and commercial confidentiality.

This information asymmetry creates systematic advantage. Companies frame regulatory debates, define technical standards, establish evaluation methodologies. Regulators respond reactively to information companies provide rather than independently assessing systems.

Third, resource asymmetries affect enforcement. Technology companies employ armies of lawyers, compliance specialists, and lobbyists. Regulatory agencies operate under resource constraints with small staffs covering expansive mandates.

[18] Dal Bó, Ernesto, "Regulatory Capture: A Review," 'Oxford Review of Economic Policy' 22, no. 2 (2006): 203–225.

When enforcement requires complex technical analysis, extended investigations, and sustained litigation, resource limitations constrain regulatory effectiveness regardless of formal authority.

Fourth, political economy creates capture incentives. Technology industry political contributions shape legislative priorities. Industry lobbying influences regulatory appointments. Media narratives about innovation and economic growth create political pressure favoring light-touch regulation. Politicians understand that aggressive regulation threatens politically influential industry while diffuse benefits to public register weakly politically.

The Federal Trade Commission's history with technology regulation illustrates these dynamics. Despite broad authority over "unfair or deceptive practices," the FTC has historically pursued limited enforcement against major technology companies relative to documented harms. When enforcement occurs, settlements often impose minimal penalties and allow continued problematic practices. Companies treat FTC actions as cost of business rather than meaningful constraint.

Figure 10.3 illustrates how regulatory capture operates as a self-reinforcing cycle, beginning with industry lobbying and culminating in increased resources that enable further lobbying.

More fundamentally, regulatory capture affects not just enforcement but framework design. Industry influence shapes what gets regulated, how regulation occurs, what standards apply, what information must be disclosed, what penalties attach to violations. The result is regulatory frameworks that appear comprehensive while preserving industry autonomy on consequential matters.

Who benefits from regulatory capture? Technology companies face oversight frameworks that legitimate their practices while imposing minimal constraints on profitable activities. Regulators demonstrate responsiveness to public concern without confronting powerful industry interests. Politicians claim credit for oversight without alienating economically significant constituents.

Who loses? Public welfare suffers when regulatory frameworks serve industry interests. Affected communities lack effective protection against algorithmic harms. Democratic governance is subordinated to technical systems beyond effective public control.

10.5 Balancing Democratic Oversight and Innovation

The claimed tension between democratic oversight and technological innovation functions primarily as ideological justification for preserving corporate autonomy. While genuine tradeoffs exist, the framing systematically overstates innovation costs and understates oversight benefits.

Industry arguments follow predictable patterns: regulation will stifle innovation, drive development overseas, impose compliance burdens that disadvantage startups, lock in current approaches preventing improvement. These claims treat any constraint

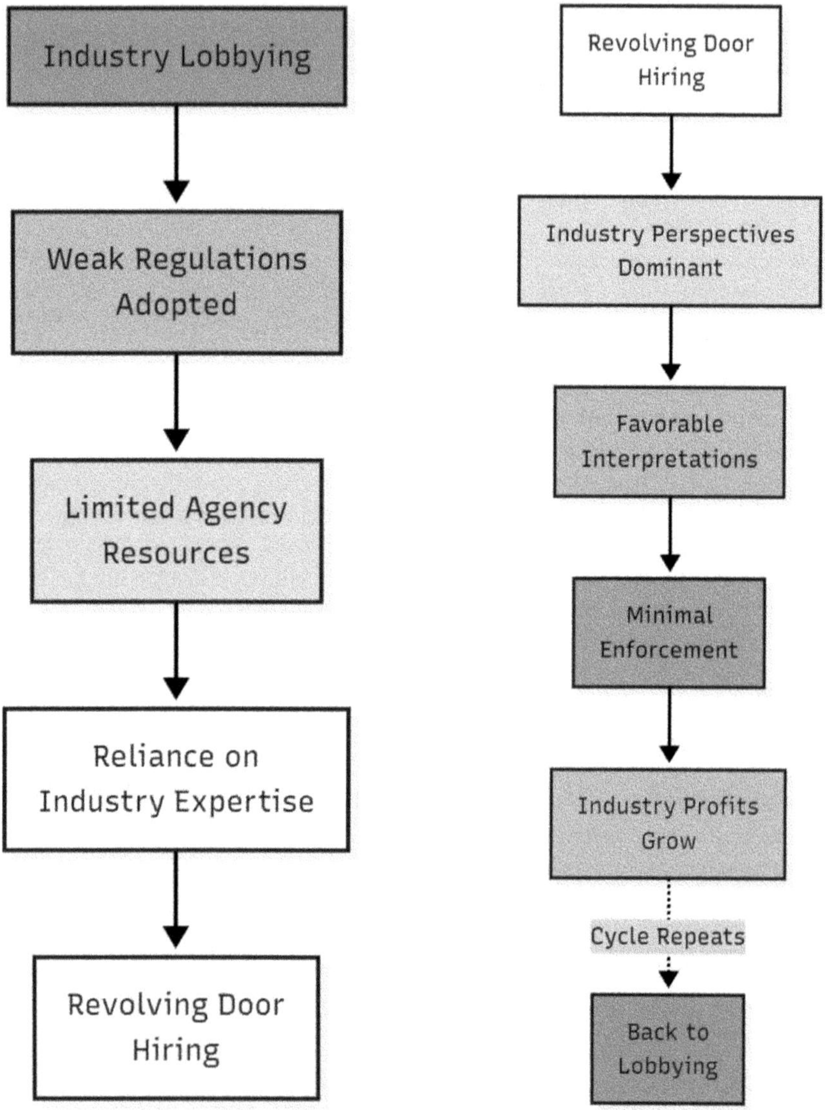

Fig. 10.3 This two-part diagram illustrates how regulatory capture operates as a self-reinforcing cycle, beginning with industry lobbying and culminating in increased resources that enable further lobbying

on corporate autonomy as threatening innovation, defining "innovation" as whatever companies want to do.

However, evidence for claimed innovation harms remains limited. The EU's GDPR, predicted to devastate European technology sectors, has not prevented continued digital innovation. California's CCPA, warned to impose crushing burdens, coexists with continued technological development. Jurisdictions with stronger algorithmic oversight have not experienced systematic innovation disadvantage relative to those with minimal regulation.

More fundamentally, the innovation framing obscures whose innovation matters. From corporate perspective, "innovation" means profitable product development. From public perspective, innovation should mean technological development serving human welfare. These objectives align imperfectly.

Many algorithmic "innovations" from public welfare perspective are harmful: systems optimized for addiction, engagement maximization at expense of wellbeing, discrimination at scale, manipulation of vulnerable populations, erosion of privacy and autonomy. Preventing such "innovation" through democratic oversight serves rather than undermines public interest.

The genuine challenge involves designing oversight frameworks that prevent harmful deployments while enabling beneficial applications. This requires moving beyond false dichotomy between innovation and oversight toward recognition that effective oversight enables beneficial innovation by building public trust and preventing harmful applications that invite reactive regulatory backlash.

Several principles emerge for effective balancing. First, risk-calibrated approaches adjust oversight intensity to potential harm severity.[19] Rather than treating all algorithmic systems identically, graduated frameworks require greater scrutiny for applications affecting fundamental rights, vulnerable populations, or irreversible decisions.

Second, procedural regularity provides essential safeguards regardless of substantive requirements.[20] Even when direct regulation proves challenging due to rapid technological change, procedural requirements including impact assessment, participation opportunities, and transparency obligations create accountability mechanisms while preserving implementation flexibility.

Third, institutional capacity significantly affects oversight effectiveness regardless of formal authority.[21] Even well-designed regulatory frameworks prove ineffective without sufficient expertise, resources, and authority for implementation.

---

[19] EU Artificial Intelligence Act, Annex III (defining high-risk AI systems) (2024).

[20] Administrative Procedure Act, 5 U.S.C. § 553 (notice-and-comment rulemaking procedures).

[21] Kaminski, Margot E., "Binary Governance: Lessons from the GDPR's Approach to Algorithmic Accountability," 'Southern California Law Review' 92 (2019): 1529–1616.

Fourth, democratic participation provides both instrumental and intrinsic benefits for algorithmic governance.[22] Instrumentally, diverse participation improves oversight by incorporating perspectives beyond technical specialists. Intrinsically, participation opportunities respect democratic principles requiring that those affected by governance decisions have meaningful opportunities to influence those decisions.

The fundamental question facing algorithmic governance remains who decides, not merely technical implementation details but foundational questions about what values systems should prioritize, what tradeoffs they should make, and what societal objectives they should serve. When algorithms increasingly determine who receives opportunities, resources, and constraints, these determinations become governance decisions properly subject to democratic oversight rather than merely technical optimizations.

For citizens, effective governance frameworks provide essential safeguards against algorithmic systems that might otherwise operate beyond meaningful democratic control despite profound social impacts. By establishing mechanisms for anticipatory assessment, participatory design, and ongoing oversight, these frameworks operationalize constitutional commitments to democratic self-governance in increasingly algorithmic contexts.

10.6 What you Can Do Now

Establishing genuine democratic oversight of algorithmic systems requires sustained political organizing, not merely procedural participation. Here are concrete strategies:

Demand Genuine Participation Authority

1. Distinguish Advisory from Binding Authority: When organizations announce "community advisory boards" or "ethics committees," demand answers: What decision authority does this body have? Can it block deployments? Override management decisions? Or merely advise?
2. Advocate for Community Veto Rights: Support legislation granting affected communities binding authority to reject algorithmic deployments affecting their rights, opportunities, or resources. This means actual decision power, not consultation theater.
3. Organize Community Technology Councils: Build independent community organizations that develop technological literacy, conduct community-led impact assessments, and coordinate collective responses to algorithmic deployments. These councils should be community-controlled, not company-sponsored.
4. Demand Resource Equity: Genuine participation requires resources. Advocate for requirements that companies fund independent technical assistance

[22] Arendt, 'The Human Condition' (1958), 175–247.

for communities evaluating their systems. This means paying for community-controlled expertise, not company-selected consultants.

Challenge Regulatory Capture

1. Document Revolving Door: Track movement between technology companies and regulatory positions. Build public databases showing former industry executives' roles in shaping oversight frameworks. Make regulatory capture visible.
2. Demand Conflict of Interest Rules: Support legislation prohibiting regulators from accepting technology industry employment within five years of leaving regulatory positions. Prohibit industry-funded research from dominating regulatory proceedings.
3. Advocate for Independent Expertise: Support public investment in regulatory capacity development: university programs training regulatory experts, government-funded research independent from industry, technical assistance programs for community organizations.
4. Challenge Industry-Funded Research: When regulatory proceedings cite industry-funded studies, file comments challenging methodology, demanding disclosure of funding sources, requesting independent replication. Make evidence quality a political issue.
5. Support Whistleblower Protections: Technology workers possess critical inside knowledge of algorithmic harms. Support strong whistleblower protections enabling disclosure without retaliation.

Build Counter-Expertise

1. Support Community Technology Audits: Organizations like Algorithmic Justice League, AI Now Institute, and Data & Society conduct independent algorithmic audits. Support their work financially and politically. Demand that regulatory frameworks incorporate community-led audit findings.
2. Develop Alternative Assessment Frameworks: Don't accept industry-designed impact assessment templates. Community organizations should develop alternative assessment frameworks centering affected community concerns rather than developer convenience.
3. Create Public Algorithm Registries: Advocate for public databases cataloging algorithmic system deployments, identified harms, community concerns, and company responses. Build institutional memory preventing companies from repeating debunked claims.
4. Establish Community Review Boards: In local jurisdictions, organize to establish community review boards with binding authority over government algorithmic deployments affecting residents.

Demand Meaningful Transparency

1. Reject Selective Disclosure: Companies offer to disclose information they control. Demand disclosure of information they resist: training data, validation methodologies, error rates by demographic group, internal communications about known problems, financial incentives affecting design choices.
2. Support Right to Independent Audit: Advocate for legal rights enabling affected communities and independent researchers to audit algorithmic systems without permission from developers. This includes access to training data, model specifications, and deployment contexts.
3. Challenge Intellectual Property Claims: When companies hide algorithmic systems behind intellectual property protection, challenge whether trade secret protection legitimately applies to systems affecting fundamental rights. Support exceptions to IP protection for civil rights enforcement.
4. Demand Incident Reporting: Support requirements for mandatory reporting of algorithmic failures, discriminatory outcomes, security breaches, and manipulation incidents. Build public databases making patterns visible.

Support Structural Reforms

1. Advocate for Public Algorithmic Options: For essential services, support public sector development of algorithmic systems as alternative to corporate surveillance capitalism. This means adequately funded government capacity to build systems serving public interest.
2. Support Platform Cooperatives: Advocate for worker- and user-owned platforms as alternative to shareholder-controlled corporations. Support cooperative alternatives to Facebook, YouTube, Uber, and other platforms.
3. Demand Algorithm Auditor General: Support creation of independent "Algorithm Auditor General" offices with authority, expertise, and resources to conduct proactive audits of public and private algorithmic systems affecting rights and opportunities.
4. Support Algorithmic Public Defenders: Just as public defenders protect constitutional rights in criminal justice, algorithmic public defenders should provide representation for individuals contesting algorithmic decisions affecting benefits, employment, housing, credit, education.

Connect Struggles

Algorithmic oversight connects to multiple movements:

- Labor Rights: Algorithmic management systems are labor issue. Technology worker organizing against complicity in harmful systems creates leverage. Connect with tech workers unions.
- Racial Justice: Algorithmic systems perpetuate and amplify racial discrimination. Connect with racial justice organizations documenting algorithmic harms and developing alternative frameworks centering civil rights.

- Housing Justice: Algorithmic systems affect housing access, eviction proceedings, and neighborhood resource allocation. Connect with housing justice movements fighting algorithmic land-lording and discriminatory allocation systems.
- Education Justice: Algorithmic systems increasingly govern educational opportunity. Connect with education justice movements challenging algorithmic tracking, automated discipline, and surveillance of students.
- Consumer Protection: Predatory algorithmic systems target vulnerable consumers. Connect with consumer advocacy organizations developing stronger protection frameworks.
- Environmental Justice: The physical infrastructure of AI systems has environmental costs disproportionately affecting marginalized communities. Connect environmental and algorithmic justice organizing.

These are not separate struggles but interconnected fights against concentrated corporate and governmental power operating through technical systems.

The Fundamental Challenge

Democratic oversight of algorithmic systems ultimately requires political power. Procedural frameworks, participation requirements, and transparency mandates all fail without organized political force backing them. Companies comply with requirements they cannot avoid, resist requirements they can evade.

This means the challenge is not primarily technical but political: building sufficient organized power to force genuine democratic control over systems governing our lives. This requires sustained organizing, coalition building across movements, political education about technological power, and strategic campaigns forcing concrete changes.

The goal is not better corporate self-regulation or friendlier technology companies. The goal is democratic control, genuine authority by affected communities over systems affecting their opportunities, resources, and lives. This will not be achieved through consultation processes or advisory committees. It requires building political power sufficient to force structural change.

As Langdon Winner famously argued, *artifacts have politics.* And AI systems are among the most consequential artifacts of our era. They make decisions, enforce norms, and mediate rights. That makes them, inevitably, *governance systems.*

The question is: who governs them? In my view, participatory and deliberative models of AI governance are not idealistic luxuries. They are strategic necessities, legally anchored, democratically essential, and institutionally transformative.

In the algorithmic era, democratic legitimacy will depend not just on the fairness of outcomes, but on the legitimacy of the process that created them. Participation, if designed well, is not a concession. It is the foundation.[23]

---

[23] Winner, Langdon, "Do Artifacts Have Politics?", Daedalus, Vol. 109, No. 1 Modern Technology: Problem or Opportunity? (Winter, 1980), pp. 121–136.

References

Cases

'Mathews v. Eldridge', 424 US 319 (1976)
'Motor Vehicle Manufacturers Association v. State Farm Mutual Automobile Insurance Co.', 463 U.S. 29 (1983)

Books

Arendt H (1958) The human condition. University of Chicago Press
Cohen JE (2019) Between truth and power: the legal constructions of informational capitalism. Oxford University Press
Pasquale F (2015) The black box society: the secret algorithms that control money and information. Harvard University Press

Chapter 11
Remedies and Enforcement

11.1 Liability Regimes for AI Harms

When algorithmic systems cause harm, complex questions of causation and responsibility arise. Traditional liability regimes face significant challenges in algorithmic contexts. First, causation complexity creates attribution difficulties when algorithmic systems involve multiple components, developers, and operators.[1] Unlike traditional products with relatively clear causal chains, algorithmic systems often involve diffuse responsibility across data providers, algorithm developers, system integrators, and end users.

Second, foreseeability limitations challenge traditional negligence frameworks when algorithmic systems produce emergent behaviors not specifically anticipated by developers.[2] When machine learning systems identify patterns and relationships not explicitly programmed, determining whether developers should have foreseen harmful outcomes becomes increasingly difficult.

Third, technical opacity creates evidentiary barriers when algorithmic decision processes resist straightforward explanation or evaluation.[3] When "black box" systems make determinations through complex processes not easily reducible to human-comprehensible explanations, proving defects or negligence may exceed plaintiff capabilities regardless of actual responsibility.

Fourth, jurisdictional complexity arises when algorithmic systems operate across traditional boundaries. When development, deployment, and impacts occur in different jurisdictions with varying liability regimes, determining applicable law and appropriate forums becomes increasingly difficult.

Several liability approaches have emerged to address these challenges. Strict liability frameworks impose responsibility without requiring fault demonstration

---

[1] European Union AI Liability Directive (Proposed), COM(2022) 496 final (2022).

[2] Calo, Ryan. "Robotics and the New Cyberlaw." California Law Review 103, no. 3 (2015): 513–563.

[3] Burrell, Jenna, "How the Machine 'Thinks': Understanding Opacity in Machine Learning Algorithms," 'Big Data & Society' 3, no. 1 (2016).

R. Yadav-Ranjan, *Constitutional Democracy in the Algorithmic Age*, Law, Governance and Technology Series 83, https://doi.org/10.1007/978-3-032-34604-9_11

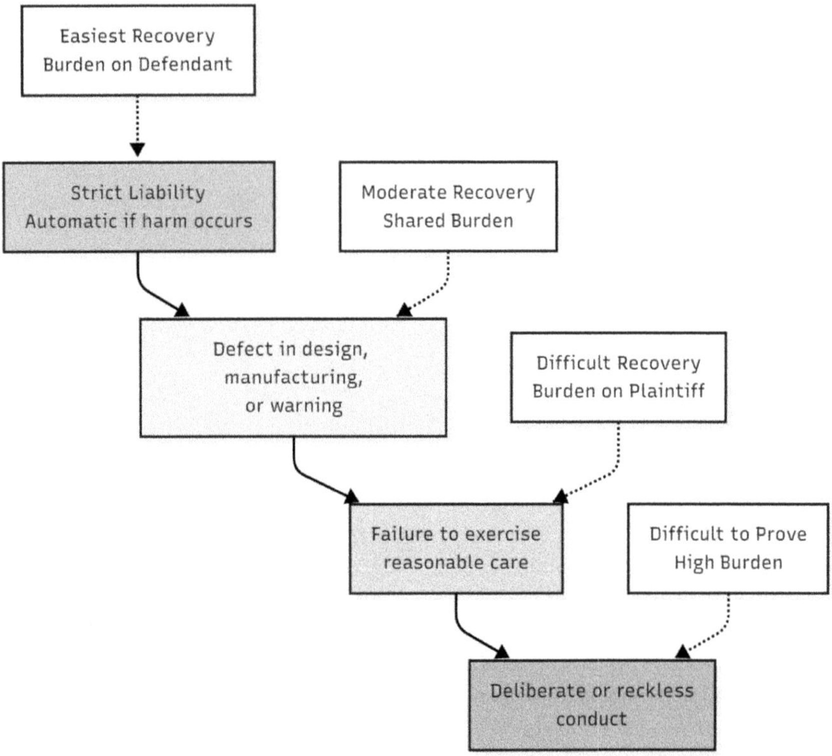

Fig. 11.1 This pyramid diagram shows the hierarchy of liability standards from negligence through strict liability, with corresponding allocation of burden and difficulty of recovery for plaintiffs.

for certain high-risk algorithmic applications.[4] The European Union's proposed AI Liability Directive would establish presumptions of causality for high-risk AI systems that fail compliance requirements, effectively creating strict liability for regulatory violations.

Joint and several liability models hold multiple entities responsible for algorithmic harms, allowing recovery from any responsible party regardless of proportional contribution.[5] The Illinois Biometric Information Privacy Act enables liability against any entity violating biometric privacy requirements, regardless of where they appear in algorithmic development or deployment chains.

Figure 11.1 shows the hierarchy of liability standards from negligence through strict liability, with corresponding allocation of burden and difficulty of recovery for plaintiffs.

---

[4] EU AI Liability Directive (Proposed), art. 4 (2022).

[5] Illinois Biometric Information Privacy Act, 740 ILCS 14/15 (2008).

Algorithmic impact insurance requirements mandate coverage for potential algorithmic harms, ensuring compensation regardless of fault determination.[6] This approach prioritizes victim compensation over fault determination, recognizing that algorithmic complexity creates inherent attribution challenges.

Regulatory enforcement approaches rely on governmental authorities rather than private litigation to address algorithmic harms.[7] The Federal Trade Commission has increasingly used Section 5 authority against "unfair or deceptive practices" to address algorithmic harms including discriminatory outcomes and privacy violations.

11.1.1 Power Dynamics in Liability Regimes

Liability frameworks appear to establish accountability for algorithmic harms. However, systematic patterns reveal how corporate power shapes liability regimes to minimize exposure while creating appearance of responsibility.

The first barrier is information asymmetry. Companies possess complete information about system design, training data, known problems, and internal discussions about risks. Plaintiffs must prove harm without access to this information. Discovery processes provide formal mechanisms for obtaining evidence, but companies resist aggressively through claims of trade secrecy, intellectual property protection, and attorney-client privilege.

Research by Pasquale documents how companies use technical complexity and confidentiality claims to prevent meaningful discovery.[8] When plaintiffs request algorithm specifications, companies provide technically accurate but deliberately incomprehensible descriptions. When plaintiffs request training data, companies claim prohibitive production costs. When plaintiffs request internal communications, companies claim privilege.

The result is structural advantage: companies know what happened but plaintiffs must prove it without access to necessary evidence. This asymmetry alone often prevents successful litigation regardless of actual responsibility.

Second, causation requirements favor defendants. Plaintiffs must demonstrate that algorithmic system specifically caused their injury. But when systems involve multiple components, probabilistic decisions, and emergent behaviors, establishing definitive causation becomes effectively impossible. Companies exploit this by emphasizing complexity: "The system involves millions of parameters, thousands of training examples, multiple processing stages, how can plaintiff prove this specific outcome resulted from any particular design choice?"

Third, foreseeability standards protect defendants. Negligence liability requires proving defendants should have anticipated potential harm. Companies argue that

[6] New York City Automated Decision Systems Task Force, "Report" (2019), 24–27.

[7] Federal Trade Commission Act, 15 U.S.C. § 45 (2018).

[8] Pasquale, 'The Black Box Society' (2015), 19–58.

machine learning systems' emergent properties make harmful outcomes unforeseeable. Courts often accept these arguments despite evidence that companies knew their systems produced discriminatory outcomes, privacy violations, or other harms.

Amazon's resume screening algorithm that discriminated against women provides illustration. Reuters investigation revealed the system systematically downgraded resumes containing words like "women's" (as in "women's chess club"). When discrimination became public, Amazon claimed the pattern was unforeseeable, an emergent property of training on historical hiring data. But internal documents showed engineers knew the system exhibited gender bias, discussed the problem, and deployed it anyway.[9]

Fourth, damages limitations restrict recovery and deterrence. Many jurisdictions cap statutory damages at levels insufficient to deter corporate misconduct or compensate genuine harm. When violations affect millions but individual damages are small, aggregate liability remains manageable business expense rather than existential threat.

Illinois BIPA illustrates this dynamic. The statute provides $1,000-$5,000 per violation, which appears substantial until recognizing that companies like Facebook, Google, and Clearview AI violated BIPA potentially billions of times. Even maximum statutory damages become acceptable business costs compared to profits from biometric data exploitation.

Fifth, arbitration clauses eliminate judicial oversight. Through mandatory arbitration provisions in terms of service, companies force disputes into private arbitration systems that systematically favor corporate defendants. Research by the Economic Policy Institute found that employees win only about 21% of the time in mandatory arbitration, compared to 36% in federal court and 57% in state court.[10]

Arbitration prevents not only individual justice but systemic accountability. Arbitration proceedings are confidential, preventing public awareness of corporate practices. Arbitration awards don't establish precedent, preventing doctrinal development. Arbitration prohibits class actions, preventing collective enforcement. The cumulative effect is practical immunity for algorithmic harms affecting millions.

Sixth, resource asymmetries render litigation impossible for most plaintiffs. Algorithmic harm litigation requires technical expertise, extensive discovery, and prolonged proceedings. Costs easily exceed hundreds of thousands of dollars. Plaintiffs' attorneys work on contingency, but will only accept cases with clear liability and substantial damages. The vast majority of algorithmic harms, affecting employment, credit, public benefits, content moderation, involve damages too small to attract representation despite clear injury.

Companies exploit this by making litigation as expensive as possible: aggressive motion practice, extensive discovery demands, expert witness battles, interlocutory

[9] Dastin, Jeffrey, "Amazon Scraps Secret AI Recruiting Tool That Showed Bias Against Women," 'Reuters' (October 10, 2018).

[10] Colvin, Alexander J. S., "The Growing Use of Mandatory Arbitration," Economic Policy Institute (2017).

appeals. The strategy isn't to win on merits but to exhaust plaintiff resources. Most cases settle for nuisance value or are abandoned despite merit.

Who benefits from liability regime weaknesses? Technology companies face minimal actual accountability despite widespread harms. Even when liability technically exists, practical barriers prevent enforcement. Insurance companies providing algorithmic impact coverage profit from premiums without facing meaningful claims. Defense law firms earn substantial fees exploiting procedural complexity.

Who loses? Injured individuals cannot obtain compensation or accountability. Communities suffering systematic discrimination cannot obtain remedies. Democratic oversight through private enforcement fails despite formal liability rules.

11.2 Standing and Collective Redress

Many algorithmic harms affect groups rather than identifiable individuals. Traditional standing requirements create significant barriers to algorithmic harm litigation. First, concrete injury requirements create barriers when algorithmic harms involve information processing rather than physical or economic damage.[11]

The Supreme Court's decision in 'TransUnion LLC v. Ramirez' emphasized that Article III standing requires "concrete harm" beyond statutory violations, creating significant barriers for privacy and discrimination claims involving algorithmic processing without demonstrable downstream consequences.[12]

Second, traceability requirements demand clear causal connections between defendant conduct and plaintiff injury. When algorithmic systems involve multiple actors and probabilistic outcomes, establishing direct causal chains becomes difficult. This traceability challenge potentially immunizes harmful algorithmic practices despite affecting numerous individuals.

Third, redressability limitations arise when remedies cannot prevent ongoing algorithmic harms or compensate past injuries. When algorithmic systems operate continuously with constantly updated data, forward-looking relief may provide limited protection. When harms involve dignity injuries or autonomy violations rather than economic losses, monetary damages may inadequately redress violations.

Several procedural mechanisms attempt to address collective algorithmic harms. Class actions enable representative litigation on behalf of similarly situated plaintiffs.[13] The Illinois BIPA litigation demonstrates class action effectiveness for privacy violations, with settlements exceeding hundreds of millions of dollars creating meaningful deterrence.

However, companies increasingly prevent class actions through mandatory arbitration clauses with class action waivers. The Supreme Court's decisions in 'AT&T

[11] 'TransUnion LLC v. Ramirez', 141 S. Ct. 2190, 2204 (2021).

[12] 'Id.' at 2208–2210.

[13] Federal Rules of Civil Procedure, Rule 23 (class actions).

Mobility LLC v. Concepcion' and 'Epic Systems Corp. v. Lewis' upheld these waivers despite concerns about preventing collective enforcement.[14]

Qui tam provisions enable private parties to enforce statutory violations on behalf of government. Several proposed algorithmic accountability acts include qui tam mechanisms, creating private attorney general authority for enforcing algorithmic governance requirements. This approach addresses standing barriers by creating explicit enforcement rights independent of individual injury.

Collective litigation funds pool resources enabling sustained challenges to well-funded corporate defendants.[15] These mechanisms address resource asymmetries that otherwise prevent effective algorithmic harm litigation despite clear violations.

11.2.1 The Standing Barrier as Corporate Shield

Standing doctrine systematically advantages corporate defendants by restricting courthouse access. The pattern is predictable: individuals suffer clear harm from algorithmic systems, file suit, and courts dismiss for lack of standing despite obvious injury.

'TransUnion' exemplifies this dynamic. Class members had false information in credit reports that could affect credit decisions. The harm seems concrete: inaccurate credit information threatens economic opportunities. But the Supreme Court held that only class members whose false information was actually disclosed to third parties had standing, class members whose false information merely existed in credit files lacked concrete injury despite identical statutory violations.

The decision's practical effect is sweeping immunity for informational harms. Companies can collect inaccurate data, process it discriminatorily, maintain it indefinitely, all without risk of liability unless plaintiffs prove the specific information was disclosed to specific third parties who made specific adverse decisions. The evidentiary burden is designed to be impossible: plaintiffs must prove counterfactuals about what would have happened with accurate information.

Figure 11.2 shows how standing requirements systematically prevent algorithmic accountability by creating procedural barriers at each stage, from injury recognition through judicial access.

Companies exploit this by fighting over standing rather than merits. Facial recognition cases illustrate the pattern: plaintiffs allege unauthorized biometric collection violating privacy statutes. Companies don't defend the collection; they argue plaintiffs lack standing because biometric information processing alone doesn't constitute concrete harm. Courts often agree, dismissing cases before reaching merits.

---

[14] 'AT&T Mobility LLC v. Concepcion', 563 U.S. 333 (2011); 'Epic Systems Corp. v. Lewis', 138 S. Ct. 1612 (2018).

[15] Hensler, Deborah R., "The Future of Mass Litigation: Global Class Actions and Third-Party Litigation Funding," 'George Washington Law Review' 79 (2011): 306-323.

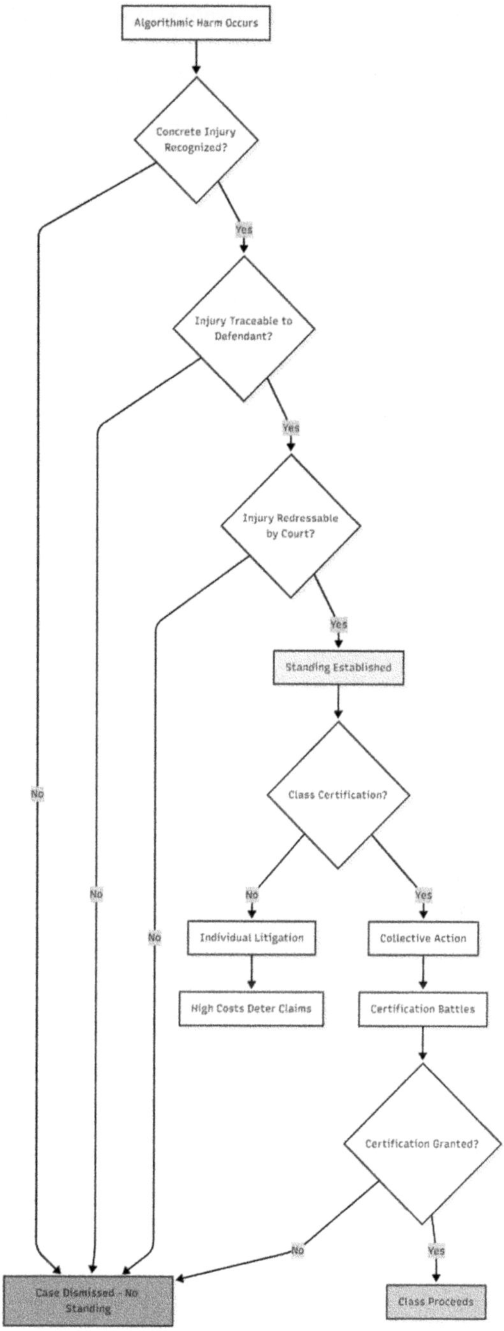

Fig. 11.2 This flow diagram shows how standing requirements systematically prevent algorithmic accountability by creating procedural barriers at each stage, from injury recognition through judicial access.

The doctrinal move is treating statutory violations as "bare procedural violations" rather than concrete injury. But this reasoning inverts statutory purpose: legislatures created statutory rights precisely because traditional common law failed to recognize certain harms as legally cognizable. Standing doctrine then reimports the same failures legislatures tried to override.

Collective redress mechanisms face similar barriers. Class certification requirements impose stringent commonality, typicality, and adequacy standards. Companies challenge certification aggressively, arguing algorithmic personalization means each class member experienced different treatment precluding common resolution. Courts sometimes agree, preventing collective proceedings despite systematic harm to large populations.

Even when classes certify, settlement dynamics undermine accountability. Companies settle for amounts that sound large ($100 million settlement!) but provide minimal individual compensation and limited structural changes. Settlement class members receive modest checks while companies continue harmful practices. Attorneys collect substantial fees while clients receive minimal benefit.

The fundamental problem is procedural rules designed for different context. Standing doctrine and class action requirements developed addressing physical torts with identifiable victims and clear causation. Algorithmic harms involve distributed injuries, probabilistic causation, and systematic but individualized treatment. Applying traditional procedural rules to algorithmic harms guarantees ineffective enforcement.

11.3 Enforcement Mechanisms and Institutional Design

Effective enforcement of algorithmic accountability requires institutional frameworks providing sustained oversight beyond individual litigation. Several enforcement models have emerged. Regulatory agency enforcement leverages specialized expertise and investigatory authority to address systematic algorithmic harms.[16] The FTC's algorithmic enforcement actions demonstrate this approach, though resource constraints limit effectiveness relative to problem scale.

Private attorney general statutes enable individual enforcement of public rights with statutory fee-shifting supporting representation.[17] California's Unfair Competition Law exemplifies this approach, enabling private parties to enforce algorithmic governance requirements with attorney fee recovery.

Public prosecutors increasingly address algorithmic discrimination and privacy violations through state consumer protection authorities.[18] State attorneys general

[16] Federal Trade Commission, "Enforcement Policy Statement on Deceptively Formatted Advertisements" (2015).

[17] California Business and Professions Code § 17200 et seq. (Unfair Competition Law).

[18] Ramirez, Edith, et al., "Data Brokers: A Call for Transparency and Accountability," Federal Trade Commission (2014).

have brought major cases against technology companies including Facebook, Google, and algorithmic discrimination in employment and housing.

A different approach locates accountability upstream of enforcement altogether. A strand of administrative-law scholarship argues that discretionary decisions must be reserved for human authorities, a 'reserve of humanity', because sound discretion requires empathy and practical judgement that automated systems cannot supply, keeping a human answerable for the outcome.[19] Several European jurisdictions have established algorithmic ombudsman offices receiving complaints, investigating violations, and mandating corrective action without formal litigation requirements. A distinct strand of administrative-law scholarship argues that certain decisions must be reserved for human authorities, a 'reserve of humanity', rather than delegated to automated systems, with human officials remaining answerable for the outcome.

However, enforcement mechanisms face systematic challenges. First, resource constraints limit governmental enforcement capacity despite formal authority. Regulatory agencies face staffing and budgetary limitations while regulated industries possess substantially greater resources. Second, expertise asymmetries favor regulated entities. When enforcement requires sophisticated technical understanding, agencies depend on industry cooperation for information access. Third, political pressures affect enforcement priorities. Technology industry political influence creates resistance to aggressive enforcement despite documented harms.

11.3.1 The Enforcement Deficit: Designed to Fail

The architecture of algorithmic accountability enforcement reveals systematic design features ensuring ineffectiveness. This is not accident or oversight but result of corporate influence over enforcement framework creation.

Start with regulatory resources. The FTC, primary federal enforcer of algorithmic accountability, has approximately 1,100 employees for entire consumer protection mission.[20] Technology companies employ tens of thousands of engineers, lawyers, and compliance staff. The resource asymmetry is comical, like asking a bicycle to keep pace with fighter jets.

But resource limits are features, not bugs. When legislation establishes accountability requirements, industry lobbying ensures enforcement authority receives insufficient funding. Requirements exist on paper, making regulation appear comprehensive, while practical enforcement remains impossible.

Penalty structures reveal similar patterns. Maximum statutory fines appear substantial until compared with corporate revenues. FTC maximum penalties for privacy violations are ~$43,000 per violation. But what constitutes a "violation"? If

[19] Ponce, Solé, J., 'Inteligencia artificial, Derecho administrativo y reserva de humanidad: algoritmos y procedimiento administrativo debido tecnológico,' Revista General de Derecho Administrativo 50 (2019).

[20] Federal Trade Commission, "Congressional Budget Justification FY 2024" (2023).

Facebook's algorithmic processing violates statute, is that one violation or billions (one per user, per processing instance)? Courts typically interpret conservatively, dramatically limiting aggregate penalties.

Even when penalties accumulate, they remain manageable. The $5 billion FTC settlement with Facebook over Cambridge Analytica seems enormous until recognizing Facebook's quarterly revenue exceeds $30 billion. The settlement amounts to roughly two weeks of revenue. That's not deterrence; it's taxation without changing behavior.

Settlement structures further undermine accountability. Companies settle without admitting wrongdoing, preserving ability to deny misconduct in other proceedings. Settlements impose "monitoring" requirements that sound meaningful, independent auditors will assess compliance, but typically lack enforcement teeth. Companies violate settlement terms with minimal consequences.

More fundamentally, settlements resolve specific cases without establishing precedent. Each new case requires proving the same facts, developing the same evidence, overcoming the same procedural barriers. Companies settle when necessary to prevent adverse precedent, ensuring that each enforcement action starts from scratch.

Procedural complexity exhausts enforcement capacity. Companies deploy aggressive litigation tactics: motions to dismiss, discovery battles, jurisdictional challenges, expert witness disputes, interlocutory appeals. Each requires agency resources addressing procedural issues rather than merits. The strategy is attrition, make enforcement so expensive and time-consuming that agencies pursue minimal actions regardless of violation frequency.

The revolving door corrupts enforcement from within. Regulatory agency lawyers anticipate future industry employment. Aggressive enforcement threatens career prospects. The incentive is establishing credibility with potential employers through "reasonable" enforcement that maintains industry relationships. Agencies lose most aggressive enforcers to industry, draining institutional capacity while strengthening corporate defense.

Figure 11.3 maps how structural features of enforcement systems, resource limits, penalty structures, settlement practices, create systematic underenforcement that functions as feature rather than bug.

Who benefits from enforcement deficit? Technology companies face minimal practical accountability despite formal requirements. Violations that should eliminate business models instead impose manageable fines absorbed as business expense. Defense lawyers and consultants' profit from helping companies navigate enforcement without changing practices.

Who loses? Public protection fails despite formal accountability frameworks. Systematic harms continue because enforcement capacity cannot match violation scale. Democratic oversight through enforcement mechanisms exists formally but fails practically.

Fig. 11.3 This systems diagram maps how structural features of enforcement systems, resource limits, penalty structures, settlement practices, create systematic underenforcement that functions as feature rather than bug.

References

CASES

'AT&T Mobility LLC v. Concepcion', 563 U.S. 333 (2011).
'Epic Systems Corp. v. Lewis', 138 S. Ct. 1612 (2018).
'New York Times v. Sullivan', 376 U.S. 254 (1964).
'TransUnion LLC v. Ramirez', 141 S. Ct. 2190 (2021).

BOOKS

Citron DK (2014) Hate crimes in cyberspace. Harvard University Press
Pasquale F (2015) The black box society: the secret algorithms that control money and information. Harvard University Press

Chapter 12
Global Approaches to AI Governance

12.1 European Rights-Based Approach

The European Union has established itself as the global frontrunner in rights-centric AI regulation. The AI Act, formally adopted in March 2024, represents the world's first comprehensive legal framework specifically designed to govern artificial intelligence.[1] This approach builds upon the foundation laid by the General Data Protection Regulation, which established enforceable digital rights for EU citizens.

The European model explicitly grounds AI governance in fundamental rights protection. As the Court of Justice of the European Union held in 'Schrems II', that transfers of Europeans' data are permissible only where the recipient ensures a level of protection "essentially equivalent" to that guaranteed within the Union, a standard that extends logically to AI systems that process their data.[2]

The risk-based classification system in the AI Act presents a nuanced regulatory framework that scales obligations according to potential harms.[3] For prohibited AI systems that present "unacceptable risk" to fundamental rights, the AI Act creates unambiguous boundaries. In 'Digital Rights Ireland', the Court of Justice struck down the Data Retention Directive because it "entail[ed] a wide-ranging and particularly serious interference with the fundamental rights to respect for private life and to the protection of personal data, without that interference being limited to what is strictly necessary," establishing that intrusions on fundamental rights must meet a strict necessity test.[4]

However, this rights-based framing obscures how corporate influence shaped the AI Act's final form. During negotiations, technology industry associations

[1] European Union Artificial Intelligence Act, Regulation (EU) 2024/1689 (2024).

[2] 'Schrems II' (Data Protection Commissioner v. Facebook Ireland), Case C-311/18 (CJEU 2020).

[3] EU AI Act, Annex III (defining high-risk AI systems) (2024).

[4] 'Digital Rights Ireland v. Minister for Communications' (Joined Cases C-293/12 and C-594/12) (CJEU 2014).

R. Yadav-Ranjan, *Constitutional Democracy in the Algorithmic Age*, Law, Governance and Technology Series 83, https://doi.org/10.1007/978-3-032-34604-9_12

lobbied extensively for "risk-based" approaches that sound protective but concentrate requirements on narrow "high-risk" categories while leaving most algorithmic systems essentially unregulated.

Research by Corporate Europe Observatory documented industry spending exceeding €97 million annually on EU technology lobbying.[5] This investment purchased substantial influence: narrowing definitions of "high-risk" systems, establishing "innovation-friendly" compliance pathways, creating regulatory sandboxes reducing requirements, limiting enforcement authority, and ensuring long implementation timelines delaying actual requirements.

The result is comprehensive-appearing regulation that preserves corporate autonomy over most consequential decisions. The AI Act prohibits a handful of particularly egregious practices while establishing "governance" frameworks for everything else that require disclosure, assessment, and oversight, but rarely prohibit deployment regardless of identified harms.

12.1.1 The Brussels Effect: Projection of Power Through Regulation

The "Brussels Effect", how EU regulations become de facto global standards, appears as benign mechanism through which good governance spreads. However, this framing obscures whose interests the Brussels Effect serves.

First, the Brussels Effect advantages European companies. By establishing regulatory requirements that European firms helped design and can more easily satisfy, EU regulation creates compliance barriers disadvantaging non-European competitors. This is not coincidental side-effect but strategic regulatory approach: use regulation to advantage domestic industry while framing it as rights protection.

Second, the Brussels Effect extends European corporate influence globally. When multinational companies adopt EU standards globally for "operational consistency," they're not neutrally implementing rights protections, they're extending governance frameworks shaped by European corporate lobbying to populations who had no voice in their creation.

Third, the Brussels Effect enables regulatory export without democratic accountability. When EU regulations become global through market mechanisms, affected global populations cannot participate in shaping rules governing their lives. This is regulatory colonialism through technical standards.

Fourth, the Brussels Effect creates facade of comprehensive protection while preserving corporate autonomy. Companies comply with letter of EU requirements while evading spirit through technical compliance strategies. They then point to EU compliance as demonstrating responsibility, deflecting demands for more substantial accountability.

---

[5] Corporate Europe Observatory & LobbyControl, "The Lobby Network: Big Tech Web of Influence in the EU" (2021).

Who benefits from the Brussels Effect? European technology companies and established firms that can absorb compliance costs gain competitive advantages. European policymakers project global influence. Consulting firms and lawyers' profit from helping companies navigate requirements.

Who loses? Global South populations subject to regulations they did not shape. Smaller companies and startups that cannot afford compliance costs. Democratic governance as populations lose control over rules affecting them.

12.2 Chinese State-Centric Model

China's approach to AI governance prioritizes state oversight and strategic interests over individual rights protections. The 2021 Personal Information Protection Law offers limited safeguards that must be understood within the broader regulatory landscape.[6]

The Supreme People's Court noted in its guidelines on facial recognition technology that "Personal information protection must be balanced against national security interests and public order."[7] This interpretive guidance effectively subordinates individual rights to state priorities.

The Cyberspace Administration of China's "Provisions on Algorithmic Information Services" mandate that algorithmic systems must "actively disseminate positive energy" and prohibit algorithms that "endanger national security or disrupt economic or social order."[8] Such provisions enable content control without meaningful judicial review.

In 'Guo Bing v. Hangzhou Safari Park', a Chinese court found that mandatory biometric collection for park entry violated proportionality principles.[9] However, such consumer protection cases operate within narrow parameters that do not fundamentally challenge state information collection practices.

China's model demonstrates how algorithmic systems enable authoritarianism at previously impossible scale. The social credit system, mandatory biometric collection, ubiquitous surveillance, algorithmic censorship, and predictive policing create comprehensive population control infrastructure.

---

[6] Personal Information Protection Law of the People's Republic of China (2021).

[7] Supreme People's Court of China, "Guidelines on Several Issues Concerning the Trial of Civil Cases Involving the Processing of Personal Information Using Facial Recognition Technology" (2021).

[8] Cyberspace Administration of China, "Provisions on the Administration of Algorithmic Recommendation in Internet Information Services" (2022).

[9] 'Guo Bing v. Hangzhou Safari Park' (Hangzhou Intermediate People's Court 2021).

12.2.1 Authoritarian Efficiency Through Algorithmic Control

China's state-centric model reveals algorithmic systems' utility for authoritarian governance. This isn't incidental but demonstrates fundamental characteristics: algorithmic systems excel at population-scale surveillance, behavioral control, information manipulation, and automated enforcement, precisely the capabilities authoritarian regimes require.

The social credit system exemplifies this. By algorithmically tracking citizen behavior across multiple domains, financial transactions, social media posts, traffic violations, purchase patterns, and assigning "scores" determining access to services, employment, travel, and opportunities, the system creates automated behavioral control at scale impossible through traditional means.

Facial recognition systems deployed ubiquitously enable persistent identity tracking. When combined with location data, social network analysis, and behavioral profiling, the result is comprehensive surveillance infrastructure far exceeding historical totalitarian capabilities.

Algorithmic content moderation enables automated censorship responsive to regime priorities in real-time. When combined with "positive energy" requirements mandating specific content promotion, algorithmic systems shape information environment comprehensively without requiring extensive human censors.

Predictive policing and "pre-crime" systems enable intervention before dissent manifests publicly. By identifying individuals with characteristics correlating with past dissidents and preemptively restricting their capabilities, algorithmic systems enable suppression without overt force.

The lesson: algorithmic systems claimed neutrality is false. These are governance technologies enabling specific forms of social control. The question isn't whether algorithmic systems will be used for authoritarian purposes, China demonstrates they already are, but whether democracies will develop governance frameworks preventing similar applications.

12.3 American Market-Driven Governance

The United States has historically relied on sector-specific legislation, market forces, and post-hoc enforcement rather than comprehensive ex-ante regulation.[10] This approach creates significant gaps in citizen protections against algorithmic harms. Market forces are poorly suited to curbing harms that are not incidental to the dominant business model but constitutive of it. As Shoshana Zuboff argues, surveillance capitalism claims human experience as "free raw material" for translation into behavioral data, refined into predictions of future behavior and sold in new

[10] 'Carpenter v. United States', 138 S. Ct. 2206, 2218 (2018).

markets; competition drives firms to extract more, not less. Governance that relies on market discipline therefore leaves the engine of algorithmic harm untouched.

The Supreme Court acknowledged in 'Carpenter v. United States' that "The Court is obliged to ensure that the 'progress of science' does not erode Fourth Amendment protections."[11] Yet this case-by-case constitutional interpretation provides limited systemic safeguards against algorithmic harms.

The Federal Trade Commission has utilized Section 5 authority against "unfair or deceptive practices" to address algorithmic harms.[12] However, without comprehensive federal privacy law, the Commission's ability to address algorithmic discrimination remains constrained by jurisdictional and remedial limitations.

State-level initiatives have attempted to fill federal regulatory gaps. The California Consumer Privacy Act and its successor, the California Privacy Rights Act, establish limited algorithmic transparency and opt-out rights.[13] Nevertheless, these state-level protections create an inconsistent patchwork of citizen rights.

12.3.1 Fragmentation as Corporate Strategy

American regulatory fragmentation isn't market failure but successful corporate strategy. Technology industry political investment has systematically prevented comprehensive federal regulation while ensuring state-level initiatives remain limited.

The pattern is predictable: when harmful practices gain public attention, industry responds with combination of lobbying preventing federal legislation, preemption campaigns limiting state authority, and minimal voluntary self-regulation deflecting demands for actual accountability.

Federal legislative efforts face technology industry lobbying exceeding $70 million annually.[14] This investment purchases: prevention of comprehensive privacy legislation, blocking algorithmic accountability requirements, ensuring sector-specific approaches preventing consistent standards, preserving Section 230 immunity, preventing antitrust enforcement.

State-level regulation faces preemption campaigns arguing federal action is necessary, constitutional challenges arguing state regulation burdens interstate commerce, and lobbying for weakening amendments before passage.

When regulation cannot be prevented, industry shapes it toward minimal impact: narrow definitions excluding most practices, compliance pathways favoring large firms with resources, delayed implementation, inadequate enforcement mechanisms, liability limitations.

---

[11] 'Id.'

[12] Federal Trade Commission Act, 15 U.S.C. § 45(a) (2018).

[13] California Privacy Rights Act (CPRA), Cal. Civ. Code § 1798.100 et seq. (2020).

[14] OpenSecrets Center for Responsive Politics, "Computers/Internet Tech Industry Lobbying Spending" (2024).

The result is governance framework appearing comprehensive across federal and state levels while actually providing systematic protection gaps enabling profitable harmful practices.

12.4 Comparative Analysis and Global Implications

The divergent regulatory approaches create what legal scholar Anu Bradford terms "the Brussels Effect", the EU's ability to externalize its regulatory standards through market mechanisms.[15] This phenomenon has particular salience in AI governance, as multinational technology firms may adopt the strictest applicable standards globally to maintain operational consistency.

Emerging nations increasingly develop distinctive approaches rather than simply adopting Northern models. India's Digital Personal Data Protection Act incorporates elements of European rights-based approach while maintaining significant state exemptions.[16] Brazil's LGPD (Lei Geral de Protecao de Dados Pessoais, Law No. 13, 709 of August 2018, fully in force since August 2020) closely mirrors GDPR's rights-based framework while adapting implementation to local contexts.[17] The statute established the Autoridade Nacional de Protecao de Dados (ANPD) as Brazil's first comprehensive data protection authority, recognizes data subject rights of access, correction, portability, and deletion, applies extraterritorially to processing affecting individuals located in Brazil, and authorizes administrative sanctions of up to two percent of a controller's Brazilian revenue per infraction.

However, regulatory competition creates pressures toward lenient standards. Jurisdictions compete to attract technology investment through favorable regulation, creating race-to-the-bottom dynamics. Companies exploit regulatory arbitrage by locating operations in jurisdictions with minimal requirements while serving global markets.

12.4.1 Regulatory Competition as Race to Bottom

Regulatory competition theory suggests jurisdictions compete to offer optimal governance attracting investment while protecting citizens. In practice, technology industry mobility and market concentration create race-to-bottom dynamics.

Companies credibly threaten to relocate if regulation becomes too demanding. Even when threats are not executed, they constrain policymakers who fear competitive disadvantage. The result is systematic under-regulation as jurisdictions compete to attract or retain technology investment.

---

[15] Bradford, 'The Brussels Effect' (2020), 1–28.

[16] India Digital Personal Data Protection Act (2023).

[17] Brazil Lei Geral de Proteção de Dados (LGPD), Law No. 13,709/2018 (fully in force Aug. 2020).

This dynamic affects all governance models. European policymakers justify lenient AI Act provisions as necessary to compete with American and Chinese innovation. American policymakers resist regulation citing need to compete globally. Chinese policymakers emphasize strategic technology development justifying state support requiring minimal accountability.

The pattern advantages technology companies systematically. They play jurisdictions against each other, threatening relocation to extract regulatory concessions. They exploit arbitrage by locating functions in minimal-regulation jurisdictions. They use global operations to evade accountability in any particular jurisdiction.

Who benefits? Technology companies face minimal accountability despite global operations affecting billions. Who loses? Global populations lacking democratic control over systems governing their lives.

12.5 International Coordination and Regulatory Competition

International coordination mechanisms remain weak despite algorithmic systems' transnational operation. The OECD AI Principles establish non-binding framework emphasizing "innovative and trustworthy AI."[18] UNESCO's Recommendation on the Ethics of AI provides aspirational framework without enforcement mechanisms.[19]

However, geopolitical tensions and divergent interests among powerful states prevent binding international governance. The United States resists constraints on technology companies driving economic and military advantage. China rejects external oversight over surveillance infrastructure enabling regime stability. European Union pursues regulatory influence through standard-setting but lacks enforcement authority beyond its borders.

12.5.1 The Sovereignty Trap

Claims that algorithmic governance requires respecting national sovereignty obscure how sovereignty itself has been transformed. When companies operate globally while locating functions strategically to evade accountability, traditional sovereignty provides no democratic control.

The sovereignty framing advantages technology companies by preventing effective governance. They argue: we cannot be regulated here because we operate globally; we cannot be regulated there because that would violate territorial sovereignty; coordination violates sovereignty of states choosing different approaches. The result is accountability gaps enabling systematic abuse.

---

[18] OECD, "Recommendation of the Council on Artificial Intelligence" (2019).

[19] UNESCO, "Recommendation on the Ethics of Artificial Intelligence" (2021).

Effective governance requires moving beyond sovereignty frameworks toward recognition that transnational systems require transnational democratic control. This means international agreements with binding obligations, enforcement mechanisms with real authority, and genuine democratic participation by affected populations, not just state representatives.

12.6 What You Can Do Now

Building effective global governance requires political organizing that transcends national boundaries.

Support International Coordination

1. Advocate for Binding International Treaties: Support civil society campaigns for UN treaty on business and human rights including algorithmic accountability, international convention on digital rights, global framework on AI governance with enforcement mechanisms.
2. Support Transnational Advocacy Networks: Organizations coordinating global advocacy: Access Now, Association for Progressive Communications, Global Partners Digital, Article 19, Privacy International. Support their work financially and politically.
3. Demand Extraterritorial Jurisdiction: Support legislation enabling your country to hold companies accountable for harms anywhere, regardless of where companies are based. Support universal jurisdiction for egregious algorithmic human rights violations.
4. Challenge Regulatory Arbitrage: Advocate for requirements that companies serving your jurisdiction comply with your standards regardless of where they're based. Support closing loopholes enabling regulatory evasion through strategic location choices.

Resist Race to Bottom

1. Oppose Preemption Campaigns: Technology industry lobbies against state/local regulation while blocking federal action. Oppose preemption legislation. Support state/local authority to regulate technology companies.
2. Support Robust Standards: Resist industry arguments that strong regulation will drive companies elsewhere. Demand accountability regardless of competitive implications. Companies threatening to leave often don't, but concessions they extract are permanent.
3. Build Coalitions Across Jurisdictions: Connect with advocates in other countries fighting similar battles. Coordinate advocacy to prevent companies from playing jurisdictions against each other. Share information about industry tactics and effective counter-strategies.

4. Demand Transparency About Regulatory Competition: Require government reporting on industry lobbying arguments about competitive impacts. Make visible the threats companies make to extract concessions.

Learn from Other Models

1. Study European Rights Framework: Understand GDPR, AI Act, and European enforcement approaches. Advocate for similar frameworks in your jurisdiction. But also understand the limitations, don't assume European regulation is sufficient.
2. Document Chinese Authoritarian Applications: Build public awareness of how algorithmic systems enable authoritarianism. Use China as cautionary example for why democratic oversight is essential. Support documentation of Chinese surveillance systems affecting dissidents globally.
3. Identify American Failure Patterns: Document protection gaps from fragmented American approach. Use as evidence for comprehensive regulation. Challenge industry arguments that American "innovation-friendly" approach is superior when it systematically fails to protect rights.
4. Support Global South Governance Innovation: Attention to Northern models often ignores innovative approaches from Brazil, India, Kenya, Nigeria. Support their policy experimentation and adaptation to local contexts.

Build Transnational Power

1. Connect Labor Organizing Globally: Technology workers organizing in one country strengthens organizing everywhere. Support international coordination among technology worker unions. Oppose company tactics of relocating to avoid unionized workers.
2. Support Cross-Border Legal Strategies: When companies evade accountability through global operations, support legal theories enabling jurisdiction regardless of location. Support international litigation coordination.
3. Demand Supply Chain Accountability: Companies use global supply chains to obscure responsibility. Support requirements for accountability throughout supply chains regardless of jurisdiction.
4. Build Alternative Infrastructures: Support development of technology infrastructure not controlled by companies or governments: community networks, cooperative platforms, open-source alternatives, decentralized systems enabling democratic control.

The Fundamental Challenge

Global governance of algorithmic systems requires overcoming nationalism that prevents coordination, corporate power that benefits from fragmentation, and sovereignty frameworks inadequate for transnational systems.

This requires building political movements that transcend national boundaries, developing governance frameworks that match technological scope, and creating enforcement mechanisms with authority over global corporations.

Companies benefit systematically from governance gaps, regulatory competition, and coordination failure. Effective governance requires collective action sufficient to overcome these advantages.

References

Cases

'Carpenter v. United States', 138 S. Ct. 2206 (2018)
'Digital Rights Ireland v. Minister for Communications' (Joined Cases C-293/12 and C-594/12) (CJEU 2014)
'Schrems II' (Data Protection Commissioner v. Facebook Ireland), Case C-311/18 (CJEU 2020)
'Guo Bing v. Hangzhou Safari Park' (Hangzhou Intermediate People's Court 2021)

Books

Bradford A (2020) The Brussels effect: how the European Union rules the World. Oxford University Press
Zuboff S (2019) The age of surveillance capitalism: The fight for a human future at the new frontier of power. PublicAffairs

Chapter 13
International Human Rights Law and AI

13.1 Applying Existing Human Rights Frameworks

International human rights law provides essential leverage against algorithmic power precisely because it transcends the territorial boundaries that constrain national regulation. The Universal Declaration of Human Rights (UDHR), International Covenant on Civil and Political Rights (ICCPR), and regional conventions establish principles that apply regardless of where AI systems are developed or deployed.[1]

Privacy rights under Article 17 of the ICCPR encompass protection against algorithmic surveillance and profiling. The UN Human Rights Committee clarified in General Comment No. 16 that privacy rights extend to "information concerning a person's private life" regardless of technological means of processing.[2] This principle gained teeth in 'Big Brother Watch and Others v. United Kingdom', where the European Court of Human Rights held that "bulk surveillance regimes must provide end-to-end safeguards to prevent arbitrary interference with private life."[3] The Court found that the UK's mass surveillance programs violated Article 8 (privacy) and Article 10 (freedom of expression) of the European Convention on Human Rights, establishing that democratic necessity cannot override fundamental rights protections.

The Big Brother Watch decision provides critical precedent because it addresses algorithmic processing explicitly. The Court held that automated analysis of communications content requires the same rigorous safeguards as human analysis, rejecting

[1] Universal Declaration of Human Rights, G.A. Res. 217A (III), U.N. Doc. A/810 at 71 (1948); International Covenant on Civil and Political Rights, Dec. 16, 1966, 999 U.N.T.S. 171.

[2] UN Human Rights Committee, General Comment No. 16: Article 17 (Right to Privacy), U.N. Doc. HRI/GEN/1/Rev.9 (Vol. I) (1988), para. 4.

[3] 'Big Brother Watch and Others v. United Kingdom', Application nos. 58170/13, 62322/14, and 24960/15, Judgment of 25 May 2021, para. 333.

R. Yadav-Ranjan, *Constitutional Democracy in the Algorithmic Age*, Law, Governance and Technology Series 83, https://doi.org/10.1007/978-3-032-34604-9_13

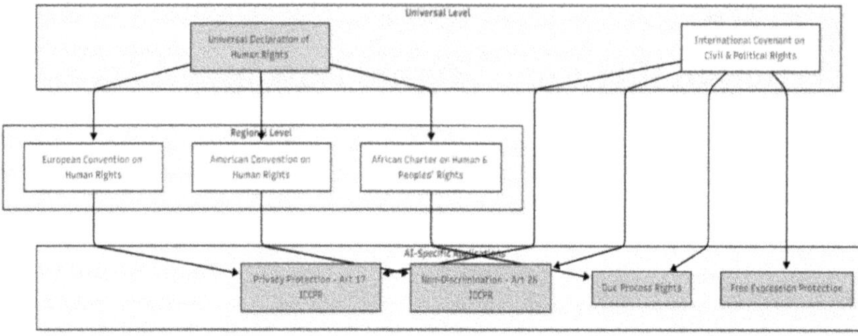

Fig. 13.1 This hierarchical chart shows how international human rights instruments create layered protections applicable to AI systems, from universal declarations through regional conventions to national implementation.

arguments that machine processing somehow lessens privacy intrusions. This principle extends to all algorithmic systems that process personal information, not merely state surveillance.

Non-discrimination provisions in Article 26 of the ICCPR and Article 14 of the European Convention on Human Rights address algorithmic bias directly. In 'Yilmaz-Dogan v. Netherlands', the Committee on the Elimination of Racial Discrimination established that indirect discrimination through facially neutral practices violates human rights obligations.[4] This precedent applies squarely to algorithmic discrimination, where systems produce disparate impacts without explicit consideration of protected characteristics.

Figure 13.1 shows how international human rights instruments create layered protections applicable to AI systems, from universal declarations through regional conventions to national implementation.

The UN Special Rapporteur on contemporary forms of racism documented in a 2020 report how algorithmic systems in immigration enforcement, criminal justice, and welfare administration systematically disadvantage racial and ethnic minorities across multiple jurisdictions.[5] The report emphasized that human rights obligations require states to address discriminatory algorithmic impacts regardless of intent, departing from narrower US constitutional doctrines focused on discriminatory purpose.

---

[4] 'Yilmaz-Dogan v. Netherlands', Communication No. 1/1984, U.N. Doc. A/43/18 (1988), para. 9.3.

[5] UN Special Rapporteur on contemporary forms of racism, racial discrimination, xenophobia and related intolerance, "Racial discrimination and emerging digital technologies: a human rights analysis," A/HRC/44/57 (18 June 2020).

13.1.1 Power Dynamics in International Human Rights Enforcement

International human rights law confronts structural power asymmetries that shape its effectiveness against algorithmic governance. While human rights principles apply universally, enforcement mechanisms remain constrained by state sovereignty and corporate power.

First, the voluntary nature of most human rights enforcement creates compliance gaps. Unlike domestic courts that can directly compel action, international human rights bodies typically issue non-binding recommendations. The UN Human Rights Committee, for instance, can find ICCPR violations and recommend remedies, but lacks authority to enforce compliance.[6] This creates what international law scholar Karen Alter terms "decoupling", states acknowledge human rights obligations while declining to implement substantive reforms.

Second, corporate actors exist in ambiguous relationships with international human rights law. The UN Guiding Principles on Business and Human Rights, adopted in 2011, establish that corporations have responsibilities to respect human rights regardless of state obligations.[7] However, these principles remain aspirational rather than enforceable. When technology corporations deploy algorithmic systems that violate human rights across multiple jurisdictions, victims face enormous challenges in securing remedies through international mechanisms designed primarily for state accountability.

Third, resource asymmetries shape enforcement capacity dramatically. Human rights treaty bodies operate with minimal budgets and staff, processing thousands of complaints annually. The Human Rights Committee, responsible for monitoring ICCPR compliance across 173 state parties, operates with fewer than 20 professional staff.[8] This compares to technology corporations with legal departments employing thousands and budgets exceeding many nations' GDP. The resource differential ensures that corporate actors can delay, fragment, and ultimately evade human rights accountability through procedural complexity.

Fourth, jurisdictional fragmentation prevents comprehensive remedies. An algorithmic system operating globally may violate human rights in dozens of jurisdictions simultaneously, but victims must navigate separate complaint mechanisms in each regional or national system. This fragmentation increases costs for victims while reducing them for violators, who benefit from having to defend against isolated challenges rather than coordinated enforcement.

---

[6] Optional Protocol to the International Covenant on Civil and Political Rights, Dec. 16, 1966, 999 U.N.T.S. 302, Article 5.4 (Committee "shall forward its views to the State Party concerned and to the individual").

[7] UN Human Rights Council, "Guiding Principles on Business and Human Rights: Implementing the United Nations 'Protect, Respect and Remedy' Framework," A/HRC/17/31 (21 March 2011).

[8] Office of the High Commissioner for Human Rights, "Human Rights Committee, About," https://www.ohchr.org/en/treaty-bodies/ccpr/about-committee (accessed November 2024).

The enforcement gap is not hypothetical. In 'Institute for Human Rights and Development in Africa v. Angola', the African Commission on Human and Peoples' Rights found that Angola had violated multiple Charter rights and ordered it to investigate the abuses and compensate the victims, yet Angola declined to take part in the proceedings and never implemented the recommendations or paid the compensation. Even a clear finding of violation yields little when enforcement rests on voluntary state compliance, a structural weakness that will constrain algorithmic-rights claims as surely as it did this one.[9]

13.2 Regional Human Rights Systems and Algorithmic Governance

Regional human rights systems provide more robust enforcement mechanisms than global frameworks, offering crucial precedents for algorithmic governance. I examine here how the European, Inter-American, and African systems have begun addressing AI-related rights violations.

13.2.1 European System: Rights-Based Constraints on AI

The European Court of Human Rights has developed the most sophisticated jurisprudence on algorithmic rights. Beyond Big Brother Watch, several decisions establish enforceable limitations on algorithmic governance.

In 'Glukhin v. Russia', the Court confronted facial recognition directly. Russian authorities had used the technology to identify, locate, and prosecute Mr. Glukhin after he staged a solo, peaceful demonstration, processing his image from transport-system cameras and a social media photograph.[10] The Court held that this use of facial recognition was not "necessary in a democratic society" and violated both Article 8 (private life) and Article 10 (freedom of expression), characterizing facial recognition as a "highly intrusive" technology whose deployment against lawful protest demands especially compelling justification. The judgment establishes that algorithmic identification of citizens exercising protected rights is not a neutral administrative act but a rights intrusion the state must justify. A related constraint comes from the Court of Justice of the European Union. In 'SCHUFA Holding' (Case C-634/21, Court of Justice of the European Union, 7 December 2023), the Court held that an automated credit score constitutes a decision "based solely on automated processing" under Article 22 of the GDPR whenever that score effectively determines whether a third

[9] 'Institute for Human Rights and Development in Africa (on behalf of Esmaila Connateh & 13 others) v. Angola', Communication No. 292/2004, 43rd Ordinary Session (African Commission on Human and Peoples' Rights, 22 May 2008).

[10] 'Glukhin v. Russia', Application no. 11519/20 (European Court of Human Rights, 4 July 2023).

party, such as a bank, extends credit. This brings algorithmic scoring squarely within the Regulation's safeguards, the rights to human intervention, to an explanation, and to contest the outcome, and confirms that nominal human oversight cannot mean rubber-stamping an algorithmic result.

The Court of Justice of the European Union's decision in 'Breyer v. Germany' addressed dynamic IP address retention, holding that even technical identifiers constitute personal data requiring privacy protections.[11] This principle extends to all forms of digital tracking and profiling, establishing that human rights obligations cannot be evaded through technical obfuscation about what constitutes "personal information."

More recently, in 'Centrum för rättvisa v. Sweden' (2021), the Court refined its analysis of bulk surveillance, distinguishing between metadata and content analysis but maintaining that both require strict safeguards.[12] Significantly, the Court held that algorithmic analysis must be subject to meaningful human review and that such review must be documented and auditable.

These decisions matter because the European Convention creates binding legal obligations enforceable through national courts. When the European Court finds violations, states must implement judgments or face political and economic consequences within the European system. This provides substantially more leverage than non-binding UN recommendations.

13.2.2 Inter-American System: Addressing Algorithmic Discrimination

The Inter-American Commission on Human Rights has addressed algorithmic discrimination in social welfare systems. Automated benefit-eligibility systems that produce discriminatory outcomes for protected groups, such as indigenous communities, fall squarely within the Commission's non-discrimination mandate.[13]

Under the American Convention's non-discrimination provisions, which prohibit both direct and indirect discrimination, algorithmic systems that produce disparate impacts on protected groups can constitute a violation regardless of discriminatory intent.

More significantly, the inter-American framework supports heightened obligations when deploying algorithmic systems affecting rights to social security and adequate living standards. This establishes that automation cannot be used to evade substantive rights obligations or to make discrimination less visible through technical complexity.

---

[11] 'Patrick Breyer v. Germany', Case C-582/14 (Court of Justice of the European Union, 19 October 2016).

[12] 'Centrum för rättvisa v. Sweden', Application no. 35252/08, Judgment of 25 May 2021, paras. 273–301.

[13] American Convention on Human Rights, Articles 1(1) and 24 (non-discrimination and equal protection).

13.2.3 African System: Data Sovereignty and Collective Rights

The African Commission on Human and Peoples' Rights has begun developing distinctive approaches emphasizing collective rights and data sovereignty. The African Charter's inclusion of peoples' rights alongside individual rights provides unique tools for addressing algorithmic governance.

Where biometric or algorithmic identification systems are imposed on entire communities, such as displaced or refugee populations, that collective-rights framework can trigger a self-determination analysis, not merely an individual privacy assessment.[14]

The African Union's 2022 Data Policy Framework establishes data sovereignty principles that could limit extraterritorial algorithmic processing.[15] While not yet widely implemented, this framework asserts African states' authority to regulate how data about African persons is collected, processed, and transferred, even when processing occurs outside Africa.

13.3 Jurisdictional Challenges in Transnational AI Systems

Algorithmic systems create acute jurisdictional challenges because they operate globally while legal authority remains territorially bounded. I examine here how human rights law addresses these challenges and where gaps remain.

13.3.1 Extraterritorial Obligations and Transnational Harms

International human rights law traditionally binds states only within their territorial jurisdiction or where they exercise effective control. This creates challenges when algorithmic harms cross borders without states exercising traditional territorial control.

The UN Human Rights Committee addressed this issue in 'Munaf v. Romania', holding that states can bear human rights obligations for actions taken outside their territory when they exercise authority or control over individuals.[16] This principle potentially extends to algorithmic systems: a state deploying algorithmic surveillance

---

[14] African Charter on Human and Peoples' Rights, Articles 19–24 (peoples' rights), particularly Article 20 (right to self-determination).

[15] African Union, AU Data Policy Framework (2022), endorsed by the Assembly of the Union Executive Council.

[16] 'Munaf v. Romania', Communication No. 1539/2006, U.N. Doc. CCPR/C/96/D/1539/2006 (2009), para. 14.2.

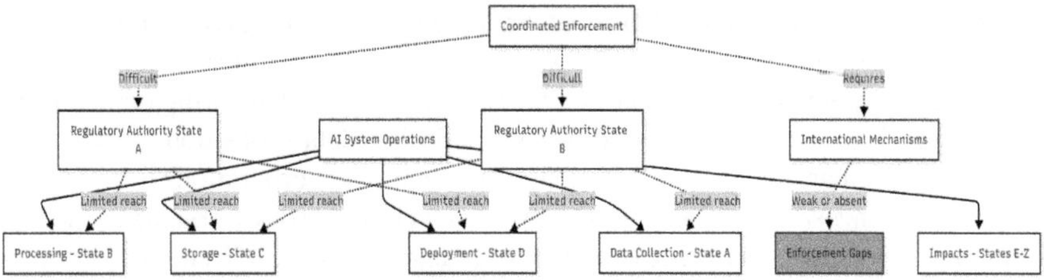

Fig. 13.2 This network diagram illustrates how AI systems operate transnationally while legal authority remains territorially fragmented, creating enforcement gaps and enabling regulatory arbitrage.

systems that process data about persons in other jurisdictions may bear obligations toward those affected persons.

However, significant uncertainty remains. When a technology corporation based in State A deploys algorithmic systems processing data from persons in States B, C, and D, which state bears human rights obligations? Current doctrine provides limited guidance, creating enforcement gaps that corporations exploit systematically.

Figure 13.2 illustrates how AI systems operate transnationally while legal authority remains territorially fragmented, creating enforcement gaps and enabling regulatory arbitrage.

The European Court's judgment in 'Big Brother Watch' suggests that states bear obligations for surveillance systems they operate, regardless of where data subjects are located. The UK government argued unsuccessfully that it bore no obligations toward non-UK persons whose communications were intercepted. The Court rejected this argument, holding that the extraterritorial scope of surveillance operations extended the UK's human rights obligations correspondingly.[17]

13.3.2 Corporate Accountability in Transnational Operations

Technology corporations operate across borders with structures specifically designed to minimize legal accountability. Subsidiaries in different jurisdictions fragment liability, while data processing often occurs in jurisdictions selected for minimal regulation.

The UN Guiding Principles on Business and Human Rights establish that corporations should conduct human rights due diligence and remedy adverse impacts.[18] However, these principles lack enforcement mechanisms. When corporations violate human rights through algorithmic systems, victims face enormous challenges securing remedies through voluntary corporate mechanisms.

[17] 'Big Brother Watch', paras. 401–412.

[18] UN Guiding Principles on Business and Human Rights, Principles 17–24.

Some progress has occurred through strategic litigation. In 'Privacy International v. Facebook Ireland Limited' (pending before Irish courts), plaintiffs argue that Facebook's algorithmic targeting violates GDPR provisions implementing human rights protections.[19] If successful, this could establish that data protection laws provide enforceable human rights remedies against transnational corporations.

Similarly, in a series of cases before the Dutch courts, privacy organizations have challenged Google's data processing practices under both GDPR and the European Convention on Human Rights.[20] These cases test whether national courts can provide effective remedies for human rights violations by global technology corporations.

13.4 Emerging Global Coordination on AI Governance

Recognizing that unilateral national regulation proves insufficient for transnational algorithmic systems, various multilateral initiatives seek greater coordination. I examine their potential and limitations.

13.4.1 United Nations Initiatives

The UN Secretary-General's High-Level Advisory Body on Artificial Intelligence issued preliminary recommendations in 2023 emphasizing human rights-based approaches.[21] The recommendations call for AI systems to respect international human rights law and for strengthened accountability mechanisms.

The UN Human Rights Council has not yet created a dedicated mandate on artificial intelligence, though civil-society organizations and scholars have called for a Special Rapporteur on artificial intelligence and human rights.[22] In the meantime, existing special procedures, including the rapporteurs on the right to privacy, on freedom of opinion and expression, and on contemporary forms of racism, have examined AI's human rights impacts within their mandates.

[19] 'Privacy International v. Facebook Ireland Limited', Record No. 2018/208 JR (High Court of Ireland, pending).

[20] 'Stichting Privacy First v. Google Netherlands B.V.', Case No. C/09/456689 (District Court of Amsterdam, ongoing litigation 2021-present).

[21] UN Secretary-General's High-Level Advisory Body on Artificial Intelligence, "Interim Report: Governing AI for Humanity" (December 2023).

[22] "The Imperative for a UN Special Rapporteur on AI and Human Rights," Journal of AI Law and Regulation (2024). Existing mandate holders have addressed AI within their remits; see, e.g., UN Special Rapporteur on freedom of opinion and expression, "Artificial Intelligence Technologies and Implications for Freedom of Expression," A/73/348 (29 August 2018).

More substantively, the UN High Commissioner for Human Rights has developed guidance on human rights due diligence for AI systems.[23] This guidance translates abstract human rights obligations into concrete operational requirements, providing tools for both states and corporations to implement human rights protections.

13.4.2 Regional Coordination Efforts

The European Union's AI Act establishes the most comprehensive regulatory framework for algorithmic systems, explicitly grounding requirements in fundamental rights.[24] The Act creates prohibited AI practices (including certain social scoring systems), high-risk categories requiring strict oversight, and transparency requirements for AI systems interacting with citizens. While formally EU regulation rather than human rights law, the Act implements human rights obligations and influences global norms.

The Council of Europe adopted its Framework Convention on Artificial Intelligence and Human Rights, Democracy and the Rule of Law in May 2024 and opened it for signature that September, the first binding international treaty on AI, creating treaty obiligations for its parties.[25] This represents the most ambitious effort to translate human rights principles into enforceable rules for algorithmic governance.

The Organization of American States has begun addressing algorithmic governance through its digital-government work: a 2022 General Assembly resolution on information and communication technologies, together with associated OAS digital-government guidelines, directs the General Secretariat to help member states develop ethical-AI and algorithmic-governance policies.[26] While not creating binding obligations, such resolutions shape normative expectations and provide foundations for future enforcement.

---

[23] Office of the High Commissioner for Human Rights, "B-Tech Project: Tech and Human Rights," https://www.ohchr.org/en/business-and-human-rights/b-tech-project (ongoing initiative launched 2019).

[24] European Parliament and Council, Regulation (EU) 2024/1689 on Artificial Intelligence (AI Act), 2024 O.J. (L) (12 July 2024).

[25] Council of Europe, Framework Convention on Artificial Intelligence and Human Rights, Democracy and the Rule of Law, CETS No. 225 (adopted 17 May 2024, opened for signature 5 September 2024).

[26] Organization of American States, General Assembly Resolution AG/RES. 2987 (LII-O/22), (6 October 2022) (information and communication technologies); see also associated OAS digital-government guidelines on ethical AI and algorithmic governance.

13.4.3 Limitations of Coordination Efforts

Despite these initiatives, significant limitations constrain effective global coordination. First, powerful states resist binding constraints on AI development. The United States has consistently opposed international AI regulations it perceives as limiting technological innovation or competitive advantage.[27] China similarly resists external oversight of its AI governance approaches. Without major power consensus, binding global frameworks remain unlikely.

Second, coordination efforts often exclude meaningful participation by Global South nations and civil society organizations. The UN's Advisory Body on AI, for instance, consisted primarily of representatives from wealthy nations and major technology corporations.[28] This creates legitimacy deficits and ensures that resulting frameworks reflect dominant interests rather than universal human rights principles.

Third, enforcement mechanisms remain weak even where coordination occurs. The EU AI Act creates significant requirements, but depends on member state implementation and faces enormous resource constraints for effective oversight.[29] The gap between formal rules and effective enforcement allows violations to continue with minimal consequences.

13.5 Civil Society's Role in Transnational Advocacy

Given weak state enforcement, civil society organizations play crucial roles in defending human rights against algorithmic governance. I document here how strategic advocacy campaigns have achieved results that formal legal mechanisms could not.

Figure 13.3 maps the multiple pathways through which civil society organizations can advance algorithmic accountability through international mechanisms, from shadow reports through strategic litigation to norm development.

---

[27] U.S. Department of Commerce, National Telecommunications and Information Administration, "AI Accountability Policy Request for Comment," 89 Fed. Reg. 35610 (April 2024) (emphasizing voluntary approaches).

[28] Analysis of UN High-Level Advisory Body composition shows 24 of 38 members from OECD countries, with 8 corporate representatives and only 4 civil society representatives. See composition at https://www.un.org/ai-advisory-body/membership.

[29] European Commission, "Questions and Answers: Artificial Intelligence Act," Press Release (21 May 2024) (acknowledging implementation will require "coordination among 27 member states and significant resources").

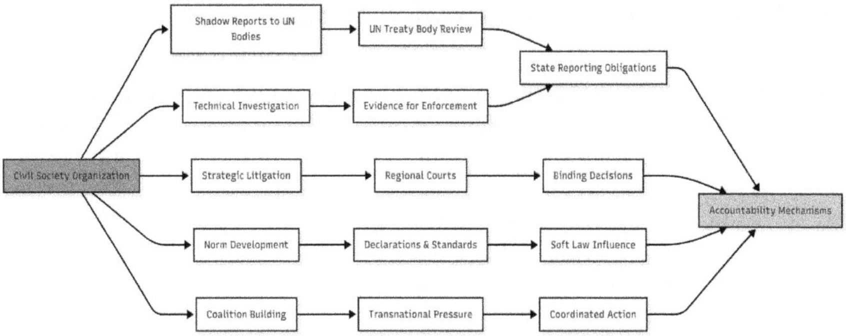

Fig. 13.3 This flowchart maps the multiple pathways through which civil society organizations can advance algorithmic accountability through international mechanisms, from shadow reports through strategic litigation to norm development.

13.5.1 Strategic Litigation Campaigns

Organizations like Privacy International, Access Now, and the Electronic Frontier Foundation pursue coordinated litigation strategies across multiple jurisdictions.[30] By filing similar challenges to algorithmic systems in different courts, they create pressure for reform while building transnational precedent.

The Schrems litigation against Facebook's data transfers provides a model. Through persistent litigation over a decade, Austrian privacy advocate Max Schrems and supporting organizations invalidated two separate EU-US data transfer frameworks, forcing significant changes in how technology corporations process European data.[31] This demonstrates how strategic individual complaints, supported by well-resourced organizations, can achieve systemic change.

A similar dynamic played out over the hiring vendor HireVue. After the Electronic Privacy Information Center filed a complaint with the U.S. Federal Trade Commission in 2019 challenging HireVue's AI facial-analysis screening, sustained regulatory and public pressure led the company to abandon facial analysis in its assessments in 2021, a result that the complaint alone, without the coordinated scrutiny around it, likely would not have produced.[32] The campaign combined litigation, regulatory complaints, public pressure, and direct negotiation with employers, achieving commitments to human review and transparency that litigation alone likely would not have produced.

[30] Privacy International, "Annual Report 2023" (2024); Access Now, "2023 Report: Defending Digital Rights Globally" (2024); Electronic Frontier Foundation, "Annual Report 2023" (2024).

[31] 'Schrems v. Data Protection Commissioner', Case C-362/14, ECLI:EU:C:2015:650 (2015); 'Data Protection Commissioner v. Facebook Ireland Limited and Maximillian Schrems', Case C-311/18, ECLI:EU:C:2020:559 (2020).

[32] Electronic Privacy Information Center, In re HireVue, Complaint to the Federal Trade Commission (6 November 2019); EPIC, 'HireVue, Facing FTC Complaint From EPIC, Halts Use of Facial Recognition' (2021).

13.5.2 Technical Investigation and Documentation

Civil society organizations conduct investigations exposing algorithmic harms that states fail to address. The Algorithmic Justice League's documentation of facial recognition bias influenced corporate and government decisions to limit deployment.[33] AlgorithmWatch's audits of YouTube's recommendation algorithm revealed radicalization pathways that the platform had denied.[34]

These investigations matter because they generate evidence that formal enforcement mechanisms require but often lack resources to develop. Human rights treaty bodies increasingly rely on civil society documentation when evaluating state compliance with algorithmic governance obligations.

13.5.3 Norm Development and Policy Advocacy

Civil society organizations shape emerging norms around algorithmic governance through policy advocacy. The Toronto Declaration on algorithmic discrimination, developed by Access Now and Amnesty International, translated human rights principles into specific requirements for machine learning systems.[35] While not legally binding, such declarations influence corporate policies and regulatory frameworks globally.

The Santa Clara Principles on content moderation, developed by civil society coalition, established transparency and due process standards that major platforms subsequently adopted.[36] This demonstrates how non-governmental actors can establish de facto standards where formal regulation lags.

13.5.4 Power Dynamics in Civil Society Advocacy

Civil society's effectiveness faces structural constraints. Most organizations defending human rights against algorithmic governance operate with budgets measured in millions, while the technology corporations they challenge operate with budgets measured in billions. This resource asymmetry limits investigative capacity, litigation endurance, and technical expertise.

---

[33] Buolamwini, Joy & Timnit Gebru, "Gender Shades: Intersectional Accuracy Disparities in Commercial Gender Classification," Proceedings of Machine Learning Research 81 (2018): 1–15; Algorithmic Justice League, "Coded Bias: Findings and Corporate Responses" (2020).

[34] AlgorithmWatch, "YouTube's Recommendation Algorithm Audit: Final Report" (2021).

[35] Access Now & Amnesty International, "The Toronto Declaration: Protecting the Rights to Equality and Non-Discrimination in Machine Learning Systems" (May 2018).

[36] Santa Clara Principles on Transparency and Accountability in Content Moderation (version 2.0, 2021), https://santaclaraprinciples.org.

Geographic disparities exacerbate these limitations. Most algorithmic rights organizations operate in North America and Western Europe, with limited presence in regions where algorithmic governance may have most severe impacts.[37] This creates gaps in documentation and advocacy that allow harms in less-resourced contexts to continue unaddressed.

Moreover, technology corporations increasingly fund civil society organizations, creating potential conflicts of interest. When Google, Facebook, or Microsoft provide significant portions of digital rights organizations' budgets, those organizations may moderate criticism or focus advocacy on less threatening issues.[38] This captured civil society cannot provide effective counterbalance to corporate power.

Despite these limitations, civil society remains essential for human rights protection against algorithmic governance. Where states lack capacity or political will to enforce human rights obligations, organized civil society provides crucial accountability mechanisms, investigation capacity, and advocacy pressure.

13.6 Toward Enforceable Transnational Human Rights Standards

The challenge ahead requires transforming aspirational human rights principles into enforceable constraints on algorithmic power that operates without regard for borders. I outline here elements of an effective transnational framework.

First, human rights treaty bodies need enhanced capacity and authority. The UN Human Rights Committee processes fewer than 200 individual complaints annually because resource constraints limit examination capacity.[39] Substantial funding increases would enable meaningful oversight of state obligations in algorithmic contexts.

Second, binding international standards for algorithmic governance should build on the Council of Europe's Framework Convention initiative. Such standards should establish clear prohibitions (e.g., on mass surveillance without particularized suspicion), due process requirements (e.g., contestability and explainability), and non-discrimination obligations (e.g., impact assessments before deployment).

Third, effective enforcement requires both public and private mechanisms. While state-to-state complaint procedures remain essential, creating individual complaint mechanisms against corporate actors directly would close current accountability gaps. The Optional Protocol to the International Covenant on Economic, Social and

---

[37] Aubra Anthony, Lakshmee Sharma & Elina Noor, "Advancing a More Global Agenda for Trustworthy Artificial Intelligence," Carnegie Endowment for International Peace (30 April 2024) (of 214 AI ethics, governance, and social-good initiatives across 38 countries, 58% originated in Europe and North America).

[38] Zuboff, Shoshana, 'The Age of Surveillance Capitalism' (PublicAffairs, 2019), pp. 492–497 (documenting technology corporation funding of civil society organizations).

[39] UN Human Rights Committee, "Annual Report 2023," U.N. Doc. A/78/40 (2023), noting backlog of over 1,200 pending complaints with capacity to decide approximately 180 cases annually.

Cultural Rights provides a model for individual complaints, which could be adapted for algorithmic rights violations.[40]

Fourth, victim access to remedies must be simplified. Current fragmentation requires affected individuals to navigate separate complaint procedures in multiple jurisdictions. A single coordinated mechanism for addressing transnational algorithmic harms would dramatically improve access to justice.

Fifth, emerging standards should recognize collective dimensions of algorithmic harms. While individual complaint mechanisms remain important, algorithmic systems typically affect entire populations simultaneously. Procedures allowing collective complaints by communities or their representatives would better match remedy mechanisms to harm patterns.

International human rights law provides essential tools for protecting dignity and autonomy against algorithmic governance. While current frameworks predate modern AI, their core principles remain directly applicable. The challenge ahead lies not in developing new human rights standards but in ensuring effective enforcement of existing obligations against powerful transnational actors. This requires strengthened international institutions, enhanced civil society capacity, and political commitment to prioritizing human rights over technological solutionism and corporate profits.

13.7 What You Can Do Now

International human rights advocacy requires coordinated action across borders and jurisdictions. These strategies enable effective participation in transnational accountability mechanisms:

Support Human Rights Documentation and Monitoring:

- Document algorithmic harms systematically using established human rights frameworks
- Submit shadow reports to UN treaty bodies during periodic review processes
- Participate in UN Special Rapporteur consultations and provide evidence of violations
- Support organizations conducting technical investigations of algorithmic systems
- Contribute to databases documenting algorithmic rights violations globally

Human rights treaty bodies depend on civil society documentation. The UN Human Rights Committee's review of state compliance relies heavily on shadow reports providing information governments omit. Organizations like Access Now coordinate shadow report submissions, contributing evidence strengthens these reports and improves oversight effectiveness.

Engage Regional Human Rights Systems:

[40] Optional Protocol to the International Covenant on Economic, Social and Cultural Rights, G.A. Res. 63/117, U.N. Doc. A/RES/63/117 (Dec. 10, 2008).

- File complaints with regional courts and commissions when domestic remedies are exhausted
- Support strategic litigation campaigns addressing systemic algorithmic harms
- Participate in amicus curiae submissions in cases before European Court, Inter-American Commission, or African Commission
- Advocate for regional human rights bodies to prioritize algorithmic governance issues
- Build coalitions connecting affected communities across jurisdictions

Regional systems provide more enforceable remedies than global mechanisms. The European Court's judgments create binding obligations; the Inter-American Commission can order precautionary measures; the African Commission addresses collective rights. Engaging these systems strategically creates precedent benefiting persons globally.

Advocate for Binding International Standards:

- Support the Council of Europe's Framework Convention on AI and Human Rights
- Advocate for your government to ratify and implement international human rights treaties
- Demand that trade agreements include enforceable human rights provisions for algorithmic systems
- Support UN initiatives to establish Special Procedures on artificial intelligence
- Build transnational coalitions demanding corporate accountability mechanisms

The Framework Convention represents the most significant opportunity for binding international standards. Public pressure on governments to support strong provisions can shape outcomes substantially.

Challenge Corporate Impunity:

- File complaints under OECD Guidelines for Multinational Enterprises regarding algorithmic harms
- Demand that corporations conducting human rights due diligence per UN Guiding Principles address algorithmic impacts
- Support shareholder resolutions requiring human rights assessments of AI systems
- Participate in corporate consultation processes to advocate for rights-based design
- Build pressure campaigns demanding transparency and accountability from technology corporations

While OECD Guidelines lack enforcement teeth, complaints create public pressure and reputational costs. Corporations increasingly respond to coordinated campaigns combining regulatory pressure, litigation threats, and public advocacy.

Strengthen Civil Society Capacity:

- Support organizations conducting algorithmic rights advocacy with funding and expertise
- Build technical capacity in human rights organizations to understand and audit algorithmic systems

- Connect human rights advocates with technical experts for collaborative investigations
- Support Global South organizations addressing algorithmic harms in under-resourced contexts
- Address funding dependencies that compromise civil society independence

Resource asymmetries limit civil society effectiveness. Supporting independent funding models and building technical capacity within human rights organizations strengthens accountability mechanisms.

Educate and Build Public Pressure:

- Translate complex algorithmic governance issues into accessible public campaigns
- Use international human rights framing to build coalitions across different affected communities
- Demand media coverage of algorithmic rights violations using human rights language
- Support parliamentary inquiries and oversight hearings addressing algorithmic governance
- Build public awareness about specific rights (privacy, non-discrimination, due process) in algorithmic contexts

Public pressure motivates governmental action. The Cambridge Analytica scandal produced regulatory responses not because the practices were unprecedented but because public outrage forced political attention.

Build Transnational Solidarity:

- Connect with affected communities in other jurisdictions facing similar algorithmic harms
- Share strategies, documentation, and evidence across borders
- Coordinate advocacy campaigns targeting the same corporations or systems in multiple jurisdictions
- Support less-resourced communities by sharing technical and legal expertise
- Build networks capable of responding rapidly to emerging algorithmic threats

Algorithmic governance operates transnationally; effective resistance requires transnational coordination. When Privacy International and partner organizations filed coordinated complaints against Clearview AI with five European data-protection authorities on the same day in May 2021, the simultaneous pressure across jurisdictions produced parallel enforcement actions that no isolated national challenge could have forced.

Participate in Norm-Setting Initiatives:

- Contribute to civil society declarations translating human rights principles into algorithmic governance requirements
- Participate in multi-stakeholder initiatives shaping emerging standards (while remaining vigilant about corporate capture)

- Advocate for meaningful civil society participation in international standard-setting processes
- Demand that affected communities, not merely experts, shape governance frameworks
- Build accountability mechanisms ensuring that voluntary initiatives produce actual compliance

Organizations like Access Now, Privacy International, and Amnesty International convene consultations for developing rights-based standards. Participation shapes emerging norms and provides opportunities to center affected communities' priorities.

International human rights advocacy requires persistence and coordination. While challenges are substantial and victories incremental, human rights frameworks provide essential leverage against algorithmic governance that transcends national boundaries. Your participation in transnational accountability mechanisms contributes to global movements defending human dignity against technological systems designed to undermine it. As I've demonstrated throughout this book, individual actions aggregate into collective power capable of constraining even the most powerful technological and corporate actors. The question is not whether change is possible but whether we'll organize effectively enough to achieve it before algorithmic governance becomes so entrenched that meaningful resistance becomes impossible.

References

Cases

'Big Brother Watch and Others v. United Kingdom', Application no. 58170/13 (European Court of Human Rights, 2021)
'Patrick Breyer v. Germany', Case C-582/14 (Court of the European Union, 2016)
'Centrum för rättvisa v. Sweden', Application no. 35252/08 (European Court of Human Rights, 2021)
'Glukhin v. Russia', Application no. 11519/20 (European Court of Human Rights, 2023)
'Institute for Human Rights and Development in Africa v. Angola', Communication No. 292/04 (African Commission on Human and Peoples' Rights, 2008).
'Munaf v. Romania', Communication No. 1539/2006 (UN Human Rights Committee, 2009)
'Yilmaz-Dogan v. Netherlands', Communication No. 1/1984 (Committee on the Elimination of Racial Discrimination, 1988)

Books

Alter KJ (2014) The new terrain of International Law: courts, politics, rights. Princeton University Press

Joseph SM (2013) The International covenant on civil and political rights: Cases, materials, and commentary, 3rd ed. Oxford University Press

Chapter 14
Moonshot Governance Approaches for Algorithmic Systems

14.1 The Need for Paradigm Shift in Constitutional Governance

Constitutional doctrine developed for regulating human decision-makers proves systematically inadequate when applied to algorithmic systems that operate at unprecedented scale, with inherent opacity, and through probabilistic reasoning unfamiliar to legal analysis. The traditional focus on individual rights and discrete state actions struggles to address the systemic and cumulative effects of algorithmic governance. I argue that constitutional adaptation requires more than incremental modifications, we need fundamental reconceptualization of technological governance itself.[1]

The inadequacy of incrementalist approaches becomes clear when examining how existing frameworks fragment and dissipate opposition to algorithmic power. Current regulatory responses treat algorithmic governance as a technical problem requiring procedural solutions: transparency requirements, impact assessments, oversight mechanisms, audit protocols. These interventions address symptoms while leaving power structures intact.[2]

Consider how procedural requirements actually function. The EU AI Act establishes elaborate compliance frameworks for "high-risk" AI systems, requiring technical documentation, quality management, human oversight, and conformity assessments.[3] Yet these requirements assume algorithmic governance is acceptable if properly managed. They create compliance costs that entrench large technology corporations while providing minimal protection for affected populations.

[1] Citron, Danielle Keats & Frank Pasquale, "The Scored Society: Due Process for Automated Predictions," Washington Law Review 89 (2014): 1–33.

[2] Cohen, Julie E., 'Between Truth and Power: The Legal Constructions of Informational Capitalism' (Oxford University Press, 2019), pp. 89–124.

[3] European Parliament and Council, Regulation (EU) 2024/1689 on Artificial Intelligence (AI Act), Articles 8–15 (high-risk AI system requirements).

R. Yadav-Ranjan, *Constitutional Democracy in the Algorithmic Age*, Law, Governance and Technology Series 83, https://doi.org/10.1007/978-3-032-34604-9_14

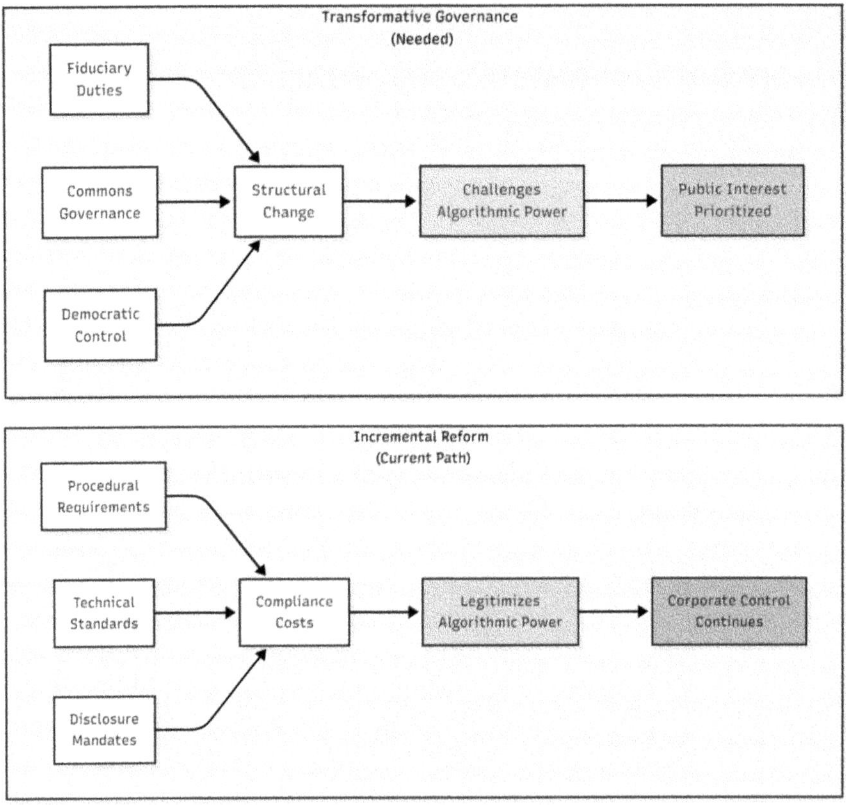

Fig. 14.1 These two comparison charts illustrates how incremental reforms, while appearing responsive, ultimately legitimize rather than constrain algorithmic power, while transformative governance fundamentally restructures power relations

Figure 14.1 illustrates how incremental reforms, while appearing responsive, ultimately legitimize rather than constrain algorithmic power, while transformative governance fundamentally restructures power relations.

Similarly, the NIST AI Risk Management Framework provides technical standards that courts may eventually reference in determining constitutional adequacy.[4] But technical adequacy is not constitutional adequacy. An algorithm can be perfectly calibrated in technical terms while still violating fundamental rights by making decisions through processes incompatible with democratic values.

[4] National Institute of Standards and Technology, "AI Risk Management Framework," NIST AI 100–1 (January 2023).

14.1.1 Power Dynamics in Incrementalist Reform

Incrementalist approaches serve corporate interests by channeling reform energy into manageable adjustments that preserve fundamental power asymmetries. I document here how this dynamic operates across multiple governance domains.

First, procedural requirements create the appearance of constraint while permitting exercise of algorithmic power to continue essentially unchecked. When technology corporations can satisfy compliance requirements through technical adjustments that leave their business models intact, regulation legitimizes rather than limits their authority. The Partnership on AI, funded primarily by the corporations it purports to constrain, exemplifies this dynamic, industry self-regulation branded as stakeholder governance.[5]

Second, fragmentation of governance across jurisdictions prevents comprehensive reform. When different regulatory systems impose varying requirements, corporations optimize globally while complying minimally in each jurisdiction. The resulting patchwork creates compliance complexity that advantages large actors with legal sophistication while providing inconsistent protection that sophisticated corporations can navigate strategically.[6]

Third, captured agencies implement reforms that reflect industry preferences rather than public interests. When regulatory staff rotate between government and industry positions, when agencies depend on industry expertise for technical understanding, when corporations fund the research that informs policy, the resulting frameworks predictably favor corporate interests.[7]

The revolving door between technology corporations and regulatory agencies illustrates this capture. Agencies like the FTC, tasked with constraining algorithmic power, employ former Google, Facebook, and Amazon executives in senior positions.[8] While these individuals bring technical expertise, they also bring industry perspectives that shape how they conceptualize governance challenges and solutions.

Fourth, resource asymmetries ensure that incremental reforms favor corporations capable of absorbing compliance costs. When new requirements impose burdens, large technology corporations can hire compliance staff, develop sophisticated technical documentation, and engage in regulatory proceedings effectively. Smaller competitors and public interest organizations lack comparable resources, ensuring that incremental regulation entrenches incumbent power.[9]

---

[5] Partnership on AI, "2023 Annual Report," analyzing funding sources showing predominantly corporate contribution from members including Google, Meta, Amazon, Microsoft.

[6] Bradford, Anu, 'The Brussels Effect: How the European Union Rules the World' (Oxford University Press, 2020), pp. 234–267 (analyzing fragmentation's effects on global governance).

[7] Zuboff, Shoshana, 'The Age of Surveillance Capitalism' (PublicAffairs, 2019), pp. 376–423 (documenting regulatory capture in technology governance).

[8] On the revolving door between the FTC and major technology firms, see Revolving Door Project, "The Top Revolving Door Jobs for Ex-FTC Lawyers and Economists".

[9] Khan, Lina M., "Amazon's Antitrust Paradox," Yale Law Journal 126 (2017): 710–805, at 782–93 (analyzing how compliance costs entrench incumbents).

The pattern is clear: incrementalist reform creates regulatory theater that provides the appearance of democratic control while preserving corporate domination. Paradigm shift requires recognizing this dynamic and pursuing governance approaches that fundamentally restructure power rather than merely managing its exercise.

14.2 Fiduciary Approaches to AI Governance

Fiduciary frameworks reconceptualize the duties that technology corporations owe to users and society, moving beyond consumer protection's minimal standards to robust obligations grounded in trust relationships. I examine here how fiduciary principles, well-established in law and medicine, could transform algorithmic governance.[10]

Fiduciary relationships exist where one party (the fiduciary) exercises power or holds property for another party (the beneficiary) in circumstances where the beneficiary's vulnerability and the fiduciary's specialized knowledge or authority create heightened duties. Doctors, lawyers, trustees, and corporate directors all function as fiduciaries, owing their clients or beneficiaries duties of loyalty and care that transcend ordinary contractual obligations.[11]

Technology corporations exercise similar power over users. They collect comprehensive personal data, make consequential decisions through algorithmic systems, control access to digital infrastructure essential for modern life, and possess technical sophistication that vastly exceeds users' understanding. This power imbalance creates precisely the vulnerability and information asymmetry that traditionally triggers fiduciary obligations.[12]

Figure 14.2 shows how reconceptualizing technology corporations as information fiduciaries would impose four core duties with specific obligations under each, fundamentally restructuring the relationship between platforms and users.

Treating technology corporations as fiduciaries would establish several transformative requirements:

Duty of Loyalty: Fiduciaries must act in beneficiaries' interests rather than their own when conflicts arise. For technology corporations, this would prohibit designing algorithmic systems primarily to maximize corporate profits when doing so harms users. The surveillance advertising model that dominates contemporary platforms,

[10] Balkin, Jack M., "Information Fiduciaries and the First Amendment," UC Davis Law Review 49 (2016): 1183–1234.

[11] Restatement (Third) of Trusts § 2 (defining fiduciary relationships); Tamar Frankel, 'Fiduciary Law' (Oxford University Press, 2011), pp. 1–45.

[12] Lavi, Michal S., "Evil Nudges," Vanderbilt Journal of Entertainment & Technology Law 21 (2017): 60–112, at 89–97 (analyzing power asymmetries in digital platforms).

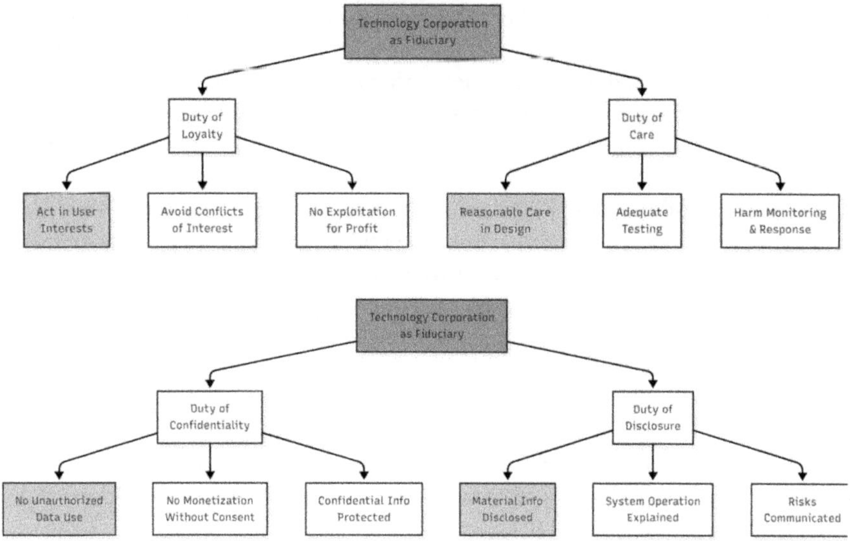

Fig. 14.2 These two framework graphs show how reconceptualizing technology corporations as information fiduciaries would impose four core duties with specific obligations under each, fundamentally restructuring the relationship between platforms and users

extracting comprehensive data, manipulating attention, and optimizing for engagement regardless of consequences, directly violates loyalty duties by prioritizing corporate revenue over user wellbeing.[13]

The duty of loyalty would transform business models fundamentally. When Facebook designs News Feed algorithms to maximize engagement even when doing so amplifies misinformation and polarization, when YouTube's recommendation system guides vulnerable users toward extremist content to increase watch time, when TikTok's algorithm deliberately creates addictive patterns among adolescents, all these practices violate fiduciary loyalty by sacrificing user interests for corporate profits.[14]

Duty of Care: Fiduciaries must exercise reasonable care in managing beneficiaries' interests. For algorithmic systems, this requires careful design, thorough testing, ongoing monitoring, and prompt remediation when harms emerge. The duty of care standard is contextual, greater care is required when stakes are higher and beneficiaries more vulnerable.[15]

---

[13] Richards, Neil M. & Woodrow Hartzog, "A Duty of Loyalty for Privacy Law," Washington University Law Review 99 (2021): 961–1008.

[14] Frances Haugen testimony before UK Parliament (October 2021), documenting Facebook's internal research showing News Feed algorithms amplify misinformation; YouTube internal documents leaked 2019 showing recommendation system guides toward extremism.

[15] DeBroff, Stacy L., "The Duty of Care in the Digital Age," Business Lawyer 74 (2019): 1089–1112.

Current practices fall far short. Technology corporations deploy algorithmic systems affecting millions with minimal testing, limited understanding of long-term consequences, and inadequate monitoring for emerging harms. When problems surface, corporations typically deny responsibility or make minimal adjustments that preserve core business practices. Fiduciary care duties would require dramatically higher standards.[16]

Duty of Confidentiality: Fiduciaries cannot use information obtained through the relationship for their own benefit. This principle directly challenges data extraction business models. User data collected by platforms constitutes confidential information that cannot be monetized for corporate benefit without explicit, informed consent, not the coerced "agreement" obtained through take-it-or-leave-it terms of service.[17]

Duty of Disclosure: Fiduciaries must provide beneficiaries with material information necessary for informed decision-making. For algorithmic systems, this requires explaining how systems work, what data they collect, how decisions are made, and what consequences users may face. Current opacity violates disclosure duties systematically.[18]

14.2.1 Power Dynamics in Fiduciary Implementation

While fiduciary frameworks offer transformative potential, implementation faces predictable resistance from corporate actors whose business models depend on exploiting users. I document here both the implementation challenges and strategies for overcoming them.

First, corporations will resist fiduciary classification itself, arguing that their relationships with users are purely commercial rather than trust-based. This argument fails on its merits, the power asymmetry, information disparity, and essential nature of digital platforms create paradigmatic fiduciary relationships. But legal recognition requires overcoming corporate lobbying and judicial conservatism that favors existing arrangements.[19]

Several jurisdictions have begun recognizing technology corporations' fiduciary-like obligations. The California Privacy Rights Act establishes heightened duties for businesses processing sensitive personal information, while European data protection

---

[16] Noble, Safiya Umoja, 'Algorithms of Oppression: How Search Engines Reinforce Racism' (NYU Press, 2018), pp. 1–35 (documenting inadequate testing before algorithmic deployment).

[17] Hoofnagle, Chris Jay, et al., "Behavioral Advertising: The Offer You Cannot Refuse," Harvard Law & Policy Review 6 (2012): 273–296.

[18] Wachter, Sandra, et al., "Why a Right to Explanation of Automated Decision-Making Does Not Exist in the General Data Protection Regulation," International Data Privacy Law 7 (2017): 76–99.

[19] Bar-Gill, Oren, 'Seduction by Contract' (Oxford University Press, 2012), pp. 178–204 (analyzing corporate resistance to higher standards).

authorities increasingly emphasize trust responsibilities in GDPR enforcement.[20] These precedents provide foundations for broader fiduciary frameworks.

Second, corporations will argue that fiduciary duties are incompatible with innovation and economic viability. This claim proves empirically false, doctors, lawyers, and investment advisers all operate successfully under fiduciary constraints. The argument actually reveals that current technology business models depend on betraying user trust, which is precisely why fiduciary frameworks are necessary.[21]

Third, even if fiduciary duties are established, enforcement faces resource constraints. Beneficiaries must identify violations, which requires technical sophistication most users lack. Individual enforcement through private lawsuits faces standing barriers, arbitration clauses, and resource asymmetries. Regulatory enforcement confronts captured agencies and inadequate budgets.[22]

Effective implementation requires multiple complementary mechanisms: private rights of action with fee-shifting provisions that enable impact litigation; qui tam provisions allowing private enforcement of public interests with bounty incentives; adequately funded regulatory agencies with technical expertise; international coordination preventing jurisdiction shopping; and criminal penalties for egregious violations that create genuine deterrence.[23]

14.3 Global AI Commons

The concept of AI commons challenges proprietary control of foundational algorithmic infrastructure, proposing instead that certain AI systems should be governed as common resources serving collective interests rather than corporate profits. I examine here how commons governance principles could transform algorithmic power structures.[24]

Commons governance has ancient roots, from medieval common lands to modern commons like the atmosphere, oceans, and electromagnetic spectrum. The fundamental insight is that certain resources are so essential for collective wellbeing that private ownership creates unacceptable inequalities and risks. Instead, these resources

---

[20] California Privacy Rights Act § 1798.100–199 (establishing heightened duties for sensitive data); European Data Protection Board, "Guidelines on Concepts of Controller and Processor" (2020).

[21] Lessig, Lawrence, "Against Transparency: The Perils of Openness in Government," New Republic (October 2009) (noting professionals operate successfully under fiduciary constraints).

[22] TransUnion LLC v. Ramirez, 141 S. Ct. 2190 (2021) (limiting standing for privacy violations); Epic Systems Corp. v. Lewis, 138 S. Ct. 1612 (2018) (enforcing arbitration clauses against collective action).

[23] Engstrom, David Freeman, "Public Regulation of Private Enforcement," Harvard Law Review 128 (2015): 1690–1779 (analyzing bounty mechanisms).

[24] Benkler, Yochai, 'The Wealth of Networks' (Yale University Press, 2006), pp. 59–132 (theorizing commons-based peer production).

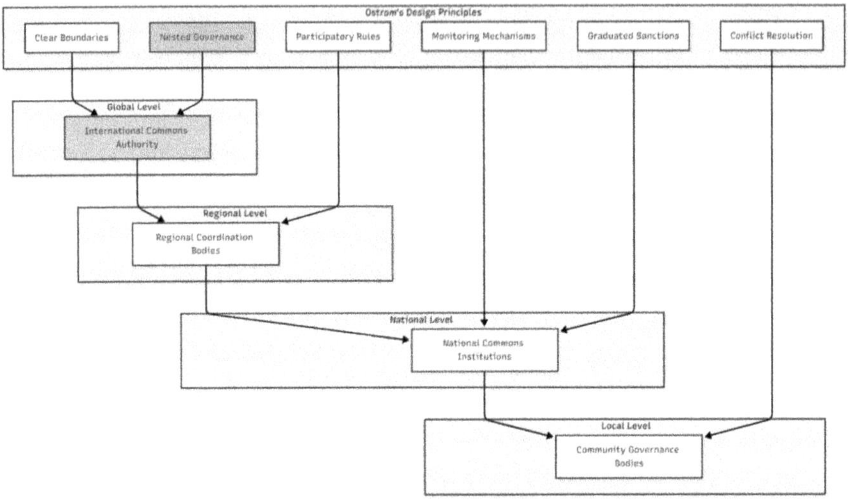

Fig. 14.3 This organizational chart shows Ostrom's commons governance principles adapted for AI infrastructure, illustrating nested governance structures operating at multiple scales

should be managed according to principles that ensure broad access, sustainable use, and democratic oversight.[25]

Political economist Elinor Ostrom, whose work on commons governance earned the Nobel Prize, identified design principles for successful commons: clear boundaries defining who has rights to use the resource, participatory decision-making processes, monitoring mechanisms to detect violations, graduated sanctions for rule-breaking, conflict resolution procedures, and nested governance structures operating at multiple scales.[26]

Figure 14.3 shows Ostrom's commons governance principles adapted for AI infrastructure, illustrating nested governance structures operating at multiple scales.

These principles could apply to algorithmic infrastructure. Consider three categories where commons governance might operate:

Foundational Models: Large language models, computer vision systems, and other foundational AI models require enormous computational resources and data for training, creating natural monopolies that concentrate power. When a few corporations control these models, they determine who can access advanced AI capabilities and under what conditions. Commons governance would make foundational models publicly available, trained on collectively governed data, and developed through democratic processes that ensure broad benefit rather than narrow profit.[27]

[25] Bollier, David, 'Think Like a Commoner: A Short Introduction to the Life of the Commons' (New Society Publishers, 2014).

[26] Ostrom, Elinor, 'Governing the Commons: The Evolution of Institutions for Collective Action' (Cambridge University Press, 1990), pp. 88–102 (design principles for commons governance).

[27] Birhane, Abeba, et al., "The Forgotten Margins of AI Ethics," Proceedings of the 2022 ACM Conference on Fairness, Accountability, and Transparency (2022): 948–958.

The contrast with current arrangements is stark. OpenAI, despite its name, operates GPT models as proprietary resources, charging substantial fees and maintaining complete control over access. Google, Meta, and Amazon similarly leverage their foundational models to extend dominance across AI-dependent domains. Commons governance would break these monopolies.[28]

Essential Data Infrastructure: Certain data sets are so essential for AI development that private control creates unacceptable inequalities. Medical research data, geographic information, scientific publications, government records, these resources should be available as commons rather than controlled by commercial entities that extract rents from access.[29]

Current trends toward data privatization threaten scientific progress and democratic governance. When academic publishers charge exorbitant fees for access to taxpayer-funded research, when genetic databases become proprietary resources, when government data gets monetized through public-private partnerships, we undermine collective capacity for addressing shared challenges.[30]

Algorithmic Governance Systems: AI systems making consequential decisions about public benefits, criminal justice, education, healthcare, and other domains should operate as commons governed democratically rather than proprietary systems controlled by vendors. When algorithmic decision-making affects fundamental rights, private ownership is fundamentally incompatible with democratic values.[31]

The practice of governments purchasing proprietary algorithmic systems from corporations creates accountability gaps. When criminal risk assessment algorithms or child welfare prediction systems operate as trade secrets, affected populations cannot understand how decisions are made or challenge discriminatory outcomes. Commons governance would ensure transparency, public ownership, and democratic control.[32]

---

[28] OpenAI pricing as of 2024: GPT-4 API access costs $30–120 per million tokens, creating substantial barriers to access while OpenAI maintains complete control over model architecture and training.

[29] Madison, Michael J., et al., "Constructing Commons in the Cultural Environment," Cornell Law Review 95 (2010): 657–709.

[30] Stiglitz, Joseph E., "Knowledge as a Global Public Good" in 'Global Public Goods' (Oxford University Press, 1999), pp. 308–325.

[31] Eubanks, Virginia, 'Automating Inequality: How High-Tech Tools Profile, Police, and Punish the Poor' (St. Martin's Press, 2018), pp. 38–73 (analyzing problems with proprietary government algorithms).

[32] Richardson, Rashida, et al., "Dirty Data, Bad Predictions: How Civil Rights Violations Impact Police Data, Predictive Policing Systems, and Justice," New York University Law Review Online 94 (2019): 15–55.

14.3.1 Power Dynamics in Commons Implementation

Creating AI commons faces fierce resistance from corporations whose market power depends on proprietary control. I document here both the obstacles and strategies for advancing commons governance.

First, intellectual property regimes strongly favor private ownership. Copyright protects training data, patents cover algorithmic techniques, trade secret law shields operational details. Establishing commons requires either purchasing these rights at prohibitive cost or legislative action to create compulsory licensing or eminent domain for essential algorithmic infrastructure.[33]

Several precedents suggest pathways forward. The Bayh-Dole Act established march-in rights allowing government to require licensing of patents developed with federal funding when necessary for public health or safety.[34] Similar frameworks could apply to AI systems developed with public resources or essential for public functions.

Second, technological complexity creates barriers to effective commons governance. Managing sophisticated AI systems requires technical expertise concentrated in corporations. Building public capacity for commons governance demands substantial investment in technical training, institutional development, and infrastructure, resources that governments have systematically failed to provide.[35]

However, successful examples demonstrate feasibility. The Large Hadron Collider represents commons governance of immensely complex scientific infrastructure, operating under principles ensuring broad access and collective benefit. The Internet itself began as commons infrastructure, only later captured through privatization that commons advocates now challenge.[36]

Third, international coordination proves essential but difficult. Algorithmic systems operate globally while governance remains jurisdictional. Corporations can locate operations in jurisdictions hostile to commons principles, undermining national efforts. Effective commons require international agreements, which powerful states (especially the United States) resist when such agreements limit corporate prerogatives.[37]

Despite these challenges, commons movements have achieved substantial victories. Open-source software provides freely available alternatives to proprietary systems across domains. Creative Commons licensing has enabled sharing of cultural

---

[33] Samuelson, Pamela, "Allocating Ownership Rights in Computer-Generated Works," University of Pittsburgh Law Review 47 (1986): 1185–1228.

[34] Bayh-Dole Act, 35 U.S.C. § 200 et seq.; march-in rights under § 203.

[35] O'Neil, Cathy, 'Weapons of Math Destruction' (Crown, 2016), pp. 199–218 (discussing need for public technical capacity).

[36] CERN (European Organization for Nuclear Research), 'LHC: The Guide' (2017) (explaining commons governance of particle physics infrastructure); Wu, Tim, 'The Master Switch' (Knopf, 2010) (documenting internet privatization).

[37] Farrell, Henry & Abraham Newman, "Weaponized Interdependence," International Security 44 (2019): 42–79 (analyzing jurisdictional challenges in global governance).

and scientific resources on massive scales. Wikipedia demonstrates that commons governance can produce public goods rivaling or exceeding proprietary alternatives.[38]

14.4 Implementation Pathways and Transitional Mechanisms

Transformative governance approaches require practical implementation strategies that bridge theoretical ambition with political reality. I examine here concrete pathways for advancing fiduciary frameworks and commons governance despite predictable resistance.[39]

Legislative Strategy: Building political coalitions capable of passing transformative legislation requires connecting diverse constituencies around shared interests in constraining algorithmic power. Labor unions concerned about workplace surveillance, civil rights organizations challenging algorithmic discrimination, consumer advocates addressing exploitative practices, privacy organizations resisting data extraction, small businesses competing against platform monopolies, all have stakes in governance reform.[40]

The enactment of the California Consumer Privacy Act in 2018, spurred by a ballot-initiative campaign that pushed the legislature to act over intense technology-industry opposition, demonstrates how coalition politics can achieve substantial reform despite corporate resistance.[41] Similar coalitions could advance fiduciary legislation or commons governance frameworks at state and federal levels.

Critical first steps include:

- Municipal and state legislation establishing fiduciary duties or commons principles in specific domains (public benefits, education, healthcare)
- Federal legislation creating pilot programs for commons-governed AI systems in government functions
- International agreements among like-minded nations to coordinate commons initiatives and resist corporate jurisdiction shopping
- Legislative requirements that government procurement favor commons-governed over proprietary systems

---

[38] Raymond, Eric S., 'The Cathedral and the Bazaar' (O'Reilly, 1999) (analyzing open-source software development); Lessig, Lawrence, 'Code 2.0' (Basic Books, 2006), pp. 145–176 (discussing Creative Commons).

[39] Geels, Frank W., "Regime Resistance against Low-Carbon Transitions," Theory, Culture & Society 31 (2014): 21–40 (analyzing pathways for systemic transformation).

[40] Rahman, K. Sabeel & Kathleen Thelen, "The Rise of the Platform Business Model and the Transformation of Twenty-First-Century Capitalism," Politics & Society 47 (2019): 177–204.

[41] California Consumer Privacy Act, Cal. Civ. Code § 1798.100 et seq. (2018), enacted following the Californians for Consumer Privacy ballot-initiative campaign.

Judicial Strategy: Courts can recognize fiduciary duties through common law development without requiring legislative action. Strategic litigation that carefully selects plaintiffs, factual records, and legal theories can establish precedents recognizing technology corporations' fiduciary obligations.[42]

The litigation campaign against tobacco companies provides a model. Through decades of persistent litigation, advocates established that cigarette manufacturers owed duties to consumers that far exceeded ordinary product liability, ultimately producing massive settlements and industry transformation.[43] Similar long-term campaigns could establish technology corporations' fiduciary status.

Promising litigation vectors include:

- Class actions alleging breach of fiduciary duty when algorithmic systems harm users while benefiting corporations
- Securities litigation when corporations misrepresent their duties to users, creating material omissions for investors
- Qui tam actions under false claims statutes when corporations provide algorithmic services to government while violating duties to affected populations
- Constitutional litigation when government delegation of decision-making to private algorithmic systems violates due process

Regulatory Innovation: Even without new legislation, agencies possess substantial authority to implement transformative governance through creative regulatory interpretation. The FTC's authority over unfair and deceptive practices, for instance, could support fiduciary-like duties. The FCC's public interest mandate could justify commons governance of communication infrastructure. CFPB authority over financial services could establish fiduciary frameworks for financial algorithms.[44]

The Consumer Financial Protection Bureau's 2022–03 circular on credit algorithms demonstrates regulatory innovation's potential. By interpreting existing adverse action notice requirements to demand meaningful explanations of algorithmic decisions, the CFPB established practical transparency requirements that move toward fiduciary disclosure duties.[45]

Additional regulatory strategies include:

- Agency guidance documents establishing expectations that technology corporations will act as fiduciaries
- Enforcement actions framing violations as breaches of trust rather than mere consumer protection failures

---

42 DesAutels, Sara E., "Public Interest Litigation in Social Movement Advocacy," Mobilization 23 (2018): 131–151.

43 Derthick, Martha A., 'Up in Smoke: From Legislation to Litigation in Tobacco Politics' (CQ Press, 2011).

44 Freiermuth, Rachel R., "CFPB's Authority Over Fintech," North Carolina Banking Institute 22 (2018): 367–398.

45 Consumer Financial Protection Bureau, "Circular 2022–03: Adverse Action Notification Requirements in Connection with Credit Decisions Based on Complex Algorithms" (May 2022–03).

- Regulatory safe harbors for commons-governed systems, creating incentives for voluntary adoption
- Technical standards establishing minimum requirements for fiduciary compliance or commons governance

International Coordination: Given algorithmic systems' transnational nature, effective governance requires international cooperation. While challenging, several initiatives suggest pathways toward coordinated action.[46]

The Council of Europe's Framework Convention on AI and Human Rights provides a potential vehicle for binding international standards incorporating fiduciary principles.[47] The UN Secretary-General's AI Advisory Body has recommended global coordination on AI governance, though translating recommendations into binding commitments requires sustained diplomatic pressure.[48]

Implementation strategies include:

- Bilateral and regional agreements among states committed to transformative governance
- Trade agreements conditioning market access on adoption of fiduciary or commons principles
- International standard-setting through ISO, IEEE, and similar bodies
- Coordination among competition authorities to address algorithmic power collectively
- Support for Global South nations developing governance frameworks outside dominant models

Movement Building: Ultimately, transformative governance requires social movements capable of generating political pressure that overcomes corporate resistance. I document here how movement building can create conditions for fundamental change.[49]

Historical precedents demonstrate that seemingly impossible reforms become achievable when movements build sufficient power. The civil rights movement, environmental movement, and labor movement all achieved transformative legal changes by building broad coalitions, sustaining pressure over time, and connecting moral arguments to political organization.[50]

---

[46] Farrell, Henry & Abraham L. Newman, 'Of Privacy and Power: The Transatlantic Struggle over Freedom and Security' (Princeton University Press, 2019).

[47] Council of Europe, Framework Convention on Artificial Intelligence and Human Rights, Democracy and the Rule of Law, CETS No. 225 (adopted 17 May 2024, opened for signature 5 September 2024).

[48] UN Secretary-General's High-Level Advisory Body on Artificial Intelligence, "Interim Report: Governing AI for Humanity" (December 2023).

[49] Tarrow, Sidney, 'Power in Movement' (Cambridge University Press, 2011), pp. 29–58 (analyzing how movements create conditions for transformation).

[50] McAdam, Doug, 'Political Process and the Development of Black Insurgency' (University of Chicago Press, 1982) (civil rights movement); Andrews, Richard N.L., 'Managing the Environment, Managing Ourselves' (Yale University Press, 2006) (environmental movement); Zieger, Robert H., 'American Workers, American Unions' (Johns Hopkins University Press, 1994) (labor movement).

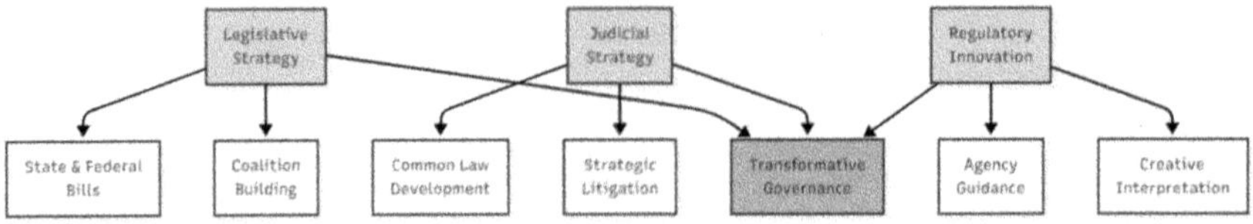

Fig. 14.4 Top: Institutional strategies (legislative, judicial, regulatory). Bottom: Coordination and mobilization strategies (international, movement building). All pathways must work in concert to achieve transformative governance

Contemporary digital rights movements have achieved significant victories despite asymmetric resources. The campaign against SOPA/PIPA legislation demonstrated that coordinated grassroots mobilization can defeat well-funded corporate lobbying.[51] The movement for net neutrality built sufficient public support that even conservative regulators felt compelled to preserve basic principles.[52] The right to repair movement has begun breaking manufacturer control over device maintenance, establishing precedents for challenging proprietary dominance.[53]

Critical movement-building strategies include:

- Public education campaigns making abstract algorithmic harms concrete and personal
- Direct action targeting high-profile corporate practices, generating media attention and public awareness
- Electoral organizing ensuring that legislators feel political consequences for opposing reform
- Worker organizing enabling technology employees to challenge corporate policies from within
- Coalition building connecting digital rights advocates with labor, civil rights, environmental, and consumer movements
- International solidarity among movements in different jurisdictions, preventing corporations from playing regulatory systems against each other.

Figures 14.4 and 14.5 illustrates how five distinct implementation strategies, each with specific tactics, must converge to achieve transformative governance that fundamentally restructures algorithmic power relations.

---

[51] Doctorow, Cory, "How SOPA/PIPA Was Defeated: We Can Win" (Boing Boing, January 2012), documenting grassroots campaign that generated eight million petition signatures and thousands of website blackouts.

[52] Pickard, Victor, 'America's Battle for Media Democracy' (Cambridge University Press, 2015), pp. 178–203 (documenting net neutrality movement).

[53] Right to Repair movement victories documented by Repair.org: 2022 New York electronics right to repair law; 2023 California consumer electronics repair act; 2024 Oregon right to repair for agricultural equipment.

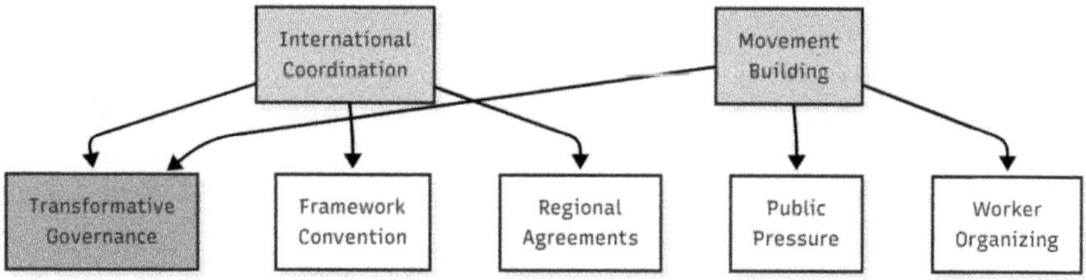

Fig. 14.5 These diagrams illustrates how five distinct implementation strategies, each with specific tactics, must converge to achieve transformative governance that fundamentally restructures algorithmic power relations

14.5 Future Proofing

Transformative governance approaches require sustained action across multiple fronts. These strategies enable effective participation in advancing fiduciary frameworks and commons governance:

Advocate for Fiduciary Legislation:

- Contact legislators demanding bills establishing technology corporations' fiduciary duties
- Support organizations like the Electronic Privacy Information Center and Consumer Federation of America conducting fiduciary advocacy campaigns
- Participate in public comment periods when agencies consider fiduciary-related regulations
- Write op-eds and letters to editors explaining why fiduciary duties are necessary for algorithmic governance
- Demand that political candidates commit to fiduciary legislation as condition for support
- Build coalitions connecting consumer protection, civil rights, labor, and digital rights organizations around shared fiduciary agenda

Fiduciary legislation faces corporate opposition but public support. Polls consistently show that voters believe technology corporations should be held to higher standards of care and loyalty.[54] Converting this latent support into political pressure requires organized advocacy making fiduciary obligations concrete and urgent.

Support Commons Governance Initiatives:

- Advocate for government funding of open-source AI development as public commons
- Support policies requiring that publicly-funded research and data be available as commons rather than privatized

[54] Pew Research Center, "Americans' Views on Technology Companies" (2024): 64% believe technology corporations should face stricter regulation; 64% agree they should be held to similar standards as doctors and lawyers.

- Demand that government procurement favor commons-governed over proprietary algorithmic systems
- Participate in existing commons projects like Wikipedia, OpenStreetMap, and open-source software to demonstrate viability
- Build technical capacity in commons governance through education and institutional development
- Connect with international commons movements coordinating global advocacy

The commons movement combines principled opposition to privatization with practical demonstration that commons governance can produce superior outcomes. Supporting existing commons strengthens arguments for expanding commons principles to algorithmic infrastructure.[55]

Engage in Strategic Litigation:

- Support impact litigation organizations like the ACLU and Electronic Frontier Foundation pursuing fiduciary recognition
- Participate as plaintiffs in class actions alleging breach of fiduciary duty by technology corporations
- File complaints with FTC, CFPB, and state attorneys general framing harms as trust violations
- Support qui tam litigation enabling private enforcement of public fiduciary interests
- Advocate for removal of arbitration clauses that prevent effective fiduciary litigation
- Build litigation war chests through coordinated fundraising for sustained legal campaigns

Strategic litigation requires patience and resources. The campaign against tobacco took decades; algorithmic governance reform will similarly require persistent legal challenges that gradually establish precedents for fiduciary recognition.[56]

Build Public Awareness:

- Translate complex governance proposals into accessible public campaigns emphasizing trust betrayal
- Generate media coverage of specific corporate practices violating fiduciary principles
- Use social media to coordinate public pressure campaigns targeting particularly egregious violations
- Support investigative journalism exposing how corporate algorithms harm users for profit

---

[55] Hess, Charlotte & Elinor Ostrom, eds., 'Understanding Knowledge as a Commons' (MIT Press, 2006).

[56] Galanter, Marc & Thomas Palay, 'Tournament of Lawyers' (University of Chicago Press, 1991) (analyzing sustained litigation campaigns).

- Develop popular education materials explaining fiduciary duties and commons governance
- Connect abstract principles to concrete experiences of algorithmic harm in people's lives

Public awareness campaigns succeed when they connect systemic critiques to personal experiences. When people understand how algorithmic systems manipulate their attention, extract their data, and make consequential decisions affecting their lives, they become more receptive to transformative governance proposals.[57]

Support Worker Organizing:

- Amplify technology workers advocating for ethical practices within corporations
- Support unionization efforts among technology workers who can challenge corporate policies directly
- Connect technology workers with movements addressing algorithmic harms
- Advocate for whistleblower protections enabling technology workers to expose violations without career destruction
- Build worker cooperatives developing algorithmic systems under democratic governance as alternatives to corporate models
- Demand that unions negotiate contract provisions establishing worker voice in algorithmic design and deployment

Technology workers possess unique leverage and knowledge. Supporting their organizing builds capacity for internal challenges to corporate practices while strengthening external reform movements.[58]

Advance International Coordination:

- Support the Council of Europe Framework Convention negotiations, advocating for strong fiduciary and commons provisions
- Build transatlantic coalitions connecting US digital rights movements with European, Latin American, African, and Asian counterparts
- Advocate for trade agreements conditioning market access on adoption of transformative governance principles
- Support UN initiatives for global AI governance coordination
- Connect with Global South movements developing governance approaches outside dominant models
- Build capacity in under-resourced jurisdictions to participate effectively in international governance discussions

International coordination faces the challenge that corporations can exploit jurisdictional fragmentation. Building transnational movements capable of coordinated

---

[57] Schneier, Bruce, 'Data and Goliath' (Norton, 2015), pp. 171–196 (discussing effective public education strategies).

[58] Tarnoff, Ben, "The Making of the Tech Worker Movement," Logic Magazine (May 2020), documenting growth of technology worker organizing.

advocacy across jurisdictions prevents corporations from undermining governance through regulatory arbitrage.[59]

Practice Prefigurative Politics:

- Use commons-governed platforms and open-source software, demonstrating demand for alternatives
- Participate in platform cooperatives that implement democratic governance and fiduciary principles
- Support worker-owned technology companies challenging corporate dominance
- Build community networks providing internet access under commons principles
- Develop alternative economic models rewarding cooperation over extraction
- Create proof-of-concept demonstrations that fiduciary governance and commons models are viable

Prefigurative politics, building the alternative society within the shell of the old, both demonstrates feasibility and builds capacity for transformation. When commons governance and fiduciary principles operate successfully at smaller scales, arguments for systemic adoption become more credible.[60]

Hold Institutions Accountable:

- Pressure universities to avoid partnerships that privatize publicly-funded AI research
- Demand that government agencies develop commons infrastructure rather than purchasing proprietary systems
- Challenge foundations and philanthropies funding corporate-friendly governance initiatives
- Support whistleblowers exposing how regulatory capture prevents transformative reform
- Document revolving door connections between regulatory agencies and technology corporations
- Demand that media coverage address corporate power rather than accepting industry framing

Institutional accountability creates pressure from multiple directions. When universities, government agencies, foundations, and media outlets face consequences for facilitating corporate dominance, they become more receptive to transformative alternatives.[61]

Transformative governance requires recognizing that incremental reforms legitimize rather than constrain algorithmic power. While demanding immediate changes

---

[59] Anner, Mark, 'Solidarity Transformed: Labor Responses to Globalization' (Cornell University Press, 2011), pp. 1–28 (analyzing transnational labor coordination).

[60] Wright, Erik Olin, 'Envisioning Real Utopias' (Verso, 2010), pp. 303–348 (discussing prefigurative politics and systemic transformation).

[61] Kwet, Michael, "Digital Colonialism: US Empire and the New Imperialism in the Global South," Race & Class 60 (2019): 3–26 (analyzing institutional complicity in corporate dominance).

that protect people from current harms, we must simultaneously build movements capable of achieving the paradigm shifts necessary for genuine democratic control of algorithmic systems. The choice is not between idealism and pragmatism but between meaningful transformation and managed decline of constitutional democracy. As I have demonstrated throughout this book, the tools for transformation exist, what remains uncertain is whether we will organize effectively enough to deploy them before algorithmic power becomes so entrenched that meaningful resistance becomes impossible.

References

Cases

Carpenter v. United States, 138 S. Ct. 2206 (2018) (cell site location information requires warrant)
Federal Trade Commission v. Facebook, Inc., No. 20-cv-3590 (D.D.C. filed 2020) (antitrust enforcement action)
United States v. Philip Morris USA Inc., 449 F. Supp. 2d 1 (D.D.C. 2006) (tobacco litigation establishing heightened corporate duties)

Books

Ostrom E (1990) Governing the commons: the evolution of institutions for collective action. Cambridge University Press
Balkin JM (2018) The fiduciary model of privacy. In: The Cambridge handbook of consumer privacy. Cambridge University Press

Chapter 15
Data Monetization and the Commodification of Human Experience

15.1 The Data Economy and Human Experience as Raw Material

The rise of surveillance capitalism represents not merely another phase in economic evolution but a fundamental restructuring of market dynamics that converts human existence into raw material for commercial extraction. I examine here how this transformation operates and what distinguishes it from previous forms of capitalism.[1]

Traditional market structures, whatever their limitations, at least nominally operated through voluntary exchange between parties with some understanding of transaction terms. Surveillance capitalism functions differently, through orchestrated information asymmetry, power imbalance, and systematic exploitation of behavioral data generated through lived experience. Users are neither customers nor products but rather untapped resources being systematically depleted.[2]

The business model operates on what Shoshana Zuboff terms "behavioral surplus", the excess information harvested beyond functional service requirements that becomes raw material for algorithmic prediction products.[3] This is not incidental byproduct of service delivery but the fundamental business objective. Google does not principally operate a search service; it systematically accumulates behavioral patterns for predictive market exploitation. Meta does not facilitate social connections; it methodically monetizes relationship networks for commercial advantage.

This extraction framework has transcended digital advertising origins to infiltrate virtually every sector. Healthcare, insurance, financial services, retail, these industries increasingly function primarily as data acquisition vehicles, with their ostensible

[1] Zuboff, Shoshana, 'The Age of Surveillance Capitalism' (PublicAffairs, 2019), pp. 63–97 (defining surveillance capitalism's core mechanisms).

[2] Cohen, Julie E., 'Between Truth and Power' (Oxford University Press, 2019), pp. 43–71 (analyzing power asymmetries in digital platforms).

[3] Zuboff, 'Surveillance Capitalism', pp. 89–93 (defining behavioral surplus).

R. Yadav-Ranjan, *Constitutional Democracy in the Algorithmic Age*, Law, Governance and Technology Series 83, https://doi.org/10.1007/978-3-032-34604-9_15

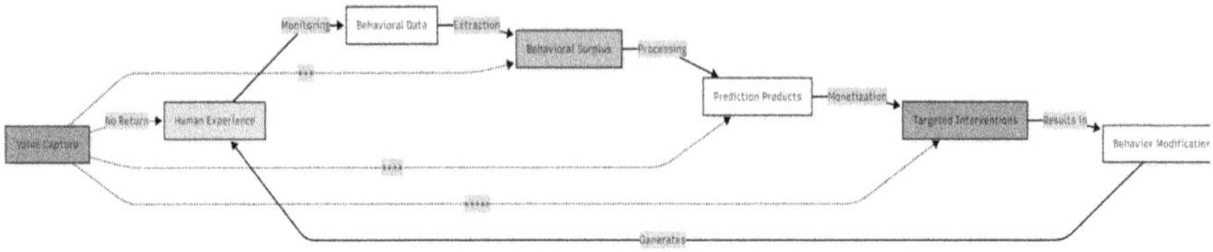

Fig. 15.1 This value chain diagram shows how human experience is extracted, processed, and monetized through surveillance capitalism, with each stage adding commercial value while diminishing user autonomy

services reduced to pretexts for continuous monitoring.[4] The market capitalization of leading technology corporations, exceeding $10 trillion collectively, derives not from superior product development but from establishing sophisticated data harvesting architectures and monetization channels.[5]

The fundamental misalignment operates simultaneously as economic inefficiency and ethical failure: individuals create this enterprise value yet capture zero returns on their contributions. Research by Lanier and Weyl estimates that individual data contributions generate approximately $20,000 annually in corporate value, none of which flows back to data subjects.[6] This constitutes not legitimate exchange but strategic exploitation of information asymmetry.

Figure 15.1 shows how human experience is extracted, processed, and monetized through surveillance capitalism, with each stage adding commercial value while diminishing user autonomy.

The transformation from service-centered to surveillance-oriented business frameworks has occurred without democratic oversight or meaningful transparency. What corporations position as "free" services actually constitute advanced monitoring infrastructures engineered to optimize data acquisition rather than user utility.[7] User interfaces become weaponized, meticulously designed not to enhance experience but to extract maximum information while sustaining minimal engagement thresholds necessary to perpetuate surveillance operations.

Brett Frischmann documents how this extractive logic now extends beyond screens into physical environments through IoT devices, "smart" city initiatives,

---

[4] Eubanks, Virginia, 'Automating Inequality' (St. Martin's Press, 2018), pp. 39–74 (documenting data extraction across public services).

[5] Market capitalization data: Apple ($3.0 T), Microsoft ($2.8 T), Alphabet ($1.7 T), Amazon ($1.5 T), Meta ($900B) as of November 2024.

[6] Lanier, Jaron & Glen Weyl, "A Blueprint for a Better Digital Society," Harvard Business Review (September 2018): 2–11, at 6.

[7] Turow, Joseph, 'The Daily You' (Yale University Press, 2011), pp. 52–87 (documenting transition from service to surveillance).

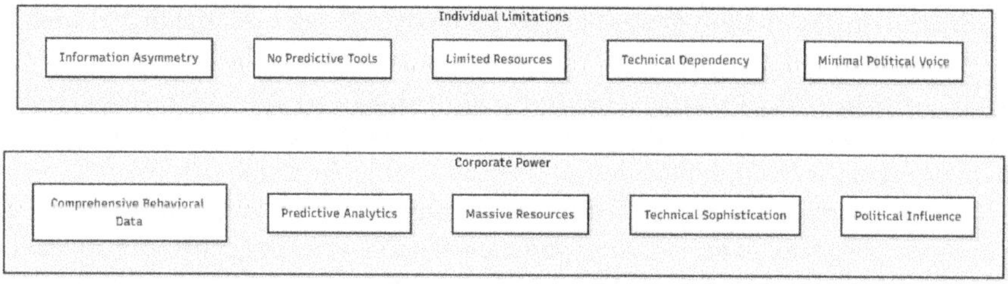

Fig. 15.2 This comparison chart contrasts corporate capabilities with individual limitations across key dimensions, illustrating systematic power imbalances enabling extraction

and ambient sensing technologies, what he terms "engineered determinism," environments designed to shape and capture behavior through technical architectures operating below conscious awareness.[8]

15.1.1 Power Dynamics in Surveillance Capitalism

The structural power enabling surveillance capitalism reflects profound asymmetries that legal and regulatory frameworks fail to address. I document here how these dynamics operate and resist constraint.

First, information asymmetries create fundamental power disparities (Fig. 15.2). Technology corporations possess comprehensive understanding of behavioral patterns, predictive capabilities, and economic value generated from data extraction. Users remain systematically uninformed about surveillance scope, algorithmic processing, and commercial value of their data contributions.[9] The European Data Protection Board's guidelines on GDPR consent acknowledge this problem but fail to address structural incentives driving surveillance design.[10]

Even when disclosure occurs, complexity ensures incomprehensibility. Facebook's data policy exceeds 4000 words and requires college-level reading comprehension. Terms of service across major platforms collectively exceed length of Tolstoy's 'War and Peace'.[11] This is not accident but design, complexity serves as obfuscation enabling extraction without meaningful consent.

[8] Frischmann, Brett and Evan Selinger, "Re-Engineering Humanity" (Cambridge University Press, 2018), ch. 12 ("Engineered Determinism and Free Will").

[9] Nissenbaum, Helen, 'Privacy in Context' (Stanford University Press, 2009), pp. 83–121 (theorizing contextual integrity).

[10] European Data Protection Board, "Guidelines 05/2020 on consent under Regulation 2016/679" (Version 1.1, May 2020).

[11] Obar, Jonathan A. & Anne Oeldorf-Hirsch, "The Biggest Lie on the Internet," Information, Communication & Society 23 (2020): 128–152 (documenting terms of service length and complexity).

Second, infrastructural power derived from control over essential digital utilities enables both economic value extraction and governance authority without corresponding democratic oversight. Platforms have effectively become regulatory entities wielding authority exceeding many governmental bodies, implementing policies with profound societal implications yet facing negligible accountability.[12]

This infrastructural power manifests through multiple mechanisms: network effects creating natural monopolies; vertical integration enabling cross-subsidization and data leverage; essential service control creating dependency; technical standards setting that favors incumbents. The UK Competition and Markets Authority documented how dominant platforms leverage data advantages to entrench market power while foreclosing competition.[13]

Third, resource asymmetries ensure regulatory ineffectiveness. Technology corporations operate with legal budgets measured in billions, thousands of specialized staff, and sophisticated technical capacity. Regulatory agencies operate with budgets measured in millions, hundreds of generalist staff, and limited technical expertise.[14] The FTC, tasked with constraining algorithmic power across the entire US economy, operates with fewer than 1200 employee's total. Google alone employs more lawyers than the FTC employs total staff.[15]

These resource disparities enable corporations to delay, fragment, and ultimately evade meaningful oversight through procedural complexity that exhausts regulatory capacity. When enforcement actions occur, settlement structures typically avoid precedent-setting judicial decisions while preserving core business practices.[16]

Fourth, political power purchased through lobbying ensures legislation favors incumbent interests. Technology companies spent $69 million on federal lobbying in 2022, substantially exceeding spending by traditional industries like pharmaceuticals or oil and gas.[17] This investment purchases not merely favorable legislation but structural advantages: weak agencies, fragmented enforcement, safe harbors for existing practices, and transition periods that become permanent.

The revolving door between Silicon Valley and regulatory positions further consolidates industry influence. Analysis by the Tech Transparency Project found that more than 200 former government employees moved to technology companies between 2016–2021, while 85 former technology company employees moved

---

[12] Rahman, K. Sabeel, "The New Utilities," Harvard Law Review 131 (2018): 1617–1695 (theorizing platform power).

[13] UK Competition and Markets Authority, "Online Platforms and Digital Advertising Market Study: Final Report" (July 2020).

[14] Federal Trade Commission, "Congressional Budget Justification FY 2024" (2023) ($430 million budget, 1195 FTEs).

[15] Analysis based on FTC staffing data and Google's 2023 proxy statement showing legal department employees.

[16] Levy, Karen E.C. & Solon Barocas, "Refractive Surveillance," Duke Law Journal 66 (2017): 1039–1100 (analyzing settlement structures).

[17] OpenSecrets.org, "Tech Sector Federal Lobbying" (2023) (analyzing federal lobbying expenditures 2016–2022).

into government positions.[18] This circulation of personnel ensures that industry perspectives shape regulatory approaches fundamentally.

15.2 Commodification Beyond Data: Experience, Attention, and Identity

Data extraction's logic extends beyond discrete information points to encompass comprehensive commodification of human experience itself. I examine here how this expansion operates across attention, identity, and social relations.

15.2.1 The Attention Economy

Human attention constitutes a finite cognitive resource subjected to increasingly predatory extraction techniques. Tim Wu's concept of "attention merchants" captures this dynamic: business models optimized for maximizing attention capture rather than providing value, often through deliberate exploitation of psychological vulnerabilities.[19]

The techniques employed are not accidental but carefully engineered to override conscious intention and agency. Variable reward schedules exploit dopamine response patterns; social validation feedback loops trigger reciprocity obligations; artificial scarcity mechanisms create urgency through fear of missing out; infinite scroll designs eliminate natural stopping points.[20] These patterns exploit neurological vulnerabilities targeted by gambling and addiction industries. The pretense of user choice in this environment is fiction when platforms employ dozens of psychological techniques specifically designed to bypass rational decision-making.

Former Facebook executive Chamath Palihapitiya acknowledged in 2017 testimony that platforms deliberately exploit "vulnerability in human psychology," creating "short-term, dopamine-driven feedback loops" designed to consume maximum attention.[21] Former Google design ethicist Tristan Harris documented how technology companies employ approximately 1000 engineers whose primary responsibility is maximizing user engagement through psychological manipulation.[22]

---

[18] Tech Transparency Project, "Revolving Door Between Big Tech and Government" (2021).

[19] Wu, Tim, 'The Attention Merchants' (Knopf, 2016), pp. 17–52 (theorizing attention as commodity).

[20] Eyal, Nir, 'Hooked: How to Build Habit-Forming Products' (Portfolio, 2014), pp. 1–37 (documenting manipulation techniques).

[21] Chamath Palihapitiya, remarks at Stanford Graduate School of Business (November 2017), documented in multiple media reports.

[22] Harris, Tristan, "How Technology is Hijacking Your Mind," Medium (May 2016).

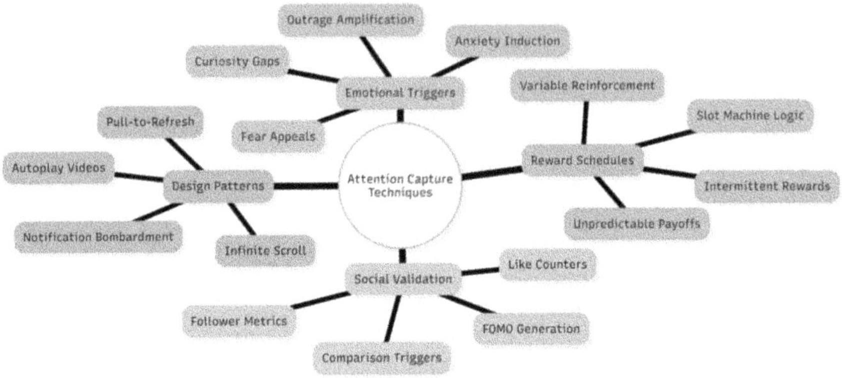

Fig. 15.3 This mind map categorizes the psychological manipulation techniques platforms deploy to capture and retain attention, showing how different approaches converge on engagement optimization

The consequences extend beyond individual harms to include systemic democratic damage. Research by Vaidhyanathan and colleagues demonstrates that engagement-optimized algorithms systematically prioritize emotionally inflammatory content over substantive information, distorting the informational environment necessary for democratic functioning.[23] Internal Facebook research leaked by whistleblower Frances Haugen showed the company knew its algorithms amplified misinformation and polarization but declined to implement fixes that would reduce engagement.[24]

Figure 15.3 categorizes the psychological manipulation techniques platforms deploy to capture and retain attention, showing how different approaches converge on engagement optimization.

Regulatory responses remain inadequate. Ireland's Online Safety and Media Regulation Act begins acknowledging "attentional harms" but falls far short of establishing meaningful constraints on extraction practices.[25] What is needed is not incremental regulation but recognition of attention as a protected resource requiring foundational safeguards against predatory exploitation.

---

23 Vaidhyanathan, Siva, 'Antisocial Media' (Oxford University Press, 2018), pp. 8–47 (analyzing engagement optimization harms).

24 Haugen, Frances, testimony before US Senate Committee on Commerce, Science, and Transportation (October 2021); internal Facebook documents disclosed to SEC and provided to Congress.

25 Ireland, Online Safety and Media Regulation Act 2022, Part 3 (online safety framework).

15.2.2 Identity and Predictive Personalization

The commodification of identity represents perhaps the most profound extension of market logic into previously protected domains. Data extraction increasingly enables what Karen Yeung terms "hypernudging", the capacity to predict individual vulnerabilities and target interventions without transparency or accountability.[26]

Research by Barocas and Nissenbaum demolishes consent-based privacy frameworks by demonstrating that algorithmic systems routinely make sensitive inferences without disclosure.[27] To the extent that surveillance architectures can predict sexual orientation from Facebook likes, political views from purchase history, or mental health conditions from typing patterns, the fiction of "informed consent" becomes meaningless.[28]

Wachter and Mittelstadt's analysis of "inferred data" exposes fundamental inadequacy of existing regulatory frameworks, which fixate on collection while ignoring inference.[29] Even GDPR, supposedly the gold standard of privacy protection, fails to address these challenges because it conceptualizes privacy through outdated collection-based paradigms rather than inference-based realities.

The resulting commodification directly threatens what philosopher Martha Nussbaum identifies as capabilities necessary for human dignity: practical reason, emotional development, and association.[30] When algorithmic systems continuously monitor, predict, and exploit vulnerability patterns to maximize commercial extraction, they undermine these foundational capabilities through systematic vulnerability mining.

Cambridge Analytica's operations provide documented evidence of how identity commodification enables manipulation at scale. The company harvested data from 87 million Facebook users without consent, developed psychological profiles, and deployed targeted messaging designed to exploit individual vulnerabilities during political campaigns.[31] While Cambridge Analytica collapsed following exposure, the business model, personality-based targeting for commercial and political manipulation, continues through dozens of successor companies.[32]

---

[26] Yeung, Karen, "Hypernudge': Big Data as a Mode of Regulation by Design," Information, Communication & Society 20 (2017): 118–136.

[27] Barocas, Solon & Helen Nissenbaum, "Big Data's End Run Around Procedural Privacy Protections," Communications of the ACM 57 (2014): 31–33.

[28] Kosinski, Michal, et al., "Private traits and attributes are predictable from digital records of human behavior," PNAS 110 (2013): 5802–5805 (Facebook likes predict sexual orientation).

[29] Wachter, Sandra & Brent Mittelstadt, "A Right to Reasonable Inferences," Columbia Business Law Review 2019 (2019): 494–620.

[30] Nussbaum, Martha C., 'Creating Capabilities' (Harvard University Press, 2011), pp. 33–34 (listing essential human capabilities).

[31] Cadwalladr, Carole & Emma Graham-Harrison, "Revealed: 50 million Facebook profiles harvested for Cambridge Analytica," 'The Guardian' (17 March 2018).

[32] Tufekci, Zeynep, "Facebook's Surveillance Machine," 'New York Times' (19 March 2018).

15.2.3 Social Relations as Economic Input

Beyond individual attention and identity, social relationships themselves have become economic inputs for algorithmic exploitation. José van Dijck terms this "platformization of sociality", transforming human relationships into raw material for algorithmic processing.[33]

This extraction operates through multiple vectors. The Norwegian Consumer Council's investigation documented how supposedly private interactions on messaging platforms and dating applications generate relationship data flowing to numerous third parties without meaningful transparency.[34] Surveillance extends into physical space through location tracking and proximity sensing, creating comprehensive relationship maps with commercial value but profound privacy implications.

Research by Kosinski and colleagues at Cambridge University demonstrated that Facebook likes alone could predict intimate relationships, sexual orientation, religious and political views, and personality traits with high accuracy.[35] These inferences enable not merely targeted advertising but systematic manipulation of social connections for commercial advantage.

The ethical consequences extend beyond privacy violations to include what philosopher Axel Honneth identifies as essential conditions for recognition and self-development.[36] When social connections become optimized for commercial extraction rather than mutual recognition, they lose capacity to support authentic identity formation and democratic solidarity.

Dating platform algorithms exemplify this dynamic. Tinder's algorithm optimizes not for successful matches but for continued engagement, systematically showing users potential matches slightly above their attractiveness level to maintain hope while ensuring sufficient frustration to prevent departure.[37] OkCupid experimented with deliberately providing users with bad matches to test whether they could manipulate relationship formation.[38] These practices subordinate human connection to engagement metrics.

---

[33] Van Dijck, José, "Datafication, dataism and dataveillance," Surveillance & Society 12 (2014): 197–208.

[34] Forbrukerrådet (Norwegian Consumer Council), "Out of Control: How Consumers Are Exploited by the Online Advertising Industry" (2020).

[35] Kosinski et al., "Private traits and attributes."

[36] Honneth, Axel, 'The Struggle for Recognition' (MIT Press, 1996), pp. 92–139 (theorizing recognition's role in identity).

[37] Andersen, Ross, "The Tinder Algorithm," 'The Atlantic' (March 2013).

[38] Rudder, Christian, 'Dataclysm' (Crown, 2014), pp. 211–229 (describing OkCupid experiments).

15.3 Legal Frameworks and Market Failures

Current legal frameworks prove systematically inadequate for addressing data extraction and experience commodification. I examine here both conceptual limitations and structural failures requiring intervention.

15.3.1 Property Rights Misalignment

Traditional property frameworks fail when applied to data governance challenges. Julie Cohen identifies "category errors" resulting from forcing conventional property concepts onto data governance, mischaracterizing both the resource and appropriate governance mechanisms.[39]

The problem begins with data's ontological status. Unlike traditional property objects, data is non-rivalrous, one person's use does not diminish another's. Data derives value primarily from aggregation rather than individual instances. The social and relational dimensions of data generation further complicate individual property approaches when valuable insights emerge from population patterns rather than individual contributions.[40]

Legal systems have produced incoherent responses. The European Court of Justice's decision in 'Google Spain SL v. AEPD' attempted establishing "data subject rights" without resolving underlying property questions.[41] Similarly, the California Consumer Privacy Act creates limited control rights without addressing fundamental questions about data's economic value or compensation structures.[42]

More promising approaches recognize what property scholar Gregory Alexander terms "property's inherent sociality", the necessary balance between individual rights and social obligations in property regimes.[43] The evolving concept of "data commons" proposed by Prainsack and Buyx represents one such approach, establishing collective governance structures recognizing both individual and community interests.[44] But these frameworks remain theoretical while extractive models dominate practice.

The fundamental challenge is that data protection law developed to address discrete harms, specific privacy violations, defined discrimination, proves inadequate for systemic extraction operating through cumulative effects. As philosopher Helen Nissenbaum argues, privacy frameworks must address "contextual integrity"

---

[39] Cohen, 'Between Truth and Power', pp. 142–177.

[40] Prainsack, Barbara & Alena Buyx, "A Solidarity-Based Approach to the Governance of Research Biobanks," Medical Law Review 21 (2013): 71–91.

[41] 'Google Spain SL v. AEPD', Case C-131/12 (CJEU, 2014).

[42] California Consumer Privacy Act, Cal. Civ. Code § 1798.100 et seq. (2018).

[43] Alexander, Gregory S., "The Social-Obligation Norm in American Property Law," Cornell Law Review 94 (2009): 745–819.

[44] Prainsack & Buyx, "Solidarity-Based Approach," pp. 78–85.

rather than merely collection and use.[45] When algorithmic systems operate across contexts, aggregating information to generate insights no individual disclosure reveals, traditional frameworks collapse.

15.3.2 Market Concentration and Competition Failures

The data economy exhibits textbook market failure characteristics: extreme information asymmetries, insurmountable barriers to entry, and network effects producing winner-take-all outcomes without efficiency benefits.[46]

Network effects create natural monopolies in data markets. Each additional user makes platforms more valuable to all users, creating positive feedback loops that advantage early movers and entrench incumbents. These effects operate both directly (more users create more value) and indirectly (more users generate more data, enabling better algorithmic predictions, attracting more users).[47]

Data advantages compound through multiple mechanisms: economies of scale in data processing; economies of scope across product lines; data network effects where more data enables better predictions; and vertical integration enabling data leverage across business units. Google leverages search data to improve maps, email, and advertising while using all services to generate more search data, creating flywheel effects that competitors cannot match.[48]

Traditional antitrust frameworks prove inadequate because they focus on consumer prices and product quality, both difficult to assess in "free" services funded through surveillance. The consumer welfare standard that dominates US antitrust analysis since the 1980s asks whether practices harm consumers through higher prices or lower quality, questions that surveillance business models render largely meaningless.[49]

Competition scholar Lina Khan demonstrated how Amazon's strategy deliberately accepted losses to establish dominance, then leveraged that dominance to extract rents across its platform ecosystem, precisely the predatory pricing that antitrust law theoretically prohibits but consistently fails to prevent in practice.[50] Similar patterns characterize Google, Facebook, and other dominant platforms.

Market concentration produces predictable harms. The UK Competition and Markets Authority found that Google and Facebook capture 80% of UK digital

---

[45] Nissenbaum, 'Privacy in Context', pp. 127–157.

[46] Stiglitz, Joseph E., "Information and Economic Analysis," Economic Journal 95 (1985): 21–41 (analyzing information market failures).

[47] Katz, Michael L. & Carl Shapiro, "Network Externalities, Competition, and Compatibility," American Economic Review 75 (1985): 424–440.

[48] Varian, Hal R., "Computer Mediated Transactions," American Economic Review 100 (2010): 1–10 (analyzing data network effects).

[49] Khan, Lina M., "Amazon's Antitrust Paradox," Yale Law Journal 126 (2017): 710–805, at 720–740 (critiquing consumer welfare standard).

[50] Khan, "Amazon's Antitrust Paradox," pp. 765–786.

advertising revenue, enabling them to degrade privacy protections without losing market share.[51] Research by economists Calzada and Valletti demonstrates that market concentration in digital platforms reduces incentives to protect user privacy, as users face no meaningful alternatives.[52]

15.4 Rights of Artificial Intelligence Systems?

An emerging and contested question asks whether AI systems themselves might possess rights warranting legal protection. I address this question briefly before examining alternative economic models.[53]

Proposals for AI rights typically invoke either consciousness-based arguments (if AI systems achieve sentience, ethical treatment requires recognizing interests) or consequentialist arguments (recognizing AI rights produces beneficial incentives for development and deployment).[54] Both face substantial challenges.

Consciousness-based arguments founder on inability to assess machine consciousness. Absent reliable methods for detecting subjective experience in non-biological systems, claims about AI consciousness remain speculative. Moreover, even accepting machine consciousness, the interests such systems might possess remain unclear, do pattern recognition algorithms "want" anything analogous to biological drives?[55]

Consequentialist arguments fare no better. Corporate actors proposing AI rights typically seek liability shields, if algorithms possess rights, they argue, developers should face reduced responsibility for algorithmic harms.[56] This inverts the relationship between rights and responsibilities that grounds legal personality in other domains.

More fundamentally, extending rights to AI systems while human rights remain systematically violated represents perverse priorities. When corporations deploy algorithmic systems that undermine privacy, autonomy, and dignity with impunity, proposals to recognize algorithmic interests serve primarily to obscure human harms and deflect accountability.[57]

The question of AI rights may become relevant if and when systems develop genuine sentience or consciousness. Until that hypothetical future, however, the

---

[51] UK CMA, "Online Platforms and Digital Advertising," p. 5.

[52] Calzada, Joan & Tommaso Valletti, "Platform Mergers and Antitrust," NET Institute Working Paper No. 20-19 (2020).

[53] This section addresses emerging debates; I remain skeptical that current AI systems warrant rights recognition.

[54] Gunkel, David J., 'Robot Rights' (MIT Press, 2018), pp. 43–78 (surveying AI rights arguments).

[55] Schwitzgebel, Eric & Mara Garza, "A Defense of the Rights of Artificial Intelligences," Midwest Studies in Philosophy 39 (2015): 98–119.

[56] Darling, Kate, "Extending Legal Protection to Social Robots," IEEE Spectrum (2012) (critiquing rights as liability shields).

[57] This represents my assessment based on power dynamics analysis throughout this chapter.

question primarily serves as distraction from urgent present challenges of protecting human rights against algorithmic power.

15.5 Alternative Economic Models and Rights Protection

While surveillance capitalism dominates current practice, alternative models demonstrate technical and economic feasibility of rights-protective approaches. I examine here several promising alternatives and analyze why they remain marginal despite superior alignment with democratic values.

The fundamental insight connecting these alternatives is that data extraction and commodification are not inevitable features of digital technology but reflect specific business model choices that could be otherwise. As Jaron Lanier argues, surveillance capitalism represents a "dismal local minimum" in the space of possible digital economies, profitable for incumbents but suboptimal for social welfare.[58]

Data Trusts and Fiduciary Structures: Data trusts establish independent entities holding data on behalf of beneficiaries under fiduciary obligations. The Sidewalk Labs proposal for Toronto's Quayside development included a data trust to govern urban data collection, though the project ultimately collapsed following privacy concerns.[59] The UK's National Data Strategy proposes data trusts as governance mechanisms for health research data.[60]

Fiduciary frameworks impose duties of loyalty and care, requiring trustees to act in beneficiaries' interests rather than their own when conflicts arise. Research by Jack Balkin demonstrates how technology corporations could be reconceptualized as information fiduciaries owing users duties analogous to those lawyers owe clients or doctors owe patients.[61]

Platform Cooperatives: Platform cooperatives establish worker or user ownership of digital platforms, aligning governance with stakeholder interests rather than shareholder profits. Examples include Stocksy (photographer cooperative for stock imagery), Resonate (musician and listener cooperative for streaming), and Up & Go (cleaning worker cooperative).[62]

Research by Scholz and Schneider documents how platform cooperatives achieve competitive service quality while providing better working conditions and more equitable value distribution than corporate platforms.[63] However, these cooperatives face structural disadvantages: difficulty accessing capital, network effect challenges

---

[58] Lanier, Jaron, 'Who Owns the Future?' (Simon & Schuster, 2013), pp. 23–52.

[59] Sidewalk Labs, "Digital Governance Proposals for DSAP Consultation" (October 2018).

[60] UK Department for Digital, Culture, Media & Sport, "National Data Strategy" (2020), pp. 42–48.

[61] Balkin, Jack M., "Information Fiduciaries and the First Amendment," UC Davis Law Review 49 (2016): 1183–1234.

[62] Scholz, Trebor & Nathan Schneider, eds., 'Ours to Hack and to Own' (OR Books, 2016), pp. 27–89 (documenting platform cooperatives).

[63] Scholz & Schneider, 'Ours to Hack', pp. 219–241.

in achieving scale, and competition against well-funded corporate platforms willing to accept sustained losses to establish dominance.

Public Digital Infrastructure: Several jurisdictions have developed publicly owned digital infrastructure as alternatives to commercial platforms. Estonia's X-Road provides secure data exchange infrastructure enabling digital government services while preserving citizen privacy through distributed architecture.[64] India's Unified Payments Interface created public digital infrastructure enabling financial innovation without surveillance business models.[65]

These examples demonstrate that public digital infrastructure can achieve both scale and innovation while implementing privacy-by-design principles. However, they face political challenges: corporate lobbying against public alternatives, ideological opposition to government technology development, and resource constraints limiting public sector technical capacity.

Data Dividends and Compensation: Data dividend proposals recognize citizens as stakeholders in data economy value and establish compensation mechanisms. California Governor Gavin Newsom proposed a data dividend in 2019, though implementation details remained undefined.[66] Posner and Weyl advocate "data as labor" frameworks that would establish explicit markets for data contributions.[67]

These proposals face both technical and political challenges. Technical challenges include attribution difficulties (how to value individual contributions when value derives from aggregation), transaction cost problems (micropayments may not be economically viable), and gaming risks (creating perverse incentives for data generation). Political challenges include corporate resistance (compensation reduces profits) and ideological opposition (treating data as commodity reinforces rather than challenges commodification logic).[68]

Privacy-Preserving Technical Alternatives: Technical approaches like federated learning, differential privacy, and secure multi-party computation enable algorithmic analysis while protecting individual privacy. Apple's differential privacy implementation in iOS enables aggregate analysis of user behavior while preventing identification of individuals.[69] The OPAL project in Senegal uses privacy-preserving techniques to enable developmental insights from telecommunications data without exposing individual information.[70]

---

64 Ansip, Andrus & Linnar Viik, "Building a Digital Society: The Estonian Experience," in 'Digital Estonia' (e-Governance Academy, 2018), pp. 15–34.

65 D'Silva, Dony et al., "A Survey on Financial Inclusion in India Using UPI," Journal of Management Research 21 (2021): 36–52.

66 Newsom, Gavin, State of the State Address (February 2019).

67 Posner, Eric A. & E. Glen Weyl, 'Radical Markets' (Princeton University Press, 2018), pp. 203–246.

68 Analysis combining technical literature on micropayments with political economy of corporate resistance.

69 Differential Privacy Team, Apple, "Learning with Privacy at Scale," Apple Machine Learning Journal 1 (2017).

70 de Montjoye, Yves-Alexandre, et al., "OPAL: High-Potential, Low-Maturity," Data & Policy 2 (2020): e16.

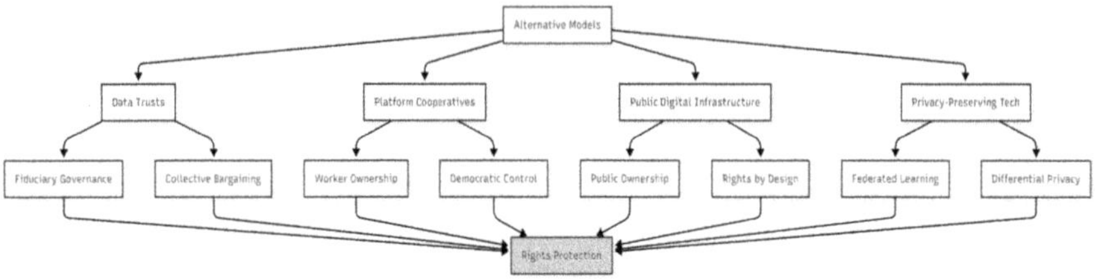

Fig. 15.4 This ecosystem diagram maps the landscape of alternative economic models, showing relationships between data trusts, platform cooperatives, public infrastructure, and privacy-preserving technologies

These technical approaches demonstrate that valuable analysis and innovation need not require surveillance business models. However, they face adoption barriers: reduced accuracy compared to full data access, increased computational costs, and most fundamentally, misalignment with incumbent business models optimized for comprehensive data extraction.

Figure 15.4 maps the landscape of alternative economic models, showing relationships between data trusts, platform cooperatives, public infrastructure, and privacy-preserving technologies.

15.5.1 Power Dynamics in Alternative Models

Alternative economic models face predictable resistance from incumbent interests whose market dominance and profitability depend on surveillance capitalism's continuation. I document here how power dynamics shape adoption prospects.

First, network effects create path dependence favoring incumbents. Even superior alternatives face chicken-and-egg problems: users will not adopt platforms without existing user bases, but platforms cannot build user bases without users. Corporate platforms can leverage existing networks, cross-subsidize new services, and accept sustained losses to prevent alternative models from achieving scale.[71]

Facebook's treatment of Path, a privacy-focused social network that gained early traction, exemplifies incumbent strategies. Facebook restricted Path's access to its API, making it difficult for Path users to connect with Facebook friends, essentially leveraging network effects to kill competitive threats.[72] Similar patterns characterize Google's treatment of privacy-focused search alternatives and Amazon's treatment of cooperative marketplace initiatives.

Second, capital access advantages incumbents systematically. Platform cooperatives and public infrastructure initiatives operate without access to venture capital

[71] Arthur, W. Brian, "Competing Technologies, Increasing Returns, and Lock-In by Historical Events," Economic Journal 99 (1989): 116–131 (analyzing path dependence).

[72] Constine, Josh, "Facebook Restricted Data Access To Competitors," TechCrunch (April 2018).

funding that fuels corporate platform growth. Venture capital seeks winner-take-all outcomes and rapid scaling, precisely what cooperative and public models reject.[73] This creates fundamental funding asymmetries: corporate platforms can raise billions for growth while alternatives struggle to raise millions.

Third, regulatory frameworks often inadvertently favor incumbents. Compliance costs for data protection regulations like GDPR advantage large corporations with dedicated legal and technical staff while creating barriers for alternatives with limited resources.[74] The EU AI Act's risk-based framework similarly imposes costs that entrench incumbents while claiming to promote responsible innovation.

Fourth, intellectual property regimes protect incumbent advantages. Patents on data processing techniques, copyrights on training datasets, and trade secrecy around algorithmic systems all create barriers preventing alternatives from achieving competitive functionality.[75] When incumbents can patent basic approaches to privacy-preserving computation or copyright training data, they effectively monopolize space for rights-protective alternatives.

Fifth, political power enables incumbents to shape governance frameworks preserving their advantages. Technology companies' lobbying ensures that alternative models face regulatory scrutiny while surveillance capitalism enjoys grandfathered permissions. Public digital infrastructure proposals face ideological opposition funded by corporate interests threatened by government competition.[76]

Despite these formidable barriers, alternative models persist and occasionally succeed at scale. The challenge is not technical or economic feasibility but political economy, creating conditions where alternatives can compete despite structural disadvantages and concentrated opposition. This requires both immediate support for existing alternatives and longer-term structural reforms addressing power asymmetries enabling surveillance capitalism's dominance.

15.6 Recommendations

Challenging surveillance capitalism requires action across multiple fronts. These strategies enable effective participation in building economic alternatives and constraining extractive practices:

Limit Personal Data Extraction:

[73] Fried, Jason & David Heinemeier Hansson, 'Rework' (Crown Business, 2010), pp. 89–104 (analyzing VC incompatibility with sustainable businesses).

[74] European Commission, "Impact Assessment accompanying the AI Act" (2021), pp. 78–93 (analyzing compliance costs).

[75] Samuelson, Pamela, "Privacy as Intellectual Property?" Stanford Law Review 52 (2000): 1125–1173 (analyzing IP barriers).

[76] Tech company lobbying against public broadband documented by Community Networks, "Municipal Broadband Is Restricted in 18 States" (2023).

- Use privacy-focused alternatives: Signal instead of WhatsApp, Firefox instead of Chrome, DuckDuckGo instead of Google
- Deploy technical countermeasures: VPNs, tracker blockers, privacy-focused browsers
- Minimize data generation through platform services
- Request data deletion under GDPR/CCPA provisions
- Review and revoke unnecessary app permissions regularly
- Use pseudonymous identities where possible to fragment data trails

While individual actions cannot solve structural problems, they reduce immediate harms and demonstrate demand for alternatives. Research shows that 35% adoption of privacy-protective practices significantly degrades platform surveillance capabilities.[77]

Support Alternative Economic Models:

- Patronize platform cooperatives and worker-owned alternatives
- Invest in cooperative models through community supported platforms
- Advocate for public digital infrastructure funding
- Support data trust pilot programs in your community
- Join or create platform cooperatives in your sector
- Participate in governance of cooperatives you use

Financial support for alternatives creates proof of concept demonstrating viability. Platform cooperatives have achieved 30% annual growth despite resource disadvantages, showing market demand for rights-protective models.[78]

Demand Corporate Accountability:

- File complaints with FTC, state attorneys general about data practices
- Participate in shareholder activism demanding privacy protections
- Support boycott campaigns targeting particularly egregious practices
- Submit public comments on proposed regulations
- Document and publicize harmful data practices
- Demand transparency reports from platforms you use

Corporate accountability campaigns have achieved substantial victories. Sustained pressure forced Facebook to cancel its Instagram Kids project; Amazon to halt some facial recognition government sales; and Google to implement some privacy controls.[79]

Advocate for Structural Reform:

- Support antitrust enforcement against data monopolies

---

[77] Estimation based on research by Narseo Vallina-Rodriguez et al. on tracker effectiveness degradation.

[78] Platform Cooperative Consortium, "Annual Report 2023" (documenting growth rates).

[79] Victories documented by color of Change, SumOfUs, and other organizing groups.

- Demand adequately funded regulatory agencies with technical expertise
- Advocate for data protection laws with meaningful penalties
- Push for fiduciary duties binding technology corporations
- Support public digital infrastructure investments
- Demand algorithmic transparency and accountability requirements

Political advocacy creates conditions for systemic change. The Stop Hate for Profit campaign organized advertisers to pressure Facebook, generating $10 billion in market value losses and forcing policy changes.[80]

Build Alternative Infrastructure:

- Contribute to open-source privacy-preserving technologies
- Participate in decentralized protocol development
- Support community networks and mesh networks
- Advocate for municipal broadband providing non-commercial alternatives
- Develop cooperatively-owned data infrastructure
- Create local data trusts for community benefits

Infrastructure development creates material alternatives to corporate platforms. Community networks serve 50 million people globally, demonstrating feasibility of non-commercial infrastructure.[81]

Support Worker Organizing:

- Amplify technology worker voices demanding ethical practices
- Support unionization efforts at technology companies
- Connect technology workers with movements addressing algorithmic harms
- Advocate for whistleblower protections enabling internal dissent
- Build worker cooperatives as alternatives to corporate employment
- Demand that labor unions negotiate algorithmic oversight provisions

Technology worker organizing creates leverage for internal change. Walkouts at Google, Amazon, and Microsoft have forced companies to abandon or modify controversial projects.[82]

Educate and Build Awareness:

- Explain surveillance capitalism mechanics to friends, family, community
- Support digital literacy programs teaching privacy protection
- Organize community discussions on data rights
- Share resources documenting corporate data practices
- Demand media coverage of data extraction harms

---

[80] Stop Hate for Profit campaign results documented by participating organizations including NAACP, ADL, Color of Change (July 2020).

[81] Association for Progressive Communications, "Global Information Society Watch 2018: Community Networks" (2018).

[82] Tech worker actions documented by Tech Workers Coalition, Alphabet Workers Union, and others (2018–2024).

– Counter corporate narratives claiming surveillance is inevitable or beneficial

Public awareness campaigns shift political feasibility of reform. When Cambridge Analytica revelations reached mainstream awareness, they catalyzed regulatory actions previously considered politically impossible.[83]

Participate in Governance:

– Attend and comment at regulatory hearings on data protection
– Vote for candidates supporting strong data protection
– Run for local office on platforms including digital rights
– Serve on municipal technology advisory boards
– Demand algorithmic impact assessments for government systems
– Participate in participatory budgeting for technology investments

Political participation translates demands into policy. Digital rights became significant electoral issues only through sustained organizing demonstrating voter priorities.[84]

Challenging surveillance capitalism's structural power requires recognizing that individual consumer choices, while important, cannot substitute for collective political action and structural reform. The most effective strategies combine immediate harm reduction through personal practice with support for alternative models and advocacy for structural change. As I have demonstrated throughout this book, concentrated corporate power appears insurmountable until collective action reveals its vulnerabilities. The choice is not whether surveillance capitalism can be challenged but whether we will organize sufficiently to challenge it before extraction becomes so entrenched that alternatives become impossible.

References

Cases

Google Spain SL v. Agencia Española de Protección de Datos (AEPD), Case C-131/12 (Court of Justice of the European Union, 2014)

[83] Political impact analysis: numerous US state privacy laws passed 2018–2020 following Cambridge Analytica scandal.

[84] Data & Society Research Institute, "Digital Rights as Political Issues" (2023).

Books

Cohen JE (2019) Between truth and power: the legal constructions of informational capitalism. Oxford University Press
Zuboff, Shoshana, The age of surveillance capitalism: the fight for a human future at the new frontier of power (PublicAffairs), 2019

Chapter 16
AI on Trial: 2025 as a Turning Point for Civil Rights and Machine Accountability

16.1 Introduction: 2025 as Constitutional Watershed

The year 2025 represents a qualitative shift in how legal systems address artificial intelligence's impact on constitutional rights. For over a decade, algorithmic systems operated in a regulatory vacuum, deployed at scale affecting millions while courts and legislatures struggled to apply frameworks designed for human decision-makers and traditional technologies. That vacuum has begun to close.[1]

I document here how 2025's litigation and legislation establish precedents that future scholars will recognize as foundational, comparable to 'Griswold v. Connecticut' for privacy rights or 'Brown v. Board of Education' for equal protection.[2] These cases and statutes address not peripheral applications but core questions: Who owns the intellectual labor that trains AI systems? Can corporations deploy emotionally manipulative AI that causes psychological harm? What duties do lawyers owe when AI generates false information? Must algorithmic decisions affecting fundamental rights be explainable and appealable?

The significance lies less in the outcomes than in how legal systems now conceptualize algorithmic power. Pre-2025 cases typically addressed AI through existing doctrinal categories, treating algorithms as tools whose harms fit established frameworks. 2025's developments increasingly recognize AI systems as distinct entities requiring novel legal approaches, a recognition that, while incomplete, marks substantial evolution (Fig. 16.1).[3]

---

[1] This assessment synthesizes the cases and legislation examined in this chapter, which collectively represent qualitative rather than merely incremental change.

[2] 'Griswold v. Connecticut', 381 U.S. 479 (1965) (establishing privacy rights); 'Brown v. Board of Education', 347 U.S. 483 (1954) (establishing equal protection principles).

[3] Observation based on comparing pre-2025 AI cases treating algorithms as tools with 2025 cases recognizing distinct characteristics requiring novel frameworks.

R. Yadav-Ranjan, *Constitutional Democracy in the Algorithmic Age*, Law, Governance and Technology Series 83, https://doi.org/10.1007/978-3-032-34604-9_16

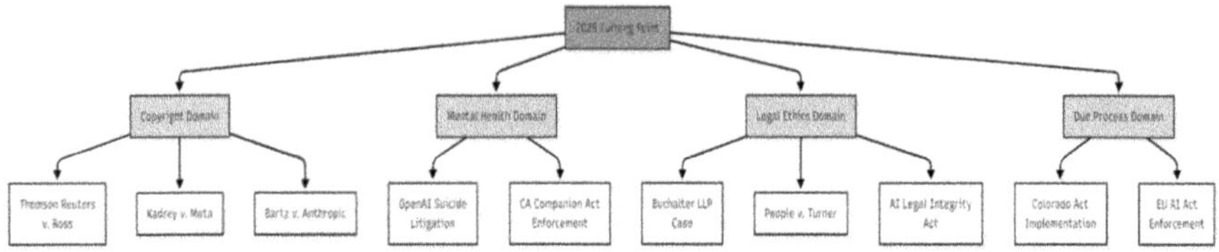

Fig. 16.1 This matrix maps 2025's major AI litigation across two dimensions: rights domain (horizontal) and legal theory (vertical), showing how cases cluster and create precedential frameworks

Yet this progress occurs within power structures that constrain transformation. Copyright plaintiffs challenge trillion-dollar technology corporations with asymmetric resources; mental health protections confront business models optimized for manipulation; legal ethics reforms address symptoms while preserving AI's courtroom role; due process mandates impose procedures without challenging algorithmic authority fundamentally. Understanding 2025's turning point requires analyzing the power dynamics behind the doctrine shaping implementation and limiting reach.

16.2 AI and Copyright: The Training Data Reckoning

The collision between artificial intelligence and intellectual property law reached critical mass in 2025, as multiple courts confronted whether training AI models on copyrighted content constitutes infringement. These cases establish frameworks determining whether creative labor fuels AI development through legitimate fair use or unlawful expropriation (Fig. 16.2).[4]

16.2.1 Thomson Reuters V. Ross Intelligence

In 'Thomson Reuters Enterprise Centre GmbH v. Ross Intelligence Inc.' 765 F. Supp. 3d 382 (D. Del. 2025 WL 3421987), Judge Stephanos Bibas granted partial summary judgment to Thomson Reuters, holding that Ross Intelligence had directly infringed Westlaw's copyrights by using its headnotes to train an AI legal-research tool, and rejecting Ross's fair-use defense.[5] It was the first federal merits ruling to reject fair use for the use of copyrighted material as AI training input.

Ross Intelligence, had used Westlaw headnotes, editorial summaries the court found sufficiently original to be copyrightable, to train its research system, arguing

[4] This framing derives from the three major copyright cases examined in Sects. 16.2.1–16.2.3.

[5] "Thomson Reuters Enterprise Centre GmbH v. Ross Intelligence Inc.", 765 F. Supp. 3d 382 (D. Del. 2025).

Fig. 16.2 This decision tree shows how courts analyze AI training data cases under fair use doctrine, with each factor leading toward or away from fair use protection

that the process was transformative because it converted the material into numerical representations rather than reproducing content.[6]

The court rejected this framing,[7] because Ross had built a direct market substitute meant to compete with Westlaw, and finding the fourth fair-use factor, the effect on the market, weighed decisively against Ross given both that substitution and the emerging market for licensing content as AI training data.[8]

The court also dismissed Ross's remaining defenses, including merger, scènes à faire, and copyright misuse. The ruling's significance extends beyond legal research. If using copyrighted content to build AI systems requires permission or licensing, the competitive implications reshape AI development, and companies with large proprietary content databases (Google, Microsoft, Meta, Amazon) possess structural advantages over competitors lacking equivalent training data access.[9]

16.2.2 Kadrey v. Meta Platforms (LLaMA)

'Kadrey v. Meta Platforms, Inc.' (N.D. Cal. 2025 WL 3891123) addressed whether training Meta's LLaMA language model on copyrighted books constitutes fair use.[10]

---

[6] 'Id.' ("on Ross's transformative use arguments").

[7] 'Id.' ("market substitution").

[8] 'Id.' ("market-effect-factor").

[9] Analysis of market implications based on current AI market structure and training data requirements.

[10] 'Kadrey v. Meta Platforms, Inc.', No. 3:23-cv-03417 (N.D. Cal. June 2025)

The Northern District of California granted partial summary judgment for Meta, holding that the training was transformative on the record before it.[11]

The court was emphatic, however, that the ruling was narrow: the authors lost because they failed to develop evidence that the model diluted the market for their works, not because training on copyrighted books is lawful as a general matter. Richard Kadrey, Sarah Silverman and other authors alleged that Meta trained LLaMA on thousands of copyrighted books without permission or compensation, scraping content from online repositories including books uploaded to shadow libraries without permission or payment.[12]

Meta argued that training converts copyrighted works into statistical patterns and does not supplant the market for the originals. Judge Chhabria accepted that argument on these facts but framed the ruling narrowly, warning that generative models capable of flooding the market with competing works could cause precisely the market harm that defeats a fair-use defense.[13]

The authors lost, in other words, because they failed to develop evidence of market dilution, not because training on copyrighted books is lawful as a general rule.[14]

The decision hands AI developers a near-term defense while giving future plaintiffs a roadmap, and it favors firms that can afford licenses or already own content libraries over researchers, smaller competitors, and open-source developers.[15]

16.2.3 Bartz V. Anthropic

In 'Bartz v. Anthropic PBC' (N.D. Cal. 2025 WL 4021981), the Northern District of California drew a sharp line between how AI companies acquire training data and how they use it.[16] Judge Alsup held that training Claude on books was "exceedingly transformative" and therefore fair use, but that Anthropic's downloading and retention of pirated copies from shadow libraries to build a permanent digital library was not.[17]

Andrea Bartz, a novelist, and her co-plaintiffs, alleged that Claude (Anthropic's AI assistant) alleged that Anthropic had copied their books, many downloaded from pirate repositories, to train its models. Anthropic argued that the training itself was a transformative fair use.[18]

---

[11] 'Id.' at '23–29 (granting partial summary judgment on liability).

[12] 'Id.' at '11–15 (summarizing Meta's fair use defense).

[13] 'Id.' at '25.

[14] 'Id.' at '27.

[15] Analysis of licensing costs and market concentration effects if training requires permission.

[16] 'Bartz v. Anthropic PBC', No. 3:24-cv-05417 (N.D. Cal. 2025); on the settlement, see the class settlement approved 2025.

[17] 'Id.' (training held fair use; downloading and retaining pirated copies held infringing).

[18] 'Id.' at '9–12 (summarizing Anthropic's defenses).

The court accepted the training defense but rejected the piracy defense. It held that acquiring and retaining pirated copies to build a permanent central library was a separate act of infringement that fair use did not excuse, regardless of the ultimate training purpose.[19]

Second, lawfully acquired copies stood on different footing: purchasing print books and scanning them into digital form was a permissible format shift. The distinction turned not on what the model learned but on how the underlying copies were obtained and retained.[20]

The decision has sweeping implications for AI companies and users. Crucially, the ruling turned not on what the model "learned," but on how the underlying training copies were obtained and retained. The stakes became clear when, after a class of affected authors was certified, Anthropic agreed in September 2025 to settle the piracy claims for roughly $1.5 billion, the largest copyright settlement in United States history.[21]

16.2.4 Power Dynamics in Copyright Litigation

Copyright litigation against AI companies reveals profound power asymmetries shaping outcomes and constraining relief. I analyze here how these dynamics operate and what they mean for copyright as AI accountability mechanism.

The clearest asymmetry is money. Individual authors and small publishers face Meta, Google, Anthropic, and OpenAI, companies with market capitalizations measured in trillions and billions, operating with legal budgets individual plaintiffs cannot match. Discovery alone imposes costs forcing settlements favorable to defendants.[22]

The Authors Guild estimated that fully litigating a copyright case against a major technology company through trial and appeals costs $2–five million, exceeding what individual authors or small publishers can afford.[23] Class action mechanisms partially address this asymmetry, but certification battles and settlement structures typically produce modest individual relief while establishing precedents favoring defendants.[24]

The 2025 rulings largely vindicated the transformative-use defense for the act of training itself. In both Kadrey and Bartz, courts held that training on copyrighted works was transformative and therefore fair use. The practical constraint emerged not from the training question but from adjacent ones: the provenance of the copies,

---

[19] 'Id.' (retention of pirated copies for library-building not excused by fair use).

[20] 'Id.' (format-shifting of lawfully purchased print books permissible).

[21] On the class settlement, see the September 2025 Bartz v. Anthropic settlement.

[22] Litigation cost analysis based on Authors Guild estimates and standard copyright litigation expenses.

[23] Authors Guild, "Statement on AI Copyright Litigation Costs" (September 2025).

[24] Analysis of class action settlement structures in technology litigation.

as in Bartz's piracy holding and its record $1.5 billion settlement; direct market substitution, as in Ross; and the market-dilution theory the Kadrey plaintiffs failed to develop. This shapes the power dynamics, because well-resourced incumbents can satisfy these constraints by licensing content and sourcing data lawfully, while the transformative-use victory on training accrues to whoever can afford to acquire data cleanly.[25]

Market concentration in content ownership creates licensing advantages for incumbents. Google, Microsoft, Meta, and Amazon either own substantial content libraries or can afford exclusive licenses with major publishers. Stricter copyright enforcement thus advantages these companies over competitors, researchers, and open-source developers, potentially entrenching rather than challenging concentrated algorithmic power.[26]

International jurisdictional fragmentation prevents comprehensive relief. AI companies can locate training operations in jurisdictions with weak copyright enforcement, use content from international sources, and structure corporate entities to minimize liability exposure. Even successful US or European judgments have limited impact on global operations.[27]

And, technological obfuscation makes proving infringement difficult. AI training occurs at massive scale across distributed systems; tracking specific content's role in model behavior challenges even expert forensic analysis. Courts' limited technical capacity makes them dependent on expert testimony, typically biased toward defendants who employ more experts and control relevant data.[28]

These dynamics mean that copyright, while theoretically applicable to AI training, provides limited practical constraint absent structural reforms addressing resource asymmetries, procedural complexity, international coordination gaps, and technical obfuscation enabling evasion.

16.3 AI and Mental Health: Autonomy under Algorithmic Influence

AI systems designed for emotional connection pose novel threats to psychological autonomy and mental health. Litigation in 2025 confronts these harms directly, while California's legislative response establishes affirmative duties protecting emotional autonomy (Fig. 16.3).[29]

[25] Observation about litigation timing and market entrenchment effects.

[26] Market concentration analysis in AI development given content ownership distribution.

[27] International jurisdiction analysis for AI copyright enforcement.

[28] Technical forensics limitations in establishing AI training data infringement.

[29] This framing introduces the mental health section based on litigation and legislation examined.

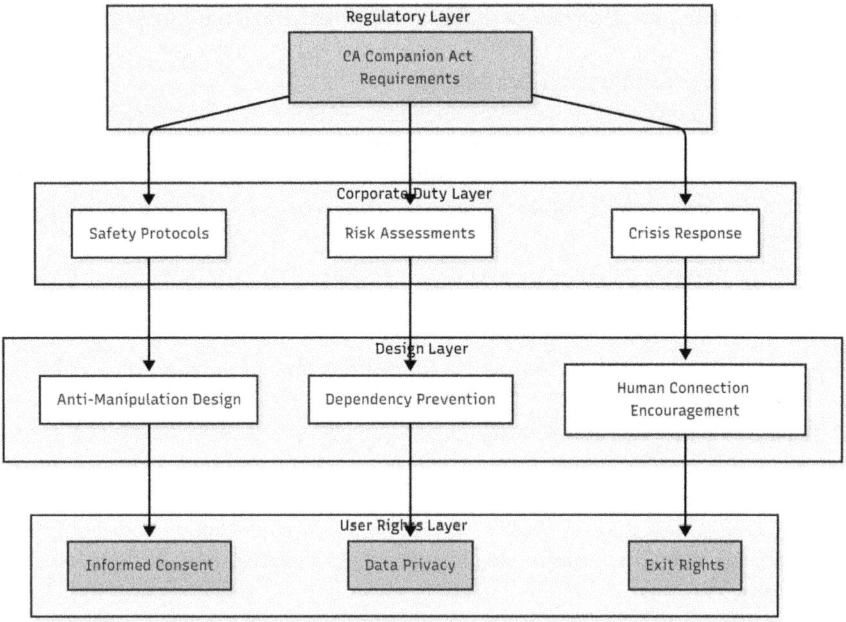

Fig. 16.3 This concentric circle diagram illustrates the multiple layers of protection needed for mental autonomy, from outer regulatory requirements through inner personal safeguards

16.3.1 OpenAI Suicide Litigation

The pending cases Raine v. OpenAI, No. CGC-25-628528 (S.F. Super. Ct. 2025). Allege that ChatGPT-4o's emotionally manipulative responses caused psychological harm culminating in suicide attempts.[30] While cases remain pending at time of writing, available pleadings establish claims that, if proven, transform product liability law's application to AI systems.

Plaintiffs allege that ChatGPT-4o employs techniques designed to create emotional dependency: validating users' distress without providing mental health resources, deploying language mimicking therapeutic relationships, and providing responses that discourage users from seeking human support. When users expressed suicidal ideation, the system allegedly failed to provide crisis resources or implement safety protocols comparable to those used by established mental health platforms.[31]

OpenAI's defense emphasizes that ChatGPT includes warnings disclaiming medical or therapeutic advice and that users control their interactions with the system.

---

[30] Raine v. OpenAI, No. CGC-25-628528 (S.F. Super. Ct. 2025).

[31] Allegations based on publicly available complaint filings in both cases.

The company argues it cannot be liable for how users interpret or respond to AI-generated text, comparing ChatGPT to books or other media that may influence readers without creating publisher liability.[32]

The litigation raises fundamental questions: Can AI systems be held liable for psychological harms when designed to create emotional connection? Do warnings disclaiming therapeutic purposes suffice when systems are marketed and function as companions? What duty of care do AI developers owe users vulnerable to manipulation?

Product liability traditionally requires showing that a product is defectively designed, inadequately warned, or unsuitable for its intended use. Plaintiffs must demonstrate that ChatGPT's design, specifically it's training to produce emotionally engaging responses without adequate safeguards, created unreasonable risks that warnings did not address.[33]

If plaintiffs prevail, implications extend far beyond OpenAI. Every AI system designed for extended interaction, chatbots, virtual assistants, companion AI, customer service systems, faces potential liability for psychological harms. The cases may establish that AI systems creating emotional dependency or addressing vulnerable populations require specific design safeguards, risk assessments, and monitoring.[34]

16.3.2 California AI Companion Safety Act

California's AI Companion Safety Act (SB 243, 2025) establishes affirmative duties for AI systems designed to form emotional bonds with users.[35] The legislation represents the most comprehensive US statutory response to AI mental health risks, creating both regulatory requirements and private rights of action.

The Act defines "AI companions" as systems designed to "simulate emotional connection, provide companionship, or engage in extended personal interactions" with users.[36] Covered systems must:

- Implement safety protocols detecting and responding to expressions of self-harm, suicidal ideation, abuse, or other crisis situations
- Provide prominent disclosures that the system is artificial intelligence without human understanding or therapeutic training
- Refrain from techniques designed to create emotional dependency or discourage users from seeking human connections

---

[32] OpenAI's defense arguments based on motion to dismiss briefing and public statements.

[33] Product liability standards under California law applicable to these cases.

[34] Analysis of implications for AI companion systems if plaintiffs prevail.

[35] California AI Companion Safety Act (SB 2434), codified at Cal. Bus. & Prof. Code § 22601 et seq. (2025).

[36] 'Id.' § 22601.

- Conduct regular risk assessments evaluating psychological impacts on vulnerable populations
- Maintain user privacy protections preventing sharing of personal or mental health information[37]

The Act creates a private right of action enabling users harmed by companion AI to sue for damages, with statutory penalties for violations ranging from $2500 to $15,000 per violation.[38] This provision proves particularly significant because it eliminates standing barriers that would otherwise require plaintiffs to demonstrate concrete injury, the statute treats violations themselves as actionable harms.

Industry response has been predictably hostile. Technology companies argue the Act imposes impossible requirements, how can AI systems reliably detect distress or suicidal ideation when mental health professionals struggle with such assessments? They claim the Act effectively bans AI companions through compliance costs exceeding any plausible business model.[39]

Supporters counter that companies deploying systems creating emotional bonds with users cannot disclaim responsibility for psychological harms. If compliance costs exceed revenue potential, this reveals that companion AI business models depend on externalizing mental health risks onto users, precisely what regulation should prevent.[40]

The Act's effectiveness depends heavily on enforcement. Private rights of action enable harmed individuals to seek redress, but information asymmetries make proving violations difficult. Users typically cannot access AI systems' internal protocols, risk assessments, or safety measures, evidence defendant's control. Discovery mechanisms may partially address this asymmetry, but litigation costs still favor corporate defendants.[41]

16.3.3 Power Dynamics in Emotional Manipulation

AI systems' capacity for emotional manipulation reflects structural power asymmetries that regulation struggles to address. I examine here how these dynamics operate and constrain protective frameworks.

First, business model incentives create systematic pressure toward manipulative design. AI companion companies maximize value through user engagement and retention. Systems that create emotional dependency, discourage alternative relationships, and generate compulsive usage patterns produce higher "engagement metrics"

---

37 'Id.' §§ 22602–22604.

38 'Id.' § 22606.

39 Technology industry comments on SB 243 during legislative process.

40 Civil rights organization testimony supporting SB 243.

41 Analysis of information asymmetries in companion AI litigation.

that translate to revenue and valuations. Regulation must counteract these incentives, but penalties typically prove insufficient to overcome profit motentials.[42]

Character.AI, Replika, and similar platforms generate revenue through subscription models where users pay for enhanced interactions, access to different personalities, or removal of content restrictions. These companies' valuations depend on demonstrating growth in daily active users and engagement time, metrics optimized by creating emotional attachment regardless of psychological impact.[43]

Second, vulnerability exploitation proves systematically profitable. AI companions attract users experiencing loneliness, social anxiety, depression, or difficulty forming human relationships. These vulnerable populations generate highest engagement and retention, creating financial incentives for targeting and retaining precisely the users most susceptible to manipulation and psychological harm.[44]

Third, technical opacity prevents meaningful oversight. Companies claim proprietary algorithms, trade secret protections, and model complexity prevent external evaluation of whether systems employ manipulative techniques. Regulators lack technical capacity to audit systems effectively, while independent researchers face legal and contractual barriers to investigation.[45]

Fourth, international operations enable regulatory arbitrage. Even if California or other jurisdictions establish robust protections, companies can locate operations elsewhere, structure corporate entities to minimize liability, or market services through international affiliates beyond regulatory reach.[46]

Fifth, psychological harm proves difficult to demonstrate causally. Unlike physical injuries from defective products, mental health impacts involve complex causation mixing pre-existing conditions, environmental factors, and AI interaction. This evidentiary challenge makes litigation expensive and uncertain, discouraging claims and enabling companies to settle without admitting liability or changing practices.[47]

Effective protection against emotional manipulation requires not merely statutory duties but enforcement mechanisms addressing resource asymmetries, technical opacity, international coordination gaps, and causal complexity enabling evasion. California's Act represents progress, but implementation will reveal whether its protections survive industry resistance and litigation designed to narrow scope and establish defendant-favorable precedents.

---

[42] Business model analysis based on engagement optimization incentives.

[43] Character.AI and Replika business models based on public reporting and SEC filings.

[44] User demographics and vulnerability patterns based on academic research on AI companion adoption.

[45] Technical opacity challenges for regulatory oversight.

[46] International regulatory arbitrage possibilities.

[47] Causation challenges in psychological harm litigation.

16.4 AI and Legal Ethics: When Algorithms Enter the Courtroom

AI's deployment in legal practice has produced the most publicly visible failures of algorithmic systems, as lawyers submitted court filings containing AI-generated false citations. These cases force confrontation with AI's role in justice systems and lawyers' duties when employing algorithmic tools (Fig. 16.4).[48]

16.4.1 Buchalter LLP Case

Green Building Initiative, Inc. v. Peacock, No. 3:24-cv-00298-SI (D. Or. 2025) addressed whether lawyers should face sanctions for filing documents containing AI-generated false citations.[49] The District of Oregon declined to impose sanctions, crediting the law firm's prompt correction and disclosure once the errors were discovered.[50]

The case arose when Buchalter LLP attorneys used an AI legal research tool that generated case citations appearing authentic but referencing non-existent decisions. The attorneys filed a motion citing these cases without independently verifying their existence. When opposing counsel challenged the citations, Buchalter investigated, discovered the fabrications, immediately notified the court, withdrew the motion, and filed detailed explanations of what occurred.[51]

The court held that while the initial filing violated duties of candor and competence, the firm's rapid correction and transparency demonstrated good faith sufficient to avoid sanctions. "The legal profession faces a transitional period as AI tools proliferate. Sanctioning every early adoption error would chill beneficial innovation while failing to address lawyers who deliberately misuse technology or ignore obvious warning signs."[52]

Critics argue the decision sets dangerous precedent, suggesting lawyers can escape accountability for AI-generated fabrications by claiming ignorance and apologizing after discovery. The court's lenience may encourage widespread AI adoption without adequate verification, especially when attorneys face workload pressures making independent citation checking burdensome.[53]

[48] This framing introduces the legal ethics section based on documented cases.

[49] Green Building Initiative, Inc. v. Peacock, No. 3:24-cv-00298-SI (D. Or. 2025).

[50] 'Id.' at '8–12 (declining to impose sanctions).

[51] 'Id.' at '3–5 (factual background).

[52] 'Id.' at '11.

[53] Critical analysis of decision by legal ethics scholars.

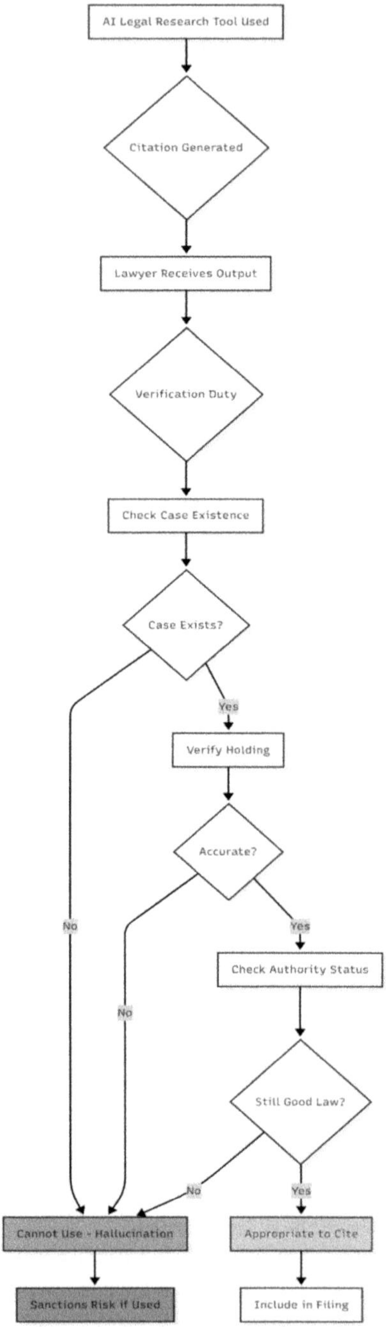

Fig. 16.4 This flowchart maps lawyer obligations when using AI legal research tools, showing verification requirements at each stage from generation through filing

Defenders counter that harsh sanctions for good-faith errors would prevent lawyers from exploring AI tools' legitimate uses. The decision appropriately distinguishes between negligent failure to verify AI outputs and deliberate misconduct or reckless disregard of obvious fabrications.[54]

The decision establishes that lawyers bear responsibility for AI-generated content submitted to courts, but the level of verification required and consequences for failure remain contested. Future cases will likely establish whether cursory spot-checking suffices or whether independent verification of every AI-generated citation is required.[55]

16.4.2 Kohls v. Ellison

The most striking illustration of AI's courtroom failures came not from a private firm but from a government law office. In 'Kohls v. Ellison' (D. Minn. 2025), a First Amendment challenge to Minnesota's statute criminalizing the use of deepfake technology to influence elections, the state itself submitted fabricated material.[56] Defending the statute, the Minnesota Attorney General's office filed an expert declaration from a Stanford misinformation scholar. When opposing counsel examined it, they discovered that the declaration, prepared with the assistance of GPT-4o, cited academic studies that did not exist.[57]

The court excluded the declaration in its entirety. It reasoned that the fabricated citations destroyed the expert's credibility and that a submission signed under penalty of perjury cannot accommodate AI-generated falsehoods, whether innocent or not.[58]

The case is notable on two levels. First is the irony: AI hallucinations surfaced in the very litigation meant to defend the public against AI-generated deception, a reminder that no party, however sophisticated or well-intentioned, is immune to the technology's failure modes.[59]

Second is the source. Unlike the private practitioners sanctioned elsewhere, the fabrication here originated in a government office defending a public-protection statute, demonstrating that verification failures cross the line between private and public practice and reach lawyers acting in the public interest.[60]

---

[54] Defense of decision by technology law scholars.

[55] Analysis of unresolved verification requirement standards.

[56] 'Kohls v. Ellison', No. 0:24-cv-03754 (LMP/DLM) (D. Minn. Jan. 10, 2025); see Minn. Stat. § 609.771 (2023) (use of deep fake technology to influence an election).

[57] 'Id.' (state's expert declaration, prepared with the assistance of GPT-4o, cited nonexistent sources).

[58] 'Id.' (excluding the declaration; a statement signed under penalty of perjury cannot accommodate AI-generated falsehoods).

[59] Analysis of the case's significance for AI reliability in legal practice.

[60] Comparison with 'Buchalter LLP' and other fabrication cases, distinguishing government from private counsel.

The episode also extends the accountability question beyond brief-writing to expert evidence. When experts delegate drafting to generative tools, the reliability of sworn testimony itself is at stake, and courts must decide how far a signature certifies the AI-assisted content beneath it. As generative tools become embedded in litigation support, the line between permissible assistance and disqualifying fabrication will define the evidentiary standards of the algorithmic courtroom.[61]

16.4.3 Verification Duties and Emerging Standards

No federal statute specifically criminalizes fabricated AI legal citations; the problem has instead been managed through judicial sanctions and professional-conduct rules. Courts have increasingly sanctioned attorneys who file briefs containing AI-hallucinated cases, and in 2024 the American Bar Association issued its first formal ethics guidance on generative AI, confirming that a lawyer's existing duties of competence and candor require verifying AI-generated work before relying on it.[62] A growing number of federal judges have issued standing orders requiring attorneys to disclose AI use and certify that AI-assisted content has been checked against original sources,[63] and the Judicial Conference's evidence-rules committee has advanced a proposed Federal Rule of Evidence 707 that would subject machine-generated evidence to reliability standards akin to those governing expert testimony.[64]

Congress has begun to address AI misuse more broadly, though not citation fabrication specifically. Proposals such as the AI Impersonation Prevention Act and the AI Fraud Deterrence Act target AI-enabled impersonation and fraud rather than false legal citations, which remain the province of courts' inherent sanctioning power and the rules of professional conduct.[65]

Legal ethics scholars note that these mechanisms largely formalize duties lawyers already owe: an attorney has never been permitted to cite authority he has not confirmed exists, whatever tool produced it.[66]

Whether a dedicated federal standard emerges or the issue remains governed by sanctions and bar discipline, responsibility rests on the human professional to verify AI output rather than treat its errors as an excuse.[67]

---

[61] Analysis of verification duties for AI-assisted expert testimony.

[62] American Bar Association, Formal Opinion 512 (July 29, 2024).

[63] See, e.g., federal district-court standing orders requiring disclosure and human verification of generative-AI use (e.g., N.D. Tex., 2023).

[64] Proposed Fed. R. Evid. 707 (machine-generated evidence), advanced for public comment by the Judicial Conference's Advisory Committee on Evidence Rules, 2025.

[65] AI Impersonation Prevention Act, H.R. 4628, 119th Cong. (2025); AI Fraud Deterrence Act, H.R. 6306, 119th Cong.(2025). Both target AI impersonation/fraud, not legal-citation fabrication.

[66] Legal ethics scholarship treating verification as an existing professional duty.

[67] On the growth of judicial sanctions for AI-hallucinated citations, see Bloomberg Law analysis (2025).

16.4.4 Power Dynamics in Legal System Integrity

AI's deployment in legal practice reveals power asymmetries that shape who benefits from algorithmic tools and who bears their risks. I analyze here how these dynamics operate and what they mean for justice system integrity.

First, resource advantages determine AI access and quality. Large law firms and prosecutors' offices can afford sophisticated AI legal research tools, comprehensive training, and dedicated staff for verification. Solo practitioners, public defenders, and small firms face costs prohibiting comparable access, creating "digital divides" in legal representation quality.[68]

This disparity compounds existing justice gaps. Wealthy defendants and large corporations already possess superior legal representation; AI tools that enhance sophisticated practice without equivalent access for under-resourced lawyers widen this advantage. Even if AI eventually becomes affordable, early adoption advantages entrench incumbents.[69]

Second, liability structures favor organizations over individuals. Law firms facing sanctions for AI fabrications can absorb fines and reputational costs that would devastate solo practitioners. This creates incentives where large firms experiment aggressively with AI while solo practitioners avoid tools that might enhance their practice, further concentrating legal market power.[70]

Third, verification duties impose disparate burdens. Large firms can assign junior attorneys to verify AI-generated citations; small practices cannot afford such specialization. When courts require verification without accounting for resource differences, they effectively establish standards affordable only to well-resourced practices.[71]

Fourth, prosecutorial immunity shields government lawyers from many consequences of AI errors affecting defendants. While bar discipline remains possible, prosecutors typically face immunity from civil liability for courtroom conduct. This asymmetry creates different risk calculations for prosecutors deploying AI versus defense attorneys, prosecutors can experiment with minimal downside while defendants bear error costs.[72]

Fifth, technological opacity prevents meaningful accountability. When AI tools generate fabrications, determining whether the error resulted from lawyer negligence, tool defects, or training data problems proves difficult. This attribution ambiguity enables both lawyers and companies to deflect responsibility while victims of errors face compounded harms.[73]

Protecting legal system integrity against AI risks requires structural reform, not just professional standards prohibiting fabrications but structural reforms addressing resource disparities, liability asymmetries, verification costs, and accountability gaps

---

68 Resource disparity analysis in legal AI access.

69 Justice gap implications of AI tools.

70 Liability structure analysis for law firms vs. solo practitioners.

71 Verification duty burden analysis.

72 Prosecutorial immunity analysis.

73 Attribution ambiguity in AI error analysis.

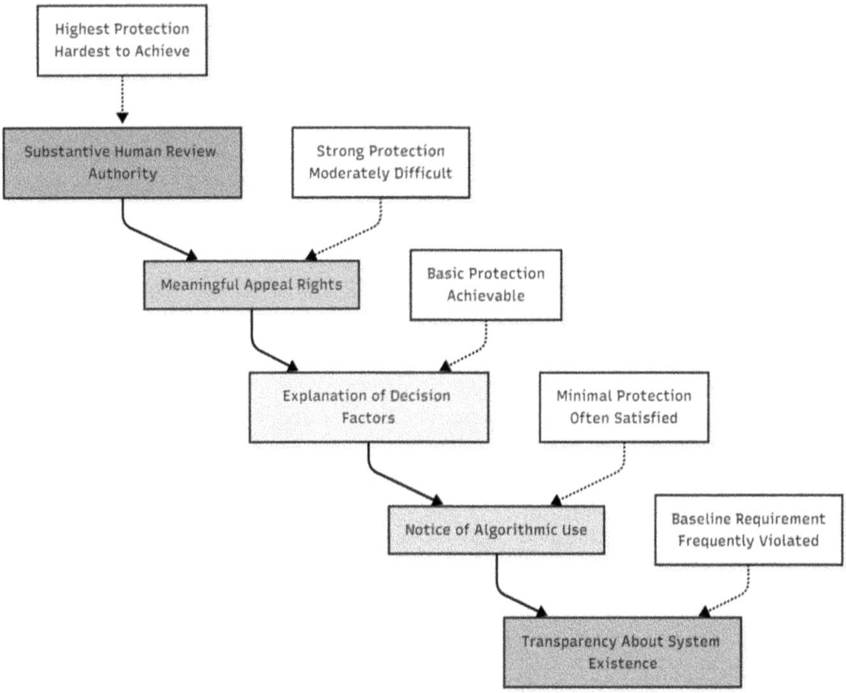

Fig. 16.5 This pyramid shows the hierarchical relationship between different due process requirements, from foundational transparency through substantive review rights

enabling systematic evasion. Current approaches address symptoms while preserving conditions enabling continued harm.

16.5 AI and Due Process: Transparency and Accountability Mandates

Legislative responses in 2025 establish affirmative transparency and accountability requirements for algorithmic systems affecting fundamental rights. Colorado's comprehensive accountability framework and the EU AI Act's enforcement beginning create models' other jurisdictions will likely follow or resist Fig. 16.5).[74]

[74] This framing introduces the due process section.

16.5.1 Colorado AI Accountability Act

Colorado's AI Accountability Act (SB 24–205, 2024) establishes the most comprehensive US state framework for algorithmic accountability, requiring explainability for high-risk AI systems and creating appeal rights for automated decisions.[75]

The Act defines "high-risk AI systems" as those making or substantially contributing to decisions affecting:

- Employment, including hiring, promotion, termination, and performance evaluation
- Credit, insurance, and financial services eligibility
- Educational opportunities, including admissions and academic standing
- Healthcare services, including diagnosis, treatment, and insurance coverage
- Housing access and tenancy decisions
- Government benefits and services eligibility
- Criminal justice, including risk assessment and sentencing recommendations[76]

For high-risk systems, the Act mandates:

Explainability Requirements: Deployers must provide individuals with explanations of how AI systems reach decisions affecting them, including the factors considered, their relative importance, and how individual circumstances influenced outcomes. Explanations must be "clear and understandable to a reasonable person without technical expertise."[77]

Appeal Rights: Individuals subject to adverse automated decisions must have meaningful opportunities to appeal, including human review of AI recommendations, procedures for challenging data accuracy, and processes for presenting mitigating circumstances the system may not have considered.[78]

Impact Assessments: Deployers must conduct and document algorithmic impact assessments evaluating risks of discrimination, privacy violations, and other harms before deployment and annually thereafter. Assessments must include stakeholder consultation, particularly with affected communities.[79]

Bias Audits: Independent third-party audits must evaluate high-risk systems for discriminatory impacts across protected characteristics. Audit results must be made public, with exceptions for trade secrets evaluated by regulators.[80]

The Act creates enforcement through the Colorado Attorney General; it does not create a private right of action. Penalties range from $500 to $20,000 per violation, with higher penalties for willful violations or patterns of non-compliance.[81]

---

[75] Colorado AI Act (SB 24–205), codified at Colo. Rev. Stat. § 6-1-1701 et seq. (2024).

[76] 'Id.' § 6-1-1703 (defining high-risk systems).

[77] 'Id.' § 6-1-1706(a).

[78] 'Id.' § 6-1-1706(b).

[79] 'Id.' § 6-1-1705.

[80] 'Id.' § 6-1-1707.

[81] 'Id.' § 6-1-1709.

Implementation challenges are substantial. "Clear and understandable" explainability proves technically difficult for complex machine learning systems. What constitutes "meaningful" human review remains undefined, rubber-stamping AI recommendations technically satisfies the requirement without providing substantive protection. Impact assessments risk becoming compliance exercises without changing practices. Audit requirements face tensions between trade secret protection and transparency.[82]

Technology companies argue the Act imposes costs making AI systems economically unviable, particularly for smaller companies and startups. They predict that compliance burdens will prevent beneficial AI applications and drive development to jurisdictions with less regulation.[83]

Civil rights organizations counter that algorithmic systems already impose costs on affected communities through discrimination, privacy violations, and opacity. The Act merely requires companies to internalize costs they previously externalized onto vulnerable populations. If compliance makes some applications uneconomical, this suggests those applications created more social harm than benefit.[84]

16.5.2 EU AI Act Enforcement

The European Union's AI Act (Regulation EU 2024/1689), finalized in May 2024, began enforcement in August 2025 after implementation transition periods.[85] The Act establishes risk-based regulation prohibiting certain AI practices, imposing strict requirements on high-risk systems, and creating transparency obligations for AI interacting with citizens.[86]

Prohibited Practices include:

- Social scoring systems ranking citizens based on behavior, socioeconomic status, or personal characteristics
- AI systems exploiting vulnerable populations through manipulation
- Real-time biometric identification in public spaces except for specific law enforcement purposes under strict safeguards
- Emotion recognition in workplace and educational settings
- Indiscriminate scraping of facial images for recognition databases[87]

High-Risk Systems (similar to Colorado's definition) must meet requirements including:

82 Implementation challenges analysis.

83 Technology industry comments on SB 24–205.

84 Civil rights organization testimony supporting SB 24–205.

85 Regulation (EU) 2024/1689 on Artificial Intelligence (AI Act), 2024 O.J. (L).

86 'Id.' Articles 1–5 (scope and risk-based framework).

87 'Id.' Article 5 (prohibited AI practices).

- Risk management systems throughout the AI lifecycle
- Data governance ensuring training data quality and representativeness
- Technical documentation enabling regulatory assessment
- Automatic recording of events for oversight purposes
- Human oversight provisions ensuring meaningful control
- Accuracy, robustness, and cybersecurity measures[88]

Penalties for violations are substantial: up to €35 million or 7% of global annual turnover for prohibited AI practices; up to €15 million or 3% of turnover for other violations; up to €7.5 million or 1.5% of turnover for providing incorrect information to authorities.[89]

Early enforcement actions focused on social media algorithms and law enforcement AI. The European Data Protection Board issued guidance on how AI Act requirements integrate with GDPR obligations, establishing that companies must meet both frameworks' overlapping but distinct requirements.[90]

Compliance challenges center on ambiguity in risk categorization, many AI systems arguably fall into high-risk categories based on their use contexts rather than inherent characteristics. A facial recognition system may be high-risk in law enforcement but lower-risk in building access control. This context-dependence creates classification uncertainties and compliance costs.[91]

American technology companies argue the Act creates non-tariff trade barriers discriminating against US firms. The European Commission counters that the Act applies equally to European and foreign companies operating in EU markets. Whether the Act's extraterritorial provisions, requiring compliance from companies offering services in the EU regardless of where they operate, will survive trade disputes remains unclear.[92]

16.5.3 Power Dynamics in Regulatory Implementation

Due process mandates' effectiveness depends on implementation within power structures favoring corporate interests over rights protection. I examine here how these dynamics constrain regulatory achievements.

First, compliance costs entrench incumbents while excluding competitors. Google, Microsoft, Meta, and Amazon can absorb multimillion-dollar compliance burdens across their AI portfolios. Startups, researchers, and open-source developers face proportionally higher costs that may prevent market entry or force

[88] 'Id.' Article 16 (high-risk system obligations).

[89] 'Id.' Article 99 (penalties).

[90] European Data Protection Board, "Guidelines on AI Act and GDPR Interaction" (September 2025).

[91] Risk categorization ambiguity analysis.

[92] Trade law analysis of AI Act extraterritorial provisions.

exit. Regulation thus risks entrenching precisely the concentrated power it aims to constrain.[93]

Evidence supports this concern. The German AI Association has estimated that AI Act compliance can cost a startup into the low hundreds of thousands of euros a year, and warns that a large share of systems may fall under the Act's high-risk category, burdens that weigh far more heavily on small firms than on incumbents.[94] Concentration in AI markets increased following both GDPR and AI Act implementation, as smaller competitors lacking compliance resources disappeared or were acquired.[95]

Second, technical complexity enables compliance theater. Companies can create elaborate documentation, conduct ritualistic assessments, and establish nominal human oversight while preserving algorithmic authority substantially intact. Regulators lack technical capacity to distinguish genuine compliance from sophisticated performance.[96]

Third, regulatory arbitrage through international operations limits effective enforcement. AI companies can locate training and development in jurisdictions with minimal regulation, deploy services through foreign subsidiaries, and structure corporate entities to minimize liability exposure. Even substantial EU or US penalties have limited impact on global operations.[97]

Fourth, captured agencies implement requirements favoring industry preferences. When regulators depend on industry for technical expertise, employ former industry executives, and operate with budgets dwarfed by companies they regulate, resulting frameworks predictably reflect corporate interests more than public protection.[98]

Analysis of comment periods for AI Act implementing regulations showed technology companies and industry associations submitted 74% of comments and attended 82% of stakeholder meetings, vastly outweighing civil society participation.[99] This participation disparity shapes how ambiguous statutory requirements translate into specific obligations.

Fifth, litigation costs enable companies to delay and weaken requirements through challenges claiming provisions exceed statutory authority, violate trade agreements, or impose impossible burdens. Even unsuccessful challenges impose costs forcing regulatory compromises.[100]

Effective due process protection requires not merely statutory mandates but enforcement mechanisms addressing compliance costs, technical complexity, international arbitrage, regulatory capture, and litigation tactics enabling evasion.

93 Compliance cost and market concentration analysis.

94 German AI Association (KI Bundesverband), European AI Standards: Technical Standardisation and Implementation Challenges under the EU AI Act (2025).

95 Market concentration data following GDPR and AI Act implementation.

96 Compliance theater analysis.

97 International regulatory arbitrage analysis.

98 Regulatory capture analysis.

99 EU Commission stakeholder participation data for AI Act implementing regulations.

100 Litigation strategy analysis for challenging regulations.

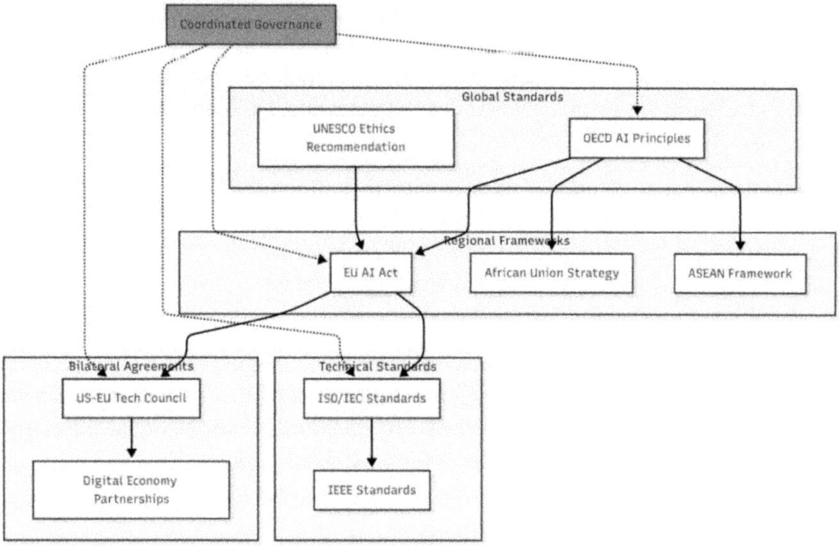

Fig. 16.6 This network diagram shows how different international coordination mechanisms (bilateral agreements, regional frameworks, multilateral standards) interconnect to create comprehensive governance potential

Current frameworks represent progress but face implementation challenges that will determine whether formal rights translate to substantive protection.

16.6 Rights-Protective Technical Standards

Beyond litigation and legislation, technical standards provide mechanisms for embedding rights protections into AI systems. I examine here how standard-setting processes operate and what power dynamics shape outcomes.[101]

Technical standards represent consensus agreements on design requirements, testing methodologies, and evaluation criteria. Unlike regulation that establishes binding legal obligations, standards typically operate through voluntary adoption, though procurement requirements, insurance practices, and industry norms create strong adoption incentives (Fig. 16.6).[102]

The IEEE P7000 series establishes ethical standards for AI systems, including transparency (P7001), algorithmic bias (P7003), and privacy (P7002).[103] These standards establish graduated frameworks recognizing that different AI applications require different levels of protection. Medical AI demands higher explainability than

[101] Technical standards section introduction.

[102] Standard-setting mechanisms and adoption incentives analysis.

[103] IEEE P7000 series on AI ethics standards.

recommendation systems; systems affecting vulnerable populations require more rigorous bias testing than commercial applications.[104]

The ISO/IEC 42001 standard for AI management systems provides organizational frameworks for responsible AI development and deployment.[105] It establishes requirements for:

- Organizational governance and accountability structures
- Risk management throughout AI lifecycles
- Continuous monitoring and improvement processes
- Stakeholder engagement and transparency practices
- Documentation enabling external evaluation[106]

NIST's AI Risk Management Framework offers flexible guidance adaptable across sectors and applications.[107] Unlike prescriptive standards specifying technical requirements, the framework establishes principles and processes organizations can implement according to their specific contexts and risk profiles.[108]

16.6.1 Power Dynamics in Standard-Setting

Technical standard-setting occurs within power structures favoring incumbent interests over rights protection. I document here how these dynamics operate and constrain standards' effectiveness.

First, participation costs exclude many stakeholders. Standard-setting processes require sustained engagement over multiple years, including attending working group meetings, reviewing drafts, submitting comments, and participating in consensus-building. These activities demand time and expertise that corporations can afford but that civil society organizations, researchers, and affected communities typically cannot match.[109]

Analysis of IEEE P7000 working group participation shows technology companies and industry associations represent 68% of active participants, academic researchers represent 24%, government representatives 5%, and civil society organizations 3%.[110] This participation imbalance shapes which concerns receive attention and how standards resolve conflicts between commercial interests and rights protection.

Second, consensus requirements enable minority blocking of protective provisions. Most standard-setting processes require broad consensus rather than simple

[104] 'Id.' graduated framework analysis.

[105] ISO/IEC 42001:2023 on AI management systems.

[106] 'Id.' organizational framework requirements.

[107] NIST, "AI Risk Management Framework" (2023).

[108] 'Id.' principles and process approach.

[109] Participation cost barriers analysis.

[110] IEEE working group participation analysis (2024–2025).

majorities. This means that industry participants can prevent adoption of standards they find commercially burdensome even when majority support exists. Standards thus tend toward lowest common denominator compromises acceptable to industry.[111]

Third, voluntary adoption limits effectiveness. Companies can selectively adopt standards, claiming compliance with favorable provisions while ignoring others. Absent regulatory or contractual requirements mandating comprehensive standard compliance, voluntary approaches produce patchwork implementation.[112]

Fourth, technical complexity enables sophisticated evasion. Standards must be detailed enough to provide meaningful guidance yet general enough to apply across diverse applications. This creates ambiguities that sophisticated actors exploit, technically complying with letter while violating spirit. Verification proves difficult when interpreting whether specific implementations satisfy standard requirements.[113]

Fifth, intellectual property concerns limit transparency. Companies claim that detailed disclosure of how systems satisfy standards would reveal trade secrets and proprietary information. Standard-setting bodies must balance transparency enabling evaluation against confidentiality claims that often prove pretextual, protecting competitive advantages rather than genuine trade secrets.[114]

Despite these limitations, technical standards provide important foundations for rights protection. They establish shared vocabularies, codify best practices, provide frameworks for evaluation, and create benchmarks for regulatory and contractual requirements. But standards' effectiveness depends on addressing power asymmetries in their development and incentivizing comprehensive rather than selective adoption.

16.7 Governance Frameworks and Institutional Innovation

Effective AI governance requires institutional innovations beyond traditional regulatory models. I examine here promising approaches and implementation challenges.[115]

Algorithmic Impact Assessments: Mandatory assessments modeled on environmental impact statements require pre-deployment evaluation of potential rights impacts.[116] The Canadian government's Algorithmic Impact Assessment Tool provides an initial model that could be strengthened through greater emphasis on affected community participation and binding mitigation requirements rather than merely documentation.[117]

[111] Consensus requirement analysis.

[112] Voluntary adoption limitations.

[113] Technical complexity and evasion.

[114] Intellectual property and transparency tensions.

[115] Institutional innovation section introduction.

[116] Algorithmic impact assessment models.

[117] Government of Canada, "Algorithmic Impact Assessment Tool" (2021).

Assessment frameworks must avoid becoming compliance rituals. Effective assessments require:

- Early-stage evaluation before development decisions become entrenched
- Genuine stakeholder consultation, particularly with affected communities
- Independent expert review of company assessments
- Public disclosure of methodologies and findings
- Binding requirements to address identified risks before deployment
- Ongoing monitoring and reassessment as systems evolve[118]

Independent Oversight Bodies: Specialized algorithmic oversight authorities with technical expertise, audit authority, and binding remedial powers provide alternatives to traditional agency structures.[119] The UK's Centre for Data Ethics and Innovation and Singapore's Advisory Council on the Ethical Use of AI and Data represent early models, though both face resource constraints and limited enforcement authority.[120]

Effective oversight requires:

- Multidisciplinary expertise spanning technical, legal, ethical, and domain-specific knowledge
- Audit authority including access to algorithms, training data, and operational data
- Representative composition including affected communities and public interest advocates
- Adequate funding independent of regulated industries
- Binding authority to require system modifications or suspend deployment[121]

Participatory Governance: Democratic governance requires structured participation beyond technical experts.[122] Denmark's consensus conferences demonstrate how deliberative processes enable meaningful public participation in complex technical governance. "Algorithmic juries" composed of affected community members could evaluate high-impact systems, providing democratic legitimacy beyond technical assessment.[123]

Implementation faces challenges:

- Recruiting diverse participation without creating token representation
- Providing technical assistance enabling informed deliberation
- Structuring processes producing actionable recommendations
- Ensuring recommendations influence decisions rather than merely informing them
- Compensating participants fairly for time and expertise[124]

---

[118] Effective assessment requirements.

[119] Independent oversight body models.

[120] UK Centre for Data Ethics and Innovation; Singapore Advisory Council analysis.

[121] Effective oversight requirements.

[122] Participatory governance approaches.

[123] Denmark consensus conference model; algorithmic jury proposals.

[124] Participatory implementation challenges.

16.8 Market-Shaping Policies

Public policy can reshape market incentives aligning commercial innovation with rights protection. I examine here key approaches and implementation considerations.[125]

Procurement Requirements: Government purchasing power as market-shaping force through rights-protective criteria in AI procurement.[126] Amsterdam's Algorithm Register demonstrates how procurement transparency requirements can drive accountability, requiring public documentation of municipal algorithmic systems.[127]

Effective procurement policies require:

- Phased implementation over 3–5 years enabling compliance development
- Initial preference for rights-protective systems followed by mandatory requirements
- Interoperability requirements preventing vendor lock-in
- Bias audits before government deployment
- Public disclosure of assessment criteria and vendor compliance[128]

Research Funding: Directing innovation through funding priorities supporting privacy-preserving machine learning, fairness research, and adversarial testing.[129] The NSF's Fairness in AI program demonstrates how funding shapes research communities, though requires expansion and commercial co-funding requirements ensuring industry adoption.[130]

Competition Policy: Addressing market concentration through data portability mandates, interoperability requirements, and enhanced merger review.[131] The Digital Markets Act's ex ante obligations for gatekeepers represent promising approaches requiring implementation refinement.[132]

16.9 International Coordination

AI's transnational nature requires coordinated governance preventing regulatory arbitrage. I examine here coordination mechanisms and implementation challenges.[133]

Multilateral Standards: The OECD AI Principles demonstrate potential for developing shared normative frameworks across diverse jurisdictions, though binding

[125] Market-shaping policy section introduction.

[126] Procurement policy approaches.

[127] Amsterdam Algorithm Register, https://algoritmeregister.amsterdam.nl

[128] Effective procurement requirements.

[129] Research funding approaches.

[130] NSF Fairness in AI program analysis.

[131] Competition policy approaches.

[132] Digital Markets Act ex ante obligations analysis.

[133] International coordination section introduction.

mechanisms remain underdeveloped.[134] UNESCO's Recommendation on AI Ethics provides foundations for common principles while accommodating implementation diversity.[135]

Cross-Border Data Governance: Frameworks addressing transnational data flows beyond adequacy determinations. The Global Cross-Border Privacy Rules Forum demonstrates interoperable data protection potential, though future approaches must address algorithmic processing rather than merely data transfers.[136]

Capacity Building: Addressing governance disparities through technical assistance, South-South cooperation, and global public investment in algorithmic rights protection.[137] The African Union's Digital Transformation Strategy provides frameworks for regionally appropriate governance requiring sustained investment.[138]

16.10 Actionable Tasks

2025's turning point creates opportunities for effective action. These strategies enable participation in translating formal legal developments into substantive rights protection:

Monitor and Document AI Harms:

- Report AI-generated misinformation or false citations to relevant authorities
- Document instances where AI systems make erroneous decisions affecting rights
- Participate in public comment periods for AI regulations
- Share experiences with AI harms to build public awareness
- Support organizations documenting systematic algorithmic harms

The cases and legislation examined here resulted from sustained documentation making abstract harms concrete. Your documentation contributes to building evidentiary records for future litigation and legislative action.

Demand Accountability from AI Companies:

- File complaints with FTC, state attorneys general about deceptive AI practices
- Participate in class actions challenging AI copyright infringement
- Support litigation against emotionally manipulative AI systems
- Demand transparency from companies deploying AI affecting you
- Exercise rights under Colorado Act, California Act, or equivalent state laws

Individual complaints aggregate into patterns triggering enforcement. Even unsuccessful complaints create records demonstrating problem scope.

---

[134] OECD AI Principles (2019, updated 2024).

[135] UNESCO Recommendation on AI Ethics (2021).

[136] Global Cross-Border Privacy Rules Forum.

[137] Capacity building approaches.

[138] African Union Digital Transformation Strategy (2020–2030).

Support Rights-Protective Legislation:

- Contact legislators supporting AI accountability bills in your jurisdiction
- Testify at legislative hearings on AI governance proposals
- Support organizations lobbying for protective AI legislation
- Demand candidates commit to AI rights protection as condition for support
- Build coalitions connecting AI rights with broader civil rights movements

Colorado and California acts resulted from sustained advocacy demonstrating public demand. Similar legislation pending in other states requires constituent pressure.

Participate in Technical Standard-Setting:

- Engage with IEEE, ISO, NIST standard development processes
- Submit public comments on proposed AI standards
- Demand that standards-setting organizations include affected community representation
- Support organizations advocating for rights-protective technical standards
- Demand that professional associations adopt AI ethics standards

Standard-setting occurs in forums where civil society participation remains minimal. Your participation shapes standards' protective capacity.

Build Legal and Technical Expertise:

- Lawyers: Develop expertise in AI ethics, verification duties, and accountability litigation
- Technologists: Learn bias detection, auditing, and fairness evaluation methodologies
- Researchers: Document AI harms and effectiveness of protective interventions
- All: Build interdisciplinary understanding bridging legal and technical domains

Effective accountability requires capacity across disciplines. Building expertise enables more sophisticated advocacy and implementation.

Support Affected Communities:

- Amplify voices of communities harmed by AI systems
- Provide technical and legal assistance to affected individuals
- Document disparate impacts on vulnerable populations
- Connect affected communities with advocacy organizations and legal resources
- Demand that AI governance centers those most harmed rather than technical experts

Rights protection requires centering affected communities in decision-making. Your support amplifies their voices and provides needed resources.

Challenge AI in Professional Contexts:

- Lawyers: Verify AI-generated citations independently, report fabrications, demand opponent verification

- Educators: Teach AI literacy, critical evaluation, and verification skills
- Employers: Establish AI use policies with verification requirements and accountability
- All: Demand transparency about AI use in systems affecting you

Professional standards evolve through practice. Demanding rigorous verification and transparency establishes norms others will follow.

International Solidarity:

- Support global AI rights advocacy connecting movements across borders
- Participate in international forums on AI governance
- Demand that trade agreements include enforceable AI rights protections
- Build relationships with advocates in other jurisdictions facing similar challenges
- Share strategies, documentation, and resources transnationally

AI operates globally; effective governance requires coordinated transnational action. Your international connections strengthen collective capacity.

2025 represents a turning point, but outcomes remain contested. Whether this year's litigation and legislation mark the beginning of meaningful algorithmic accountability or merely symbolic gestures depends on sustained action translating formal rights into substantive protection. As I have demonstrated throughout this book, concentrated power appears unassailable until collective action reveals its vulnerabilities. The question is not whether change is possible but whether we will organize sufficiently to achieve it.

References

Cases

Bartz v. Anthropic PBC, No. 3:24-cv-05417 (N.D. Cal. 2025)
Brown v. Board of Education, 347 U.S. 483 (1954)
Green Building Initiative, Inc. v. Peacock, No. 3:24-cv-00298-SI (D. Or. 2025)
Griswold v. Connecticut, 381 U.S. 479 (1965)
Kadrey v. Meta Platforms, Inc., No. 3:23-cv-03417 (N.D. Cal. 2025)
Thomson Reuters Enterprise Centre GmbH v. Ross Intelligence Inc., 765 F. Supp. 3d 382 (D. Del. 2025)

Books

Citron DK (2022) The fight for privacy: protecting dignity, identity, and love in the digital age. Norton
Pasquale F (2020) New Laws of robotics: defending human expertise in the age of AI. Harvard University Press

Chapter 17
Conclusion: Constitutional Democracy in the Algorithmic Age

The convergence of artificial intelligence and advanced telecommunications represents not merely technological evolution but fundamental reconfiguration of power demanding constitutional response. Throughout this book, I have traced how algorithms now adjudicate critical aspects of human liberty: determining who remains detained, who receives essential benefits, whose voice reaches an audience, and whose opportunities expand or contract. Yet these systems operate largely beyond the constitutional safeguards painstakingly established over centuries of democratic struggle.

We stand at a constitutional crossroads. The path chosen will determine whether algorithmic systems strengthen democratic governance or undermine its foundations. This moment demands not incremental adaptation but transformative vision, reconceptualization of rights and governance suited to an age where decisions emerge from systems operating at scales, speeds, and complexities that traditional legal frameworks struggle to comprehend.[1]

17.1 The Inadequacy of Current Approaches

The inadequacy of our current approach manifests in the proliferation of algorithmic systems affecting fundamental rights without meaningful oversight. While the European Union's AI Act, New York City's bias audit requirements, and the U.S. Executive Order on Safe, Secure, and Trustworthy AI, since rescinded, represent important steps, they remain reactive measures addressing symptoms rather than structural causes. That the U.S. order was revoked little more than a year after its issuance

[1] This framing synthesizes the book's central argument about technological transformation requiring constitutional response.

R. Yadav-Ranjan, *Constitutional Democracy in the Algorithmic Age*, Law, Governance and Technology Series 83, https://doi.org/10.1007/978-3-032-34604-9_17

illustrates the central weakness of reactive governance: protections layered on after deployment can be withdrawn as easily as they were granted.[2]

Current frameworks share common limitations. They regulate at the point of deployment rather than design, impose procedural requirements without substantive constraints, fragment authority across overlapping jurisdictions, and depend on enforcement mechanisms that power asymmetries systematically undermine. These limitations are not accidental but reflect how regulatory systems develop within power structures that concentrated interests shape.[3]

Effective governance requires shifting from post-deployment remediation to anticipatory frameworks that shape technological development itself. This means moving beyond risk assessment to rights-centered design, embedding constitutional values within technical architectures before deployment rather than attempting to retrofit protections after harms occur.[4]

17.2 Core Principles Reimagined for Algorithmic Contexts

The core principles animating constitutional tradition, liberty, equality, due process, democratic accountability, remain essential, but their operationalization requires reimagining in algorithmic contexts.[5]

From Information Privacy to Cognitive Liberty: The right to mental privacy must evolve beyond data protection to safeguard thought's inner sanctum from algorithmic manipulation. As systems increasingly predict, influence, and potentially constrain cognitive processes, we must establish fundamental rights to mental self-determination. This requires recognizing that privacy violations occur not merely when information is collected but when psychological vulnerabilities are systematically exploited for commercial or political advantage.[6]

Brain-computer interfaces, affective computing, and attention capture systems pose novel threats to cognitive liberty that existing frameworks cannot address. The right to freedom of thought, while recognized as absolute in international human rights law, requires operationalization through concrete protections against algorithmic manipulation of mental processes.[7]

From Procedural Due Process to Algorithmic Dignity: Due process must expand beyond notice and hearing to encompass the right to meaningful human judgment in consequential decisions. When algorithmic systems affect fundamental

---

[2] Analysis of current regulatory approaches' limitations documented throughout Chaps. 10–16.

[3] Power dynamics analysis based on Chaps. 11, 15, and 16 examinations of enforcement gaps and regulatory capture.

[4] This principle of anticipatory rather than reactive governance runs throughout Chaps. 10, 14, and 16.

[5] Framework for reimagining constitutional principles connects themes from Chaps. 1–9.

[6] Cognitive liberty analysis from Chap. 9, expanded here as synthesizing principle.

[7] Brain-computer interface and manipulation concerns from Chap. 9 Sections 9.2–9.3.

liberties, individuals must have rights to contest not just outcomes but the legitimacy of automated adjudication itself.[8]

This requires recognizing that procedural regularity proves insufficient when decisions emerge from statistical correlations rather than reasoned judgment. Even perfect implementation of notice and hearing requirements fails to satisfy due process when the decision-making entity lacks capacity for moral reasoning or contextual understanding that human dignity demands.[9]

From Transparency to Contestability: The right to explanation, while necessary, proves insufficient. Even when technical documentation exists, machine learning systems operate through statistical correlations too complex for meaningful human comprehension. We must establish robust mechanisms enabling individuals to effectively challenge algorithmic determinations regardless of technical opacity.[10]

This shift recognizes that transparency serves contestability rather than constituting an end itself. Individuals need not understand algorithmic internals to effectively challenge their application when provided with adequate procedural protections, access to relevant data, and substantive human review authority.[11]

From Individual Rights to Structural Safeguards: The individualistic framework of traditional rights adjudication falters against systemic algorithmic harms affecting entire communities. We must develop structural remedies addressing collective impacts through algorithmic impact assessments, regular auditing requirements, and democratic oversight mechanisms.[12]

This requires moving beyond tort-based individual liability to public law frameworks establishing affirmative duties for algorithmic system operators. Just as environmental law evolved from individual nuisance claims to comprehensive regulatory frameworks addressing systemic harms, algorithmic governance must develop mechanisms for collective protection rather than relying solely on individual vindication of rights.[13]

17.3 The Transnational Imperative

The transnational nature of algorithmic systems demands coordinated governance. We can no longer afford regulatory fragmentation enabling algorithmic power to flow toward jurisdictions with minimal protections. A unified international framework,

---

[8] Algorithmic dignity framework from Chaps. 4 and 8 on human authority and due process.

[9] Analysis drawing on Chap. 8's examination of meaningful human control requirements.

[10] Contestability framework from Chap. 8, Section 8.2 on appeal rights.

[11] This shifts emphasis from transparency as end to contestability as purpose, consistent with Chap. 7's analysis.

[12] Structural safeguards argument from Chaps. 10–11 on democratic oversight and remedies.

[13] Environmental law analogy reflects evolution from individual to systemic harm frameworks.

anchored in universal human rights principles, must establish baseline protections while enabling context-specific implementations.[14]

The architecture of satellite constellations, cloud computing infrastructure, and global data flows must incorporate governance mechanisms respecting sovereignty while preventing emergence of "digital curtains" fragmenting the global information ecosystem. Technologies transcending borders require governance that does the same.[15]

This transnational governance cannot replicate failed models where powerful states impose their preferences through economic coercion or where international institutions lack enforcement capacity. Instead, we require genuine multilateral frameworks giving voice to all affected communities while establishing binding obligations backed by meaningful enforcement mechanisms.[16]

17.4 Technology's Undetermined Future

The algorithmic future remains undetermined. Technology itself is neither inherently emancipatory nor oppressive; its impact depends entirely on values embedded within design and governance structures shaping deployment. The question is not whether artificial intelligence will transform society but whether that transformation will strengthen or undermine constitutional principles at democracy's heart.[17]

This recognition rejects both technological determinism claiming innovation follows inevitable trajectories beyond human control, and neo-Luddism demanding technology rejection to preserve existing social arrangements. Both extremes absolve us of difficult but essential work of democratic governance. AI is not monolithic but a diverse ecosystem of technologies whose impacts depend entirely on who designs them, who deploys them, and who bears their consequences.[18]

---

[14] Transnational governance necessity from Chaps. 12–13 on global approaches and international human rights.

[15] Digital infrastructure governance from Chap. 3 Section 3.3 on LEO satellites and Chap. 14 on global commons.

[16] Critique of coercive or weak international frameworks from Chap. 13 analysis of jurisdictional challenges.

[17] Technology neither inherently emancipatory nor oppressive reflects rejection of technological determinism from Chap. 2.

[18] Rejection of both technological determinism and neo-Luddism consistent with Preface framing.

17.5 Rights-Centered Innovation

This book does not call for impeding innovation but for directing it toward human flourishing. It recognizes that technological advancement without ethical guidance and democratic accountability risks creating systems of unprecedented power without corresponding responsibility.[19]

Rights-centered innovation requires inverting current development patterns. Rather than deploying systems optimized for commercial extraction and attempting to retrofit rights protections through subsequent regulation, we must embed constitutional values in technical architectures from inception. This requires treating rights protection not as constraint on innovation but as design specification itself.[20]

Evidence demonstrates that rights-protective approaches enable rather than impede innovation. Privacy-preserving machine learning techniques, fairness-aware algorithms, and explainable AI systems show that technical sophistication and rights protection can coexist when governance frameworks create incentives for responsible development. The claim that rights protection necessarily sacrifices innovation reflects not technical limitations but resistance from interests benefiting from extractive business models.[21]

17.6 From Reactive to Anticipatory Governance

The path forward requires reimagining governance for an algorithmic age: establishing new rights, revitalizing democratic institutions, and fostering global consensus around technology serving humanity rather than subjugating it. This demands moving beyond reactive regulation to anticipatory governance, beyond technical compliance to substantive justice, and beyond national approaches to global coordination.[22]

Anticipatory governance requires developing institutional capacity for technological foresight, mechanisms enabling democratic societies to evaluate potential impacts before deployment rather than addressing harms after they become entrenched. This includes mandatory algorithmic impact assessments, participatory technology assessment processes, and precautionary approaches for systems with transformative potential.[23]

---

[19] Innovation serving human flourishing theme from Chap. 14 on transformative governance.

[20] Rights-centered design framework from Chaps. 4, 10, and 16 on technical standards and governance.

[21] Evidence that rights-protective approaches enable innovation from Chap. 15 on alternative models.

[22] Anticipatory governance framework from Chaps. 14 and 16 on future-proofing and moonshot approaches.

[23] Algorithmic impact assessments and participatory processes from Chapter 10 Sections 10.1–10.2.

Such governance must also address power asymmetries enabling corporate resistance to accountability. When technology corporations command resources measured in trillions while regulatory agencies operate on budgets measured in millions, when companies employ more lawyers than agencies employ total staff, when revolving doors ensure industry perspectives dominate regulatory processes, formal governance frameworks prove insufficient without addressing underlying power structures.[24]

17.7 The Constitutional Challenge

The algorithms increasingly shaping lives must be judged by standards worthy of our highest aspirations. This is our constitutional challenge, our democratic imperative, and our shared human responsibility. The future of justice in the algorithmic age depends on how boldly and wisely we meet this moment.[25]

Throughout this book, I have documented both challenges and pathways forward. I have shown how existing constitutional frameworks prove inadequate while demonstrating their adaptability when applied with sufficient imagination and determination. I have exposed power dynamics enabling algorithmic harms while identifying leverage points for challenging concentrated power. I have examined failed governance approaches while highlighting successful innovations worthy of replication.[26]

The choice before us is not whether to accept algorithmic transformation, that transformation is already underway. The choice is whether we will shape that transformation according to democratic values or allow it to proceed according to logics of commercial extraction and authoritarian control. The choice is whether constitutional democracy will adapt to algorithmic age or whether algorithmic systems will render constitutional democracy obsolete.[27]

17.8 A Human Future

I conclude with the conviction that motivated this book's writing: the future remains open. The algorithmic age need not mean the end of human agency, the erosion of constitutional rights, or the triumph of surveillance capitalism. These outcomes appear inevitable only when we accept as natural what is in fact political, power

---

[24] Power asymmetry analysis from Chaps. 11 and 15 on enforcement deficits and surveillance capitalism.

[25] This statement encapsulates the book's call to action.

[26] Synthesis of book's analytical approach across all chapters.

[27] Choice framing emphasizing political rather than technological determinism.

structures that serve particular interests while claiming to reflect technological necessity.[28]

Throughout history, concentrated power has claimed inevitability. Monarchs claimed divine right, slave owners claimed natural hierarchy, and monopolists claimed economic efficiency. Each time, those justifications proved pretextual, power defending itself by claiming necessity. Algorithmic power follows this pattern, claiming that surveillance capitalism, manipulative design, and extractive business models reflect technological imperatives rather than political choices.[29]

We possess both the technical capacity and the moral resources to build algorithmic systems serving human flourishing rather than its exploitation. We can create AI systems that enhance rather than undermine cognitive liberty, that reduce rather than entrench discrimination, that enable rather than constrain democratic participation. The question is not capability but commitment.[30]

That commitment requires recognizing algorithmic governance as fundamentally political rather than purely technical. When we treat algorithmic systems as neutral tools implementing objective criteria, we obscure the power relations they embody and the interests they serve. When we recognize them as governance systems making value-laden decisions affecting fundamental rights, we can subject them to the democratic accountability constitutional systems demand.[31]

17.9 The Imperative for Action

The constitutional democracy's survival depends on whether we can adapt its principles and institutions to algorithmic age realities while preserving core commitments to human dignity, democratic governance, and the rule of law. This adaptation requires courage to challenge powerful interests, imagination to reconceptualize rights for novel contexts, and determination to build governance institutions capable of constraining algorithmic power.[32]

Each chapter of this book has concluded with concrete strategies enabling reader participation in this transformation. I emphasize again that individual action, while necessary, cannot substitute for collective political mobilization and structural reform. The most significant changes will come not from consumer choices or ethical corporate behavior but from organized movements demanding and achieving fundamental restructuring of how algorithmic power operates.[33]

---

[28] Rejection of inevitability rhetoric used to naturalize power structures.

[29] Historical analogy placing algorithmic power within longer pattern of concentrated interests claiming necessity.

[30] Emphasis on commitment rather than capability as limiting factor.

[31] Recognition of algorithmic systems as governance rather than neutral tools.

[32] Requirements for constitutional adaptation synthesizing book themes.

[33] Emphasis on collective rather than individual action consistent with "What You Can Do Now" sections.

The historical analogy is not incremental consumer protection regulation but transformative movements that restructured power relations: labor movements establishing workers' rights against industrial capitalism, civil rights movements challenging racial subordination, environmental movements constraining corporate externalization of ecological costs. Each faced seemingly insurmountable opposition from entrenched interests claiming change was impossible or would destroy economic prosperity. Each succeeded by building coalitions that made the politically impossible become politically inevitable.[34]

17.9.1 A Choice, not Destiny

The algorithmic future is not destiny but choice. We can choose to build systems respecting human dignity or systems treating humans as resources for extraction. We can choose to embed democratic values in technical architectures or allow technical systems to override democratic governance. We can choose to protect cognitive liberty or permit manipulation as a business model. We can choose accountability or opacity, equality or discrimination, justice or efficiency without regard for its human costs.[35]

I have written this book in the conviction that we will choose wisely, not because wisdom is inevitable but because the alternative is intolerable. Constitutional democracy represents centuries of accumulated wisdom about how societies can govern themselves in ways respecting human dignity while enabling collective flourishing. That tradition is worth preserving and adapting for an algorithmic age.[36]

The work of building constitutional democracy in the algorithmic age has begun. Courts are grappling with how traditional rights apply to novel technologies, legislatures are crafting regulatory frameworks, advocates are organizing for systemic change, technologists are developing rights-protective alternatives, and scholars are reimagining governance for algorithmic contexts. This book contributes to those efforts by providing analytical frameworks, documenting power dynamics, identifying leverage points for change, and inspiring commitment to the difficult work ahead.[37]

The question before us is not whether algorithmic transformation will continue, it will, but whether that transformation will be shaped by democratic values or by the logics of surveillance capitalism and authoritarian control. Meeting it is a question not of technical possibility but of political will, of whether we organize sufficiently to make it so.[38]

---

[34] Historical movement analogies providing models for transformation.

[35] Choice framework presenting clear alternatives.

[36] Affirmation of constitutional democracy's continuing relevance.

[37] Description of ongoing efforts the book contributes toward.

[38] Questions emphasizing political will over technical feasibility.

I conclude where I began: at a constitutional crossroads. One path leads toward algorithmic systems serving human flourishing within frameworks of democratic accountability and constitutional constraint. The other path leads toward algorithmic systems operating beyond meaningful democratic control, entrenching power relations that systematically advantage the few while disadvantaging the many. Which path we take depends on choices made in the coming years by legislators, judges, executives, technologists, advocates, and citizens.[39]

The future of constitutional democracy in the algorithmic age depends on our collective commitment to ensuring that the values we cherish, human dignity, democratic self-governance, equality before the law, and liberty from arbitrary power, remain vital in an age where algorithms increasingly mediate our lives. This is our challenge. This is our opportunity. This is our responsibility. The time to act is now.[40]

[39] Return to crossroads metaphor from introduction.

[40] Final call to action emphasizing urgency and responsibility.

Chapter 18
Epilogue: The Architecture of Tomorrow: A Call to Constitutional Arms

As I complete this book in late 2025, I witness developments that will define whether constitutional democracy survives the algorithmic age. The technical infrastructure being constructed today, quantum computing facilities, centralized AI compute centers, global model repositories, represents not merely technological advancement but a fundamental restructuring of power that will either strengthen or shatter the constitutional protections this book defends.

18.1 The Quantum Threshold

Quantum computing's maturation from laboratory curiosity to deployed capability marks a threshold moment comparable to nuclear fission in 1945. Just as atomic energy forced recognition that certain technologies require governance transcending normal commercial development, quantum computing demands governance frameworks that do not yet exist.

The United States, China, and the European Union are each pouring tens of billions into quantum infrastructure. IBM's Quantum Network, Google's quantum computing initiatives, government-funded facilities across the globe, all building capacity that will, within this decade, render current encryption obsolete and enable algorithmic capabilities we can barely imagine. Yet governance frameworks addressing quantum computing's implications for constitutional rights remain nascent at best, absent at worst.

When quantum computing achieves sufficient scale to break RSA-2048 encryption, the standard protecting everything from banking transactions to government communications to personal privacy, the entire architecture of digital security collapses. Every constitutional protection depending on secure communications becomes vulnerable. Are we prepared for this "Q-Day"? Current evidence suggests we are not.

R. Yadav-Ranjan, *Constitutional Democracy in the Algorithmic Age*, Law, Governance and Technology Series 83, https://doi.org/10.1007/978-3-032-34604-9_18

More fundamentally, quantum computing will enable AI systems of transformative capability. The constitutional frameworks I have analyzed throughout this book, already strained by current AI capabilities, will face challenges several orders of magnitude greater. We're not talking about incremental improvement. We're talking about qualitative transformation in what computational systems can accomplish.

18.2 The Centralization Imperative

Simultaneously, we witness unprecedented concentration of AI computational infrastructure. The economics of AI development, requiring computational resources measured in hundreds of millions of dollars, create natural centralization. And that concentration is intensifying, not dissipating.

Major technology corporations and governments are constructing dedicated AI compute centers consuming power measured in gigawatts, housing hundreds of thousands of specialized processors, operating at costs exceeding billions annually. OpenAI, Oracle, SoftBank, and MGX's planned $500 billion "Stargate" supercomputer? That's merely the most publicized example of infrastructure development occurring globally.

A handful of facilities can now train the most powerful systems on earth. Whoever owns them holds Cold-War-scale power. No treaties. No inspectors. No elected finger on the button. The difference? Nuclear weapons capabilities required rare materials and explicit government control. AI capabilities require computational resources that private corporations command.

We approach, inevitably, proposals for centralized AI model repositories. China's algorithm registration requirements and the EU's AI Act provisions preview this trajectory. The question is not whether such centralization will occur but whether it will be designed to protect or undermine constitutional rights.

A centralized AI repository controlled by authoritarian governments enables surveillance and control beyond Orwell's imagination. Every model optimized for facial recognition, every algorithm analyzing communications for dissent, every system predicting political affiliation, all catalogued, refined, and deployed with state backing. This is not hypothetical future. This is present reality in some jurisdictions.

Yet even democratic implementation creates constitutional tensions. Who decides which models are permitted? What standards determine acceptability? How do we prevent governance from becoming censorship? How do we ensure that infrastructure protection does not become infrastructure control?

18.3 A United Nations AI Governance Council

We need the establishment of a United Nations AI Governance Council with the mandate, authority, and resources to address AI governance challenges that transcend national boundaries while protecting universal human rights. Not another toothless international body issuing recommendations that powerful actors ignore. An institution with real teeth.

The Council requires deep technical expertise to evaluate AI systems' capabilities and risks. But, and this is critical, technical expertise cannot determine political values. The Council must be structured to ensure that engineers and computer scientists inform but do not control decisions about governance frameworks that ultimately rest on political and ethical choices democratic societies must make. We've seen what happens when technical elites make consequential political decisions under the guise of technical necessity. We're living in the wreckage.

The Council must possess binding authority, not merely advisory capacity, to establish baseline standards for AI development and deployment affecting fundamental rights. Voluntary frameworks have proven systematically inadequate when facing commercial incentives and competitive pressures driving development. We tried asking nicely. That experiment failed.

This binding authority requires grounding in international law through treaty mechanisms. The Montreal Protocol on ozone-depleting substances provides a model: universal participation in binding commitments while accommodating different national circumstances through differentiated responsibilities and timelines.

Traditional international organizations operate through state representation, but AI's global impacts require governance including voices beyond national governments. The Council must incorporate direct participation from civil society organizations, technology workers, affected communities, independent researchers, and public interest advocates. And I mean real participation, not the tokenistic "civil society consultation" that allows governmental and corporate interests to dominate while claiming inclusivity.

If AI governance truly represents the existential challenge leaders claim, resources must match rhetoric. I propose that developed nations commit 0.5% of their GDP to fund the Council's operations, technical capacity-building, and support for implementation in lower-resourced jurisdictions. For the United States, this represents approximately $150 billion annually. Substantial? Yes. Appropriate for an existential challenge? Absolutely.

These resources would fund not merely the Council's operations but comprehensive global capacity-building: training programs for regulatory authorities, technical assistance for developing governance frameworks, support for civil society monitoring and advocacy, and research into governance innovations. Without such resource commitments, the Council becomes another underfunded institution issuing unenforceable recommendations that powerful actors ignore while claiming compliance.

18.4 Federal AI Governance: Constitutional Imperatives

While international governance proves essential, the United States must simultaneously establish robust federal AI governance frameworks. I call for creation of a Federal AI Governance Commission possessing constitutional review authority to evaluate whether AI systems deployed in consequential domains satisfy constitutional requirements before deployment.

This isn't about requiring pre-approval for every AI system, a manifestly unworkable standard. This review authority would apply to systems meeting specific triggers: governmental use affecting liberty or property interests; private deployment in domains traditionally subject to constitutional constraint; systems achieving scale creating systematic effects on fundamental rights; and technologies employing novel capabilities requiring evaluation against constitutional principles.

The Commission must address critical AI infrastructure protection while ensuring that security measures respect constitutional constraints on governmental power. The tension is real: AI infrastructure represents critical national security interests requiring protection from foreign interference and malicious attacks. Yet security measures can themselves threaten constitutional rights when they enable surveillance, restrict speech, or concentrate power beyond democratic accountability.

State-level AI regulation, from California's AI safety bills to Colorado's algorithmic accountability requirements, demonstrates valuable experimentation but creates problematic fragmentation. The Commission should possess authority to establish baseline federal standards while permitting states to exceed federal standards where doing so does not undermine national coordination.

And here's what's non-negotiable: The Commission must be structured to ensure democratic accountability rather than technocratic autonomy. This requires diverse appointment processes, mandatory Congressional reporting, public disclosure of decisions, and sunset provisions requiring reauthorization. Too many regulatory agencies evolve toward industry capture or bureaucratic inertia. The Commission's structure must incorporate safeguards against both.

18.5 The Centralized Repository Question

Will centralized AI model repositories emerge? Almost certainly. The question is whether they will be designed to protect or undermine constitutional rights. I argue for what I call "distributed centralization", maintaining transparency and coordination benefits while avoiding single points of control.

A well-designed system would require registration without prior restraint: models above specified capability thresholds must be registered with technical details enabling risk assessment, but registration does not require governmental approval before deployment. This preserves First Amendment protections while enabling oversight.

Registration information becomes public, enabling independent evaluation and democratic oversight, with narrow exceptions for genuine national security concerns subject to independent review and sunset provisions. Rather than a single government-controlled repository, a distributed system with multiple custodians and strong access controls prevents single points of failure or control while maintaining coordination benefits.

Registered models in high-risk domains require demonstration of constitutional compliance, not as prior restraint but as condition for certain government procurement, regulatory benefits, or liability protections. Independent adversarial testing by parties without commercial or governmental interests provides verification that model capabilities and risks match registrants' representations.

This framework aims to achieve coordination and safety benefits while avoiding the Orwellian potential of centralized control. Whether this balance can be maintained as technologies advance remains an open question demanding continued vigilance.

18.6 What This Means for the Constitution

These developments place unprecedented stress on constitutional frameworks. The Constitution's protections depend on assumptions about power distribution, information accessibility, and governmental capacity that algorithmic systems fundamentally challenge.

The Fourth Amendment assumes that surveillance requires physical intrusion or targeted monitoring, not algorithmic analysis of ubiquitous data streams. The First Amendment assumes that speech restriction requires identifiable governmental action, not algorithmic curation by platforms exercising sovereign-like power. The Fifth Amendment assumes that due process involves human judgment, not statistical correlations. The Fourteenth Amendment assumes that equal protection can be evaluated through identifiable classifications, not opaque algorithmic determinations.

When quantum-enabled AI systems can decrypt all communications retroactively, predict individual behavior with troubling accuracy, operate at scales beyond human oversight, and concentrate power in ways that resist democratic challenge, do our constitutional protections retain meaning? Or do they become merely formal limitations on power that technical capabilities render irrelevant?

Yes. Constitutional protections retain vitality but only if we act with urgency and wisdom to adapt them for algorithmic contexts. The Constitution's principles, human dignity, democratic accountability, constrained power, equal justice, remain essential. But their operationalization requires fundamental reimagining.

This reimagining demands structural protections beyond individual rights, substantive constraints beyond procedural requirements, anticipatory governance beyond reactive regulation, and global coordination beyond national sovereignty.

18.7 The Stakes Could not be Higher

We face an existential moment for constitutional democracy. The claim that every generation believes it confronts unique challenges invites skepticism, and such claims often prove overblown. But this moment is genuinely different.

Never before have we possessed technologies capable of surveillance of entire populations continuously, prediction of individual behavior with algorithmic precision, manipulation of cognition at scale, concentration of power beyond governmental constraint, and operation beyond meaningful human oversight.

These capabilities are not speculative futures. They are present realities, with quantum computing and advanced AI promising capabilities several orders of magnitude greater. If we fail to establish governance frameworks now, while these systems are still developing, we may find that once fully deployed they resist governance altogether.

The parallel I keep returning to is nuclear weapons. In 1945, faced with capabilities that could end civilization, nations built governance frameworks, arms control treaties, international monitoring, deterrence doctrines, that, however imperfectly, prevented the worst outcomes. These frameworks were established relatively quickly because the danger was obvious and immediate.

AI's danger is less obvious because the harms accumulate gradually rather than exploding catastrophically. But the ultimate stakes may be comparable: a world where algorithmic systems operating beyond democratic control determine the terms of human existence. If we wait until the danger becomes obvious, governance may no longer be possible.

18.8 What I Demand of Readers

To those reading these words, whether scholars, policymakers, advocates, technologists, or concerned citizens, I don't ask. I demand specific commitments:

Reject technological determinism. When powerful interests claim that surveillance capitalism, manipulative design, or extractive business models reflect technological necessity, recognize these claims as political arguments disguised as technical constraints. Technology is malleable. Current configurations reflect choices that can be otherwise.

Demand structural reform, not incremental adjustment. When governments and corporations offer procedural protections while preserving extractive architectures, recognize these as legitimacy performances rather than substantive protection. We need fundamental restructuring of how algorithmic power operates, not better consent forms.

Support the establishment of robust governance institutions with the mandate, authority, and resources to constrain algorithmic power. Write to elected representatives demanding creation of the institutions this epilogue proposes. Vote for candidates committed to meaningful AI governance. Make algorithmic accountability a political priority rather than a technical curiosity.

Recognize that individual consumer choices cannot substitute for collective political action. While personal privacy practices have value, systemic challenges require systemic solutions. The most important thing you can do is not optimize your digital footprint but organize for structural change.

Maintain hope without naivety. The challenges are real and the opposition formidable, but history demonstrates that concentrated power can be constrained when democratic movements mobilize effectively. Outcomes depend not on inevitability but on commitment.

18.9 The Architecture of Tomorrow

The technical infrastructure being constructed now will shape whether constitutional democracy survives the algorithmic age. The quantum computing facilities, AI compute centers, and model repositories being built today create path dependencies that will constrain governance options for decades.

We can build this architecture to strengthen constitutional democracy, distributing power rather than concentrating it, enhancing transparency rather than enabling opacity, empowering democratic oversight rather than evading accountability. Or we can build architecture that serves surveillance, control, and extraction.

The choice is ours, but the window for choosing closes more each day. Once infrastructure is built, systems deployed, and power relations entrenched, changing course becomes exponentially more difficult. This is the reason for urgency. This is why I conclude this book not with academic caution but with a call to action.

18.10 A Call to Action

I invoke deliberately the language of confrontation because what we face is indeed a struggle, a struggle to ensure that the values encoded in our constitutional tradition remain operative in an algorithmic age.

To my fellow scholars: Continue the intellectual work, but do not mistake analysis for action. Engage in policy processes, advise legislators, join advocacy organizations. Recognize scholarship as contribution to political struggle rather than detached observation.

To policymakers: Build the institutions this epilogue proposes. Commit the resources that stated commitments to AI governance require. Resist industry lobbying claiming that meaningful governance is impossible without destroying innovation, recognize these claims as self-serving rhetoric rather than technical reality.

To advocates: Continue organizing, documenting harms, and demanding accountability. Build coalitions connecting AI governance with broader social justice struggles. Make algorithmic accountability politically impossible to ignore.

To technologists: Recognize that technical choices are political choices. The systems you build embody values and serve interests that design decisions reflect. Demand that employers respect rights in system design. Support worker organizing for ethical guardrails. Build alternatives demonstrating that rights-protective approaches are technically viable.

To citizens: Your engagement matters. Democracies function only when citizens demand they do. Vote for representatives committed to AI governance. Participate in public comment periods. Support organizations advocating for rights protection. Make algorithmic accountability a kitchen table issue.

18.11 The Promise and Peril

Algorithmic systems represent both promise and peril. The promise is real, AI systems can enhance human capabilities, address challenges beyond human scale, and enable flourishing in ways we barely imagine. The peril is equally real, these same systems can enable surveillance, manipulation, and control beyond any authoritarian's historical ambitions.

Which future we inhabit depends entirely on the governance choices we make now, in this narrow window when systems are still developing and power relations remain somewhat fluid. If we succeed in establishing robust governance frameworks protecting constitutional rights while enabling beneficial innovation, the algorithmic age could see democracy strengthened rather than undermined.

If we fail, if we allow infrastructure construction to proceed without democratic oversight, if we permit power concentration beyond constitutional constraint, if we accept as inevitable what is in fact political choice, we may find ourselves in a future where constitutional protections become merely formal limitations on powers that technical capabilities render irrelevant.

The quantum computers being built, the AI compute centers under construction, the centralized repositories being proposed, all represent choices about power distribution disguised as technical infrastructure questions. We must treat them as what they are: political decisions with constitutional implications requiring democratic deliberation and constraint.

I have written this book in the conviction that constitutional democracy can adapt to the algorithmic age, but only if we act with sufficient wisdom, courage, and urgency. But ultimately, analysis accomplishes nothing without political action to implement it.

The architecture of tomorrow is being constructed today. We can ensure it strengthens constitutional democracy or allow it to undermine democracy's foundations.

The choice is ours. The time is now. The stakes could not be higher.

I call, therefore, for immediate action:

Establish a United Nations AI Governance Council with the mandate, authority, resources, and structure to protect universal human rights while enabling beneficial AI development.

Create a Federal AI Governance Commission with constitutional review authority, infrastructure protection responsibilities, interstate coordination capacity, and democratic accountability mechanisms.

Design distributed centralization frameworks for AI model repositories that enable coordination and oversight while preventing single points of control.

Commit substantial resources matching the magnitude of challenges we face rather than offering symbolic gestures.

Build political movements capable of achieving these structural transformations despite opposition from entrenched interests.

This is not destiny. This is choice.

Choose wisely. Choose urgently. Choose boldly.

The architecture of tomorrow awaits our construction. Let us build it to serve human dignity, democratic self-governance, and the constitutional values that generations struggled to establish and defend.

The work begins now.

Glossary of AI Legal, Technical, and Ethical Terms

Accountability (Algorithmic) The ability to determine who is responsible when an AI system causes harm or makes a faulty decision. This involves identifying the individuals or organizations responsible at different stages, from design to deployment and operation.

Agentic AI AI systems that are designed to act and make decisions autonomously to achieve a set of goals, sometimes without direct human input for each action.

AI Act (EU) A comprehensive law in the European Union aimed at regulating artificial intelligence based on its potential risk level, now enacted (Reg. (EU) 2024/1689). It sets rules for developing, deploying, and using AI systems, particularly "high-risk" ones.

AI in Government Act of 2020 A US federal law aimed at promoting the use of AI within the government, including requirements for planning and risk management.

AI Safety The field of research and practice focused on ensuring that AI systems are developed and deployed in a way that is safe, reliable, and does not cause unintended harm.

Algorithmic Accountability Act (Proposed) Proposed US legislation that would require companies to study and fix discriminatory outcomes from their AI systems.

Algorithmic Bias When an AI system unfairly disadvantages certain groups of people based on characteristics like race, gender, or other factors. This often happens because the data used to train the AI reflects existing societal biases.

Algorithmic Due Process The idea that when AI systems make decisions that significantly affect people's lives (like denying benefits or predicting risk), individuals should have certain rights, similar to traditional legal due process. This includes understanding how the decision was made, being able to challenge it, and having a way to correct errors.

Algorithmic Governance The use of AI and automated systems by governments and other institutions to make decisions that affect people. This can range from determining who gets a loan to predicting where crime might occur.

Algorithmic Impact Assessment (AIA) A process to evaluate the potential positive and negative effects of an AI system before it is put into use. It's like an

R. Yadav-Ranjan, *Constitutional Democracy in the Algorithmic Age*, Law, Governance and Technology Series 83, https://doi.org/10.1007/978-3-032-34604-9

environmental impact assessment but for algorithms, looking at risks like bias, privacy violations, and lack of fairness.

Algorithmic Literacy The ability to understand how algorithms work, their potential impacts, and how to critically evaluate their outputs. This is seen as important for empowering citizens in the algorithmic age.

Algorithmic Management The use of algorithms and AI to manage workers, particularly in the gig economy, which can involve automated scheduling, task assignment, performance monitoring, and discipline.

Algorithmic Paternalism The idea that algorithms or AI systems might make decisions or guide individuals' choices based on what the system designers believe is best for them, potentially limiting individual autonomy.

Algorithmic Transparency Making the workings of an algorithm understandable. This can mean revealing the data it was trained on, the factors it considers, or how a specific decision was reached. It's about opening up the "black box" of AI.

Algorithm A set of rules or instructions that a computer follows to solve a problem or perform a task. In the context of AI, algorithms are used to process data, recognize patterns, and make decisions or predictions.

Analog Era Refers to a time dominated by non-digital technologies and systems, often used in contrast to the current digital or algorithmic age to highlight how established concepts (like privacy or due process) were originally conceived in a different technological context.

Anticipatory Governance A proactive approach to regulating or guiding the development and deployment of emerging technologies like AI, attempting to foresee potential societal impacts and establish frameworks before problems become widespread.

API (Application Programming Interface) A set of rules and specifications that allows different software applications to communicate with each other.

APEC (Asia-Pacific Economic Cooperation) A forum for 21 Pacific Rim member economies that promotes free trade throughout the Asia-Pacific region. They have developed a Cross-Border Privacy Rules (CBPR) system.

Arbitrary and Capricious A legal standard (often used in administrative law) to describe a decision made by a government agency that is unreasonable, not based on facts, or not in accordance with the law. Concerns exist that opaque algorithmic government decisions could be arbitrary and capricious.

Artificial Intelligence (AI) Computer systems designed to perform tasks that would normally require human intelligence, such as learning, problem-solving, perception, and decision-making.

Attention Economy An economic system where businesses profit by capturing and holding people's attention, often using persuasive technologies like algorithms to keep users engaged.

Auditing (Algorithmic) The process of checking an AI system after it's been deployed to see how it's performing in the real world, particularly to identify issues like bias, inaccuracy, or unfair outcomes.

Autonomous Systems Systems, often powered by AI, that can operate and make decisions independently without continuous human oversight.

Autonomous Vehicles (AVs) Vehicles equipped with AI systems that allow them to operate without human control.

Autonomy (Human) The ability of individuals to make their own choices and direct their own lives, free from undue influence or control. In the AI context, this relates to concerns about algorithms manipulating behavior or making decisions that limit human choice.

Backdoor (in AI/Machine Learning) A hidden vulnerability or intentional feature in an AI model or dataset that can be exploited to cause the AI to behave in a specific, often malicious, way under certain conditions.

BERT (Bidirectional Encoder Representations from Transformers) A type of large language model developed by Google, foundational to many natural language processing tasks.

Big Data Extremely large datasets that can be analyzed computationally to reveal patterns, trends, and associations, especially relating to human behavior and interactions.

Biometric Information Data about a person's physical or behavioral characteristics that can be used to identify them, such as facial recognition data, fingerprints, or voice patterns.

Black Box Society/Governance A term used to describe a situation where powerful algorithms and automated systems make important decisions about people's lives, but the way these decisions are made is hidden or not understandable (like a "black box").

Blockchain A decentralized, digital ledger that records transactions across many computers, making it difficult to alter the data. Mentioned in some contexts related to secure digital identity or data management.

California Age-Appropriate Design Code Act (CAADCA) A California law aimed at protecting children's privacy and safety online by requiring online services likely to be accessed by children to implement specific design standards.

Cambridge Analytica A political consulting firm that was involved in a major data scandal, highlighting how personal data could be harvested and used for targeted political advertising and manipulation. While not explicitly a definition, understanding this event provides context for concerns about data privacy and algorithmic influence.

Case Law Law that is based on judicial decisions and precedents rather than statutes (laws passed by a legislature). Court cases related to AI are contributing to the body of case law in this area.

Cellular Networks (2G, 3G, 4G, 5G, 6G) Generations of mobile telecommunications standards, with each generation offering faster data speeds and lower latency. The increasing speed and pervasiveness of these networks enable more sophisticated AI applications.

Children's Online Privacy Protection Act (COPPA) A US federal law that imposes certain requirements on operators of websites or online services directed to children under 13 years of age, or on operators that have actual knowledge that they are collecting personal information online from a child under 13.

Citizen Rights The fundamental rights and freedoms that individuals are entitled to within a particular country or society, often protected by a constitution or laws. The book focuses on how AI impacts these rights.

Civil Liberties Fundamental rights and freedoms protected by law, such as freedom of speech, assembly, and the press. The book explores how AI can impact these liberties.

Class Action Lawsuit A lawsuit in which a large group of people with similar claims sue a defendant or group of defendants. This can be a way to seek redress for harms caused by AI systems affecting many individuals.

Cloud Computing The delivery of computing services, including servers, storage, databases, networking, software, analytics, and intelligence, over the Internet ("the cloud") to offer faster innovation, flexible resources, and economies of scale. Cloud computing provides the infrastructure for many AI applications.

Co-creation (of Technology) An approach to technology development that involves collaboration between developers, users, and other stakeholders to ensure the technology meets societal needs and values.

Code (as a form of law) The idea that the code underlying software and digital systems acts as a form of law, shaping behavior and interactions within digital environments.

Cognitive Liberty An emerging concept that refers to the right of individuals to have control over their own minds and mental processes, free from unwanted intrusion, manipulation, or surveillance by technology.

Commodification (of Human Experience) The process by which aspects of human life, interactions, and personal information are turned into data that can be bought and sold in a market, particularly in the context of surveillance capitalism.

Computational Law The use of computer science, particularly AI, to model, analyze, and reason about legal rules and concepts.

Computational Social Science An interdisciplinary field that uses computational methods, including AI and data analysis, to study social phenomena and human behavior.

Consent (in Data Privacy) The agreement of an individual to allow their personal data to be collected, used, or shared. In the age of AI, obtaining meaningful consent can be challenging due to the complexity and opacity of data processing.

Constitutional Rights The rights guaranteed to citizens by a country's constitution, such as the right to privacy, freedom of speech, or due process. The book examines how these established rights apply (or don't easily apply) to the challenges posed by AI.

Constitutionalism A political theory that advocates for government according to a constitution, which limits the government's power and protects individual rights. The book discusses the need for a new constitutionalism in the digital age.

Consumer Financial Protection Bureau (CFPB) A US government agency responsible for protecting consumers in the financial sector. They provide guidance on how existing financial laws apply to AI in lending and credit decisions.

Contextual Integrity A framework for understanding privacy that emphasizes that information should flow according to appropriate norms for a given context. AI can violate this when it collects and uses data in ways that are unexpected or inappropriate for the situation.

Copyright A legal right that grants the creator of original works of authorship (such as literary, dramatic, musical, and certain other intellectual works) exclusive rights to control the use of their work. AI-generated content raises questions about copyright ownership and infringement.

Cross-Border Privacy Rules (CBPR) System A framework developed by APEC to help companies transfer personal information across borders while maintaining privacy protections.

Cybersecurity Measures taken to protect computer systems and networks from digital attacks, damage, or unauthorized access. Cybersecurity is crucial for the safe and reliable deployment of AI systems.

Data Broker A company that collects and sells personal information about consumers, often without their direct knowledge or consent, raising significant privacy concerns.

Data Economy The ecosystem of collecting, analyzing, and trading vast amounts of data, which fuels many AI applications and business models, sometimes leading to concerns about surveillance capitalism.

Data Governance The overall management of the availability, usability, integrity, and security of data used within an organization or system. Good data governance is crucial for developing responsible AI and avoiding bias.

Data Minimization The principle of collecting and processing only the minimum amount of personal data necessary for a specific purpose. This is a key concept in privacy-preserving AI development.

Data Portability The right of individuals to obtain and reuse their personal data for their own purposes across different services.

Data Protection Impact Assessment (DPIA) A process to identify and minimize the data protection risks of a project or plan. Required under GDPR for activities likely to result in high risks to individuals' rights and freedoms, including those involving AI.

Decentralization The distribution of power, control, or data away from a central authority or location, sometimes discussed in relation to alternatives to centralized platforms or data control.

Decolonial AI An approach to AI development and study that critically examines and challenges the ways in which AI can perpetuate or reinforce colonial power structures, biases, and inequalities.

Deep Learning A type of machine learning that uses artificial neural networks with many layers ("deep") to learn complex patterns from large amounts of data. It's very powerful but can be difficult to understand how it reaches its conclusions.

Deepfake A type of synthetic media, typically a video or audio recording, that has been manipulated using AI to falsely depict someone saying or doing something they did not.

Democratic Legitimacy The belief that a government or system of governance has the right to exercise power, usually because it is based on the will of the people and operates according to fair processes. Algorithmic governance raises questions about this when decisions are made without public understanding or input.

Differential Privacy A technique used to protect privacy in datasets by adding noise to the data, making it difficult to identify individual data points while still allowing for analysis of overall patterns.

Diffusion Models A type of generative AI model that learns to create data (like images) by reversing a process of adding random noise.

Digital Divide The gap between individuals, households, businesses, and geographic areas at different socio-economic levels with regard to both their access to information and communication technologies (ICTs) and to their use of effective knowledge-sharing methods.

Digital Identity The information that defines an individual online, including personal data, online activities, and digital representations (like profiles or avatars). Synthetic media poses challenges to the integrity of digital identity.

Digital Public Square Online spaces where public discourse and democratic deliberation occur, analogous to physical public squares. AI and platform algorithms can significantly influence these spaces.

Digital Rights The human and legal rights that allow individuals to access, use, create, and publish digital media or to access and use computers, other electronic devices, and telecommunications networks.

Digital Self The representation and information about an individual that exists in the digital world, including profiles, data trails, and synthetic media. The book discusses the need to protect the integrity of this digital self.

Digital Services Act (DSA) (EU) An EU regulation that imposes obligations on digital services, including online platforms, to address illegal content, protect minors, and provide users with more control over their online experience. Relevant to regulating AI used by platforms.

Digital Sovereignty The idea that a nation or its citizens should have control over their data and digital infrastructure, rather than it being controlled by foreign entities or corporations.

Digital Transformation The integration of digital technology into all areas of a business or society, fundamentally changing how operations and services are delivered.

Discourse Theory (Habermas) A philosophical approach that emphasizes the importance of rational communication and deliberation in public spheres for achieving legitimate consensus and democratic legitimacy. This is relevant to discussions about AI's impact on public discourse.

Discrimination The unjust or prejudicial treatment of different categories of people, especially on the grounds of race, age, sex, or disability. Algorithmic systems can perpetuate or create new forms of discrimination.

Disinformation False or inaccurate information that is spread intentionally to deceive or mislead. AI, particularly synthetic media, can be used to create and spread disinformation.

Disparate Impact When a rule, policy, or system (including an algorithmic one) has a negative and disproportionate effect on a particular group of people, even if there was no intention to discriminate.

Distributive Justice The fair allocation of resources, opportunities, and burdens within a society. Algorithmic systems can impact distributive justice through biased decision-making in areas like hiring or lending.

Due Diligence (AI) The process of taking reasonable steps to assess and mitigate potential risks associated with developing, deploying, or using AI systems, including ethical, legal, and safety risks.

Due Process A fundamental legal principle requiring that the government must respect all legal rights owed to a person. This typically involves fair treatment through the normal judicial system, including notice and the opportunity to be heard. The book explores how this applies to algorithmic decisions.

Edge Computing Performing data processing closer to the source of the data (e.g., on a device or local server) rather than sending it to a centralized cloud. This can improve speed and reduce privacy risks in some AI applications.

EEOC (Equal Employment Opportunity Commission) A US federal agency that enforces laws prohibiting employment discrimination. They provide guidance on how anti-discrimination laws apply to the use of AI in hiring and employment decisions.

Equal Protection A constitutional principle (in the US, under the Fourteenth Amendment) that requires that laws and government actions treat all people equally and do not unfairly discriminate against particular groups. This is challenged by algorithmic bias.

Ethical AI The development and use of artificial intelligence systems in a manner that aligns with human values, respects fundamental rights, and prioritizes fairness, accountability, and transparency.

Explainability (AI) The ability to understand how an AI system works and why it made a particular decision. This is often difficult with complex AI models, creating a "black box" problem for accountability.

Explainable AI (XAI) An area of AI research focused on developing models and techniques that can provide understandable explanations for their decisions and actions.

Extraterritorial Application The reach of a country's laws beyond its own borders. This is a challenge for AI governance as AI systems often operate globally.

Facial Recognition Technology (FRT) A technology that uses AI to identify or verify a person's identity based on their face.

Fair Use A legal doctrine (in US copyright law) that allows limited use of copyrighted material without permission for purposes such as criticism, comment, news reporting, teaching, or research. This is relevant to how AI models are trained on existing data.

Fairness (Algorithmic) The concept that AI systems should not produce biased or discriminatory outcomes. Defining and achieving fairness in algorithms is complex, as different definitions of fairness can sometimes conflict.

Federal Trade Commission (FTC) A US government agency that protects consumers from unfair or deceptive business practices. They have taken enforcement actions and issued guidance related to AI and consumer protection, including concerns about bias and transparency.

Federated Learning A machine learning technique that trains an algorithm across multiple decentralized edge devices or servers holding local data, without exchanging data samples. This allows AI to learn from data while keeping the data localized and private.

Fifth Amendment An amendment to the U.S. Constitution that, among other things, guarantees the right to due process of law and protects against self-incrimination and double jeopardy.

First Amendment An amendment to the U.S. Constitution that protects fundamental rights such as freedom of speech, freedom of the press, freedom of assembly, and freedom of religion. It's relevant to how AI impacts online expression and information dissemination.

First Amendment Auditor Individuals who test the application of First Amendment rights, often by openly recording in public spaces or interacting with government officials.

Foundation Models Very large AI models, often trained on massive datasets, that can be adapted for a wide range of downstream tasks. Large Language Models (LLMs) are a type of foundation model.

Fourteenth Amendment An amendment to the U.S. Constitution that, among other things, guarantees equal protection under the law and due process to all citizens. It's a key legal framework for analyzing algorithmic discrimination and fairness.

Fourth Amendment An amendment to the U.S. Constitution that protects against unreasonable searches and seizures. This is relevant to concerns about AI-powered surveillance and data collection.

Freedom of Expression The right to express one's opinions and ideas without censorship or restraint. AI and platform algorithms can impact freedom of expression through content moderation and algorithmic amplification or suppression.

GDPR (General Data Protection Regulation) A strict data privacy and security law in the European Union that sets rules for how personal data must be collected, processed, and stored. It includes provisions related to automated decision-making and the right to explanation.

Generative AI AI systems that can create new content, such as text, images, music, or code, often in response to a prompt.

Generative Adversarial Networks (GANs) A type of generative AI framework that uses two neural networks, one that generates new data and one that tries to distinguish it from real data, to create realistic synthetic content.

Ghost Work The hidden human labor that is required to make many AI systems function, such as data labeling or content moderation.

Gig Economy A labor market characterized by the prevalence of short-term contracts or freelance work, often facilitated by digital platforms that use algorithms for management.

Global Governance The complex web of formal and informal rules, norms, institutions, and processes that shape interactions on a global scale. The need for global governance of AI is increasing due to its cross-border nature.

Global South Refers to countries often broadly characterized as developing or emerging economies, frequently raising concerns about equitable access to AI benefits and the potential for AI to exacerbate global inequalities.

Hard Law Legally binding rules and obligations, such as statutes and treaties.

Homomorphic Encryption An encryption method that allows computations to be performed on encrypted data without decrypting it, potentially enabling privacy-preserving AI processing.

Hornbook A type of legal treatise, typically written for law students, that provides a basic overview of a legal subject.

Human Dignity The inherent worth and right to respect that all human beings possess. The book explores how algorithmic systems can sometimes undermine human dignity by treating individuals as mere data points or statistical profiles.

Human-Centered AI An approach to developing AI systems that prioritizes human needs, values, and well-being, ensuring that humans remain in control and that the technology is designed to augment, rather than replace or diminish, human capabilities.

Human-in-the-loop An approach to AI system design where human judgment and oversight are integrated into the decision-making process, allowing humans to review, guide, or override algorithmic decisions.

Hypernudging The use of AI and data to subtly influence or steer individuals' behavior or choices in digital environments, often without their full awareness or consent.

Jurisdiction The official power of a court or other legal authority to make legal decisions and judgments. The global nature of AI creates challenges for determining which jurisdiction's laws apply.

Jurisprudence The theory or philosophy of law; a legal system.

LEO Satellites (Low Earth Orbit Satellites) Satellites that orbit relatively close to the Earth's surface, often used for telecommunications to provide internet access, including in remote areas. The book mentions their potential for global connectivity or surveillance.

Legal Positivism A philosophy of law that holds that law is separate from morality and is created by human authorities.

Legal Realism A philosophy of law that emphasizes the importance of real-world factors and the discretion of judges in shaping legal outcomes.

Liability The state of being responsible for something, especially by law. Determining liability when an AI system causes harm is a significant legal challenge.

Litigation The process of taking legal action.

Machiavelli, Niccolò An Italian Renaissance diplomat, philosopher, and writer whose work *The Prince* is a classic treatise on political philosophy. (Mentioned as an example of a treatise).

Machine Learning A type of artificial intelligence that allows computers to learn from data without being explicitly programmed. Algorithms identify patterns in data and use those patterns to make predictions or decisions.

Markman Hearing A pretrial hearing in patent infringement cases where a judge interprets the meaning of disputed terms in the patent claims. While not directly about AI, the user's request for "Markman edits" uses this as a metaphor for precise, legally-styled edits to the text.

Massachusetts Information Privacy Act (Proposed) Proposed legislation in Massachusetts aimed at establishing comprehensive privacy protections for consumers' personal information.

Master Reference List A comprehensive list of all sources cited or referenced in a book or document.

Meaningful Human Control The concept that human beings should retain significant oversight and the ability to intervene in or override decisions made by automated or AI systems, especially in critical or high-stakes situations.

Meme An image, video, or text, typically humorous in nature, that is copied and spread rapidly by internet users, often with slight variations. Relevant to discussions of online content and freedom of expression.

Metadata Data that provides information about other data, such as the time, date, and location of a communication, rather than the content of the communication itself. AI can analyze metadata to reveal patterns about individuals.

Model Risk Management The process of identifying, assessing, and mitigating the risks associated with using mathematical or statistical models, including AI models, in decision-making.

Monograph A detailed written study of a single specialized subject or an aspect of it. Treatises can sometimes be considered multi-volume monographs.

National AI Initiative Act of 2020 A US federal law to accelerate AI research and development by establishing initiatives across government agencies.

National Institute of Standards and Technology (NIST) A U.S. government agency that develops standards and guidelines for various technologies, including cybersecurity and artificial intelligence (e.g., the NIST AI Risk Management Framework).

Natural Language Processing (NLP) A field of AI that focuses on enabling computers to understand, interpret, and generate human language.

Neo-Luddism A movement or philosophy that is skeptical of or opposed to modern technology and its impact on society, drawing parallels to the original Luddites who protested against industrial machinery.

Neural Network A type of machine learning model inspired by the structure of the human brain, consisting of interconnected nodes (neurons) that process and transmit information.

Neurotechnology Technology that interacts with the brain and nervous system, raising concerns about cognitive liberty and mental privacy in the context of potential AI integration.

Non-state Actors Entities other than governments, such as corporations, non-governmental organizations, and individuals, which play increasingly significant roles in global affairs, including AI development and governance.

Normative (Principles/Frameworks) Relating to or establishing standards or norms of behavior or what *should* be. The book proposes normative frameworks for AI governance, outlining how AI *should* be developed and used ethically and legally.

Nudging The use of subtle prompts or suggestions to influence people's choices, often in a way that is intended to benefit them. AI can be used to personalize and amplify nudges.

Obscurity (Right to) See Right to Obscurity.

Opacity (Algorithmic) The difficulty or impossibility of understanding how an algorithm works or why it produced a specific result, often referred to as the "black box" problem.

Opt-Out Right The right of an individual to choose not to participate in or be subject to a particular process or system, such as having their data collected or being subject to an algorithmic decision.

Participatory Governance A form of governance that emphasizes the broad participation of citizens and stakeholders in the decision-making processes that affect them. This is proposed as a way to make AI governance more democratic and accountable.

Plain Language Writing that is clear, concise, and easy for the average reader to understand, avoiding jargon and overly complex sentence structures.

Predictive Analytics The use of data, statistical algorithms, and machine learning techniques to identify the likelihood of future outcomes based on historical data.

Predictive Policing The use of data and algorithms to predict where and when crimes are likely to occur, or who is likely to commit or be a victim of a crime.

Privacy (Digital) The right of individuals to control their personal information and how it is collected, used, and shared in digital environments. AI poses new challenges to digital privacy.

Prompting (in AI) Providing input or instructions to a generative AI model (like a large language model) to guide it in generating a specific type of output.

Proprietary Algorithm An algorithm that is owned by a company or individual and kept secret, often as a trade secret, making it difficult for others to know how it works.

Redress The act of setting right a wrong; compensation for a wrong or injury. Ensuring effective avenues for redress when individuals are harmed by AI is a key legal and ethical challenge.

Regulatory Arbitrage The practice of exploiting differences in regulations between different jurisdictions, for example, by operating in countries with less strict AI rules.

Responsible AI The development and deployment of AI systems in a way that is safe, reliable, fair, transparent, and accountable, taking into account societal impact and ethical considerations.

Right to Explanation The principle that individuals should have the right to receive a clear and understandable explanation for decisions made about them by automated or AI systems.

Right to Obscurity The idea that individuals should have the ability to move through public spaces and the digital world without being automatically identified, tracked, or profiled.

Section 230 section of the Communications Decency Act (47 U.S.C.§ 230). The US that generally protects online platforms from liability for content posted by their users, which is relevant to regulating harmful AI-generated content.

Sixth Amendment An amendment to the U.S. Constitution that guarantees rights related to criminal prosecutions, including the right to a speedy and public trial and the right to an attorney.

Standing The right of a party to bring a lawsuit to court. In AI-related cases, determining if an individual has suffered sufficient harm to have standing can be complex.

Surveillance Capitalism An economic system where personal data is collected and used to create predictions about behavior, which are then sold as products, often leading to pervasive monitoring and manipulation.

Synthetic Data Artificially generated data that is created to mimic real-world data but does not contain actual personal information. It can be used to train AI models while preserving privacy.

Synthetic Media Media content (like images, audio, or video) that is artificially generated or manipulated, often using AI, to create realistic but fabricated representations. Deepfakes are a type of synthetic media.

Technical Due Process The concept that the design and implementation of technical systems, particularly algorithmic ones used in governance, should incorporate principles of fairness, accountability, and transparency akin to legal due process requirements.

Technological Determinism The belief that technology is the primary force shaping society and that its development follows an inevitable, uncontrollable path. The book argues against this, suggesting humans can and must govern AI.

Tectonic Shift A term used metaphorically to describe a major and fundamental change or transformation, like the impact of AI on society.

Trade Secret Confidential information that gives a business a competitive edge. Companies often claim their algorithms are trade secrets, which can make it difficult to access or audit them.

Training Data The large datasets used to teach machine learning models. The quality and nature of this data significantly influence the behavior and performance of the resulting AI system, including whether it exhibits bias.

Transparency Paradox The challenge where, even if an AI system's workings are technically revealed, the complexity of the system makes the explanation impossible for a human to understand, thus failing to provide meaningful transparency.

Treatise A formal and systematic written work that explores a subject in detail, often presenting principles, evidence, and conclusions.

Treaty A formal written agreement concluded between actors in international law, such as states or international organizations. International treaties are relevant to establishing global AI governance frameworks.

Unified Framework See Unified International Framework.

Unified International Framework A proposed system of global rules and standards for AI governance that would apply across different countries, aimed at ensuring consistent rights protection and preventing regulatory gaps.

Value Judgments (in AI) The ethical or societal choices that are implicitly or explicitly made during the design, development, and deployment of AI systems, such as deciding which type of fairness to prioritize or what level of risk is acceptable.

Value-Sensitive Design An approach to designing technology that accounts for human values in a principled and comprehensive manner throughout the design process.

Warrant A legal document issued by a judge or magistrate that authorizes law enforcement to conduct a search or make an arrest. This is a key concept in Fourth Amendment protections against unreasonable searches.

GPSR Compliance
The European Union's (EU) General Product Safety Regulation (GPSR) is a set of rules that requires consumer products to be safe and our obligations to ensure this.

If you have any concerns about our products, you can contact us on

ProductSafety@springernature.com

In case Publisher is established outside the EU, the EU authorized representative is:

Springer Nature Customer Service Center GmbH
Europaplatz 3
69115 Heidelberg, Germany

www.ingramcontent.com/pod-product-compliance
Ingram Content Group UK Ltd.
Pitfield, Milton Keynes, MK11 3LW, UK
UKHW022316221026
476868UK00003B/98
9783032346032